The Puritan Tradition in America
1620-1730

Library of New England

The Puritan Tradition in America, 1620–1730

Edited by
Alden T. Vaughan

REVISED EDITION

University Press of New England
Hanover and London

University Press of New England, Hanover, NH 03755
© 1972 by Alden T. Vaughan
Previously published in paperback in 1972 by Harper & Row Publishers, Inc., and in
cloth in 1972 by the University of South Carolina Press.
University Press of New England paperback published in 1997.
Printed in the United States of America   5   4   3   2   1
CIP data appear at the end of the book

Excerpts from *The Laws and Liberties of Massachusetts* reprinted
with the permission of the Henry E. Huntington Library.

LIBRARY OF CONGRESS CATALOGING-IN-PUBLICATION DATA
The Puritan tradition in America, 1620–1730 : Revised edition / edited by Alden T.
Vaughan.
    p.   cm. — (Library of New England)
Previously published: New York : Harper & Row, [1972].
Includes bibliographical references.
ISBN 0–87451–852–0 (alk. paper)
1. Puritans—New England—History—Sources. 2. New England—
History—Sources.   I. Vaughan, Alden T. 1929– . II. Series.
F7.P987 1997
285'.9'0974—dc21   97–23558

For
Perry Miller,
Samuel Eliot Morison,
and
Edmund S. Morgan,
who transformed the study of
American Puritanism

Contents

Introduction

"Everyone who inspects the national consciousness of . . . Americans today," historian Alan Simpson proposed in 1955, "finds Puritanism a part of its makeup, whether the inspection is made by ourselves or by stangers who look at us with incredulity."[1] Even if Simpson's assessment appears less obvious today than it did at midcentury, students of our "national character"—however imprecise that term may be—generally agree that deeply embedded in the assumptions and aspirations of modern America lies a hefty legacy of Puritan New England. To some observers that legacy enhances modern America, to others it appears deplorable. Similar judgments also mark the long debate over Puritanism's impact in the seventeenth and early eighteenth centuries, yet no student of early America questions its importance and vitality—for good or ill—in that bygone era when New England was a bastion of Puritan faith and practice. *The Puritan Tradition in America, 1620–1730* tells the story, largely through the participants' own words, of the emergence of the Puritan movement among English evangelical reformers of the late sixteenth century, the migration of a substantial branch of its adherents to North America in the early seventeenth century, and the first century of the movement's evolution in New England.

Any study of Anglo-American Puritanism confronts at the outset a confounding problem of definition: the movement was so amorphous, so multifaceted, and so dynamic that any definition of it and its adherents seems inadequate. As an English rhymester lamented in the early seventeenth century: "Long hath it vext our Learned age to scan / who rightly might be term'd a PURITAN."[2]

The definitional challenge lies in the distinction between the Puritan experience in both England and America and the broader English culture from which it evolved and with which it coexisted, and,

1. *Puritanism in Old and New England* (Chicago, 1955), 99.
2. Anonymous broadside, London (?), 1614.

in addition, the differences (and, increasingly noticed by scholars, the similarities) between New England's branch of Puritanism and the parallel but somewhat different English Puritan mainstream. Because early New Englanders shared the legacy of Tudor-Stuart England with their stay-at-home cousins, both Puritan and non-Puritan, on one level the migrant was simply a transplanted English man or woman. Similarly, New England Puritans abundantly shared beliefs and practices with Puritans in old England, yet the Puritan New Englander was set apart not only by the decision to move to America and the ordeal of getting there—profound experiences in their own right—but by the religious and secular events that occurred *in* America. Put another way: The cultural heritage brought to New England by most of the early settlers was initially Elizabethan-Stuart English, and their religious commitment was to a radically reformed Protestantism. In America, both the culture and the Protestantism were reshaped in myriad ways, large and small. During the seventeenth and early eighteenth centuries, there emerged in the Massachusetts Bay Colony, and similarly but not identically in the other New England colonies, a distinctly "New England Way"—a label that is usually applied to Puritan church polity but is apt as well for most facets of the region's society and culture.

My use of "Puritan" in this book acknowledges the word's shifting and flexible uses through time and place. I apply it to the English reformers in the last third of the sixteenth century who remained within the Church of England's broad fold but who insisted on further reforms, regardless of the particular denomination they prefigured, for it was not until the middle of the seventeenth century and beyond that the broad fabric of Puritanism was clearly rent into Presbyterians, Congregationalists or Independents, Baptists, Quakers, and a multitude of minor sects. It therefore seems pointless for this documentary history to dwell on the variations within Puritanism before the Great Migration to New England. (It is tempting to use a lowercase *p* for the early period.)[3]

Puritanism's role changed rapidly in the New World from a loosely bordered factional movement to a hegemonic faith and administra-

---

3. Some authors reject capitalization of "puritan" altogether. See, for example, Samuel Eliot Morison, *Builders of the Bay Colony* (Boston, 1930), and Patrick Collinson, *The Elizabethan Puritan Movement* (Berkelely, Calif., 1967). I hold that in New England, and largely too in old England after ca. 1630, the puritan movement had become a bona fide national church and hence should be labelled Puritan. For consistency's sake, I have used a capital P throughout.

tion. Although New England's founders disagreed on many matters, by the time they formalized their New Zion's basic structure in the 1640s, Congregationalists (though the term was rarely used at the time) could be distinguished from Presbyterians and those denominations from the emerging Baptists and later from Quakers. And since these were distinctions the New Englanders increasingly insisted on making, I employ "Puritan" in the American context to mean only the movement's Congregational wing, despite the depth of its common heritage with other Reformed groups. On the other hand, I include in the ranks of Puritanism the Plymouth separatists, for as followers of John Robinson they were only quasi-separatist, and in the "free aire of a New World" the Pilgrim and Puritan colonies became almost indistinguishable, participating alike in the formation of New England's fundamental civil and ecclesiastical institutions and presenting a virtually united front against their perceived enemies at home and abroad.

Largely freed from the fetters of English laws, customs, and the Anglican hierarchy, New England Puritans established an experiment in Christian living that reconstructed not only church polity and procedures but most of society's institutions and everyday practices. A substantial majority (arguably) of New England's early settlers believed that their espousal of Puritan doctrines reshaped their minds and souls; it set them apart from other English folk, other mortals in fact, and gave meaning and direction to their lives. Of course, the Puritans of the sixteenth and seventeenth centuries are not history's only example of a people whose religion pervaded their outlook and actions and distinguished them from their fellow nationals. Perhaps most Jews have always shared this experience, and at various times certain Christian reformers lost none of their national characteristics but gained some distinguishing qualities of belief and behavior. Their critics derided them with pejorative labels, some of which became widely accepted and, in a few instances, ennobling: hence, among English Christians of the seventeenth century, the persistence of "Puritans" and "Quakers" and, in the eighteenth, of "Methodists."

Puritanism, as I suggested above, was much more than a set of theological convictions and forms of worship. The central Puritan religious experience—the soul's conversion or rebirth—required adherents to reform their whole lives. Puritanism asked them to look with new eyes at the nature and structure of government, at the role of communities, at the obligations of families; to have new attitudes toward work, toward leisure, toward witches and the wonders of the world. In most cases, Puritanism did not cause its adherents to hold views distinctly different from nonbelievers but rather to see almost everything in a subtly but signficantly new light, sometimes distinct in kind (as in their attitudes toward the relationship of church and state or toward the value and function of education), sometimes in intensity (as in their attitudes toward witchcraft or excess profit or the role of parents). But put all the subtle differences together and the man or woman stands out as a Puritan. Despite the pitfalls of definition and measurement, we should not forget today what English folk on both sides of the Atlantic knew two and a half centuries ago: the Puritan could usually be recognized without much difficulty. There were, to be sure, figures who lived on the edge of the movement, in England and America, but the same can be said of any group and any "ism." Some humans cannot be classified.

Critics of a broad definition of Puritanism have argued that its historians define in reverse, that they label whatever a self-professed Puritan does as "Puritanism." It is true, of course, that John Winthrop's having lived his religion intensely does not make intensity of belief an exclusively Puritan characteristic. Yet if all, or at least most, men and women who claimed to be Puritans shared such an intensity, and if they also shared other characteristics in a degree not common among people unsympathetic to the Puritan movement, we have impressive evidence that Puritanism and those characteristics go hand in hand; or, in sum, that a discernible cluster of attitudes and habits is part of the Puritan personality. On such an assumption, this documentary includes selections on, for example, the early New Englanders' attitudes toward political and social order, toward education, toward science and superstition. Any non-Puritan might have shared many or all of those views while abhorring Puritan theology. It seems, however, more than coincidental that the first New Englanders' attachment to formal learning resulted in an early, broad, and relatively competent system of schooling, in marked contrast to other British American colonies where, despite scattered sentiment in favor of educational institutions, nothing parallel to New England's emerged until well into the eighteenth century. So too with the Puritans' least admirable actions: although virtually all seventeenth-century British Americans believed in witchcraft, only the Puritan colonists cared intensely enough to extinguish dozens of human lives in the hope of re-

ducing Satan's minions. A final example: most people of English heritage in all colonies and in the mother country surely believed in
well-ordered families. What justifies including here a selection on the
Puritan family is the relative frequency and vigor with which Puritans
harped on the subject in sermons, pamphlets, laws, and governmen-
tal pronouncements.

A Puritan, then, on either side of the Atlantic, was not quite like
other people. Probing endlessly the implications of Christian doctrine for himself or herself and for the whole society, the believer
tried to force both to act accordingly. Of course both self and society
often resisted, which accounts not only for the psychic tensions so
characteristic of the Puritan mind but also for society's contentious-
ness wherever Puritans abounded.

Although each piece in the Puritan's unique makeup may have
been small, taken together they formed a mindset that emboldened
tens of thousands of English men and women to forsake their homeland and embark for New England, to fashion there a remarkable so-
cial/religious experiment that would last for several generations and
be influential for several centuries. The bulk of English Puritans, of
course, chose not to emigrate. While their overseas cousins pursued
their "errand into the wilderness," the stay-at-homes flourished in
their own right. With help from numerous non-Puritan allies, they
seized control of Parliament, executed Archbishop William Laud and
King Charles, fought in Oliver Cromwell's Ironsides, and briefly enjoyed hegemony over the British Isles. Puritanism, on both sides of
the Atlantic, was an intensely political movement.

Yet when all is said and done, Puritanism was more a matter of religious faith than of anything else. Accordingly, this historical collection is heavily laced with extracts from church platforms, sermons,
and other documents of a similar nature, in addition to more mun-
dane sources—diaries, letters, laws, town records—that indirectly reveal religious aspects of the Puritan outlook. This is not an anthology
of church documents; it is, rather, a documentary history of a people
for whom religious matters were intensely important and whose society reflected that importance throughout its social, economic, and
political fabric.

Since the dawn of Puritanism in the sixteenth century, debate has
raged over the benevolence or banefulness of its experiment in Amer-

ica.[4] Looked at through the eyes of transient New Englanders unpersuaded by the Puritan ethos and their historiographic descendants, the early history of New England was at best misguided, at worst appalling. Conforming to neither the religious nor the political norms of the mother country—the Puritans' critics charge—New England's leaders imposed a self-righteous, quasi-independent, intolerant regime on all who entered their corner of the New World, a corner to which they had no right of absolute rule. American Puritans acted, this interpretation suggests, much as English Puritans did in the 1640s and 1650s when Oliver Cromwell showed what Puritan rule could be on a national level. But even Cromwell did not go so far toward a tyranny over body and mind; he slew enemies without mercy but at least his friends enjoyed some leeway in matters of conscience and behavior. Not so in New England, where both church and state made every man, woman, and child conform to Puritan precepts. An occasional brave soul—Roger Williams and Mary Dyer are favorite examples—challenged the political and ecclesiastical oligarchies and paid a high price for their effrontery. In the end, the combined power of the suppressed majority revolted quietly from below, while the restored crown and an antagonized parliament, applying imperial pressure from across the sea, hobbled the Puritan stronghold in New England. By the end of the seventeenth century, this version argues, the extension of the franchise to non-church members and the end of Congregationalism's monopoly on the region's places of worship gradually turned New England from a Puritan oligarchy into a Yankee democracy. Certain traits would persist: the work ethic, an emphasis on moral uprightness (perhaps hypocritically, but an emphasis

4. The historiographic overview of American Puritanism on the following several pages is intended as a broad context for this documentary collection as well as a guide to further reading. For an excellent narrative overview, see Francis J. Bremer, *The Puritan Experiment: New England Society from Bradford to Edwards* (New York, 1976; rev. ed., Hanover, N.H., 1995). Earlier but still useful reviews of Puritan historiography include Edmund S. Morgan's chapter in Ray A. Billington, ed., *The Reinterpretation of Early American History* (San Marino, Calif., 1966); Michael McGiffert, "American Puritan Studies in the 1960s," *William and Mary Quarterly*, 3d ser. XXVII (1970); David D. Hall, "Understanding the Puritans," in Herbert J. Bass, ed., *The State of American History* (Chicago, 1970); Laura B. Ricard, "New England Puritan Studies in the 1970s," *Fides et Historia*, XXV (1982); David D. Hall, "Religion and Society: Problems and Reconsiderations," in Jack P. Greene and J. R. Pole, eds., *Colonial British America: Essays in the New History of the Early Modern Era* (Baltimore, 1984), and "On Common Ground: The Coherence of American Puritan Studies," *William and Mary Quarterly*, 3d ser. XLIV (1987); and Francis J. Bremer, "From the Old World to the New," in Martin Kaufman et al., *A Guide to the History of Massachusetts* (Westport, Conn., 1988). See also the ongoing "Bibliographies of New England History," especially Roger Parks, ed., *New England: A Bibliography of Its History* (Hanover, N.H., 1989).

nonetheless), a suspicion of outsiders, taciturnity, and even religious intolerance, for Congregational churches continued to have favored status and to impose handicaps on other faiths well into the nineteenth century.

This stereotype, formulated by both amateur and professional historians of the nineteenth and twentieth centuries, drew from abundant seventeenth-century sources. There were, for example, Anglican Thomas Morton's amusing caricature of the Puritans in *New English Canaan* (1637); Baptist Samuel Gorton's caustic critique of Puritan polity in *Simplicities Defence against . . . that Seven-Headed Church-Government in New-England* (1646); Presbyterian John Child's complaints of persecution in *New England's Jonas Cast Up at London* (1647); and Quaker George Bishop's bitter accusations in *New England Judged . . .* (1661). Such attacks on Congregational New England found ready readers in their day and were fodder for later critical analyses of the Puritan colonies. Yet despite frequent voices of dissent, the dominant theme in early American historical writing remained laudatory of early New England.

The apotheosis of the Puritan fathers and their colonies had begun with their own historians, for among the early Puritans historians were legion. Governor William Bradford, whose account of the Pilgrim colony is often considered the best of the Puritan chronicles, was also the first; close behind was John Winthrop's version of the Bay Colony's history from its settlement in 1630 to his death in 1649. (Although Winthrop's history was not published in full until the 1820s nor Bradford's until the 1850s, both manuscripts circulated widely among historians of their own and later times.[5]) Equally favorable to the Puritan enterprise was Edward Johnson of Woburn, Massachusetts, whose *Wonder-working Providence of Sion's Saviour in New England* appeared in 1654; and William Hubbard, who wrote an "official" *General History of New England* in 1679. The capstone came in 1702 with Cotton Mather's monumental, though pretentious, *Magnalia Christi Americana*. It epitomized the Puritan craving for reassurance that New England was under God's special providence and that the New Englanders were His favorite people. From these

---

5. The best of the many editions of Bradford is Worthington Chauncy Ford, ed., *History of Plymouth Plantation* (2 vols., Boston, 1912), although Samuel Eliot Morison's edition, *Of Plymouth Plantation, 1620–1647* (New York, 1952) is more accessible and readable. For Winthrop's history, see the excellent recent edition, *Journal of John Winthrop, 1630–1649*, ed. Richard S. Dunn, James Savage, and Laetitia Yeandle (Cambridge, Mass., 1996), of which an abridged paperback edition is also available.

and other Puritan texts flowed abundant material for subsequent New Englanders to tell of the founding generations as the Puritan chroniclers would themselves have wanted it.

The new American nation's search for national heroes and a usable past completed the apotheosis begun by the founding generation and nurtured by such eighteenth-century filiopietists as Thomas Prince and Daniel Neal.[6] In the nineteenth century, George Bancroft, the first "professional" historian—a profession he crammed into a lifetime full of other professions—unabashedly proclaimed that New England was the source of most American democratic institutions and that, as to character, "Puritanism was a life-giving spirit; activity, thrift, intelligence, followed in its train; and, as for courage, a coward and a Puritan never went together."[7] Such hyperbole dismayed a few historians, including Richard Hildreth, whose widely praised *History of the United States* (1849–1852) portrayed early New England less sympathetically. Still, John Gorham Palfrey's *History of New England* (1858–1890), an enthusiastic defense of the Puritans, probably enjoyed wider circulation than did Hildreth's less impassioned study. By the third quarter of the century, the New England Puritans' reputation had reached an all-time high.

The pendulum soon swung back. An early sign was Brooks Adams's curious harangue, *The Emancipation of Massachusetts* (1887); far from being the source of democratic and egalitarian concepts, Adams contended, Puritanism fostered religious and political intolerance. Only with the overthrow of theocratic rule in the late seventeenth century and the infusion of secular influence in the eighteenth did "emancipation" come to the Bay Colony.

Five years later, Brooks's brother Charles Francis Adams, Jr., chimed in with *Three Episodes in Massachusetts History* and a year after that with *Massachusetts, Its Historians and Its History*. Charles was by far the better historian; his work is more judicious, better researched, and more gracefully written. But he, like Brooks, would have none of the ancestor worship that might have been expected from one of New England's oldest and "best" families. "Massachusetts had its ice age," wrote Adams, "sterile, forbidding, unproductive, its history dotted only with boulders and stunted growth. . . . It is

---

6. Thomas Prince, A *Chronological History of New-England, in the Form of Annals* (Boston, 1736); Daniel Neal, *The History of New-England* . . . (2 vols., London, 1720).

7. George Bancroft, *History of the United States of America: From the Discovery of the Continent*, author's last rev. (6 vols., New York, 1892) I, 318.

barely possible that New England, contrary to all principle and precedent, may have profited by the harshness and bigotry which for a time suppressed all freedom of thought in Massachusetts; but it is far more likely that the slow results afterwards there achieved came notwithstanding that drawback, rather than in consequence of the discipline it afforded."[8] Only with the coming of the Revolution and the Enlightenment, Adams argued, did the somber, intolerant, conformist, and morbid influence of the Puritans fade. (Critics of the Adamses might ponder the coincidence of their concluding date for the colony's dark ages and the emergence to prominence of John Adams.) In 1908, a speaker addressing the Ancient Order of Hibernians of Worcester, Massachusetts, went a giant rhetorical step farther than than the Adamses:

The toleration and liberty that [the Puritans] established are the kind foreshadowed in the compact signed on board the Mayflower—the right to dominate over all and to persecute, to execute, and drive hence all who did not yield implicit obedience to their morbid opinions and wishes. The story of detention in the stocks, of burning holes through tongues with red-hot irons, of cropping ears, of hanging, of banishment, and penal enactments, darken and disgrace the pages of early New England history. . . . It is clear from the admissions of the Pilgrims and Puritans themselves that they were arrogant, narrow, bigoted, intolerant, mercenary, and sinful.[9]

Little wonder that the Progressive historians in the second and third decades of the twentieth century delighted in debunking the Puritans.

Perhaps the most damaging blow to the Puritan reputation came from another Adams, though not a member of the New England clan. Brooklynite James Truslow Adams garnered a Pulitzer Prize for his *Founding of New England* (1921), which remains a lucid and generally reliable account of New England history to 1691. But Adams had little respect for the Puritan experiment and doubted even its motives: except for a few theocratic leaders, it was not God but cod the early New Englanders sought. An oligarchy emerged, in Adams's version, dominated by the clergy and in blatant disregard of

8. Charles Francis Adams, *Massachusetts, Its History and Its Historians: An Object Lesson* (Boston, 1893), 109–110.
9. George McAleer, *An Hour with the Puritans and Pilgrims*, reprinted in McAleer, *Gathered Waiflets* (Worcester, Mass., 1913), quotations from pp. 113, 127.

the theological and political wishes of the vast non-Puritan majority, whom Adams estimated at 80 percent of the total population. Several of Adams's prominent contemporaries voiced similar views, most notably Charles A. Beard and Vernon Louis Parrington. But it was H. L. Mencken who put into popular parlance the sentiments that scholars advanced to smaller audiences when he defined Puritanism as "the haunting fear that someone, somewhere, may be happy."[10]

Soon after Mencken's barb, a reaction began against the Progressive historians' excessive present-mindedness and economic determinism. Kenneth Murdock's *Increase Mather: The Foremost American Puritan* (1925) took the first step. From most scholars it drew high praise; predictably it met with skepticism from the historians whose interpretation it sought to overturn. Parrington called Murdock's biography

an extraordinarily painstaking document that has added to our knowledge of Increase Mather's life and work, but it was unhappily conceived in the dark of the moon, a season congenial to strange quirks of fancy. . . . It would have us believe that in spite of all the smoke that gathered about Increase Mather's militant pilgrimage through life, there was never any fire of his kindling; that in spite of all the puddles through which the priestly politician splashed to reach his ends, no spot or stain ever smutched his gown. The contention may be sound, but it puts credulity to the strain, and unless one has something of a Mather stomach for marvels, one is likely to indulge in the luxury of doubt.[11]

Parrington notwithstanding, Murdock launched a new trend in American historiography, initially dominated by two of his Harvard colleagues, that has lasted, despite considerable modification and occasional dissent, to the present.

More significant in the long run than Murdock's biography of Mather was Samuel Eliot Morison's volume of biographical essays, *Builders of the Bay Colony* (1930). Morison highlighted Puritan society's variety and complexity and restored religion—faith and practice—to a central position in the founding and development of Massachusetts. Implicit throughout Morison's book is a rebuttal of J. T. Adams's overly economic and fundamentally unsympathetic view,

10. *The Vintage Mencken*, ed. Alistaire Cooke (New York, 1990), 233.
11. Vernon Louis Parrington, *Main Currents in American Thought.Volume I: 1620–1800: The Colonial Mind* (New York, 1927), 100.

and in a witty appendix Morison refuted Adams directly on the portion of Massachusetts settlers who shared the Puritan ethos, joined a church, and hence (if male) acquired the political franchise. During the 1930s and 1940s, Morison produced several volumes on the history of Harvard College that continued the Puritans' rehabilitation, especially in descriptions of their educational and social institutions. His *Puritan Pronaos* (1936; reissued in 1956 as *The Intellectual Life of Colonial New England*) further resuscitated the Puritans' intellectual reputation, especially its secular components.[12]

By the time Morison's later volumes reached the public, Perry Miller of the Harvard English department had emerged as the revisionist movement's most impressive spokesman. *Orthodoxy in Massachusetts, 1630-1650* (1933) stressed the roots of Puritan thought in the theological evolution of English Protestantism. His *New England Mind: The Seventeenth Century* (1939) set Puritan ideology into the context of medieval and reformation developments and established Miller as one of the foremost intellectual historians of the twentieth century. With a companion volume, *The New England Mind: From Colony to Province* (1953), Miller completed what Murdock and Morison had begun: a return of theology and philosophy to center stage in the emergence of Puritanism in late Elizabethan England and its subsequent transference and modification in the New World. So vast was Miller's contribution that his work has remained ever since the baseline for Puritan studies. Initially that scholarship was solidly in Miller's camp; works by Morison, Edmund Morgan, and others in the 1940s and 1950s generally expanded rather than challenged the Miller paradigm.[13]

Historians in the 1930s through 1950s generally eschewed sterile arguments over the banefulness or benevolence of America's Puritan experiment and concentrated instead on understanding its complexity and explaining its theological and institutional variations. Miller's generation portrayed the Puritans less critically than did the Progressive historians yet generally acknowledged the characteristics and

12. In addition to the two books cited in this paragraph, Morison's writings on early New England include *The Founding of Harvard College* (Cambridge, Mass., 1935), a book of wider scope than its title might suggest, and *Harvard College in the Seventeenth Century* (2 vols., Cambridge, Mass., 1936).

13. Edmund S. Morgan's important contributions include *The Puritan Family: Religion and Domestic Relations in Seventeenth-Century New England* (Boston, 1944; rev. ed., New York, 1966); *The Puritan Dilemma: The Story of John Winthrop* (Boston, 1958); *Visible Saints: The History of a Puritan Idea* (New York, 1963); and *Roger Williams: The Church and the State* (New York, 1967).

episodes that had drawn criticism from earlier scholars. In general, Puritan studies insisted that New England society, while restrictive in the sense that outspoken critics of the Congregational Way were unwelcome and sometimes banished, in practice proved flexible, varied, and often contentious, and (for the seventeenth century) moderately tolerant. They demonstrated too the tenacity and vitality of the Puritan ethos, which made a major contribution to the quality of New England life. And that life was never all work and no play. It had color, romance, music, and laughter—if not to the point of hilarity, at least to an extent denied by the old stereotypes, a far cry from C. F. Adams's view of a society "singularly barren,—almost inconceivably sombre."[14] In sum, Miller's generation agreed, Puritanism gave to New England a rigorous intellectual theology that provided the dynamic impetus to the region's political, economic, and cultural institutions.

Beginning in the 1960s, a new generation of scholars reached beyond Miller, and although they often acknowledged a deep debt to him and to his contemporaries, the younger authors were critical of Miller's research and conclusions. Initially they accused Miller of seeing too much intellectual system in the Puritan mind, of ascribing to it too much theological uniqueness, and of treating New England Puritanism as a static phenomenon.[15] With each passing decade, new studies in history, religion, and literature have further modified and expanded an interpretation that had seemed so persuasive. It would be misleading, however, to view the scholarship of the 1960s and beyond as essentially an attack on an earlier school, merely another turn of the wheel. At bottom, the new scholars have been less concerned with challenging the wisdom of their elders (though there is inevitably a bit of that) than with correcting misreadings of the evi-

14. Adams, *Massachusetts History and Historians*, 64. Cf. the writings of Morison and Morgan, especially the former's brief pamphlet, *Those Misunderstood Puritans* (North Brookfield, Mass., 1992). Revision of the Victorian and Progressive era stigmatization of the Puritans as rigid and humorless continues to the present in studies such as Bruce C. Daniels, *Puritans at Play: Leisure and Recreation in Colonial New England* (New York, 1995).

15. Most of the scholarly books on Puritanism since Miller's time have addressed his contributions, sometimes to praise, often to chide. Among the many specific issues that drew warm debate was the extent of Miller's research sample—i.e., how thoroughly did he read the sermonic and other literature from which he drew the composite "New England mind"? Cf. especially George Selement, "Perry Miller: A Note on His Sources in *The New England Mind*," *William and Mary Quarterly*, 3d ser. XXXI (1974), and James Hoopes, ed., *Sources for the The New England Mind: The Seventeenth Century* (Williamsburg, Va., 1981). The substance of Miller's scholarship is defended in Francis T. Butts, "The Myth of Perry Miller," *American Historical Review*, LXXXVII (1982). Miller's life and writings were assessed in a memorial issue of *The Harvard Review*, II, no. 2 (Winter-Spring 1964); see also the later tribute by Ann Douglas, "The Mind of Perry Miller," *The New Republic*, LXVIII (1982).

dence and with answering questions ignored or only tangentially addressed by the historians of the 1930s through 1950s.

Some scholars, solidly trained in theology as well as history, have
challenged Miller's view of Calvinism and the relationship between
English Puritanism and the Reformed tradition; William Ames,
William Perkins, and the American Puritans who drew on their works
now appear less unique than Miller portrayed them.[16] Under fire too
have been the validity of Miller's emphasis on covenant-centered theology, his concentration on "non-separating Congregationalists" as
the forerunners of the New England Puritans,[17] and his explication
of Puritan "declension" in the late seventeenth and early eighteenth
centuries.[18] Important reservations have also been imposed on
Miller's explanation of Puritan uses of typology—a form of biblical
metaphor employed by many New England theologians, especially
(so Miller contended) by Roger Williams.[19] And while most of the
early revisionism was aimed at Miller—the most imposing target—

16. The literature on the English background is vast and, of course, still growing. Especially
important are the several books and articles by Patrick Collinson, among them *The Elizabethan
Puritan Movement* (Berkeley, Calif., 1967), *The Religion of Protestants: The Church in English
Society, 1559–1625* (Oxford, 1982), *Godly People: Essays on English Protestantism and Puri-
tanism* (London, 1983), and *The Birthpangs of Protestant England: Religious and Cultural
Change in the Sixteenth and Seventeenth Centuries* (Houndmills, Eng., 1988). Other important
contributions include Peter Lake, *Moderate Puritans and the Elizabethan Church* (Cambridge,
1983); William Hunt, *The Puritan Moment: The Coming of Revolution in an English County*
(Cambridge, Mass., 1983); David Underdown, *Revel, Riot, and Rebellion: Popular Politics and
Culture in England, 1603–1660* (Oxford, 1985); Nicholas Tyack, *Anti-Calvinists: The Rise of
English Arminianism, c. 1590–1640* (Oxford, 1987); Diarmaid MacCulloch, *The Later Reformation in England, 1547–1603* (London, 1990); Christopher Hill, *The English Bible and the
Seventeenth-Century Revolution* (London, 1993); and Peter Lake and Kenneth Fincham, eds.,
The Early Stuart Church, 1603–1642 (Stanford, Calif., 1993). Still useful, though modifed in
some repects by subsequent scholarship, are William Haller, *The Rise of Puritanism* (New York,
1938), and M. M. Knappen, *Tudor Puritanism: A Chapter in the History of Idealism* (Chicago,
1939). The Netherland's important contibution to evolving Puritanism is examined in Keith L.
Springer, *The Learned Doctor William Ames: Dutch Backgrounds of English and American Puritanism* (Urbana, Ill., 1972).
17. For example, Jens G. Møller, "The Beginnings of Covenant Theology," *Journal of Ecclesiastical History*, XIV (1963); David D. Hall's introduction to the Harper Torchbook edition of
Miller's *Orthodoxy* (1970); and Michael McGiffert, "Grace and Works: The Rise and Division
of Covenant Divinity in Elizabethan Puritanism," *Harvard Theological Review*, LXXV (1982).
18. That Puritanism adapted rather than declined has been argued in many books and articles, including Robert C. Pope, *The Half Way Covenant: Church Membership in Puritan New
England* (Princeton, N.J., 1969); Emory Elliott, *Power and the Pulpit in Puritan New England*
(Princeton, N.J., 1975); and Stephen Foster, *The Long Argument: English Puritanism and the
Shaping of New England Culture, 1570–1700* (Chapel Hill, N.C., 1991). For a clarification
and defense of Miller's position, see Butts, "Myth of Perry Miller," 680-686.
19. The literature on Puritan uses of typology is extensive. Representative examples include
Sacvan Bercovitch, "Typology in Puritan New England: The Williams-Cotton Controversy Re-
assessed," *American Quarterly*, XIX (1967); and Mason Lowance, *The Language of Canaan:
Metaphor and Symbol in New England from the Puritans to the Transcendentalists* (Cambridge,
Mass., 1980).

some of it, at least implicitly, undercuts the work of Miller's contemporaries. Historians even argue over such fundamental issues as the distinction between Anglican and Puritan outlooks.[20]

Among the frequently voiced criticisms of Miller was that he based his analysis of the New England mind on a narrow sample of published sermons. In 1986, Harry Stout's New England Soul, an exhaustive study of approximately two thousand sermons, most of them in manuscript, revealed the printed texts' unrepresentativeness. Whereas most surviving manuscript sermons (including many thousands that Stout did not analyze) are from Sunday services, the printed sermons—especially after the founding decades—are "occasional" pieces, crafted especially for elections or executions, days of fast or thanksgiving, and similar events. They accordingly had specific, often secular, purposes; far more meaningful to the intellectual and emotional lives of New Englanders were the many thousand hours of preaching that each parishioner heard in his or her lifetime, most of it reiterating basic Puritan doctrine.[21] Given such extensive exposure to the clergy's direct and indirect influence, it is unsurprising that individual Puritans exhibited a more intense personal piety than Miller had recognized. Not every New Englander, of course, absorbed the entire theological package. Vestiges of old folk beliefs merged in many minds with the preacher's formal lessons, yet by and large popular religion and Puritan doctrine coincided in New England.[22]

The revisions proposed by Stout, Charles Hambrick-Stowe, and Charles Cohen applied primarily to Miller's New England Mind, but Miller's first book, Orthodoxy in Massachusetts, 1630-1650 (1933)

20. In additon to some of the works cited in n. 17 above, see the disparate positions of C. H. and Katherine George, The Protestant Mind of the English Reformation, 1570–1640 (Princeton, N.J., 1961); John F. H. New, Anglican and Puritan: The Basis of Their Opposition, 1558–1640 (Stanford, Calif., 1964); David Little, Religion, Order, and Law: A Study in Pre-Revolutionary England (New York, 1969); and Darrett B. Rutman, American Puritanism: Faith and Practice (Philadelphia, 1970).

21. Harry S. Stout, New England Soul: Preaching and Religious Culture in Colonial New England (New York, 1986).

22. The major works on the substance and expression of Puritan piety are Charles E. Hambrick-Stowe, The Practice of Piety: Puritan Devotional Disciplines in Seventeenth-Century New England (Chapel Hill, N.C., 1982), and Charles L. Cohen, God's Caress: The Psychology of Puritan Religious Experience (New York, 1986). The most important exposition of popular religious thought is David D. Hall, Worlds of Wonder, Days of Judgment: Popular Religious Belief in Early New England (New York, 1989). See also Patricia Caldwell, The Puritan Conversion Narrative: The Beginnings of American Expression (Cambridge, 1983); and George Selement, Keepers of the Vineyard: The Puritan Ministry and Collective Culture in Colonial New England (Lanham, Md., 1984).

and the title essay of his *Errand into the Wilderness* (1956) came under respectful fire too. *Orthodoxy* had addressed, among other matters, the distinction between English and American Puritanism and the motives for migration to New England. Both of these topics remain vital in contemporary Puritan studies, although largely along lines that Miller did not follow. Historians, as noted above, have long questioned Miller's concept of "non-separating Congregationalism" and have emphasized instead the similarity and continuity of thought between the movement's English and American wings and their ongoing seventeenth-century dialogue. Especially influential in explaining Anglo-American interconnectedness have been the writings of Stephen Foster and Francis Bremer.[23] At the same time, students of the Puritan migration have greatly expanded our understanding of why several thousand English men and women chose to migrate, who they were, where they came from, and the disparate local or regional backgrounds that led to various socioeconomic patterns in early New England.[24]

Several topics that received sparse attention from Miller's generation became lively foci of debate in the 1970s and beyond. Community studies, which had blossomed with the "new social history" of the

23. Foster, *The Long Argument*; Francis J. Bremer, ed., Puritanism: *Transatlantic Perspectives on a Seventeenth-Century Anglo-American Faith* (Boston, 1993), and Bremer, *Congregational Communion: Clerical Friendship in the Anglo-American Puritan Community, 1610–1692* (Boston, 1994). See also Janice Knight, *Orthodoxies in Massachusetts: Rereading American Puritanism* (Cambridge, Mass., 1994). Among the many books that examine New England's theological rifts are Emery Battis, *Saints and Sectaries: Anne Hutchinson and the Antinomian Controversy* (1962); William K. B. Stoever, *"A Faire and Easie Way to Heaven": Covenant Theology and Antinomianism in Early Massachusetts* (Middletown, Conn., 1978); Philip F. Gura, *A Glimpse of Sion's Glory: Puritan Radicalism in New England, 1620–1660* (Middletown, Conn., 1984); and Carla Gardina Pestana, *Quakers and Baptists in Colonial Massachusetts* (Cambridge, 1991).

24. Among the book-length studies that try to explain the cultural roots of the "great migration" are David Grayson Allen, *In English Ways: The Movement of Societies and the Transferal of English Local Law and Custom to Massachusetts Bay in the Seventeenth Century* (Chapel Hill, N.C., 1981); David Cressy, *Coming Over: Migration and Communication between England and New England in the Seventeenth Century* (Cambridge, 1987); the first section of David Hackett Fischer, *Albion's Seed: Four British Folkways in America* (New York, 1989); Virginia DeJohn Anderson, *New England's Generation: The Great Migration and the Formation of Society and Culture in the Seventeenth Century* (New York, 1991); and Roger Thompson, *Mobility and Migration: East Anglian Founders of New England* (Amherst, Mass., 1994). More concerned with the character of the early New England experience are Theodore Dwight Bozeman, *To Live Ancient Lives: The Primitivist Dimension in Puritanism* (Chapel Hill, N.C., 1988); Andrew Delbanco, *The Puritan Ordeal* (Cambridge, Mass., 1989); and Avihu Zakai, *Exile and Kingdom: History and Apocalypse in the Puritan Migration to America* (Cambridge, 1992). For the first fruits of an ongoing genealogical survey of the early immigrants, see Robert Charles Anderson, *The Great Migration Begins: Immigrants to New England, 1620–1633* (3 vols., Boston, 1995).

late 1960s and after, attracted a bumper crop in 1970, including Kenneth Lockridge's study of Dedham, Massachusetts, Philip Greven's of Andover, John Demos's of Plymouth Colony, and Michael Zuckerman's of a score of eighteenth-century New England villages.[25] A few subsequent books bolstered the early findings, but most of the post-1970 publications offered different perspectives. Stephen Innes found the roots of Springfield, Massachusetts, to be essentially commercial rather than religious, while Christine Heyrman uncovered a growing rather than declining piety in two coastal Massachusetts communities.[26] The likelihood of additional studies of New England communities (some of which seem not to have been very Puritan) decreased as the availability of adequate town records diminished; in fact, the apparently disparate community characterstics may reflect nothing so much as the survival of church records in some instances, commercial records in others. Yet several distinct types of New England communites appear to have existed simultaneously, based partly on location, partly on size, partly on their stage of socioeconomic development, and partly too on the backgrounds—both ideological and agricultural—of the town's founders.[27]

25. Kenneth A. Lockridge, A New England Town: The First Hundred Years (New York, 1970); Philip Greven, Jr., Four Generations: Population, Land, and Family in Colonial Andover, Massachusetts (Ithaca, N.Y., 1970); John Demos, A Little Commonwealth: Family Life in Plymouth Colony (New York, 1970); and Michael Zuckerman, Peaceable Kingdoms: New England Towns in the Eighteenth Century (New York, 1970). Important pre-1970 town studies include Sumner Chilton Powell, Puritan Village: The Formation of a New England Town (Middletown, Conn., 1963), and Darrett B. Rutman, Winthrop's Boston: Portrait of a Puritan Town, 1630–1649 (New York, 1965).

26. Stephen Innes, Labor in a New Land: Economy and Society in Seventeenth-Century Springfield (Princeton, N.J., 1983); Christine Leigh Heyrman, Commerce and Culture: The Maritime Communities of Colonial Massachusetts, 1690–1750 (New York, 1984). See also the strikingly different views of Salem in Richard P. Gildrie, Salem, Massachusetts, 1626–1683: A Covenant Community (Charlottesville, Va., 1975), and Christine Alice Young, From 'Good Order' to Glorious Revolution: Salem, Massachusetts, 1628–1689 (Ann Arbor, Mich., 1980).

27. Among the many attempts to typologize the villages, towns, and cities of early New England (often in books and articles that also address other aspects of early New England) are: Kenneth A. Lockridge, "Land, Population, and the Evolution of New England Society, 1630–1790," Past and Present, no. 39 (1968); Edward M. Cook, "Local Leadership and the Typology of New England Towns," Political Science Quarterly, LXXXVI (1971); Bruce Daniels, The Connecticut Town: Growth and Development, 1635–1790 (Middletown, Conn., 1979); and Stephen Innes, Creating the Commonwealth: The Economic Culture of Puritan New England (New York, 1995). Darrett B. Rutman sets New England towns in a wider context in "Assessing the Little Communities of Early America," William and Mary Quarterly, 3d ser. XLIII (1986). For economic motives that influenced town founding, see, in addition to the Innes book cited above, John Frederick Martin, Profits in the Wilderness: Entrepreneurship and the Founding of New England Towns in the Seventeenth Century (Chapel Hill, N.C., 1991). A very different approach to early New England communites is Joseph S. Wood, "Village and Community in Early Colonial New England," Journal of Historical Geography, VIII (1982).

Although scholarly interest in community studies declined after the bountiful early 1970s, other aspects of New England's social history gained momentum. Women's spiritual and secular lives and the wider context of gendered assumptions and language—neglected in most earlier studies of New England's patriarchal society—received overdue attention, most notably in seminal works by Laurel Ulrich and Amanda Porterfield.[28] Many of the books and articles that have shed useful light on women's lives focus less on women than on families or on childhood, where the wife/mother roles were obviously crucial.[29] New interest in early American law has illuminated women's legal roles in Puritan society[30]; while studies of colonial literacy have shed useful light on the extent of schooling and literacy among females.[31]

Another reflection of the broad social and historiographic trend in the 1970s was the increasing attention to early Puritan attitudes and policies toward Indians and African Americans. Two books of the 1950s and 1960s—Douglas Leach's on King Philip's War and Alden Vaughan's on the period from 1620 to the eve of the war—were taken

---

28. Laurel Thatcher Ulrich, *Good Wives: Image and Reality in the Lives of Women in Northern New England, 1650–1750* (New York, 1982); Amanda Porterfield, *Female Piety in Puritan New England: The Emeregence of Religious Humanism* (New York, 1992). Other important studies include Roger Thompson, *Women in Stuart England and America: A Comparative Study* (London, 1974), and *Sex in Middlesex: Popular Mores in a Massachusetts County, 1649–1699* (Amherst, Mass., 1986); Lyle Koehler, *A Search for Power: The "Weaker Sex" in Seventeenth-Century New England* (Urbana, Ill., 1980); and, for the English context, Patricia Crawford, *Women and Religion in England, 1550–1720* (London, 1993).

29. The modern study of New England families began with Morgan's *Puritan Family*; thereafter little additional work appeared until the 1970s. The bulk of it has been published in scholarly journals, but several books are relevant, including Levin Ludwig Schucking, *The Puritan Family: A Social Study from the Literary Sources*, trans. Brian Battershaw (London, 1969), and Ilana Krausman Ben-Ames, *Adolescence and Youth in Early Modern England* (New Haven, 1994), primarily about English Puritans; Philip Greven, *The Protestant Temperament: Patterns of Child-Rearing, Religious Experience, and the Self in Early America* (New York, 1977); and C. John Sommerville, *The Discovery of Childhood in Puritan New England* (Athens, Ga., 1993). On Puritan attitudes toward death, especially among children, see David E. Stannard, *The Puritan Way of Death: A Study in Religion, Culture, and Social Change* (New York, 1977); and Gordon E. Geddes, *Welcome Joy: Death in Puritan New England* (Ann Arbor, Mich., 1981).

30. For example, Peter Hoffer and N. E. H. Hull, *Murdering Mothers: Infanticide in England and New England* (New York, 1981), and Cornelia Hughes Dayton, *Women before the Bar: Gender, Law, and Society in Connecticut, 1639–1789* (Chapel Hill, N.C., 1995). Other studies of the law in Puritan society, although not addressed primarily to women's lives, are revealing nonetheless. See, for example, David Thomas Konig, *Law and Society in Puritan Massachusetts: Essex County, 1629–1692* (Chapel Hill, N.C., 1979).

31. For example, Kenneth A. Lockridge, *Literacy in Colonial New England: An Enquiry into the Social Context of Literacy in the Early Modern West* (New York, 1974); and E. Jennifer Monaghan, "Literacy Instruction and Gender in Colonial New England," *American Quarterly*, XL (1988).

to task by Francis Jennings and his disciples in the 1970s and 1980s; the causes and aftermaths of New England's "Indian Wars" remain a hotly contested chapter of Puritan historiography.[32] So too do Puritan missionary efforts. Despite a growing sophistication about the nature of religious affiliation and alienation, there is little agreement about the fundamental motives of either the missionaries or the converts, or, for that matter, about the number of converts.[33] Although no consensus has emerged on either the military or missionary aspects of early New England history, there is general agreement that these issues are part and parcel of the Puritan movement, not secular events that were irrelevant to Puritan values and perspectives. Most scholars who charge that the New Englanders were the worst violators of Indian rights and lives, as well as those who argue that the New England record is relatively benign, center their explanations on Puritan ideology. To the former it appears dehumanizing; to the latter, ameliorating.[34] Similarly, New England's treatment of its small African

32. Douglas Edward Leach, *Flintlock and Tomahawk: New England in King Philip's War* (New York, 1958); Alden T. Vaughan, *New England Frontier: Puritans and Indians, 1620–1675* (Boston, 1965; 3rd ed., Norman, Okla., 1995); Francis Jennings, *The Invasion of America: Indians, Colonialism, and the Cant of Conquest* (Chapel Hill, N.C., 1975); Neal Salisbury, *Manitou and Providence: Indians, Europeans, and the Making of New England, 1500–1643* (New York, 1982); Russell Bourne, *The Red Kings' Rebellion: Racial Politics in New England, 1675–1678* (New York, 1990); Alfred A. Cave, *The Pequot War* (Amherst, Mass., 1996).

33. The extensive writings on this topic include James Axtell, *The Invasion Within: The Contest of Cultures in Colonial North America* (New York, 1985), esp. pp. 138–150, and the same author's *After Columbus: Essays in the Ethnohistory of Colonial North America* (New York, 1988); Robert James Naeher, "Dialogue in the Wilderness: John Eliot and the Indian Exploration of Puritanism as a Source of Meaning, Comfort, and Ethnic Survival," *New England Quarterly*, LXII (1989); Richard W. Cogley, "Idealism vs. Materialism in the Study of Puritan Missions to the Indians," *Method and Theory in the Study of Religion*, III (1991); and Charles L. Cohen, "Conversion among Puritans and Amerindians," in Bremer, ed., *Transatlantic Perspectives*.

34. For a discussion of the contrasting views, see the introduction to the third edition of Vaughan, *New England Frontier*. Among the important issues other than military and missionary that have attracted scholarly attention in the last quarter of the twentieth century are the law, addressed in, among other works, Yasuhide Kawashima, *Puritan Justice and the Indian* (Middletown, Conn., 1986), and James Warren Springer, "American Indians and the Law of Real Property in Colonial New England," *American Journal of Legal History*, XXX (1986). Captivities of Puritans by Indians and the resulting narratives (an especially lively topic for specialists in early American literature) are examined in many recent books and articles, including Alden T. Vaughan and Daniel K. Richter, "Crossing the Cultural Divide, 1620–1763," in Vaughan, *Roots of American Racism*; Mitchell Robert Breitwieser, *American Puritanism and the Defense of Mourning: Religion, Grief, and Ethnology in Mary Rowlandson's Captivity Narrative* (Madison, Wisc., 1991); and John Demos, *The Unredeemed Captive: A Family Story from Early America* (New York, 1994).

The uses and abuses of the natural environment are examined in William Cronon, *Changes in the Land: Indians, Colonists, and the Ecology of New England* (New York, 1983), and Carolyn Merchant, *Ecological Revolutions: Nature, Gender, and Science in New England* (Chapel Hill, N.C., 1989).

American population and the region's early embrace of slavery (Samuel Sewell's challenge to it in 1700 notwithstanding) have been cast in a Puritan context by most of the authors who have attempted to reconstruct the early black experience.[35]

Recent work on early New England ethnohistory is perhaps exceeded in volume only by the books and articles on witchraft. Most of them, not surprisingly, have addressed the Salem episode—a popular and professional staple for more than a century. Paul Boyer and Stephen Nissenbaum's *Salem Possessed* (1974), by combining many of the best features of a community study with a sociological analysis of the witchraft frenzy, revived scholarly interest in a subject that was beginning to go fallow. About the same time, New England's earlier witchcraft cases began to attract keen interest for their presumably more representative reflection of the ongoing Puritan concern with demonology and magic. John Demos's meticulous analysis of all New England cases before Salem is the landmark contribution; other scholars have combined the early cases with the Salem outburst to form comprehensive analyses of the phenomenon; and several recent works offer fresh approaches to the events of 1692. In the past quarter-century, the Puritanism/witchcraft connection has been approached from a remarkable variety of perspectives, with neither a consensus on the subject nor a cessation of contributions in sight.[36]

In recent decades, biographical appoaches to early New England have enjoyed a revival. Predictably, the Mathers have been prime grist: their roles were central to the Puritan experiment and their writings are voluminous. In addition to Kenneth Silverman's prize-win-

35. Robert C. Twombly and Robert H. Moore, "Black Puritan: The Negro in Seventeenth-Century Massachusetts," *William and Mary Quarterly*, 3d ser. XXIV (1967); Winthrop D. Jordan, *White over Black: American Attiudes toward the Negro, 1550–1812* (Chapel Hill, N.C., 1968); Bernard Rosenthal, "Puritan Conscience and New England Slavery," *New England Quarterly*, XLVI (1973); and, with a different focus, William D. Pierson, *Black Yankees: The Development of an Afro-American Subculture in Eighteenth-Century New England* (Amherst, Mass., 1988).

36. Among the many important books on witchraft (space precludes a listing here of the periodical literature) are Chadwick Hansen, *Witchcraft at Salem* (New York, 1969); Boyer and Nissenbaum, *Salem Possessed: The Social Origins of Witchcraft* (Cambridge, Mass., 1974); John Putnam Demos, *Entertaining Satan: Witchcraft and the Culture of Early New England* (New York, 1982); Richard Weisman, *Witchraft, Magic and Religion in Seventeenth-Century Massachusetts* (Amherst, Mass., 1984); Carol Karlsen, *The Devil in the Shape of a Woman: Witchcraft in Colonial New England* (New York, 1987); Richard Godbeer, *The Devil's Dominion: Magic and Religion in Early New England* (Cambridge, 1992); Bernard Rosenthal, *Salem Story: Reading the Witch Trials of 1692* (New York, 1993); Elaine G. Breslaw, *Tituba, Reluctant Witch of Salem: Devilish Indians and Puritan Fantasies* (New York, 1996); and Peter C. Hoffer, *The Devil's Disciples: Makers of the Salem Witchcraft Trials* (Baltimore, 1996).

ning life of Cotton Mather, other important contributions to the Mather resuscitation (several early biographies, and Miller's works too, treated them harshly) include David Levin's fresh look at Cotton's early career; B. R. Burg's brief summary of Richard Mather's life; Robert Middlekauff's ambitious intellectual biography of the family's first three generations in New England; and Michael Hall's major reassessment of Increase Mather, which supplants Kenneth Murdock's 1925 book as the standard "life."[37] A few other clergymen have drawn biographical attention, most notably Thomas Hooker and John Cotton, and a few collective biographical studies have brought deserved attention to some of the lesser known preachers.[38] A few other overlooked figures from early New England—including, finally, a few Native Americans—have been treated in useful new essays.[39]

In 1987, David Hall suggested as the agenda for subsequent Puritan studies "the struggle for power—the politics of culture" within the broad context of Puritan language and theology.[40] A decade later, Darren Staloff's *The Making of an American Thinking Class* makes a major step toward fulfilling Hall's challenge. Staloff explains how the Puritans constructed "an early ideological one-party state" through the clergy's monopoly on biblical exegesis (of profound importance in a society committed to biblical guidance); the clergy's frequent and influential consultations with the magistrates on matters of state; the limitation of the colony-wide franchise to church members; the magistrates' legislative veto in the General Court and their role as executive council when the court was in recess, and the magistrates' simultaneous authority as the colony's high court. In Staloff's meticu-

---

37. Kenneth Silverman, *The Life and Times of Cotton Mather* (New York, 1984); David Levin, *Cotton Mather: The Young Life of the Lord's Remembrancer, 1663–1703* (Cambridge, Mass., 1978); B. R. Burg, *Richard Mather of Dorcester* (Lexington, Ky., 1976); Robert Middlekauff, *The Mathers: Three Generations of Puritan Intellectuals, 1596–1728* (New York, 1971); Michael G. Hall, *The Last American Puritan: The Life of Increase Mather* (Middletown, Conn., 1988). Relevant volumes in Twayne's United States Authors series include Mason I. Lowance, *Increase Mather* (New York, 1974), and B. R. Burg, *Richard Mather* (Boston, 1982).

38. Frank Shuffleton, *Thomas Hooker, 1586–1647* (Princeton, N.J., 1977); Sargent Bush, Jr., *The Writings of Thomas Hooker: Spiritual Adventure in Two Worlds* (Madison, Wisc., 1980); Everett Emerson, *John Cotton*, rev. ed. (Boston, 1990), in the Twayne series; Francis J. Bremer, *Shaping New Englands: Puritan Clergymen in Seventeenth-Century England and New England* (New York, 1994), also in the Twayne series.

39. See, for example, Philip Ranlet, *Enemies of the Bay Colony* (New York, 1995), a book that intentionally plays on the title and method of Morison's *Builders* but presents a very different picture; and some of the essays in Robert S. Grumet, ed., *Northeastern Indian Lives, 1632–1816* (Amherst, Mass., 1996).

40. Hall, "On Common Ground," 229.

lous explication, Puritan theology shaped the Massachusetts Colony's early political institutions and political culture.[41] Studies of the other New England colonies, especially New Haven, might reveal similar patterns throughout the region.

A quarter-century ago, Michael McGiffert concluded in an essay on Puritan studies since Miller's death in 1963, that "Puritan and New England historiography is remarkable more for vitality than for coherence." That generalization seems less applicable on the eve of the twenty-first century. In 1986, the emergent dean of Puritan studies, David Hall, discerned considerable "common ground" in recent works on Puritan theology.[42] Yet in many other areas of Puritan culture and society, there is more carping than common ground. That may be inevitable in so diverse a field, where scholars approach a frustratingly diffuse subject from widely disparate backgrounds and perspectives. Puritanism, like any "ism," encompasses divergent, even contradictory, qualities and personalities; it changes over time; it has subtle and far-reaching intellectual and social ramifications. This persistent illusiveness helps to account for the vitality and longevity of Puritan scholarship and of the Puritan tradition in America.

In selecting documents for this book, I have tried to eschew any particular school of interpretation, though inevitably the organization and choice of sources and the phrasing of the introductory sections reflect my preference for certain viewpoints. In the opening pages of this introduction, I explained some of the convictions that underlie my general criteria of selection. A few additional observations here may help the reader understand my choice of specific documents and the editorial apparatus I applied to them.

First, the matter of geographical distribution: Although some of the documents are drawn from New Haven, Connecticut, and Plymouth, most are taken from the writings and records of Massachusetts. In part this imbalance reflects the greater availability of Massachusetts sources. The Bay Colony was the largest in area and population; it boasted more clergymen and magistrates, who in turn wrote more sermons and other religious tracts, penned more letters and memoirs and histories, and enacted more legislation. The abundance of Mass-

---

41. Staloff, *The Making of an American Thinking Class: Intellectuals and Intelligensia in Puritan Massachusetts* (New York, 1997). An important but quite different political analysis is T. H. Breen, *The Character of a Good Ruler: A Study of Puritan Political Ideas in New England, 1630–1730* (New Haven, 1970).

42. For citations to these articles, see note 4 above.

achusetts materials in this collection reflects also the Bay Colony's central role. For better or for worse, "the Governor and Company of the Massachusetts Bay in New England," as it was officially styled, dominated the evolution of American Puritanism. Inevitably, then, the bulk of selections in this collection emanated from Massachusetts. Nor have I treated Puritan settlements elsewhere than in New England; Puritan outposts in the southern colonies and in the West Indies, transient and tangential to the mainstream of Puritan migration, have been omitted, although their stories lend interest and significance to the larger issue of European migration to America and sometimes shed important comparative light on the New England experience.[43]

There is at least one substantial omission that I made with great reluctance: the writings of English and Continental clergymen from whom the New England Puritans drew their inspiration. The Puritans themselves would undoubtedly lament the absence of texts by Peter Martyr, Thomas Cartwright, John Preston, and Petrus Ramus, and the inclusion of only one selection each from William Ames and William Perkins. Equally missed would be the *Institutes* of Calvin and key passages from the Geneva Bible or its English variations. I omitted them here because there simply was not room for everything and because the complex intellectual and theological heritage on which the Puritans drew does not lend itself to brief excision in a documentary history. Readers who wish greater familiarity with the roots of the Puritan mind should read the modern analyses by William Haller, Perry Miller, Patrick Collinson, and a host of recent contributors to our understanding of English Puritanism. Equally important are the early Puritan texts themselves. Fortunately, modern anthologies and edited versions of many whole works make accessible the writings of many theologians that held places of honor on every Puritan bookshelf.[44]

This book's limited attention to belletristic literature also deserves explanation. I have included few selections from the essentially aes-

43. See especially Babette M. Levy, *Early Puritanism in the Southern and Island Colonies* (Worcester, Mass., 1960), and Karen Ordahl Kupperman, *Providence Island, 1630–1641: The Other Puritan Colony* (New York, 1993).

44. Among the many accessible editions, some in fascimile, some in modernized and annotated form, are William Ames, *The Marrow of Theology*, ed. John D. Eusden (Boston, 1968), of which a small portion is reprinted in this volume; Everett H. Emerson, ed., *English Puritanism: From John Hooper to John Milton* (Durham, N.C., 1968); and Leonard J. Trinterud, ed., *Elizabethan Puritanism* (New York, 1971). Facsimile editons of many individual texts were published by Arno Press in 1972 as the "Research Library of Colonial Americana."

thetic writings produced in early New England; Thomas Tillam's brief poem on his arrival in New England, included here for its content rather than its style, constitutes an exception as may, depending upon one's definition, several other selections. My reason for omitting what may loosely be called *belles lettres* (an imprecise term in any context but especially so in the seventeenth century) is a belief that the size and function of this volume regrettably precludes it. Moreover, that broad genre of Puritan literature is available in several other anthologies. More than half a century ago, Perry Miller and Thomas H. Johnson published a broad and extensive collection of Puritan writing, which Miller later condensed into an even handier collection; both anthologies are available in most college and many public libraries.[45] More recently, Alan Heimert and Andrew Delbanco published an admirable selection of Puritan writings,[46] but, like the Miller collections, it scants the political, economic, and social documents through which *The Puritan Tradition in America* sketches the political, social, and (to some extent) the economic contexts of the Puritans' American experiment.

My choice of editorial format also deserves comment. Scholars no longer insist that modern editions reproduce the idiosyncracies of spelling and punctuation that make the reading of seventeenth-century works so laborious. Modern readers are entitled to a modern format—not bowdlerized or expurgated, but a readable text that preserves the flavor and sense of the original without the barriers to understanding imposed by erratic orthography and inconsistent or outmoded punctuation. Today's reader wants, I believe, an insight into the Puritan experience rather than an exercise in typographical gymnastics; I suspect that John Winthrop or Cotton Mather or Thomas Prince would approve of the style promoted by Samuel Eliot Morison in his edition of William Bradford's *Of Plymouth Plantation* and here used with minor variations. The goal of Puritan writing was didactic—to get the message across as widely and as profoundly as possible. I hope the adjustments I have made in the documents will facilitate that purpose. However, I could not resist exposing the reader to a few samples of seventeenth-century orthography, and to that end quotations appearing in chapter introductions and head-

45. Perry Miller and Thomas H. Johnson, eds, *The Puritans: A Sourcebook of Their Writings* (2 vols., New York, 1938; rev. ed., 1963); Perry Miller, ed., *The American Puritans: Their Prose and Poetry* (Garden City, N.Y., 1956).
46. *The Puritans in America: A Narrative Anthology* (Cambridge, Mass., 1985).

notes are offered in the most pristine printed form I could find, though even there I have substituted *i* for *j*, *u* for *v*, and *th* for the thorn *y* where appropriate; all superscript letters have been lowered to the line; and unusual abbreviations have been expanded. Readers who remain curious to see what the documents looked like in an entirely untampered condition are referred to such relics of nineteenth-century printing as *The Records of the Governor and Company of the Massachusetts Bay in New England* (1853-1854), or, better still, to the barely legible manuscripts in public and private depositories.

For permission to reprint materials still under copyright I am indebted to the following: the American Antiquarian Society for Thomas Tillam's poem "Uppon the first sight of New England" and portions of Cotton Mather's "Angel of Bethesda"; the Colonial Society of Massachusetts for extracts from the autobiography of Thomas Shepard; the Henry E. Huntington Library and Art Gallery, San Marino, California, for extracts from *The Laws and Liberties of Massachusetts*; *The New England Quarterly* and Josephine B. Stearns for a portion of Raymond Phineas Stearns's transcription of a letter from John Woodbridge, Jr., to Richard Baxter; the Pilgrim Press for portions of William Ames, *The Marrow of Theology*, translated from the third Latin edition, 1629, and edited by John D. Eusden (Philadelphia: Pilgrim Press), copyright © 1968 by United Church Press; and Yale University Press for a selection from Franklin B. Dexter's *Documentary History of Yale* (New Haven, 1916).

On a more personal level I am deeply indebted to several friends, students, and colleagues who have contributed immeasurably to the making of this book. They are too numerous all to be mentioned by name, and their help has been too varied to be adequately described; I hope they will take some comfort in seeing this book in print and in knowing that they shared in its creation. I extend special thanks to the late Richard B. Morris and to Robert T. Handy, David H. Flaherty, and Francis J. Bremer for their perceptive readings of the entire manuscript of the first edition. Francis J. Bremer, Darren Staloff, Virginia Mason Vaughan, and an anonymous reader for the University Press of New England offered wise counsel on the revised edition. Finally, I have indicated on the dedication page my intellectual debt to three scholars among the many from whom I continue to learn about the Puritan experience.

Editor's Note to the Revised Edition

This documentary collection was first published in a paperback edition in 1972 by Harper and Row as The Puritan Tradition in America, 1620–1730, a volume in "The Documentary History of the United States" under the general editorship of Richard B. Morris, and was issued simultaneously in a limited hardcover edition by the University of South Carolina Press. For the revised edition I have rewritten the introductory essay, corrected some minor errors, and substituted two documents: no. 3 ("The Intensity of Puritan Piety") and no. 23 ("The Trial of Anne Hutchinson"). I would have added a few other documents to the revised edition had not the production costs been prohibitive.

During the quarter century between the first and second editions of this book, a number of documentary collections have appeared on specific aspects of early New England history that shed important light on Puritanism's varied roles. Readers are encouraged to consult these useful anthologies for insight into topics that receive sparse attention in The Puritan Tradition in America: on individual piety and the conversion experience, George Selement and Bruce C. Wooley, eds., Thomas Shepard's "Confessions" (Boston, 1981), and Michael McGiffert, ed., God's Plot: Puritan Spirituality in Thomas Shepard's Cambridge, rev. ed. (Amherst, Mass., 1994); on Anne Hutchinson and the religious/political upheavals of the 1630s, David D. Hall, ed., The Antinomian Controversy 1636–1638: A Documentary History, rev. ed. (Durham, N.C., 1990); on Puritan preaching, Phyllis M. Jones and Nicholas R. Jones, eds., Salvation in New England: Selections from the Sermons of the First Preachers (Austin , Tex., 1977); on witchcraft, Paul Boyer and Stephen Nissenbaum, eds., Salem-Village Witchcraft: A Documentary Record of Local Conflict in Colonial New England (Belmont, Calif., 1972), and, with a wider focus, David D. Hall, ed., Witch-Hunting in Seventeenth-Century New England: A Documentary History, 1638–1692 (Boston, 1991); on Puritan perceptions of war with the Indians, Richard Slotkin and James K. Folsom, eds., So Dreadfull a Judgment: Puritan Responses to King Philip's War, 1676–1677 (Middletown, Conn., 1978); and on captivity by Indians and the resulting narratives, Alden T. Vaughan and Edward W. Clark, eds., Puritans among the Indians: Accounts of Captivity and Redemption, 1676–1724 (Cambridge, Mass., 1981).

I

Uprooting

PURITANISM EMERGED in the second half of the sixteenth century as a demand for change within the English church. The process of reformation had not gone far enough, some thought; further purification would be necessary before the Church of England resembled the church of the early Christians. Critics of the reformers dubbed them "puritans," "precisionists," or other terms intended to discredit them. By the late 1570s the terms of derision had taken on a measure of dignity, and the reformers somewhat grudgingly accepted "Puritan" as their label.

Even before the appearance of the Puritan movement, major changes in the structure of the church had been effected by Henry VIII when he broke with Rome in 1534 and established himself as the religious as well as the civil head of the realm. Theological tampering, however, had been discouraged by the "Defender of the Faith," a title Leo X had bestowed on Henry in 1532 for his attacks on Lutheranism. But during the reign of youthful Edward VI (r.1547–1553), Archbishop Thomas Cranmer advanced a number of moderate Protestant reforms by publishing an English prayer book and discarding many rituals and appurtenances associated with Roman Catholicism. Then Edward's brief reign was followed by a Catholic revival under Mary Tudor (r.1553–1558), who earned the sobriquet "Bloody Mary" for her sanguinary treatment of Protestants. Numerous Anglicans, many of them young preachers and students already bent on reform, fled to the continent where they established refugee communities in such centers of Calvinist thought as Zurich, Frankfort, and Geneva. In 1558 Elizabeth brought Protestantism into favor once again, but with her accession a struggle resumed over the form it should take in England. The legacy was unclear: the Church of England had undergone over a half-century of flux; there was little precedent for Elizabeth to follow. Her initial inclination, as reported by the Spanish ambassador, was to restore religion to the form in which her father had left it. But events since Henry's death made that an improbable goal.

Well before the famous rift between Henry VIII and the Pope culminated in Parliament's decision of 1534, that henceforth the King and his successors would be "Protector and only Supreme Head of the Church and Clergy of England," there had been a movement for reform in the English church. Though muted and sometimes proscribed, the thrust toward ecclesiastical reform by men such as William Tyndale, John Frith, and John Bale had been persistent and energetic. That thrust had been reinforced in the late 1540s by visiting European scholars such as Peter Martyr and Martin Bucer, and it now received a vigorous spurt from the several hundred returning exiles, often referred to as "Marian Exiles," who came home when Protestant Elizabeth succeeded Catholic Mary. Convinced of the necessity of a more purified church than had existed during Edward's reign, and imbued with evangelical fervor and new ideas as a result of their stay in Europe, many of the returning refugees enthusiastically joined the effort to persuade the Queen that the church needed radical reformation.

Elizabeth had other ideas. Although a sincere Protestant, her theological views were relatively conservative, and—more importantly—they were clearly subordinate to her temporal ambitions. Elizabeth wanted stability not strife, and to get it she readily curbed religious extremists of any persuasion. An increasingly complex contest ensued, in which reformers of widely varying convictions vied with the Queen and the Anglican hierarchy for substantial changes in the Church's practices and, as the century wore on, in its fundamental structure as well. And from the outset, what appeared on the surface to be a purely religious affair held profound implications for English political, social, and economic life. In an age that cared deeply about its religious forms and doctrines, and in a society where religious institutions were inextricably involved in what we now consider the secular areas of life, what began as a mild storm within the national church would lead, before the movement was a century old, to a tempest throughout English society.

1. Emergence of a Puritan Faction

Within five years of her accession, the Queen had produced her "Elizabethan settlement." In 1559 an Act of Supremacy restored royal leadership to the church, in the same year the Act of Uniformity required all Englishmen to attend orthodox services, and in 1563 the adoption of the Thirty-nine Articles fixed the basic doctrines and forms of worship. To many reformers the settlement seemed a disappointing compromise that must be overturned. Their objection was not to royal supremacy, mandatory services, or fixed doctrines but to the specific content of the articles which clung tenaciously to "popish" forms.

A. Puritans and Parliament

With Elizabeth intent on moderation and most of the Anglican hierarchy impervious to further adjustment, only Parliament remained as an avenue of change. So it was that in 1572 a group of reformers in the House of Commons introduced a bill to legalize nonconformity of the kind dubbed "Puritan" by its detractors. Although suppressed by the Queen, who decreed that no more bills concerning religion could be introduced without her approval, the measure did bring issues into the open. It also gave rise to a pamphlet by two young Puritan preachers—John Field (d.1588) and Thomas Wilcox (c.1549–1608)—entitled An Admonition to Parliament (1572), which for the first time gave clear and full public statement to the aims of the more radical wing of the reform faction.

Source: W. H. Frere and C. E. Douglas, eds., Puritan Manifestoes (London, 1907), 8–14, 20, 35–37.

Seeing that nothing in this mortal life is more diligently to be sought for and carefully to be looked unto[1] than the restitution of true religion and reformation of God's church: it shall be your parts (dearly beloved) in this present Parliament assembled, as much as in you lieth to promote the same, and to employ your whole labor and study not only in abandoning all popish remnants both in ceremonies and regiment, but also in bringing in and placing in God's Church those things only which the Lord Himself[2] in His word commandeth. . . .

1. 2 Reg. 23; 2 Chron. 17; 29:29,30,31; Psal. 132:2,3,4; Matth. 21:12; John 2:15.
2. Deut. 4:2; 12:32. [In order to conserve space, further Biblical references, with which this document abounds, have been omitted. Editor.]

May it therefore please your wisdoms to understand we in England are so far off from having a church rightly reformed, according to the prescript of God's word, that as yet we are not come to the outward face of the same. . . . The outward marks whereby a true Christian church is known are preaching of the word purely, ministering of the sacraments sincerely, and ecclesiastical discipline which consisteth in admonition and correction of faults severely.

Touching the first, namely the ministry of the word, although it must be confessed that the substance of doctrine by many delivered is sound and good, yet herein it faileth, that neither the ministers thereof are according to God's word proved, elected, called, or ordained, nor the function in such sort so narrowly looked unto as of right it ought and is of necessity required. For whereas in the old church [i.e., in the early years of Christianity] a trial was had both of their ability to instruct, and of their godly conversation also, now, by the letters commendatory of some one man, noble or other, tag and rag, learned and unlearned, of the basest sort of the people (to the slander of the gospel in the mouths of the adversaries) are freely received. In those days no idolatrous sacrificers or heathenish priests were appointed to be preachers of the gospel, but we allow and like well of popish mass mongers, men for all seasons, King Henry's priests, King Edward's priests, Queen Mary's priests, who of a truth (if God's word were precisely followed) should from the same be utterly removed. Then they taught others, now they must be instructed themselves, and therefore like young children they must learn catechisms.

Then election was made by the common consent of the whole church; now every one picketh out for himself some notable good benefice, he obtaineth the next advowson by money or by favor, and so thinketh himself to be sufficiently chosen. Then the congregation had authority to call ministers; instead thereof now they run, they ride, and by unlawful suit and buying prevent other suitors also. Then no minister placed in any congregation but by the consent of the people; now that authority is given into the hands of the bishop alone, who by his sole authority thrusteth upon them such as they many times as well for unhonest life, as also for lack of learning, may and do justly dislike. Then none admitted to the ministry but a place was void beforehand, to which he should be called; but now bishops (to whom the right of ordering ministers doth at no hand appertain) do make 60, 80, or a 100 at a clap, and send them abroad into the country like masterless men. Then, after just trial and vocation, they were admitted to their function by laying on of the hands of the company of the eldership only; now there is (neither of these being looked unto) required an alb, a surplice, a vestment, a pastoral staff, beside that ridiculous and (as they use it to their new creatures) blasphemous saying "receive the Holy Ghost." Then every pastor had his flock and every flock his shepherd, or else shepherds; now they do not only run frisking from place to place (a miserable disorder in God's church) but covetously join living to living, making shipwreck of their own consciences, and being but one shepherd (nay, would to God they were shepherds and not wolves) have many flocks. Then the ministers were preachers; now bare readers, and if any be so well disposed to preach in their own charges, they may not without my Lord's license. In those days known by voice, learning, and doctrine; now they must be discerned from other by popish and anti-Christian apparel, as cap, gown, tippet, etc. Then, as God gave utterance, they preached the word only; now they read homilies, articles, injunctions, etc. Then it was painful, now gainful. Then poor and ignominious, now rich and glorious. And therefore titles, livings, and offices by anti-Christ devised are given to them, as Metropolitan, Archbishop, Lord's Grace, Lord Bishop, Suffragan, Dean, Archdeacon, Prelate of the Garter, Earl, County Palatine, Honor, High Commissioners, Justices of Peace and Quorum, etc. All which, together with their offices, as they are strange and un-heard of in Christ's church—nay plainly in God's word forbidden —so are they utterly, with speed, out of the same to be removed.

Then ministers were not tied to any form of prayers invented by man, but as the spirit moved them, so they poured forth hearty supplications to the Lord. Now they are bound of necessity to a prescript order of service and Book of Common Prayer in which a great number of things contrary to God's word are contained, as baptism by women, private communions, Jewish purifyings, observ-ing of holy days, etc., patched (if not all together, yet the greatest piece) out of the Pope's portuis. Then feeding the flock diligently, now teaching quarterly. Then preaching in season and out of season, now once in a month is thought sufficient; if twice, it is judged a work of supererogation. Then nothing taught but God's word, now princes' pleasures, men's devices, popish ceremonies, and anti-Christian rites in public pulpits defended. Then they sought them, now they seek theirs.

These and a great many other abuses are in the ministry remaining, which unless they be removed and the truth brought in, not only God's justice shall be poured forth, but also God's church in this realm shall never be builded. For if they which seem to be workmen are no workmen in deed, but in name, or else work not so diligently and in such order as the workmaster commandeth, it is not only unlikely that the building shall go forward, but altogether impossible that ever it shall be perfited. The way therefore to avoid these inconveniences and to reform these deformities is this: your wisdoms have to remove advowsons, patronages, impropriations, and bishops' authority, claiming to themselves thereby right to ordain ministers and to bring in that old and true election which was accustomed to be made by the congregation. You must displace those ignorant and unable ministers already placed, and in their rooms appoint such as both can and will by God's assistance feed the flock. You must pluck down and utterly overthrow without hope of restitution the Court of Faculties, from whence not only licenses to enjoy many benefises are obtained, as pluralities, trialities, totquots, etc., but all things for the most part as in the Court of Rome are set on sale—licenses to marry, to eat flesh in times prohibited, to lie from benefices and charges, and a great number beside of such like abominations. Appoint to every congregation a learned and diligent preacher. Remove homilies, articles, injunctions, a prescript order of service made out of the mass book. Take away the lordship, the loitering, the pomp, the idleness, and livings of bishops, but yet employ them to such ends as they were in the old church appointed for. Let a lawful and a godly seigniory look that they preach not quarterly or monthly, but continually, not for filthy lucre sake, but of a ready mind. So God shall be glorified, your consciences discharged, and the flock of Christ (purchased with His own blood) edified.

Now to the second point, which concerns ministration of sacraments. In the old time, the word was preached before they were ministered; now it is supposed to be sufficient if it be read. Then they were ministered in public assemblies, now in private houses. Then by ministers only, now by midwives and deacons equally. But because in treating of both the sacraments together we should deal confusedly, we will therefore speak of them severally. And first for the Lord's Supper, or holy communion:

They had no introit, for Celestinus a Pope brought it in about the year 430. But we have borrowed a piece of one out of the mass book. They read no fragments of the epistle and gospel; we use both. The Nicene Creed was not read in their communion; we have it in ours. There was then accustomed to be an examination of the communicants, which now is neglected. Then they ministered the sacrament with common and usual bread; now with wafer cakes, brought in by Pope Alexander, being in form, fashion, and substance like their god of the altar. They received it sitting, we kneeling according to Honorius' decree. Then it was delivered generally and indefinitely, "Take ye and eat ye," we particularly and singularly, "Take thou and eat thou." They used no other words but such as Christ left; we borrow from papists, "the body of our Lord Jesus Christ which was given for thee," etc. They had no gloria in excelsis in the ministry of the sacrament then, for it was put to afterward. We have now. They took it with conscience. We with custom. They shut men by reason of their sins from the Lord's Supper. We thrust them in their sin to the Lord's Supper. They ministered the sacrament plainly. We pompously, with singing, piping, surplice and cope wearing. They simply as they receive it from the Lord. We sinfully, mixed with man's inventions and devices. And as for baptism, it was enough with them if they had water, and the party to be baptised faith, and the minister to preach the word and minister the sacraments. Now we must have surplices devised by Pope Adrian, interrogatories ministered to the infant, godfathers and godmothers, brought in by Hyginus, holy fonts invented by Pope Pius, crossing and such like pieces of popery which the church of God in the Apostles' times never knew (and therefore not to be used) nay (which we are sure of) were and are man's devices brought in long after the purity of the primitive church. . . .

[The Second Admonition]

A view of popish abuses yet remaining in the English Church for which godly ministers have refused to subscribe. . . .

THE FIRST ARTICLE

First, that the book commonly called the Book of Common Prayer for the Church of England, authorized by Parliament, and all and every the contents therein be such as are not repugnant to the word of God.

Albeit, right honorable and dearly beloved, we have at all times borne with that which we could not amend in this book, and have used the same in our ministry so far forth as we might, reverencing those times and those persons in which and by whom it was first authorized, being studious of peace and of the building up of Christ's church, yet now being compelled by subscription to allow the same, and to confess it, not to be against the word of God in any point but tolerable. We must needs say as followeth: that this book is an unperfect book, culled and picked out of that popish dung hill, the mass book, full of all abominations. For some and many of the contents therein be such as are against the word of God, as by His grace shall be proved unto you. And by the way we cannot but much marvel at the crafty wiliness of those men whose parts it had been first to have proved each and every content therein to be agreeable to the word of God, seeing that they enforce men by subscription to consent unto it, or else send them packing from their callings. . . .

THE SECOND ARTICLE

That the manner and order appointed by public authority about the administration of the sacraments and common prayers, and that the apparel by sufficient authority appointed for the ministers within the Church of England be not wicked nor against the word of God, but tolerable, and being commanded for order and obedience sake, are to be used.

For the order of administration of sacraments and common prayer, enough is said before: all the service and administration is tied to a surplice, in cathedral churches they must have a cope, they receive the communion kneeling, they use not for the most part common bread according to the word of God and the statute, but starch bread according to the injunction. They commonly minister the sacraments without preaching the word.

And as for the apparel, though we have been long borne in hand and yet are that it is for order and decency commanded, yet we know and have proved that there is neither order nor comeliness, nor obedience in using it. There is no order in it, but confusion; no comeliness, but deformity; no obedience, but disobedience, both against God and the Prince. We marvel that they could espy in their last synod that a gray amice, which is but a garment of dignity, should be a garment (as they say) defiled with superstition and yet that copes, caps, surplices, tippets, and such like baggage, the preaching signs of popish priesthood, the Pope's creatures kept in the same form to this end to bring dignity and reverence to the ministers and sacraments, should be retained still and not abolished. But they are as the garments of the idol, to which we should say, avaunt and get thee hence. They are as the garments of Balamites, of popish priests, enemies to God and all Christians. They serve not to edification, they have the shew of evil (seeing the popish priesthood is evil), they work discord, they hinder the preaching of the gospel, they keep the memory of Egypt still amongst us, and put us in mind of that abomination whereunto they in times past have served, they bring the ministry into contempt, they offend the weak, they encourage the obstinate. Therefore can no authority by the word of God, with any pretense of order and obedience, command them nor make them in any ways tolerable, but by circumstances they are wicked and against the word of God. . . .

THE THIRD ARTICLE

That the articles of religion which only concern the true Christian faith and the doctrine of the sacraments, comprised in a book imprinted *Articles*, whereupon it was agreed by both archbishops, etc., and every of them contain true and godly Christian doctrine.

For the *Articles* concerning that substance of doctrine using a godly interpretation in a point or two, which are either too sparely or else too darkly set down, we were and are ready according to duty to subscribe unto them. [*Marginal note:* The right government of the church can not be separated from the doctrine.] We would to God that as they hold the substance together with us, and we with them, so they would not deny the effect and virtue thereof. Then should not our words and works be divorced, but Christ should be suffered to reign—a true ministry according to the word instituted, discipline exercised, sacraments purely and sincerely ministered. . . .

Amen.

Shortly after the appearance of the Admonition, Field and Wilcox were incarcerated in Newgate; they remained in prison for almost a year. During that time neither their spirits nor the movement waned. New Puritan pamphleteers joined the fray, while the two prisoners urged that "it is no tyme to blanch, nor to sewe cushens under mens elbowes, or to flatter them in their synnes. . . ." Scores of friends visited the au-

thors of the Admonition, and sympathetic London merchants proffered financial aid. Meanwhile the Admonition and other pamphlets were "in every man's hand and mouth." But the Puritan victory, if it could be called that, proved short lived. Elizabeth continued to frown on Puritan activities, and for the next several decades the movement remained a noisy but largely ineffectual protest. The attempt to use Parliament as a vehicle of ecclesiastical reform would have to await more propitious times.

During the balance of Elizabeth's reign, the Puritan faction, though out of official favor and without major political influence, grew both in numbers and in diversity. Because there was no Puritan "party" in an organized sense, the movement remained varied and diffuse. Puritans disagreed among themselves on many matters, and even among the Puritan-minded clergy there were sharp differences as to the proper course of action. Ministers who favored further purification of the church had to decide whether to reform from within or withdraw from it; a few chose the latter course and became "separatists"; most took the less radical option and retained their positions in the church while attempting to influence the hierarchy toward change and at the same time practicing in the relative security of their own parishes a liberal form of Anglicanism.

Increasingly the Puritan faction could be recognized by its emphasis on preaching, either through the usual Sunday sermons or through privately sponsored "lectureships," and by its penchant for theological discussions, labeled "prophesyings," open to the public. More and more English men and women were becoming exposed to Puritan concepts of liturgy, organization, and faith. In the face of such growth, the orthodox leaders of the church struck back. Under the leadership of John Whitgift, Archbishop of Canterbury from 1583 to 1604, church and state joined hands to suppress nonconformist publications such as the pseudonymous tracts of "Martin Marprelate" and to prosecute leading Puritan spokesmen such as Thomas Cartwright, who as early as 1570 had been ousted from his professorship at Cambridge for advocating widespread changes in church polity. Many Puritans became discouraged, for even though their faction now boasted numerous adherents in Parliament, the obstinacy of the hierarchy, and especially of the Crown, made the prospects for church reform remote.

B. Puritans and the King

Hope dawned anew in 1603 with the accession of James I to the throne of England. As James VI of Scotland, where a Calvinist theology had held official sway since 1560, the new King adhered to Presbyterian doctrines which differed little from the religious preferences of most English Puritans and coincided fully with the views of some. If James supported his own religious heritage, Puritanism would have a powerful new ally.

But James did not. Although he acknowledged the legitimacy of Puritan grievances by receiving their Millenary Petition (so called from the thousand signatures it presumably contained), and although he answered the petition by calling a conference of orthodox and Puritan spokesmen, the Puritans gained few meaningful concessions from the new monarch. At a meeting held in January, 1604, at Hampton Court, the King vigorously sided with the bishops. James saw that an episcopal hierarchy and religious uniformity bolstered monarchial authority; Presbyterianism, he blustered, "agreeth with a monarchy as God and the Devil. Then Jack and Tom and Will and Dick shall meet, and at their pleasures censure me and my councel. . . ." Insisting on "one doctrine and one discipline, one religion in substance and in ceremony," he warned the Puritans to conform or be harried out of the land. At least so reads the most widely circulated report on the conference, written by a participating bishop who may well have exaggerated the hostility of James to the Puritan position. The following less familiar but briefer account of the conference also reflects a strongly Anglican bias that saw the conference as a thorough rout of Puritans.

Source: Roland G. Usher, The Reconstruction of the English Church (2 vols., New York, 1910), II, 335–338.

The Conference began upon the sixteenth day of January at eleven and continued until five of the clock. None suffered to be present but the Council and such as were agents thereunto summoned. The King made a speech unto them, wherein he signified his desire to establish truth of religion. And forasmuch as they (speaking of the Puritans) had excepted against the present state of religion and church discipline as erroneous and imperfect, he was desirous to hear the objections, that if they were approved and allowed to be just and equal they might be reformed accordingly.

Whereupon Dr. Reynolds as the mouth of the rest answered the King's speech, and excepted against many points which he derived from these general heads: (1) Articles of Religion; (2) Subscription to the Articles and Book of Common Prayer; (3) Sufficiency and Residency of the Ministry; (4) Jurisdiction of the Bishops and Chancellors. In the Articles, he made exception and a contradiction between the Article of Predestination and falling from faith, affirming the one to overthrow the other. The second against the Article of Sacraments, because that our church renounceth confirmation and yet the Book of Common Prayer alloweth it.

To the first, Dr. Overall craved audience and replied as a party particularly aimed at therein. The King granted him very willingly licentiam loquendi and was fully satisfied by him, advising in the conclusion that this addition might be put to the Article, that the elect might often fall from grace and faith.

To the second, the Bishop[s] of Winchester and London answered that confirmation was rejected as a sacrament, and in the prayer book allowed as a holy and godly practice of the Apostles in the primitive church.

After that he [Dr. Reynolds] made some exception against the translation of our Bible and the reading of the Apocrypha, the former was a little debated, and so passed over as a matter of no great moment. And yet the King [was] content to allow some new translation if the Bishops would consent thereunto; as for the Apocrypha, he allowed and justified the use thereof.

The second main and general point of subscription the King did utterly reject and would no way yield to their request to be freed from subscription. Here were handled all matters of controversy, as caps, surplice, rings, and crosses, and after much opposition and replies the King made a peremptory conclusion for the allowance and continuance of all these particulars as decent and expedient. Mr. Knewstubs was fierce against and so was Dr. Andrews as fierce for the cross, and the King was most resolute for it.

They made a petition: to be exempted from the superstitious surplice in regard to the weakness of many consciences which thereby were driven from their function. But the King replied with derision of their allegation, and said that those weak consciences were such as ought to strengthen others, and in all matters of faction shewed themselves most headstrong, proud, and violent.

The third point was judged impossible, because there were not ministers sufficient to furnish every parish, nor every parish able to find a sufficient minister. And so that point was passed over.

For their last point of jurisdiction, their desire was that the Bishops should not execute it alone by themselves but jointly with the presbytery of their brethren, the pastors and ministers of the church. Whereunto the King replied merrily saying he would have the presbytery buried in silence for these seven years and if then he grew idle, lazy, fat, and pursy, "I will set up presbytery," saith he, "to exercise my body and my patience; otherwise it shall never up for me, and so rest contented for that matter."

This is the truth and nothing but the truth; if any contradict this, you may resist him. They had a cold pull of it and are utterly foiled. They are grieved at nothing so much as the continuance of a popish relic of the surplice. It is thought they sue for connivance in [its] behalf, and rather lose their livings than wear it, God grant it.

Puritan Actors in these points:
- Dr. Reynolds, Oxen, the principal mouth and speaker
- Dr. Sparks, spoke very sparingly
- Mr. Chaderton, mute as any fish
- Knewstubs, fierce against the cross
- Patrick Galloway, silent in all things

Anti-Puritans:
- Dr. Andrewes
- Overall
- Edes
- Thomson
- Barlow
- Kings
- Montaine
- Ravis
- Abbotts

Supervisors of this Conference:
- Bishop[s] of London
- of Winchester
- Bancroft
- Bilson

Dr. Feythe (Feilde) went in with the Puritans; he never spoke but once, and that altogether against them.

Furthermore, Chaderton must conform, and his irregular college to wear the surplice and receive the communion kneeling or else be put out of it. The King imposed this by reason of information given him from the Lord Henry. The Chancellors of both the universities must send their letters down, that none shall be admitted without subscription.

This is the triumph they so long expected. Dr. Reynolds and his brethren are utterly condemned for silly men.

Some minor reforms in liturgy and ecclesiastical discipline did follow the Hampton Court Conference, and at the request of the Puritan spokesmen the Church undertook a new translation of the Bible. While the King James version of the Bible, published in 1611, could not be considered a Puritan document, many Puritan scholars had a hand in it, and on the whole it proved acceptable to the reform wing of the church. Nor did King James harry the Puritans out of England. That task awaited his son, Charles I.

Far less encouraging was the attitude of the bishops. Not only did they circulate hostile accounts of the conference, but more importantly, under Archbishop Richard Bancroft, they continued the suppression of dissent that had marked the Elizabethan era. The Puritan movement remained underground, making itself felt through prolific writings, evangelical preaching, and innumerable local "conventicles"—nonconformist gatherings not sanctioned by ecclesiastical law.

2. Emergence of Puritan Theology

In the half-century between the Admonition to Parliament and the first major migrations to New England, Puritanism added new dimensions to its attack on orthodox Anglicanism. Whereas the early stages had stressed differences of procedure and paraphernalia, by 1580 the emphasis had shifted to matters of church organization, and by early in the seventeenth century to matters of fundamental theology. Much of the change in emphasis can be attributed to the writings of a new generation of English theologians such as Thomas Cartwright (1535–1603), William Perkins (1558–1602), John Preston (1587–1628), and William Ames (1576–1633). It was Ames to whom the New Englanders would look with special reverence, for he not only added some new ideas and new emphases to dissenting thought but codified more clearly than any of his contemporaries the growing body of Puritan doctrine. Although Ames did not join the exodus to New England, he kept in close touch with its leaders, and it was probably his early death that deprived New England of his presence. As Cotton Mather put it, Ames "was intentionally a New-England man, though not eventually." (His widow and children arrived in Massachusetts in 1637; his two sons attended Harvard in the 1640s.)

While Ames's ideas on predestination and on the nature of the conversion experience did not differ radically from Anglican interpretation, Puritan thinking owed much to his emphasis on the selective nature of eternal salvation and the restriction of church membership to those who had been chosen by God for life everlasting, and on the sequential steps to salvation: justification, adoption, sanctification, and glorification. He also stressed the Covenant of Grace and the role of the Holy Spirit in religious experience, as well as the duty of man to live soberly and industriously in accordance with Divine Law. Ames's most influential work, Medulla Theologica, first appeared in 1623 in Latin and went through almost a score of subsequent printings, including English and Dutch translations. During the next century it was widely used by both English and American Puritans, the latter employing it as a textbook at Harvard and Yale and treating it almost as a catechism for adult New Englanders.

Source: William Ames, The Marrow of Theology, trans. by John D. Eusden (Philadelphia, 1968), 152–153, 160–165, 167–169, 171–172.

XXV. Predestination

1. The application of redemption to some men and not to all and the manifest difference which, therefore, arises between men

in the dispensation of grace gives to us a first intimation of God's predestination of men.

2. Predestination has existed from eternity. Eph. 1:4, *He has chosen us before the foundations of the world were laid;* 2 Tim. 1:9, *Which grace was given us before all ages.* It operated in the very beginning of God's work, but there is no inward difference in the predestined until the actual application of it. Eph. 2:3, *And we were by nature the children of wrath as well as others;* 1 Cor. 6:11, *And such were some of you.* Predestination before the application of grace puts nothing in the persons predestined but lies hidden only in the One who predestines.

3. Predestination is a decree of God concerning the eternal condition of men which shows his special glory, Rom. 9:22, 23, *Willing to show his wrath and make his power known, he suffered with much patience the vessels of wrath prepared to destruction, in order to make known the riches of his glory for the vessels of his mercy, which he has prepared for glory.* 1 Thess. 5:9, *God has not appointed us to wrath, but to obtain mercy.*

4. It is called destination because there is a sure determination of the order of means for the end. Because God determined this order by himself before any actual existence of things, it is called not simply destination but predestination. . . .

6. Predestination is accompanied by the greatest wisdom, freedom, firmness, and immutability. These are found in all the decrees of God.

7. The basis of predestination is unmovable and indissoluble. 2 Tim. 2:19, *The foundation of God stands sure, having this seal. The Lord knows who are his.* On that basis the number of the predestined (not only the formal number, or numerand, as they say, i.e., how many shall be saved and how many not, but also the material number, or numerate, i.e. who the men are) is certain with God not only in the certainty of his foreknowledge but in the certainty of the means he has ordered. Luke 10:20, *Rejoice that your names are written in the heavens.*

8. Predestination does not necessarily presuppose that either its end or object exists; rather it causes it to exist. Predestination orders that it should be. 1 Peter 1:20, *Christ foreknown before the foundations of the world are laid.*

9. Hence it depends upon no cause, reason, or outward condition, but proceeds purely from the will of him who predestines.

Matt. 11:26, *Even so, Father, because it pleases thee;* Rom. 9:16, 18, *It is not of him that wills or of him that runs but of God who shows mercy. . . . He has mercy on whom he will and chooses those whom he will harden.*

10. Hence it is not necessary, nor does it agree with the Scriptures, to appoint any previous quality in man which might be considered the formal object of predestination. No condition in any man decides that others should be excluded. It is sufficient only to understand that men, equal among themselves, are the object of the decree; the difference inherent in the decree does not depend upon man, but the differences found in men are the result of the decree. . . .

XXVII. Justification

1. Participation in the blessings of the union with Christ comes when the faithful have all the things needed to live well and blessedly to God. Eph. 1:3, *He has blessed us with every spiritual blessing;* Rom. 8:32, *He who spared not his own son . . . how shall he not freely with him give us all things also?*

2. This participation therefore brings a change and alteration in the condition of believers from the state of sin and death to the state of righteousness and eternal life. 1 John 3:14, *We know that we are translated from death to life.*

3. This change of state is twofold, relative and absolute (or real).

4. The relative change occurs in God's reckoning. Rom. 4:5, *And to him who does not work, but believes in him who justifies the ungodly, his faith is imputed as righteousness.* 2 Cor. 5:19, *God was in Christ reconciling the world to himself, not counting their offenses.*

5. The change, of course, has no degrees and is completed at one moment and in only one act. Yet in manifestation, consciousness, and effects, it has many degrees; therein lie justification and adoption.

6. Justification is the gracious judgment of God by which he absolves the believer from sin and death, and reckons him righteous and worthy of life for the sake of Christ apprehended in faith. Rom. 3:22, 24, *The righteousness of God by faith in Jesus Christ in all and upon all that believe . . . they are freely justi-*

fied by his grace . . . through the redemption made by Jesus Christ.

7. It is the pronouncing of a sentence, as the word is used, which does not denote in the Holy Scriptures a physical or a real change. There is rather a judicial or moral change which takes shape in the pronouncing of the sentence and in the reckoning. Prov. 17:15, He that justifies the wicked; Rom. 8:33, Who shall lay anything to the charge of God's elect? It is God who justifies. . . .

14. This justification comes about because of Christ, but not in the absolute sense of Christ's being the cause of vocation. It happens because Christ is apprehended by faith, which follows calling as an effect. Faith precedes justification as the instrumental cause, laying hold of the righteousness of Christ from which justification being apprehended follows; therefore, righteousness is said to be from faith, Rom. 9:30; 10:6. And justification is said to be by faith, Rom. 3:28.

15. This justifying faith is not the general faith of the understanding by which we give assent to the truth revealed in the Holy Scriptures, for that belongs not only to those who are justified, nor of its nature has it any force to justify, nor produce the effects which are everywhere in Scripture given to justifying faith. . . .

23. Not only are past sins of justified persons remitted but also those to come, Num. 23:25. God sees no iniquity in Jacob or perverseness in Israel. Justification has left no place for condemnation. John 5:24, He who believes has eternal life and shall not come into condemnation—justification gives eternal life surely and immediately. It also makes the whole remission obtained for us in Christ actually ours. Neither past nor present sins can be altogether fully remitted unless sins to come are in some way remitted.

24. The difference is that past sins are remitted specifically and sins to come potentially. Past sins are remitted in themselves, sins to come in the subject or the person sinning.

25. Yet those who are justified need daily the forgiveness of sins. This is true because the continuance of grace is necessary to them; the consciousness and manifestation of forgiveness increases more and more as individual sins require it; and the execution of the sentence which is pronounced in justification may thus be carried out and completed. . . .

XXVIII. Adoption

1. Adoption is the gracious judgment of God wherein he gives the faithful the dignity of sonship because of Christ. John 1:12, *As many as receive him to these he gives the right*, ἐξουσία, *to be made the sons of God, to those who believe in his name.* . . .

6. Although adoption follows from faith, justification comes in between. Adoption of its own nature requires and presupposes the reconciliation found in justification.

7. The faithful can expect heaven, so to speak, by a double title, namely, the title of redemption through justification and the title, as it were, of sonship through adoption.

8. It should, however, be understood that the title of redemption is the foundation of this right and adoption adds to it excellence and dignity.

9. Here is the first difference between divine adoption and human. Human adoption relates to a person who, as a stranger, has no right to the inheritance except through adoption. But believers, though by natural birth they have no right to the inheritance of life, are given it because of rebirth, faith, and justification.

10. There is also a second difference. Human adoption is only an outward designation and bestowal of external things. But divine adoption is so real a relationship that it is based on an inward action and the communication of a new inner life. . . .

XXIX. Sanctification

So much for justification and adoption, which relate to the relative change of state for believers. Now we consider the real change, wherein justification is manifested and its consequences, so to speak, brought into being.

1. The real change of state is an alteration of qualities in man himself. 2 Cor. 5:17, *Old things have passed away; all things are new.*

2. The change is not in relation or reason, but in genuine effects seen in degrees of beginning, progress, and completion. 2 Cor. 4:16, *The inner man is renewed day by day.*

3. This alteration of qualities is related to either the just and

honorable good of sanctification, or the perfect and exalted good of glorification. Rom. 6:22, *You have your fruit in holiness and your end in everlasting life.*

4. Sanctification is the real change in man from the sordidness of sin to the purity of God's image. Eph. 4:22–24, *Put off that which pertains to the old conversation, that old man, corrupting itself in deceivable lusts, and be renewed in the spirit of your mind. Put on that new man who according to God is created to righteousness and true holiness.*

5. Just as in justification a believer is properly freed from the guilt of sin and his life given him (the title to which is, as it were, settled in adoption), so in sanctification the same believer is freed from the sordidness and stain of sin, and the purity of God's image is restored to him. . . .

13. The starting point of sanctification is the filthiness, corruption, or stain of sin. 2 Cor. 7:1, *Let us purge ourselves from all filthiness of flesh and spirit, being led to holiness in the fear of God.*

14. Its end is the purity of God's image (said to be fashioned or created once more in *Knowledge, righteousness, and holiness,* Eph. 4:24) or *Conformity to the law of God,* Jas. 1:25; *Newness of life,* Rom. 6:4; the *New creature,* 2 Cor. 5:17 and Gal. 6:15; and the *Divine nature,* 2 Peter 1:4.

15. The end is called a new and divine creature. First, because it is not produced by those principles which are in us by nature, as is characteristic of all the arts pursued with industry and discipline— it comes out of the new principle of life communicated by God to us in our calling. Second, because our natural disposition is of a completely different kind from what it was before. Third, because it takes for its model the highest perfection found in God himself. . . .

XXX. Glorification

We have spoken of sanctification, one part of the alteration of qualities which relates to a just and honorable good. We now consider the other part, glorification, which relates to perfect and exalted good.

1. Glorification is the real change in man from misery, or the

punishment of sin, to eternal happiness. Rom. 8:30, *Those whom he justified he also glorified.*

2. It is called a real change so that it may be distinguished from the blessedness which is only potential in election, calling, justification, and adoption or illustrated in holy works. Rom. 4:6, *David declares the man to be blessed to whom God reckons righteousness;* Ps. 65:4, *Blessed is he whom thou choosest and bringest to dwell in thy courts;* Matt. 5:3, *Blessed are the poor in spirit.*

3. Since the starting point is misery or the punishment of sin, it is called redemption, 1 Cor. 1:30; Eph. 1:14; Gal. 3:13; Heb. 2:14, 15.

4. Redemption is a real deliverance from the evils of punishment, which is actually nothing but the carrying out of the sentence of justification. For in justification we are pronounced just and awarded the judgment of life. In glorification the life that results from the pronouncement and award is given to us: We have it in actual possession. . . .

3. The Intensity of Puritan Piety

Adherence to the doctrines espoused by Ames and other English clergymen was almost always accompanied by profound personal piety. Puritan preachers, not surprisingly, were widely noted for the depth of their commitment to reformed Christianity and for its pervasive effect on their daily lives. The laity exhibited similar characteristics, as the following selections from John Winthrop's "Experiencia" suggest. The future governor of the Massachusetts Bay Colony recorded these autobiographical reflections during his own period of emerging faith: a brief entry from 1613 that expresses Winthrop's determination to conduct his daily life by Christian precepts, and entries from 1616 that reveal his and his second wife's pious response to her impending and untimely death.

Source: Robert C. Winthrop, *Life and Letters of John Winthrop* (2 vols., Boston, 1864) I: 73–74, 80–89.

May 23, 1613. When my condition was much straightened, partly through my long sickness, partly through want of freedom, partly through lack of outward things, I prayed often to the Lord for deliverance, referring the means to Himself, and with all I often promised to

ance, referring the means to Himself, and with all I often promised to put forth myself to much fruit when the Lord should enlarge me. Now that He hath set me at great liberty, giving me a good end to my tedious quartan, freedom from a superior will and liberal maintenance by the death of my wife's father (who finished his days in peace the 15 of May, 1613):

I do resolve, first, to give myself, my life, my wit, my health, my wealth to the service of my God and Savior, who by giving Himself for me, and to me, deserves whatsoever I am or can be, to be at His commandment and for His glory:

2. I will live where He appoints me.

3. I will faithfully endeavor to discharge that calling which He shall appoint me unto.

4. I will carefully avoid vain and needless expenses that I may be the more liberal to good uses.

5. My property and bounty must go forth abroad, yet I must ever be careful that it begin at home.

6. I will so dispose of my family affairs as my morning prayers and evening exercises be not omitted.

7. I will have a special care of the good education of my children.

8. I will banish profaneness from my family.

9. I will diligently observe the Lord's Sabbath both for the avoiding and preventing worldly business and also for the religious spending of such times as are free from public exercises, viz. the morning, noon, and evening.

10. I will endeavor to have the morning free for private prayer, meditation, and reading.

11. I will flee idleness and much worldly business.

12. I will often pray and confer privately with my wife.

* * * * *

On Saturday being the last of November 1616, Thomasine, my dear and loving wife, was delivered of a daughter, which died the Monday following in the morning. She took the death of it with that patience that made us all to marvel, especially those that saw how careful she was for the life of it in her travail. That day, soon after the death of the child, she was taken with a fever which shaked her very much and set her into a great fit of coughing, which by Tuesday morning was well allayed, yet she continued aguish and sweating, with much hoarseness, and her mouth grew very sore and much troubled with blood falling from her head into her mouth and throat. . . .

On Thursday in the night she was taken with death, and about midnight or somewhat after called for me and for the rest of her friends. When I came to her she seemed to be fully assured that her time was come, and to be glad of it, and desired me to pray, which I did; and she took comfort therein and desired that we would send for Mr. Sands, which we did. In the meantime, she desired that the bell might ring for her, and diverse of the neighbors came into her, which when she perceived she desired me that they might come to her one by one, and so she would speak to them all, which she did as they came, quietly and comfortably. When the bell began to ring, some said it was the 4 o'-clock bell, but she conceiving that they sought to conceal it from her that it did ring for her; she said it needed not, for it did not trouble her. Then came in Mr. Nicolson whom she desired to pray, which he did.

When Mr. Sands was come she reached him her hand, being glad of his coming (for she had asked often for him). He spake to her of diverse comfortable points, whereunto she answered so wisely and comfortably, as he and Mr. Nicolson did both marvel to hear her, Mr. Sands saying to me that he did not look for so sound judgment in her. He said he had taken her always for a harmless young woman, and well affected, but did not think she had been so well grounded. Mr. Nicolson, seeing her humbleness of mind and great comfort in God, said that her life had been so innocent and harmless as the devil could find nothing to lay to her charge. Then she desired Mr. Sands to pray, but not pray for life for her; he answered that he would pray for grace. . . .

The fever grew very strong upon her, so as when all the time of her sickness before she was wont to say she thanked God she felt no pain, now she began to complain of her breast and troubles in her head, and after she had slumbered a while and was awaked, she began to be tempted, and when I came to her she seemed to be affrighted, used some speeches of Satan's assaulting her, and complained of the loss of her first love, etc.; then we prayed with her, as she desired. After prayer she disliked that we prayed for life for her, since we might see it was not God's will that she should live.

Her fever increased very violently upon her, which the devil made advantage of to molest her comfort, but she declaring unto us with what temptations the devil did assault her, bent herself against them, praying with great vehemence for God's help and that He would not take away His loving kindness from her, defying Satan and spitting at him, so as we might see by her setting of her teeth and fixing her eyes, shaking her head and whole body, that she had a very great conflict with the adversary.

After she a little paused, and that they went about to cover her hands which lay open with her former striving, she began to lift up herself, desiring that she might have her hands and all at liberty to glorify God and prayed earnestly that she might glorify God, although it were in hell. Then she began very earnestly to call upon all that were about her, exhorting them to serve God, etc. (And whereas all the time of her sickness before she would not endure the light but would be careful to have the curtains kept close, now she desired light, and would have the curtain towards the window set open, and so to her end was much grieved when she had not either the daylight or candlelight, but the firelight she could not endure to look upon, saying that it was of too many colors like the rainbow.) . . .

To her mother she said that she was the first child that she should bury, but prayed her that she would not be discomforted at it; when her mother answered that she had no cause to be discomforted for her, for she should go to a better place and she should go to her father, she replied that she should go to a better father than her earthly father.

Then came my father and mother, whom she thanked for all their kindness and love towards her.

Then she called for my children and blessed them severally, and would needs have Mary brought that she might kiss her, which she did.

Then she called for my sister Luce, and exhorted her to take heed of pride and to serve God.

Then she called for her servants. To Robert she said, you have many good things in you, I have nothing to accuse you of; be faithful and diligent in your service.

To Anne Pold she said that she was a stubborn wench, etc., and exhorted her to be obedient to my mother.

To Elizabeth Crouff she said, take heed of pride and I shall now release you, but take heed what service you go into.

To Anne Addams she said, thou hast been in bad serving long in an alehouse, etc.; thou makest no conscience of the Sabbath; when I would have had thee gone to church thou wouldst not, etc.

Then came Mercy Smith to her, to whom she said thou art a good woman; bring up thy children well, you poor folks commonly spoiled your children in suffering (them) to break God's Sabbaths, etc. . . .

Her pain increased very much in her breast, which swelled so as they were forced to cut the tyings of her waistcoat to give her ease. Whilst she lay in this estate she ceased not (albeit she was very hoarse, and spake with great pain) one while to exhort, another while to pray.

Her usual prayer was "Come Lord Jesus; When Lord Jesus, etc."; her exhortation was to stir up all that saw her to prepare for death, telling them that they did not know how sharp and bitter the pangs of death were, with many like speeches.

In this time she prayed for the church, etc., and for the ministry, that God would bless good ministers and convert such ill ones as did belong to IIim and weed out the rest. After this we might perceive that God had given her victory, by the comfort which she had in the meditation of her happiness, in the favor of God in Christ Jesus. Towards afternoon her great pains remitted, and she lay very still and said she saw her time was not yet come, she should live 24 hours longer; then when any asked her how she did, she would answer prettily well, but in her former fit to that question she would answer that she was going the way of all flesh. Then she prayed me to read by her. When I asked her where, she answered, in some of the holy gospels, so I began in John the 14 and read on to the end of the 17th chapter. And when I paused at the end of any sweet sentence, she would say "this is comfortable"; if I stayed at the end of any chapter for her to take rest, she would earnestly call to read on. . . .

That Sabbath noon, when most of the company were gone down to dinner, when I discoursed unto her of the sweet love of Christ unto her and of the glory that she was going unto, and what an holy everlasting Sabbath she should keep and how she should sup with Christ in paradise that night, etc., she showed by her speeches and gestures the great joy and steadfast assurance that she had of those things. When I told her that her Redeemer lived and that she should see Him with those poor dim eyes, which should be bright and glorified, she answered cheerfully, she should. When I told her that she should leave the society of friends which were full of infirmities and should have communion with Abram, Isaac, and Jacob, all the prophets and apostles and saints of God, and those holy martyrs (whose stories when I asked her if she remembered she answered yea), she would lift up her hands and eyes and say, yea she should. Such comfort had she against death that she steadfastly professed that if life were set before her she would not take it.

When I told her that the day before was 12 months she was married to me and now this day she should be married to Christ Jesus, who would embrace her with another manner of love than I could, "O husband," said she, and spoke as if she were offended, for I perceived she did mistake me, "I must not love thee as I love Christ." . . .

About 5 of the clock, Mr. Nicolson came to her and prayed with her, and about the end of his prayer, she fetched 2 or 3 sighs and fell asleep in the Lord . . .

She was a woman wise, modest, loving, and patient of injuries, but her innocent and harmless life was of most observation. She was truly religious, and industrious therein; plain-hearted and free from guile, and very humble-minded; never so addicted to any outward things (to my judgment) but that she could bring her affections to stoop to God's will in them. She was sparing in outward show of zeal, etc., but her constant love to good Christians and the best things, with her reverent and careful attendance of God's ordinances, both public and private, with her care for avoiding of evil herself and reproving it in others did plainly show that truth and the love of God did lie at the heart. Her loving and tender regard of my children was such as might well become a natural mother. For her carriage towards myself, it was so amiable and observant as I am not able to express; it had this only inconvenience, that it made me delight too much in her to enjoy her long.

4. Reasons for Forsaking England

As Puritan beliefs and practices gained adherents, so did the determination of the Anglican establishment to uproot the spreading dissent. The church tried several tactics: issuing decrees against unorthodox practices, increasing supervision over local clergymen, and removing ministers from their livings. Perhaps as many as three hundred ministers lost their posts in the aftermath of the Hampton Court Conference, when every minister was required to subscribe to all of the Thirty-nine Articles. As a last resort, offending clergymen were hailed before Courts of High Commission, which examined theological and ecclesiastical matters and inflicted punishments, including excommunication, on the guilty.

Charles I's dissolution of Parliament in March 1629 dealt a heavy blow to Puritan hopes for church reform. Repression now seemed imminent in politics as well as in religion. In June 1629, attorney and manor lord John Winthrop (1588–1649) gave up his position in the Court of Wards and prepared for an exodus from England, observing sadly that "this lande growes wearye of her Inhabitantes." But the challenge of emigration was immense; it would be costly, dangerous, and uncertain. More important, it had to be justifiable to the Puritan conscience. Winthrop therefore drafted a series of papers for circulation to prospective colonists in which he succeeded in blending sacred and secular motives into a holy cause.

Reasons to be considered for justifying the undertakers of the intended plantation in New England and for encouraging such whose hearts God shall move to join with them in it.

First, it will be a service to the church of great consequence to carry the gospel into those parts of the world, to help on the coming in of fullness of the Gentiles, and to raise a bulwark against the kingdom of anti-Christ which the Jesuits labor to rear up in those parts.

2. All other churches of Europe are brought to desolation, and our sins, for which the Lord begins already to frown upon us, do threaten us fearfully, and who knows but that God hath provided this place to be a refuge for many whom he means to save out of the general calamity. And seeing the church hath no place left to fly into but the wilderness, what better work can there be than to go before and provide tabernacles and food for her, against she cometh thither?

3. This land grows weary of her inhabitants, so as man who is the most precious of all creatures is here more vile and base than the earth we tread upon, and of less price among us than a horse or a sheep; masters are forced by authority to entertain servants, parents to maintain their own children. All towns complain of the burthen of their poor, though we have taken up many unnecessary, yea unlawful, trades to maintain them. And we use the authority of the law to hinder the increase of people, as urging the execution of the state against cottages and inmates, and thus it is come to pass that children, servants, and neighbors (especially if the[y] be poor) are counted the greatest burthen, which if things were right it would be the chiefest earthly blessing.

4. The whole earth is the Lord's garden, and He hath given it to the sons of men with a general condition, Gen. 1:28, "Increase and multiply, replenish the earth and subdue it," which was again renewed to Noah. The end is double moral and natural: that man might enjoy the fruits of the earth, and God might have his due glory from the creature. Why then should we stand here striving for places of habitation (many men spending as much labor and cost to recover or keep sometimes an acre or two of land as would procure them many hundred as good or better in an other country) and in the meantime suffer a whole continent as fruitful and convenient for the use of man to lie waste without any improvement?

5. We are grown to that height of intemperance in all excess of riot, as no man's estate almost will suffice to keep sail with his equals, and he who fails herein must live in scorn and contempt. Hence it comes that all arts and trades are carried in that deceitful and unrighteous course, as it is almost impossible for a good and upright man to maintain his charge and live comfortably in any of them.

6. The fountains of learning and religion are so corrupted (as beside the unsupportable charge of the education) most children (even the best wits and fairest hopes) are perverted, corrupted, and utterly overthrown by the multitude of evil examples and the licentious government of those seminaries, where men strain at gnats and swallow camels, use all severity for maintenance of capes and other complements, but suffer all ruffian-like fashion and disorder in manners to pass uncontrolled.

7. What can be a better work and more honorable and worthy a Christian than to help raise and support a particular church while it is in the infancy, and to join his forces with such a company of faithful people as by a timely assistance may grow strong and prosper, and for want of it may be put to great hazard, if not wholly ruined.

8. If any such who are known to be godly, and live in wealth and prosperity here, shall forsake all this to join themselves to this church, and to run a hazard with them of a hard and mean condition, it will be an example of great use both for removing the scandal of worldly and sinister respects which is cast upon the adventurers, to give more life to the faith of God's people in their prayers for the plantation, and to encourage others to join the more willingly in it.

9. It appears to be a work of God for the good of His church, in that He hath disposed the hearts of so many of His wise and faithful servants (both ministers and others) not only to approve of the enterprise but to interest themselves in it, some in their persons and estates, others by their serious advice and help otherwise. And all by their prayers for the welfare of it, Amos 3. The Lord revealeth His secrets to His servants the prophets; it is likely He hath some great work in hand which He hath revealed to His prophets among us, whom He hath stirred up to encourage His servants to this plantation, for He doth not use to seduce His people by His

own prophets but commits that office to the ministry of false prophets and lying spirits.

Divers objections which have been made against this plantation with their answers and resolutions.

Objection 1: We have no warrant to enter upon that land which hath been so long possessed by others.

Answer 1: That which lies common and hath never been replenished or subdued is free to any that will possess and improve it, for God hath given to the sons of men a double right to the earth: there is a natural right and a civil right. The first right was natural when men held the earth in common, every man sowing and feeding where he pleased, and then as men and the cattle increased they appropriated certain parcels of ground by enclosing, and peculiar manurance, and this in time gave them a civil right. Such was the right which Ephron the Hittite had in the field of Machpelah, wherein Abraham could not bury a dead corpse without leave, though for the out parts of the country which lay common he dwelt upon them and took the fruit of them at his pleasure. The like did Jacob, which fed his cattle as bold in Hamor's land (for he is said to be the lord of the country) and other places where he came as the native inhabitants themselves. And that in those times and places men accounted nothing their own but that which they had appropriated by their own industry appears plainly by this: that Abimelech's servants in their own country, when they oft contended with Isaac's servants about wells which they had digged, yet never strove for the land wherein they were. So likewise between Jacob and Laban: he would not take a kid of Laban's without his special contract, but he makes no bargain with him for the land where they feed, and it is very probable if the country had not been as free for Jacob as for Laban, that covetous wretch would have made his advantage of it and have upbraided Jacob with it, as he did with his cattle. And for the natives in New England, they enclose no land, neither have any settled habitation, nor any tame cattle to improve the land by, and so have no other but a natural right to those countries. So as if we leave them sufficient for their use, we may lawfully take the rest, there being more than enough for them and us.

Secondly, we shall come in with the good leave of the Natives, who find benefit already by our neighborhood and learn of us to improve part to more use than before they could do the whole. And by this means we come in by valuable purchase, for they have of us that which will yield them more benefit than all the land which we have from them.

Thirdly, God hath consumed the Natives with a great plague in those parts so as there be few inhabitants left.

Objection 2: It will be a great wrong to our church to take away the good people, and we shall lay it the more open to the judgment feared.

Answer 1: The departing of good people from a country doth not cause a judgment but foreshew it, which may occasion such as remain to turn from their evil ways that they may prevent it, or to take some other course that they may escape it.

Secondly, such as go away are of no observation in respects of those who remain, and they are likely to do more good there than here. And since Christ's time, the church is to be considered as universal without distinction of countries, so as he who doeth good in any one place serves the church in all places in regard of the unity.

Thirdly, it is the revealed will of God that the gospel should be preached to all nations, and though we know not whether those barbarians will receive it at first or not, yet it is a good work to serve God's providence in offering it to them; and this is fittest to be done by God's own servants, for God shall have glory by it though they refuse it, and there is good hope that the posterity *shall by this means be gathered into Christ's sheepfold.*

Objection 3: We have feared a judgment a great while, but yet we are safe. It were better therefore to stay till it come, and either we may fly then, or if we be overtaken in it, we may well content ourselves to suffer with such a church as ours is.

Answer: It is likely this consideration made the churches beyond the seas, as the Palatinate, Rochelle, etc., to sit still at home and not to look out for shelter while they might have found it. But the woeful spectacle of their ruin may teach us more wisdom, to avoid the plague when it is foreseen, and not to tarry as they did till it overtake us. If they were now at their former liberty, we might be sure they would take other courses for their safety, and though half of them had miscarried in their escape, yet had it not been so miserable to themselves nor scandalous to religion as this desperate backsliding, and abjuring the truth, which many of the ancient professors among them, and the whole posterity which remain, are now plagued into.

Objection 4: The ill success of other plantations may tell us what will become of this.

Answer 1: None of the former sustained any great damage but Virginia; which happened through their own sloth and security.

2. The argument is not good, for thus it stands: some plantations have miscarried, therefore we should not make any. It consists in particulars and so concludes nothing. We might as well reason thus: many houses have been burnt by kilns, therefore we should use none; many ships have been cast away, therefore we should content ourselves with our home commodities and not adventure men's lives at sea for those things which we might live without; some men have been undone by being advanced to great places, therefore we should refuse our preferment, etc.

3. The fruit of any public design is not to be discerned by the immediate success; it may appear in time that former plantations were all to good use.

4. There were great and fundamental errors in the former which are like to be avoided in this, for first their main end was carnal and not religious; secondly, they used unfit instruments—a multitude of rude and misgoverned persons, the very scum of the people; thirdly, they did not establish a right form of government.

Objection 5: It is attended with many and great difficulties.

Answer: So is every good action. The heathen could say *ardua virtutis via.* And the way of God's kingdom (the best way in the world) is accompanied with most difficulties. Straight is the gate and narrow is the way that leadeth to life. Again, the difficulties are no other than such as many daily meet with and such as God hath brought others well through them.

Objection 6: It is a work above the power of the undertakers.

Answer 1: The welfare of any body consists not so much in quantity as in due portion and disposition of parts, and we see other plantations have subsisted divers years and prospered from weak means.

2. It is no wonder, for great things may arise from weak, contemptible beginnings; it hath been oft seen in kingdoms and states

and may as well hold in towns and plantations. The Waldenses were scattered into the Alps and mountains of Piedmont by small companies, but they became famous churches whereof some remain to this day; and it is certain that the Turks, Venetians, and other states were very weak in their beginnings.

Objection 7: The country affords no natural fortifications.

Answer: No more did Holland and many other places which had greater enemies and nearer at hand, and God doth use to place His people in the midst of perils that they may trust in Him and not in outward means and safety; so when He would choose a place to plant His beloved people in, He seateth them not in an island or other place fortified by nature, but in a plain country beset with potent and bitter enemies round about, yet so long as they served Him and trusted in His help they were safe. So the Apostle Paul saith of himself and his fellow laborers, that they were compassed with dangers on every side and were daily under the sentence of death that they might learn to trust in the living God.

Objection 8: The place affordeth no comfortable means to the first planters, and our breeding here at home have made us unfit for the hardship we are like to endure.

Answer 1: No place of itself hath afforded sufficient to the first inhabitants; such things as we stand in need of are usually supplied by God's blessing upon the wisdom and industry of man, and whatsoever we stand in need of is treasured in the earth by the Creator and is to be fetched thence by the sweat of our brows.

2. We must learn with Paul to want as well as to abound; if we have food and raiment (which are there to be had), we ought to be contented. The difference in quality may a little displease us, but it cannot hurt us.

3. It may be by this means God will bring us to repent of our former intemperance, and so cure us of that disease which sends many amongst us untimely to their graves and others to hell; so He carried the Israelites into the wilderness and made them forget the flesh pots of Egypt, which was sorry pinch to them at first, but he disposed to their good in the end. Deut. 30: 3, 16.

Objection 9: We must look to be preserved by miracle if we subsist, and so we shall tempt God.

Answer 1: They who walk under ordinary means of safety and supply do not tempt God, but such will be our condition in this plantation therefore, etc. The proposition cannot be denied; the assumption we prove thus: that place is as much secured from ordinary dangers as many hundred places in the civil parts of the world, and we shall have as much provision beforehand as such towns do use to provide against a siege or dearth, and sufficient means for raising a succceeding store against that is spent. If it be denied that we shall be as secure as other places, we answer that many of our sea towns, and such as are upon the confines of enemies' countries in the continent, lie more upon and nearest to danger than we shall. And though such towns have sometimes been burnt or spoiled, yet men tempt not God to dwell still in them, and though many houses in the country amongst us lie open to thieves and robbers (as many have found by sad experience), yet no man will say that those which dwell in such places must be preserved by miracle.

2. Though miracles be now ceased, yet men may expect more than ordinary blessing from God upon all lawful means, where the work is the Lord's and He is sought in it according to His will, for it is usual with Him to increase or weaken the strength of the means as He is pleased or displeased with the instruments and the action, else we must conclude that God hath left the government of the world and committed all power to the creature, that the success of all things should wholly depend upon the second causes.

3. We appeal to the judgment of the soldiers if five hundred men may not in one month raise a fortification which with sufficient munition and victual they may make good against 3,000 for many months, and yet without miracle.

4. We demand an instance if any prince or state hath raised 3,000 soldiers and victualed for six or eight months, with shipping and munition answerable, to invade a place so far distant as this is from any foreign enemy, and where they must run a hazard of repulse and no booty or just title of sovereignty to allure them.

Objection 10: If it succeed ill, it will raise a scandal upon our profession.

Answer: It is no rule in philosophy (much less in divinity) to judge the action by the success. The enterprise of the Israelites against Benjamin succeeded ill twice, yet the action was good and prospered in the end. The Earl of Begiers in France and the Earl of

Toulouse miscarried in the defense of a just cause of religion and their hereditary right against the unjust violence of the Earl Montford and the Pope's legate; the Duke of Saxony and the Landgrave had ill success of the gospel against Charles the Fifth wherein the Duke and his children lost their whole inheritance to this day. The King of Denmark and other princes of the union had ill success in the defense of the Palatinate and the liberty of Germany, yet the profession suffered not with their persons, except it were with the adversaries of religion; and so it was no scandal given.

B. Particular Considerations

It was not enough for Winthrop to convince others to leave England. He also had to convince himself, for many in England were reluctant to part with so able a man. "The church and common welthe hcere at home, hathe more neede of your beste abyllytie in these dangerous tymes, then any remote plantation," wrote an old friend. "All your kynsfolkes and moste understandinge friendes wyll more rejoyce at your stayenge at home." Winthrop nonetheless found the following reasons for seeking asylum in America.

Source: Massachusetts Historical Society, *Proceedings*, XII (1871–1873), 237–239.

1. It is come to that issue as in all probability the welfare of the plantation depends upon my assistance, for the main pillars of it being gentlemen of high quality and eminent parts, both for wisdom and godliness, are determined to sit still if I desert them.

2. My means here are so shortened (now my three eldest sons are come to age) as I shall not be able to continue in this place and employment where I now am. And a soldier may with honor quit his ground rather than be forced from it. And with what comfort can I live with seven or eight servants in that place and condition where for many years I have spent three or four hundred pounds yearly and maintained a greater charge? And if I should let pass this opportunity, that talent which God hath bestowed on me for public service were like to be buried. [*Marginal note:* When a man is to wade through a deep water, there is required tallness as well as courage, and if he finds it past his depth and there open a gap another way, he may take it.]

3. I have a lawful calling, outward from the chief of the plantation, approved by godly and judicious divines, and inward by the

inclination of mine own heart to the work; and there is in this the like mediate call from the king, which was in the other. [*Marginal note:* When God intends a man to a work, he sets a bias on his heart so as though he be tumbled this way and that way, yet his bias still draws him to that side, and there he rests at last.]

4. My wife and such of my children as are come to years of discretion are voluntarily disposed to the same course.

5. In my youth I did seriously consecrate my life to the service of the church, intending the ministry, but was diverted from that course by the counsel of some whose judgment I did much reverence. But it hath often troubled me since, so as I think I am the rather bounden to take the opportunity for spending the small remainder of my time to the best service of the church which I may.

6. Which way the stream of God's providence leads a man to the greatest good, he may, nay, he must go.

It is a scandal to our religion that we shew not as much zeal in seeking the conversion of the heathen as the Papists do; they stick not to employ of their most able men, while we send only such as we can best spare or are a burden to us. [*Marginal note:* The removing of a scandal from a whole church and religion itself is to be preferred before the benefit of any particular church.]

The constant practice in all other like cases must be a rule in this: in all foreign expeditions we stick not to employ of our best statesmen, and we grudge not the want of their service at home while they are employed for the good of other churches abroad.

Objection: Many speak ill of the country, of the barrenness, etc., of it.

Answer: So did the spies of the land of Canaan.

Objection: But should a man leave his country where he is so well beloved and break through the tears and desires of so many good people?

Answer: So did Paul, Acts [21:13], "What do you weeping and breaking my heart," etc.?

The welfare of this commonwealth stands upon two main pillars: religion and law.

Gen. 1:28, "And the Lord blessed them and said increase and multiply and replenish the earth and subdue it." God did not replenish the earth at first with men but gave them His commission to multiply and replenish and subdue it, which is warrant enough for anyone that lives in a country where the people are a burden to seek out and replenish and subdue other places which lie waste, that God may have the glory of the creature there also, and man may enjoy the fruit of the earth which was given him by this general commission. If it be objected that such should go as have no lands, etc., it is easily answered: such cannot go alone; some of ability must go to convey them over.

5. Harried Out of the Land

For many clergymen of a Puritan persuasion, life in England became increasingly intolerable after William Laud ascended to the See of London in 1628. Five years later, he became Archbishop of Canterbury. From his new positions of authority, and with the enthusiastic backing of Charles I, Laud and his associates clamped down hard on dissenting ministers, forcing them to conform to orthodox practices or lose their posts. In 1630, Laud charged Thomas Shepard (1605–1649), later pastor of the First Church in Cambridge, Massachusetts, to "neither Preach, Read, Marry, Bury, or exercise any Ministerial Function in any Part of my Diocess; for if you do, and I hear of it, I'll be on your back . . . and everlastingly disenable you."

Some Puritan clergymen succumbed to ecclesiastical authority. Some defied it, moving from town to town one step ahead of Laud's investigators. After 1630, many gave up the struggle and shipped for New England, where the Puritans had established an outpost at Massachusetts Bay. Shepard's autobiography records the evolution of an emigrant.

Source: Colonial Society of Massachusetts, *Publications*, XXVII (1932), 368–371, 373–376.

I went, half a year before I was Master of Arts, to Mr. Thomas Weld's house at Terling, in Essex, where I enjoyed the blessing of his and Mr. Hooker's ministry at Chelmsford. But before I came there I was very solicitous what would become of me when I was Master of Arts, for then my time and portion would be spent. But when I came thither and had been there some little season, until I was ready to be Master of Arts, one Dr. Wilson had purposed to set up a lecture and give £30 per annum to the maintenance of it. . . . The town of Earls Colne, being three miles off from Essex, hearing that there was such a lecture to be given freely, and considering that the lecture might enrich that poor town, they did therefore . . . come to the place where the ministers met, viz., at Terling in Essex, and desired that it might be settled there for three years. . . .

Having preached upon that sabbath day out of 2 Cor. 5:19, all the town gave me a call and set to their hands in writing, and so I saw God would have me to be there.

But when I had been there a while and the Lord had blessed my labors to divers in and out of the town, especially to the chief house in the town, the Priory, to Mr. Harlakenden's children . . . Satan then began to rage and the commissary's registers and others began to pursue me and to threaten me, as thinking I was a Nonconformable man (when for the most of that time I was not resolved either way but was dark in those things). Yet the Lord, having work to do in this place, kept me, a poor ignorant thing, against them all until such time as my work was done, by strange and wonderful means. . . .When I had preached awhile at Earls Colne, about half a year, the Lord saw me unfit and unworthy to continue me there any longer, and so the Bishop of London, [George] Mountain, being removed to York and Bishop Laud (now Archbishop) coming to his place—a fierce enemy to all righteousness and a man fitted of God to be a scourge to his people—he presently (having been not long in the place) but sent for me up to London, and there never asking me whether I would subscribe (as I remember) but what I had to do to preach in his diocese (chiding also Dr. Wilson for setting up this lecture in his diocese), after many railing speeches against me forbade me to preach, and not only so but if I went to preach anywhere else his hand would reach me. And so God put me to silence there which did somewhat humble me, for I did think it was for my sins the Lord set him thus against me. Yet when I was thus silenced the Lord stirred me up friends; the house of the Harlakendens were so many fathers and mothers to me, and they and the people would have me live there though I did nothing but stay in the place.

But remaining about half a year after this silencing among them, the Lord let me see into the evil of the English ceremonies—cross, surplice, and kneeling. And the Bishop of London (viz., Laud) coming down to visit, he cited me to appear before him at the

Court at Reldon, where I appearing he asked me what I did in the place, and I told him I studied. He asked me what? I told him the Fathers. He replied I might thank him for that, yet charged me to depart the place. I asked him whither I should go. To the university, said he. I told him I had no means to subsist there, yet he charged me to depart the place. . . . The Bishop having thus charged me to depart, and being two days after to visit at Dunmow in Essex, Mr. Weld, Mr. Daniell Rogers, Mr. Ward, Mr. Marshall, Mr. Wharton consulted together whether it was best to let such a swine to root up God's plants in Essex and not to give him some check. Whereupon it was agreed upon privately at Braintree that some should speak to him and give him a check. So Mr. Weld and I travelling together had some thoughts of going to New England, but we did think it best to go first unto Ireland and preach there, and to go by Scotland thither. But when we came to the church, Mr. Weld stood and heard without (being excommunicated by him). I, being more free, went within and after sermon Mr. Weld went up to hear the Bishop's speech, and being seen to follow the Bishop, the first thing he did was to examine Mr. Weld what he did to follow him and to stand upon holy ground. Thereupon he was committed to the pursuivant and bound over to answer it at the High Commission. But when Mr. Weld was pleading for himself and that it was ignorance that made him come in, the Bishop asked him whether he intended to go, whether to New England, and if so whether I would go with him.

While he was thus speaking, I came into the crowd and heard the words. Others bid me go away, but neglecting to do it a godly man pulled me away with violence out of the crowd. And as soon as ever I was gone, the apparitor calls for Mr. Shepard, and the pursuivant was sent presently after to find me out. But he that pulled me away (Mr. Holbeach by name, a schoolmaster at Felsted in Essex) hastened our horses and away we rid as fast as we could. And so the Lord delivered me out of the hand of that lion a third time. And now I perceived I could not stay in Colne without danger, and hereupon receiving a letter from Mr. Ezekiel Rogers, then living at Rowley in Yorkshire, to encourage me to come to the knight's house called Sir Richard Darley, dwelling at a town called Buttercramb, and the knight's two sons, viz. Mr. Henry and Mr. Richard Darley, promising me twenty pounds a year for their part, and the knight promising me my table, and the letters sent to me crying with that voice of the man of Macedonia, come and help us. Hereupon I resolved to follow the Lord to so remote and strange a place; the rather because I might be far from the hearing of the malicious Bishop Laud, who had threatened me if I preached anywhere . . . so with much grief of heart I forsook Essex and Earls Colne and they me, going as it were now I knew not whither. . . .

In the year 1632 [my wife] was unwilling to stay at Buttercramb and I saw no means or likelihood of abode there, for Bishop Neale coming up to York, no friends could procure my liberty of him without subscription. And hereupon the Lord gave me to call to Northumberland, to a town called Heddon, five miles beyond Newcastle which when I considered of and saw no place but that to go unto, and saw the people very desirous of it, and that I might preach there in peace, being far from any bishops, I did resolve to depart thither. And so, being accompanied with Mr. Allured, to the place I came, not without many fears of enemies, and my poor wife full of fears. It was not a place of subsistence with any comfort to me there, but the good Lord, who all my life followed me, made this place the fittest for me. And I found many sweet friends and Christian acquaintance. . . . But after we were settled the Bishop put in a priest who would not suffer me to preach publicly any more. Hereupon means was made to the Bishop of Durham, Bishop Morton, and he professed he durst not give me liberty because Laud had taken notice of me. So I preached up and down in the country and at last privately in Mr. Fenwick's house, and there I stayed till Mr. Cotton, Mr. Hooker, Stone, Weld went to New England. And hereupon most of the godly in England were awakened and intended much to go to New England. And I, having a call by divers friends in New England to come over, and many in old England desiring me to go over, and promising to go with me, I did thereupon resolve to go thither. . . .

The reasons which swayed me to come to New England were many: (1) I saw no call to any other place in old England, nor way of subsistence in peace and comfort to me and my family; (2) Divers people in old England of my dear friends desired me to go to New England, there to live together, and some went before and wrote to me of providing a place for a company of us, one of which was John Bridge. And I saw divers families of my Christian friends who were resolved thither to go with me; (3) I saw the Lord departing from England when Mr. Hooker and Mr. Cotton were gone, and I saw the hearts of most of the godly set and bent that way, and I did think I should feel many miseries if I stayed behind; (4) My judgment was then convinced not only of the evil of ceremonies, but of mixed communion and joining with such in sacraments, though I ever judged it lawful to join with them in preaching; (5) I saw it my duty to desire the fruition of all God's ordinances, which I could not enjoy in old England; (6) My dear wife did much long to see me settled there in peace and so put me on to it; (7) Although it was true, I should stay and suffer for Christ, yet I saw no rule for it now the Lord had opened a door of escape. Otherwise I did incline much to stay and suffer, especially after our sea storms; (8) Though my ends were mixed and I looked much to my own quiet, yet the Lord let me see the glory of those liberties in New England and made me purpose if ever I should come over to live among God's people as one come out from the dead, to His praise, though since I have seen as the Lord's goodness so my own exceeding weakness to be as good as I thought to have been. And although they did desire me to stay in the North and preach privately, yet (1) I saw that this time could not be long without trouble from King Charles; (2) I saw no reason to spend my time privately, when I might possibly exercise my talent publicly in New England; (3) I did hope my going over might make them follow me; (4) I considered how sad a thing it would be for me to leave my wife and child (if I should die) in that rude place of the North where was nothing but barbarous wickedness generally, and how sweet it would be to leave them among God's people, though poor; (5) my liberty in private was daily threatened, and I thought it wisdom to depart before the pursuivants came out, for so I might depart with more peace and less trouble and danger to me and my friends; and I knew not whether God would have me to hazard my person and comfort of me and all mine for a disorderly manner of preaching privately in those parts. So after I had preached my farewell sermon at Newcastle, I departed. . . .

II

First Footholds in New England

A FULL DECADE before John Winthrop and his fellow Puritans sailed to America, a group of more radical English dissenters had planted the first permanent British outpost in New England. In the late sixteenth century, a reform faction that refused to remain longer within the Church of England became known as "separatist," or "Brownist" after one of its leaders, Robert Browne. The Puritans, on the other hand, considered themselves still within the church—deeply disturbed by its faults but hopeful for its eventual improvement. But when it came to matters of theology and ecclesiastical polity, the two groups were almost indistinguishable, though neither group seemed aware of the fact until they inspected each other in the congenial isolation of the New World. There the similarities of their religious and social systems rapidly over-shadowed their differences. It is now clear that the Pilgrims, as the separatist emigrants to America have been labeled, were an integral part of the Puritan heritage in America.

The story of the separatist congregation of Scrooby, England, is familiar: how in the first years of the seventeenth century it fled to the less restrictive atmosphere of Holland, how it struggled there for more than a decade to preserve both its religious independence and its cultural Englishness. The former came under constant threat from English authorities and the prospect of Spanish victory against the Dutch; the latter was in constant jeopardy from the economic and social realities of living in a foreign land. Finally the congregation, then at Leyden and expanded by later emigrants, decided to try America.

For nearly a decade after their arrival in 1620, the Pilgrims were almost the sole European settlers in New England. A few scattered outposts of fishermen and traders dotted the coast from Cape Cod to Maine, but not many of them proved permanent, and none had their origins in religious exodus. Thus the small colony at New Plymouth served as the first Puritan experiment in the New World. By the end of 1630, however, the settlements around

Massachusetts Bay had suddenly overshadowed the Pilgrim colony, as the Great Migration turned southern New England into the Puritans' New Canaan.

6. Plymouth Plantation

The decision of the Leyden separatists to move to America came after much soul-searching and debate. Because the cost of transporting everyone and of caring for elderly and invalid members while building new homes in the wilderness prohibited the immediate migration of the whole congregation, they decided to send a small advance party. Negotiations with English officials and financiers dragged on for several years and, when finally completed, did not run smoothly. But the separatists eventually gained permission to settle where they would be left alone.

A. Pilgrim Exodus

In 1609, William Bradford (1588–1657) fled from England to the Low Countries. By 1620, he had emerged as a prominent member of the Leyden congregation and a leader of the segment that migrated to America. He also turned historian. His history Of Plimouth Plantation chronicled the story of his people from England to Europe to America; it survives as the most detailed record of their perambulations and as a remarkable piece of literary craftsmanship. Here Bradford explains the reasons for the Pilgrims' removal from Leyden, their perilous voyage across the Atlantic, and the first steps toward creating a new society in America—including the famous civil compact signed on board the Mayflower.

Source: William Bradford, *History of Plymouth Plantation, 1620–1647* (2 vols., Boston, 1912), I, 52–60, 149–152, 155, 162, 189–196.

After they had lived in this city about some eleven or twelve years (which is the more observable being the whole time of that famous truce between that state and the Spaniards), and sundry of them were taken away by death and many others began to be well stricken in years (the grave mistress of experience having taught them many things), those prudent governors with sundry of the sagest members began both deeply to apprehend their present dangers and wisely to foresee the future and think of timely remedy. In the agitation of their thoughts, and much discourse of things hereabout, at length they began to incline to this conclusion: of removal to some other place. Not out of any newfangledness or other such like giddy humor by which men are oftentimes transported to their great hurt and danger, but for sundry weighty and solid reasons, some of the chief of which I will here briefly touch.

And first, they saw and found by experience the hardness of the place and country to be such as few in comparison would come to them, and fewer that would bide it out and continue with them. For many that came to them, and many more that desired to be with them, could not endure that great labor and hard fare, with other inconveniences which they underwent and were contented with. But though they loved their persons, approved their cause and honored their sufferings, yet they left them as it were weeping, as Orpah did her mother-in-law Naomi, or as those Romans did Cato in Utica who desired to be excused and borne with, though they could not all be Catos. For many, though they desired to enjoy the ordinances of God in their purity and the liberty of the gospel with them, yet (alas) they admitted of bondage with danger of conscience, rather than to endure these hardships. Yea, some preferred and chose the prisons in England rather than this liberty in Holland with these afflictions. But it was thought that if a better and easier place of living could be had, it would draw many and take away these discouragements. Yea, their pastor would often say that many of those who both wrote and preached now against them, if they were in a place where they might have liberty and live comfortably, they would then practice as they did.

Secondly. They saw that though the people generally bore all these difficulties very cheerfully and with a resolute courage, being in the best and strength of their years, yet old age began to steal on many of them; and their great and continual labors, with other crosses and sorrows, hastened it before the time, so as it was not only probably thought, but apparently seen, that within a few years more they would be in danger to scatter, by necessities pressing them, or sink under their burdens, or both. And therefore according to the divine proverb, that a wise man seeth the plague when it cometh, and hideth himself (Proverbs 22:3) so they like skillful and beaten soldiers were fearful either to be entrapped or surrounded by their enemies so as they should neither be able to fight nor fly. And therefore thought it better to dislodge betimes to some place of better advantage and less danger, if any such could be found.

Thirdly. As necessity was a taskmaster over them so they were forced to be such, not only to their servants but in a sort to their dearest children, the which as it did not a little wound the tender hearts of many a loving father and mother, so it produced likewise sundry sad and sorrowful effects. For many of their children that were of best dispositions and gracious inclinations, having learned to bear the yoke in their youth and willing to bear part of their parents' burden, were oftentimes so oppressed with their heavy labors that though their minds were free and willing, yet their bodies bowed under the weight of the same and became decrepit in their early youth, the vigor of nature being consumed in the very bud as it were. But that which was more lamentable, and of all sorrows most heavy to be borne, was that many of their children, by these occasions and the great licentiousness of youth in that country; and the manifold temptations of the place, were drawn away by evil examples into extravagant and dangerous courses, getting the reins off their necks and departing from their parents. Some became soldiers, others took upon them far voyages by sea, and others some worse courses tending to dissoluteness and the danger of their souls, to the great grief of their parents and dishonor of God, so that they saw their posterity would be in danger to degenerate and be corrupted.

Lastly (and which was not least), a great hope and inward zeal they had of laying some good foundation, or at least to make some way thereunto, for the propagating and advancing the gospel of the kingdom of Christ in those remote parts of the world; yea, though they should be but even as stepping-stones unto others for the performing of so great a work.

These and some other like reasons moved them to undertake this resolution of their removal, the which they afterward prosecuted with so great difficulties, as by the sequel will appear.

The place they had thoughts on was some of those vast and unpeopled countries of America, which are fruitful and fit for habitation, being devoid of all civil inhabitants, where there are only savage and brutish men which range up and down, little otherwise than the wild beasts of the same. This proposition being made public and coming to the scanning of all, it raised many variable opinions amongst men and caused many fears and doubts amongst themselves. Some, from their reasons and hopes conceived, labored to stir up and encourage the rest to undertake and prosecute the same; others again, out of their fears, objected against it and sought to divert from it, alleging many things, and those neither unreasonable nor unprobable—as that it was a great design and subject to many unconceivable perils and dangers, as, besides the casualties of the sea (which none can be freed from), the length of the voyage was such as the weak bodies of women and other persons worn out with age and travail (as many of them were) could never be able to endure, and yet if they should, the miseries of the land which they should be exposed unto would be too hard to be borne and likely, some or all of them together, to consume and utterly to ruinate them. For there they should be liable to famine and nakedness and the want, in a manner, of all things. The change of air, diet, and drinking of water would infect their bodies with sore sicknesses and grievous diseases. And also those which should escape or overcome these difficulties should yet be in continual danger of the savage people, who are cruel, barbarous, and most teacherous, being most furious in their rage and merciless where they overcome, not being content only to kill and take away life, but delight to torment men in the most bloody manner that may be, flaying some alive with the shells of fishes, cutting off the members and joints of others by piecemeal and broiling on the coals, eat the collops of their flesh in their sight whilst they live, with other cruelties horrible to be related. And surely it could not be thought but the very hearing of these things could not but move the very bowels of men to grate within them and make the weak to quake and tremble.

It was further objected that it would require greater sums of money to furnish such a voyage and to fit them with necessaries than their consumed estates would amount to; and yet they must as well look to be seconded with supplies as presently to be transported. Also many precedents of ill success and lamentable miseries befallen others in the like designs were easy to be found, and not forgotten to be alleged, besides their own experience—in their former troubles and hardships in their removal into Holland—and how hard a thing it was for them to live in that strange place, though it was a neighbor country and a civil and rich commonwealth.

It was answered that all great and honorable actions are accompanied with great difficulties and must be both enterprised and overcome with answerable courages. It was granted the dangers were great, but not desperate. The difficulties were many, but not invincible, for though there were many of them likely, yet they were not certain. It might be sundry of the things feared might never befall; others by provident care and the use of good means might in a great measure be prevented; and all of them, through the help of God, by fortitude and patience, might either be borne or overcome. True it was that such attempts were not to be made and undertaken without good ground and reason, not rashly or lightly as many have done for curiosity or hope of gain, etc. But their condition was not ordinary; their ends were good and honorable, their calling lawful and urgent, and therefore they might expect the blessing of God in their proceeding. Yea, though they should lose their lives in this action, yet might they have comfort in the same and their endeavors would be honorable. They lived here but as men in exile and in a poor condition; and as great miseries might possibly befall them in this place, for the twelve years of truce were now out and there was nothing but beating of drums and preparing for war, the events whereof are always uncertain. The Spaniard might prove as cruel as the savages of America, and the famine and pestilence as sore here as there, and their liberty less to look out for remedy.

After many other particular things answered and alleged on both sides, it was fully concluded by the major part to put this design in execution and to prosecute it by the best means they could. . . .

September 6. [Their] troubles being blown over, and now all being compact together in one ship, they put to sea again with a prosperous wind, which continued divers days together, which was some encouragement unto them; yet, according to the usual manner, many were afflicted with seasickness. And I may not omit here a special work of God's providence. There was a proud and very profane young man, one of the seamen, of a lusty, able body, which made him the more haughty; he would always be contemning the poor people in their sickness and cursing them daily with grievous execrations, and did not let to tell them that he hoped to help to cast half of them overboard before they came to their journey's end, and to make merry with what they had; and if he were by any gently reproved, he would curse and swear most bitterly. But it pleased God, before they came half seas over, to smite this young man with a grievous disease of which he died in a desperate manner, and so was himself the first that was thrown overboard. Thus his curses light on his own head, and it was an astonishment to all his fellows for they noted it to be the just hand of God upon him.

After they had enjoyed fair winds and weather for a season, they were encountered many times with cross winds and met with many fierce storms with which the ship was shroudly shaken, and her upper works made very leaky; and one of the main beams in the midships was bowed and cracked, which put them in some fear that the ship could not be able to perform the voyage. So some of the chief of the company, perceiving the mariners to fear the sufficiency of the ship as appeared by their mutterings, they entered into serious consultation with the master and other officers of the ship, to consider in time of the danger, and rather to return than to cast themselves into a desperate and inevitable peril. And truly there was great distraction and difference of opinion amongst the mariners themselves; fain would they do what could be done for their wages' sake (being now near half the seas over) and on the other hand they were loath to hazard their lives too desperately. But in examining of all opinions, the master and others affirmed they knew the ship to be strong and firm under water; and for the buckling of the main beam, there was a great iron screw the passengers brought out of Holland, which would raise the beam into his place; the which being done, the carpenter and master affirmed that with a post put under it, set firm in the lower deck and otherways bound, he would make it sufficient. And as for the decks and upper works, they would caulk them as well as they could, and though with the working of the ship they would not long keep staunch, yet there would otherwise be no great danger, if they did not overpress her with sails. So they committed themselves to the will of God and resolved to proceed.

In sundry of these storms the winds were so fierce and the seas so high, as they could not bear a knot of sail, but were forced to hull for divers days together. And in one of them, as they thus lay at hull in a mighty storm, a lusty young man called John Howland, coming upon some occasion above the gratings, was, with a seele of the ship, thrown into [the] sea. But it pleased God that he caught hold of the topsail halyards, which hung overboard and ran out at length, yet he held his hold (though he was sundry fathoms under water) till he was hauled up by the same rope to the brim of the water, and then with a boat hook and other means got into the ship again and his life saved. And though he was something ill with it, yet he lived many years after and became a profitable member both in church and commonwealth. In all this voyage there died but one of the passengers, which was William Butten, a youth, servant to Samuel Fuller, when they drew near the coast.

But to omit other things (that I may be brief): after long beating at sea they fell with that land which is called Cape Cod, the which being made and certainly known to be it, they were not a little joyful. After some deliberation had amongst themselves and with the master of the ship, they tacked about and resolved to stand for the southward (the wind and weather being fair) to find some place about Hudson's River for their habitation. But after they had sailed that course about half the day, they fell amongst dangerous shoals and roaring breakers, and they were so far entangled therewith as they conceived themselves in great danger; and the wind shrinking upon them withal, they resolved to bear up again for the Cape and thought themselves happy to get out of those dangers before night overtook them, as by God's good providence they did. And the next day they got into the Cape Harbor where they rid in safety. . . .

Being thus arrived in a good harbor, and brought safe to land, they fell upon their knees and blessed the God of Heaven who had brought them over the vast and furious ocean, and delivered them from all the perils and miseries thereof, again to set their feet on the firm and stable earth, their proper element. And no marvel if they were thus joyful, seeing wise Seneca was so affected with sailing a few miles on the coast of his own Italy, as he affirmed, that he had rather remain twenty years on his way by land than pass by sea to any place in a short time, so tedious and dreadful was the same unto him.[1] . . .

1. Epistle 53.

Being thus arrived at Cape Cod the 11th of November, and necessity calling them to look out a place for habitation (as well as the master's and mariners' importunity), they having brought a large shallop with them out of England, stowed in quarters in the ship, they now got her out and set their carpenters to work to trim her up, but being much bruised and shattered in the ship with foul weather, they saw she would be long in mending. Whereupon a few of them tendered themselves to go by land and discover those nearest places, whilst the shallop was in mending; and the rather because as they went into that harbor there seemed to be an opening some two or three leagues off, which the master judged to be a river. It was conceived there might be some danger in the attempt, yet seeing them resolute, they were permitted to go, being sixteen of them well armed under the conduct of Captain Standish, having such instructions given them as was thought meet. . . .

I shall a little return back, and begin with a combination made by them before they came ashore, being the first foundation of their government in this place. Occasioned partly by the discontented and mutinous speeches that some of the strangers amongst them had let fall from them in the ship—that when they came ashore they would use their own liberty, for none had power to command them, the patent they had being for Virginia and not for New England, which belonged to another government with which the Virginia Company had nothing to do—and partly that such an act by them done (this, their condition, considered) might be as firm as any patent, and in some respects more sure.

The form was as followeth:

IN THE NAME OF GOD, AMEN.

We whose names are underwritten, the loyal subjects of our dread Sovereign Lord King James, by the grace of God of Great Britain, France, and Ireland King, Defender of the Faith, etc.

Having undertaken, for the glory of God and advancement of the Christian faith and honor of our king and country, a voyage to plant the first colony in the northern parts of Virginia, do by these presents solemnly and mutually in the presence of God and one of another, covenant and combine ourselves together into a civil body politic, for our better ordering and preservation and furtherance of the ends aforesaid; and by virtue hereof to enact, constitute, and frame such just and equal laws, ordinances, acts, constitutions, and offices, from time to time, as shall be thought most meet and convenient for the general good of the colony, unto which we promise all due submission and obedience. In witness whereof we have hereunder subscribed our names at Cape Cod, the 11th of November, in the year of the reign of our Sovereign Lord King James, of England, France, and Ireland the eighteenth, and of Scotland the fifty-fourth. Anno Domini 1620. . . .

After this they chose, or rather confirmed, Mr. John Carver (a man godly and well approved amongst them) their governor for that year. And after they had provided a place for their goods, or common store (which were long in unlading for want of boats, foulness of the winter weather, and sickness of divers), and begun some small cottages for their habitation, as time would admit, they met and consulted of laws and orders, both for their civil and military government, as the necessity of their condition did require, still adding thereunto as urgent occasion in several times, and as cases did require.

In these hard and difficult beginnings they found some discontents and murmurings arise amongst some, and mutinous speeches and carriages in other; but they were soon quelled and overcome by the wisdom, patience, and just and equal carriage of things, by the governor and better part, which clave faithfully together in the main. But that which was most sad and lamentable was that in two or three months' time half of their company died, especially in January and February, being the depth of winter and wanting houses and other comforts, being infected with the scurvy and other diseases which this long voyage and their inaccommodate condition had brought upon them, so as there died some times two or three of a day in the foresaid time, [so] that of one hundred and odd persons, scarce fifty remained. And of these, in the time of most distress, there was but six or seven sound persons who to their great commendations, be it spoken, spared no pains, night nor day, but with abundance of toil and hazard of their own health, fetched them wood, made them fires, dressed them meat, made their beds, washed their loathsome clothes, clothed and unclothed them—in a word, did all the homely and necessary offices for them which dainty and queasy stomachs cannot endure to hear named, and all this willingly and cheerfully, without any grudging in the least, showing herein their true love unto their friends and brethren, a rare example and worthy to be remembered. Two of these seven were Mr. William Brewster, their reverend elder, and Myles Standish, their captain and military commander, unto whom myself and many others were much beholden in our low and sick condition. And yet the Lord so upheld these persons as in this general calamity they were not at all infected either with sickness or lameness. And what I have said of these I may say of many others who died in this general visitation, and others yet living; that whilst they had health, yea, or any strength continuing, they were not wanting to any that had need of them. And I doubt not but their recompense is with the Lord. . . .

B. Survival and Success

By the spring of 1621, less than a score of able-bodied men were still alive in Plymouth. Survival now depended on adequate crops and additional recruits, and to both matters the Pilgrims gave their energy. In one of the earliest promotional tracts written from America, Edward Winslow (1595–1655) conveniently overlooked the recent hardships in describing for an English audience the events of the Pilgrims' first year in New England. Originally in the form of a letter, Winslow's description was soon published in London as an addendum to his and William Bradford's lengthier Relation or Journal of the Beginning and Proceedings of the English Plantation at Plimouth. Of particular interest in the selection that follows is the only known description of the first thanksgiving.

Source: Alexander Young, Chronicles of the Pilgrim Fathers of the Colony of Plymouth from 1602 to 1625 (Boston, 1841), 230–238.

. . . In this little time that a few of us have been here, we have built seven dwelling-houses, and four for the use of the plantation, and have made preparation for divers others. We set the last spring some twenty acres of Indian corn, and sowed some six acres of barley and peas, and according to the manner of the Indians we manured our ground with herrings, or rather shads, which we have in great abundance and take with great ease at our doors. Our corn did prove well, and, God be praised, we had a good increase of Indian corn, and our barley indifferent good, but our peas not worth the gathering, for wc fcared they were too late sown. They came up very well, and blossomed, but the sun parched them in the blossom.

Our harvest being gotten in, our governor sent four men on fowling, that so we might after a special manner rejoice together after we had gathered the fruit of our labors. They four in one day killed as much fowl as, with a little help beside, served the company almost a week. At which time, amongst other recreations, we exercised our arms, many of the Indians coming amongst us, and among the rest their greatest king, Massasoit, with some ninety men, whom for three days we entertained and feasted. And they went out and killed five deer, which they brought to the plantation and bestowed on our governor, and upon the captain and others. And although it be not always so plentiful as it was at this time with us, yet by the goodness of God, we arc so far from want that we often wish you partakers of our plenty.

We have found the Indians very faithful in their covenant of peace with us, very loving and ready to pleasure us. We often go to them, and they come to us; some of us have been fifty miles by land in the country with them, the occasions and relations whereof you shall understand by our general and more full declaration of such things as are worth the noting. Yea, it hath pleased God so to possess the Indians with a fear of us, and love unto us, that not only the greatest king amongst them, called Massasoit, but also all the princes and peoples round about us, have either made suit unto us or been glad of any occasion to make peace with us, so that seven of them at once have sent their messengers to us to that end. Yea, an isle at sea, which we never saw, hath also, together with the former, yielded willingly to be under the protection and subjects to our Sovereign Lord King James, so that there is now great peace amongst the Indians themselves, which was not formerly, neither would have been but for us. And we for our parts walk as peaceably and safely in the wood as in the highways in England. We entertain them familiarly in our houses, and they as friendly bestowing their venison on us. They are a people without any religion or knowledge of any God, yet very trusty, quick of apprehension, ripe-witted, just. The men and women go naked, only a skin about their middles.

For the temper of the air, here it agreeth well with that in England, and if there be any difference at all, this is somewhat hotter in summer. Some think it to be colder in winter, but I cannot out of experience so say; the air is very clear and not foggy, as hath been reported. I never in my life remember a more seasonable year than we have here enjoyed, and if we have once but kine, horses, and sheep, I make no question but men might live as contented here as in any part of the world. For fish and fowl, we have great abundance; fresh cod in the summer is but coarse meat with us; our bay is full of lobsters all the summer and affordeth variety of other fish; in September we can take a hogshead of eels in a night, with small labor, and can dig them out of their beds all the winter. We have mussels and others at our doors. Oysters we have none near, but we can have them brought by the Indians when we will. All the spring-time the earth sendeth forth naturally very good sallet herbs. Here are grapes, white and red, and very sweet and strong also; strawberries, gooseberries, raspas, etc.; plums of three sorts, with black and red being almost as good as a damson; abundance of roses, white, red, and damask, single, but very sweet indeed. The country wanteth only industrious men to employ, for it would grieve your hearts if, as I, you had seen so many miles together by goodly rivers uninhabited, and withal to consider those parts of the world wherein you live to be even greatly burthened with abundance of people. These things I thought good to let you understand, being the truth of things as near as I could experimentally take knowledge of, and that you might on our behalf give God thanks who hath dealt so favorably with us.

Our supply of men from you came the 9th of November 1621, putting in at Cape Cod, some eight or ten leagues from us. The Indians that dwell thereabout were they who were owners of the corn which we found in caves, for which we have given them full content, and are in great league with them. They sent us word there was a ship near unto them, but thought it to be a Frenchman, and indeed for ourselves we expected not a friend so soon. But when we perceived that she made for our bay, the governor commanded a great piece to be shot off, to call home such as were abroad at work. Whereupon every man, yea, boy, that could handle a gun, were ready, with full resolution that if she were an enemy we would stand in our just defense, not fearing them. But God provided better for us than we supposed. These came all in health, not any being sick by the way (otherwise than by sea-sickness) and so continue at this time, by the blessing of God. The goodwife Ford was delivered of a son the first night she landed, and both of them are very well.

When it pleaseth God, we are settled and fitted for the fishing business, and other trading; I doubt not but by the blessing of God the gain will give content to all. In the mean time, that we have gotten we have sent by this ship, and though it be not much, yet it will witness for us that we have not been idle, considering the smallness of our number all this summer. We hope the merchants will accept of it, and be encouraged to furnish us with things needful for further employment, which will also encourage us to put forth ourselves to the uttermost.

Now because I expect your coming unto us with other of our friends, whose company we much desire, I thought good to advertise you of a few things needful. Be careful to have a very good bread-room to put your biscuits in. Let your cask for beer and water be iron-bound for the first tire if not more; let not your meat be dry-salted—none can better do it than the sailors. Let your meal be so hard trod in your cask that you shall need an adz or hatchet to work it out with. Trust not too much on us for corn at this time, for by reason of this last company that came, depending wholly upon us, we shall have little enough till harvest; be careful to come by some of your meal to spend by the way—it will much refresh you. Build your cabins as open as you can, and bring good store of clothes and bedding with you. Bring every man a musket or fowling-piece; let your piece be long in the barrel, and fear not the weight of it, for most of our shooting is from stands. Bring juice of lemons, and take it fasting; it is of good use. For hot waters, aniseed water is the best, but use it sparingly. If you bring any thing for comfort in the country, butter or sallet oil, or both, is very good. Our Indian corn, even the coarsest, maketh as pleasant meat as rice, therefore spare that unless to spend by the way. Bring paper and linseed oil for your windows, with cotton yarn for your lamps. Let your shot be most for big fowls, and bring store of powder and shot. I forbear further to write for the present, hoping to see you by the next return, so I take my leave, commending you to the Lord for a safe conduct unto us. Resting in him,

Your loving friend,

E. W.

Plymouth, in New England, this 11th of December, 1621.

7. Genesis of the Bay Colony

In the same year that the separatist-Puritans sailed for America, a corporate reorganization took place in the mother country aimed at encouraging further settlement in New England. The Council for New England replaced the moribund Plymouth Company of 1606; the new organization made grants to several groups of investors including one in 1628 to the New England Company, dominated by East Anglian Puritans. Led by John White, a Dorchester clergyman, the new company introduced a subtle but profound shift in the role of what was ostensibly a commercial venture. While still hopeful of profitable cargoes from the New World, the principal investors in the company cared more for making their section of America a haven for disgruntled Puritans. In 1628 they sent John Endecott to be resident governor of their territory; in 1629 three hundred colonists and two Puritan clergymen joined the company's embryonic settlement at Salem, Massachusetts.

A. Creation of the Massachusetts Bay Company

Fearing the interference of Sir Ferdinando Gorges and other members of the Council for New England who were not necessarily in sympathy with a Puritan project, in 1629 the men who secured title to the region between the Charles and the Merrimack Rivers used their political influence to obtain from Charles I a royal charter. In theory, this gave permanent control of the company and its colony to the stockholders and especially to its officers. The charter also set forth the political structure of the colony within which the Puritan experiment would have to function.

Source: Francis N. Thorpe, ed., *The Federal and State Constitution, Colonial Charters, and Other Organic Laws* (7 vols., Washington, 1909), III, 1846, 1849–1858, 1860.

Charles, by the Grace of God, King of England, Scotland, France, and Ireland, Defender of the Faith, etc. To all whom these presents shall come . . . know ye that . . . we have given and granted, and by these presents do for us and our heirs and successors give and grant unto . . . Sir Henry Rosewell, Sir John Young, Sir Richard Saltonstall, Thomas Southcott, John Humphrey, John Endecott, Simon Whetcombe, Isaac Johnson, Samuel Aldersey, John Ven, Matthew Craddock, George Harwood, Increase Nowell, Richard Perry, Richard Bellingham, Nathaniel

Wright, Samuel Vassall, Theophilus Eaton, Thomas Goffe, Thomas Adams, John Browne, Samuel Browne, Thomas Hutchins, William Vassall, William Pynchon, and George Foxcroft, their heirs and assigns, all that part of New England in America which lies and extends between a great river there, commonly called Monomack River, alias Merrimack River, and a certain other river there, called Charles River, being in the bottom of a certain bay there, commonly called Massachusetts, alias Mattachusetts, alias Massatusetts Bay . . . from the Atlantic and western sea and ocean on the east part to the South Sea on the west part. . . .

And forasmuch as the good and prosperous success of the plantation of the said parts of New England . . . next under the blessing of Almighty God and the support of our royal authority, upon the good government of the same, to the end that the affairs and businesses which from time to time shall happen and arise concerning the said lands and the plantation of the same may be the better managed and ordered . . . we will and ordain that the said Sir Henry Rosewell [et al.] . . . and all such others as shall hereafter be admitted and made free of the Company and Society hereafter mentioned shall from time to time and at all times forever hereafter be by virtue of these presents one body corporate and politic in fact and name, by the name of the Governor and Company of the Massachusetts Bay in New England. . . . We do for us, our heirs, and successors make, ordain, constitute, and confirm by these presents, and that by that name they shall have perpetual succession, and that by the same name they and their successors shall and may be capable and enabled as well to implead, and to be impleaded, and to prosecute, demand, and answer, and be answered unto, in all and singular suits, causes, quarrels, and actions of what kind or nature soever. And also to have, take, possess, acquire, and purchase any lands, tenements, or hereditaments, or any goods or chattels, and the same to lease, grant, demise, alien, bargain, sell, and dispose of as other our liege people of this our realm of England, or any other corporation or body politic of the same may lawfully do. . . .

And our will and pleasure is . . . that from henceforth forever there shall be one Governor, one Deputy Governor, and eighteen Assistants of the same Company, to be from time to time constituted, elected, and chosen out of the freemen of the said Company, for the time being in such manner and form as hereafter in these presents is expressed, which said officers shall apply themselves to take care for the best disposing and ordering of the general business and affairs of, for, and concerning the said lands and premises hereby mentioned to be granted, and the plantation thereof, and the government of the people there. And for the better execution of our royal pleasure and grant in this behalf, we do, by these presents . . . nominate, ordain, make, and constitute our well beloved the said Matthew Craddock to be the first and present Governor of the said Company, and the said Thomas Goffe to be Deputy Governor of the said Company, and the said Sir Richard Saltonstall . . . [etc.] to be the present Assistants of the said Company, to continue in said several offices respectively for such time, and in such manner as in and by these presents is hereafter declared and appointed.

And further, we will . . . that the said Governor, Deputy Governor, and Assistants of the said Company for the time being shall or may once every month, or oftener at their pleasures, assemble and hold and keep a Court or Assembly of themselves, for the better ordering and directing of their affairs, and that any seven or more persons of the Assistants, together with the Governor or Deputy Governor so assembled, shall be said, taken, held, and reputed to be and shall be a full and sufficient Court or Assembly of the said Company for the handling, ordering, and dispatching of all such businesses and occurrents as shall from time to time happen touching or concerning the said Company or plantation; and that there shall or may be held and kept by the Governor or Deputy Governor of the said Company, and seven or more of the said Assistants for the time being, upon every last Wednesday in Hilary, Easter, Trinity, and Mich'as Terms respectively forever, one great general and solemn assembly, which four general assemblies shall be styled and called the four great and General Courts of the said Company. In all and every, or any of which said great and General Courts so assembled . . . whereof the Governor or Deputy Governor and six of the Assistants, at the least to be seven, shall have full power and authority to choose, nominate, and appoint such and so many others as they shall think fit and that shall be willing to accept the same to be free of the said Company and body, and them into the same to admit. . . .

And, our will and pleasure is . . . that yearly once in the year forever hereafter, namely the last Wednesday in Easter Term, yearly, the Governor, Deputy Governor, and Assistants of the said Company and all other officers of the said Company shall be in the General Court or Assembly to be held for that day or time, newly chosen for the year ensuing by such greater part of the said Company for the time being then and there present. . . .

And, our further will and pleasure is . . . that all and every the subjects of us, our heirs, or successors which shall go to and inhabit within the said lands and premises hereby mentioned to be granted, and every of their children which shall happen to be born there or on the seas in going thither or returning from thence, shall have and enjoy all liberties and immunities of free and natural subjects within any of the dominions of us, our heirs, or successors to all intents, constructions, and purposes whatsoever as if they and every of them were born within the realm of England. . . .

And, we do . . . grant . . . that it shall . . . be lawful to and for the Governor or Deputy Governor and such of the Assistants and freemen of said Company for the time being as shall be assembled in any of their General Courts aforesaid, or in any other courts to be specially summoned and assembled for that purpose, or the greater part of them (whereof the Governor or Deputy Governor and six of the Assistants to be always seven) from time to time, to make, ordain, and establish all manner of wholesome and reasonable orders, laws, statutes, and ordinances, directions, and instructions not contrary to the laws of this our realm of England, as well for settling of the forms and ceremonies of government and magistracy fit and necessary for the said plantation and the inhabitants there, and for naming and setting of all sorts of officers, both superior and inferior, which they shall find needful for that government and plantation . . . and for impositions of lawful fines, mulcts, imprisonment, or other lawful correction, according to the course of other corporations in this our realm of England, and for the directing, ruling, and disposing of all other matters and things whereby our said people, inhabitants there, may be so religiously, peaceably, and civilly governed as their good life and orderly conversation may win and incite the natives of [the] country to the knowledge and obedience of the only true God and Saviour of mankind and the Christian Faith, which in our royal intention and the adventurers' free profession is the principal end of this plantation. . . .

In witness whereof we have caused this our letters to be made patents.

Witness ourself, at Westminster, the fourth day of March in the fourth year of our reign. . . .

Charles Caesar

B. Transfer of the Charter

Because the charter failed to specify where the corporation must meet, some of the Puritan leaders of the company proposed to carry the charter, and hence the legal seat of government, to America. In England the company would be subject to scrutiny by the crown and to influence by non-Puritan stockholders. Taken to New England the charter would serve as the constitution of a Puritan Zion. A crucial step in the spread of the Puritan tradition to America took place on July 28, 1629, in the home of Thomas Goffe, deputy-governor of the corporation. At the close of the regular stockholders' meeting, Governor Matthew Craddock "read certaine propositions conceived by himselfe; viz., that for the advancement of the plantation, the inducing & encouraging persons of worth & qualitie [to] transplant themselves and famylyes thether, & for other weighty reasons . . . to transferr the government of the plantation to those that shall inhabite there. . . ." Debate followed, and the members finally agreed to delay decision until the next meeting. On August 29 the propositions known as the Cambridge Agreement (printed below) were signed by twelve leading members; two days later the general meeting voted its approval; and a year later John Winthrop and most of the stockholders carried their precious charter to New England. Henceforth, until revocation of the charter in 1684, the Massachusetts Bay Colony enjoyed an almost independent status, free from interference by company officers or stockholders in the mother country and almost free from encroachment by theEnglishgovernment.

Source: Robert C. Winthrop, *Life and Letters of John Winthrop* . . . (2 vols., Boston, 1864–1865), I, 344–345.

Upon due consideration of the state of the plantation now in hand for New England, wherein we (whose names are hereunto subscribed) have engaged ourselves, and having weighed the greatness of the work in regard of the consequence, God's glory and the church's good; as also in regard of the difficulties and discouragements which in all probabilities must be forecast upon the prosecution of this business; considering withal that this whole adventure grows upon the joint confidence we have in each other's fidelity and resolution herein, so as no man of us would have adventured it without assurance of the rest: now for the better encouragement of ourselves and others that shall join with us in this action, and to the end that every man may without scruple dispose of his estate and affairs as may best fit his preparation for this voyage, it is fully and faithfully agreed amongst us, and every of us doth hereby freely and sincerely promise and bind himself in the word of a Christian and in the presence of God who is the searcher of all hearts, that we will so really endeavor the prosecution of this work as by God's assistance we will be ready in our persons, and with such of our several families as are to go with us, and such provisions as we are able conveniently to furnish ourselves withal, to embark for the said plantation by the first of March next, at such port or ports of this land as shall be agreed upon by the Company, to the end to pass the seas (under God's protection) to inhabit and continue in New England. Provided always that before the last of September next the whole government together with the patent for the said plantation be first by an order of court legally transferred and established to remain with us and others which shall inhabit upon the said plantation. And provided also that if any shall be hindered by such just and inevitable let or other cause to be allowed by three parts of four of these whose names are hereunto subscribed, then such persons for such times and during such lets to be discharged of this bond. And we do further promise every one for himself that shall fail to be ready through his own default by the day appointed, to pay for every day's default the sum of £3 to the use of the rest of the Company who shall be ready by the same day and time.

This was done by order of Court, the 29th of August, 1629.

RICHARD SALTONSTALL	ISAAC JOHNSON	JOHN WINTHROP
THOMAS DUDLEY	JOHN HUMPHREY	WILLIAM PYNCHON
WILLIAM VASSALL	THOMAS SHARPE	KELLAM BROWNE
NICHOLAS WEST	INCREASE NOWELL	WILLIAM COLBRON

C. Problems of Settlement

The Bay Colony escaped some of the hardship suffered by the first settlers at Plymouth, but better planning and more prosperous backing did not prevent a brief period of suffering and a discouragingly high mortality rate. The first year of settlement in Massachusetts cost dearly in lives, health, and fortunes. Deputy Governor Thomas Dudley (1577–1653) described the situation in a letter to the Countess of Lincoln, with whom he had become acquainted while steward of the Earl of Lincoln's estate in England. The Lincoln family had a deep interest in the Puritan experiment. Two of the Earl's sisters joined the migration (including the Lady Arbella Johnson whose name graced Winthrop's flagship); the Countess's father, Viscount Saye and Sele, was instrumental in the beginning of English settlement on the Connecticut River at Fort Saybrook.

Source: New Hampshire Historical Society, *Collections,* IV (1834), 229–235.

. . . [In the] year 1629 we sent divers ships over with about 300 people and some cows, goats, and horses, many of which arrived safely. These by their too large commendations of the country and the commodities thereof invited us so strongly to go on that Mr. Winthrop of Suffolk (who was well known in his own country and well approved here for his piety, liberality, wisdom, and gravity) coming in to us, we came to such resolution that in April, 1630, we set sail from old England with four good ships. And in May following eight more followed, two having gone before in February and March, and two more following in June and August, besides another set out by a private merchant. These seventeen ships arrived all safe in New England for the increase of the plantation here this year 1630—but made a long, troublesome, and costly voyage, being all wind-bound long in England and hindered with contrary winds after they set sail, and so scattered with mists and tempests that few of them arrived together. Our four ships which set out in April arrived here in June and July, where we found the colony in a sad and unexpected condition, above eighty of them being dead the winter before, and many of those alive weak and sick; all the corn and bread amongst them all hardly sufficient to feed upon a fortnight, insomuch that the remainder of the 180 servants we had the two years before sent over, coming to us for victuals to sustain them, we found ourselves wholly unable to feed them by reason that the provisions shipped for them were taken out of the ship they were put in, and they who were trusted to ship them in another failed us and left them behind; whereupon necessity enforced us to our extreme loss to give them all liberty, who had cost us about 16 or 20 pounds a person furnishing and sending over.

But bearing these things as we might, we began to consult of the place of our sitting down, for Salem, where we landed, pleased us not. And to that purpose some were sent to the Bay to search up the rivers for a convenient place, who upon their return reported to have found a good place upon Mystic; but some other of us seconding these to approve or dislike of their judgment, we found a place [that] liked us better three leagues up Charles river, and thereupon unshipped our goods into other vessels and with much cost and labor brought them in July to Charlestown. But there receiving advertisements by some of the late arrived ships from London and Amsterdam of some French preparations against us (many of our people brought with us being sick of fevers and scurvy, and we thereby unable to carry up our ordnance and baggage so far), we were forced to change counsel and for our present shelter to plant dispersedly, some at Charlestown which standeth on the north side of the mouth of Charles river; some on the south side thereof, which place we named Boston (as we intended to have done the place we first resolved on); some of us upon Mystic, which we named Medford; some of us westwards on Charles river, four miles from Charlestown, which place we named Watertown; others of us two miles from Boston in a place we named Roxbury; others upon the river of Saugus between Salem and Charlestown; and the western men four miles south from Boston at a place we named Dorchester. This dispersion troubled some of us, but help it we could not, wanting ability to remove to any place fit to build a town upon, and the time too short to deliberate any longer lest the winter should surprise us before we had builded our houses.

The best counsel we could find out was to build a fort to retire to in some convenient place if an enemy pressed thereunto, after we should have fortified ourselves against the injuries of wet and cold. So ceasing to consult further for that time, they who had health to labor fell to building, wherein many were interrupted with a sickness and many died weekly, yea almost daily. Amongst whom were Mrs. Pynchon, Mrs. Coddington, Mrs. Phillips, and Mrs. Alcock, a sister of Mr. Hooker's. Insomuch that the ships being now upon their return, some for England, some for Ireland, there was as I make it not much less than an hundred (some think many more) —partly out of dislike of our government, which restrained and punished their excesses, and partly through fear of famine, not seeing other means than by their labor to feed themselves—which returned back again. And glad were we so to be rid of them. Others also afterwards hearing of men of their own disposition which were planted at Pascataway went from us to them, whereby though our numbers were lessened yet we accounted ourselves nothing weakened by their removal. Before the departure of the ships, we contracted with Mr. Peirce, master of the *Lyon* of Bristow, to return to us with all speed with fresh supplies of victuals, and gave him directions accordingly. With this ship returned Mr. Revelle, one of the five undertakers here for the joint stock of the company; and Mr. Vassall, one of the assistants, and his family; and also Mr. Bright, a minister, sent hither the year before.

The ships being gone, victuals wasting, and mortality increasing, we held divers fasts in our several congregations, but the Lord would not yet be deprecated, for about the beginning of September died Mr. Gager, a right godly man, a skillful surgeon, and one of the deacons of our congregation; and Mr. Higginson, one of the ministers of Salem, a zealous and a profitable preacher—this of a consumption, that of a fever—and on the 30th of September died Mr. Johnson, another of the five undertakers (the Lady Arbella, his wife, being dead a month before). This gentleman was a prime man amongst us, having the best estate of any, zealous for religion and greatest furtherer of this plantation. He made a most godly end, dying willingly, professing his life better spent in promoting this plantation than it would have been any other way. He left to us a loss greater than the most conceived. Within a month after died Mr. Rossiter, another of our assistants, a godly man, and of a good estate, which still weakened us more; so that there now were left of the five undertakers but the Governor, Sir Richard Saltonstall, and myself, and seven other of the assistants. And of the people who came over with us, from the time of their setting sail from England in April, 1630, until December following, there died by estimation about 200 at the least—so low hath the Lord brought us!

Well, yet they who survived were not discouraged, but bearing God's corrections with humility and trusting in his mercies, and considering how after a greater ebb he had raised up our neighbors at Plymouth, we began again in December to consult about a fit place to build a town upon, leaving all thoughts of a fort because upon any invasion we were necessarily to lose our houses when we should retire thereunto; so after divers meetings at Boston, Roxbury, and Watertown, on the 28th day of December we grew to this resolution to bind all the assistants (Mr. Endecott and Mr. Sharpe excepted, which last purposeth to return by the next ships into England) to build houses at a place a mile east from Watertown, near Charles river, the next spring, and to winter there the next year, that so by our examples and by removing the ordnance and munition thither, all who were able might be drawn thither, and such as shall come to us hereafter to their advantage be compelled so to do, and so if God would, a fortified town might there grow up, the place fitting reasonably well thereto.

I should before have mentioned how both the English and Indian corn being at ten shillings a strike, and beaver being valued at six shillings a pound, we made laws to restrain the selling of corn to the Indians and to leave the price of beaver at liberty, which was presently sold for ten and twenty shillings a pound. I should also have remembered how the half of our cows and almost all our mares and goats sent us out of England died at sea in their passage hither, and that those intended to be sent us out of Ireland were not sent at all. All which together with the loss of our six months' building, occasioned by our intended removal to a town to be fortified, weakened our estates, especially the estates of the undertakers, who were three or four thousand pounds engaged in the joint stock, which was now not above so many hundreds. Yet many of us labored to bear it as comfortably as we could, remembering the end of our coming hither and knowing the power of God who can support and raise us again, and useth to bring His servants low that the meek may be made glorious by deliverance. Ps. 112.

8. Puritanism and the Great Migration

Prompted by political and religious repression, social unrest, and economic hardship, almost 50,000 English men and women left for the New World during the decade and a half before 1643. Some 20,000 went to New England and, combined with the natural increase so typical of early colonies, swelled the population of that section by about 1645 to perhaps 40,000. There is now no way of knowing why so many chose the rocky coast of New England rather than the balmier West Indies or Southern colonies; for most there was undoubtedly a mixture of motives. But the writings that survive make clear the importance of religious convictions in the decisions of many to seek asylum in the Puritan colonies. It can be seen in diaries, letters, biographies, and even in the colonists' earliest efforts at poetry. The following brief poem, penned in 1638 by Thomas Tillam (?–c. 1670), an obscure settler, reflects the mixture of deep faith, hope, and caution that marks the Puritan outlook.

Source: American Antiquarian Society, *Proceedings*, new ser. LIII (1944), 331.

Upon the First Sight of New England
June 29, 1638

Hail holy land wherein our holy Lord
hath planted his most true and holy word;
Hail happy people who have dispossesed
yourselves of friends, and means, to find some rest
for your poor wearied souls, oppressed of late
for Jesus' sake, with envy, spite, and hate;
To you that blessed promise truly's given
of sure reward, which you'll receive in Heaven.
Methinks I hear the lamb of God thus speak:
Come my dear little flock, who for my sake
have left your country, dearest friends, and goods
and hazarded your lives o'th raging floods.
Possess this country; free from all annoy
here I'll be with you, here you shall enjoy
my Sabbaths, sacraments, my ministry
and ordinances in their purity.
But yet beware of Satan's wily baits;
he lurks among you, cunningly he waits
to catch you from me. Live not then secure
but fight 'gainst sin, and let your lives be pure.
Prepare to hear your sentence thus expressed:
Come ye my servants of my Father Blessed.

9. God's Favors to New England

The Great Migration lasted until events at home caused English Puritans to take new hope that purification of the church and reformation of the state could both be accomplished through Parliament and Oliver Cromwell's "New Model" army. In the meantime, New England flourished. The conditions complained of by Thomas Dudley soon disappeared as fresh supplies and new economic opportunities—especially in the export of furs, fish, and timber—brought a modest degree of prosperity. Increasing familiarity with the dangers and benefits of the wilderness also helped to reduce mortality and encourage further immigration. By 1640, Puritan adherents could claim four colonies in New England. Partly because of minor religious differences but largely in response to the search for more land and new centers of commerce and fellowship, Connecticut emerged in the mid-1630s and New Haven a few years later.

Rhode Island, founded in 1636, had its origins in dissent from the religious and political formulas of Massachusetts Bay, but it too reflected an element in the Puritan heritage brought to New England in the Great Migration. Most of the settlers in the smallest colony had come to America to escape from Anglican conformity; their complaint with Massachusetts was that it imposed an orthodoxy that was equally intolerable. Rhode Island remained a minor thorn in the side of mainstream Puritans, but joined in common cause against foreign threats and Indian hostility.

In the following extract from an anonymous pamphlet effusive praise for the Puritan colonies reflects the optimism born of early success, as well as the New Englanders' compulsion to convince old England that the experiment was going well.

Source: *New England's First Fruits* (London, 1643; reprinted New York, 1865), 36–47.

Thus far hath the good hand of God favored our beginnings; see whether He hath not engaged us to wait still upon His goodness for the future by such further remarkable passages of His providence to our plantation in such things as these:

1. In sweeping away great multitudes of the natives by the smallpox a little before we went thither, that He might make room for us there.

2. In giving such marvelous safe passage from first to last, to so many thousands that went thither the like hath hardly been ever observed in any sea voyages.

3. In blessing us generally with health and strength, as much as ever (we might truly say) more than ever in our native land, many that were tender and sickly here are stronger and heartier there. That whereas divers other plantations have been the graves of their inhabitants, and their numbers much decreased, God hath so prospered the climate to us that our bodies are haler, and children there born stronger, whereby our number is exceedingly increased.

4. In giving us such peace and freedom from enemies, when almost all the world is on a fire, that (excepting that short trouble with the Pequots) we never heard of any sound of wars to this day. And in that war which we made against them, God's hand from heaven was so manifested that a very few of our men in a short time pursued through the wilderness, slew, and took prisoners about 1,400 of them, even all they could find, to the great terror and amazement of all the Indians to this day; so that the name of the Pequots (as of Amalech) is blotted out from under heaven, there being not one that is, or (at least) dare call himself, a Pequot.

5. In subduing those erroneous opinions carried over from hence by some of the passengers, which for a time infested our church's peace, but (through the goodness of God) by conference, preaching, a general assembly of learned men, magistrates' timely care, and lastly by God's own hand from heaven (in most remarkable strokes upon some of the chief fomenters of them), the matter came to such an happy conclusion that most of the seduced came humbly and confessed their errors in our public assemblies and abide to this day constant in the truth. The rest that remained obstinate, finding no fit market there to vent their wares, departed from us to an island far off, some of whom also since that time have repented and returned to us, and are received again into our bosoms. And from that time not any unsound, unsavory, and giddy fancy have dared to lift up his head, or abide the light amongst us.

6. In settling and bringing civil matter to such a maturity in a short time amongst us, having planted fifty towns and villages, built thirty or forty churches and more ministers' houses, a castle, a

college, prisons, forts, cartways, causes many, and all these upon our own charges, no public hand reaching out any help; having comfortable houses, gardens, orchards, grounds fenced, corn fields, etc., and such a form and face of a commonwealth appearing in all the plantation that strangers from other parts—seeing how much is done in so few years—have wondered at God's blessing on our endeavors.

7. In giving such plenty of all manner of food in a wilderness, insomuch that all kinds of flesh—amongst the rest, store of venison in its season; fish, both from sea and fresh water; fowl of all kinds, wild and tame; store of white meat—together with all sorts of English grain, as well as Indian, are plentiful amongst us. As also roots, herbs, and fruit, which being better digested by the sun are far more fair, pleasant, and wholesome than here.

8. In prospering hemp and flax so well that it's frequently sown, spun, and woven into linen cloth (and in a short time may serve for cordage), and so with cotton-wool (which we may have at very reasonable rates from the islands), and [of] our linen yarn we can make dimities and fustians for our summer clothing. And having a matter of 1,000 sheep which prosper well, to begin withal, in a competent time we hope to have woolen cloth there made. And great and small cattle being now very frequently killed for food, their skins will afford us leather for boots and shoes and other uses; so that God is leading us by the hand into a way of clothing.

9. In affording us many materials (which in part already are and will in time further be improved) for staple commodities to supply all other defects, as:

(1) furs, beaver, otter, etc;
(2) clapboard, hoops, pipestaves, masts;
(3) English wheat and other grain for Spain and West Indies, and all other provisions for victualing of ships;
(4) fish, as cod, haddock, herrings, mackerel, bass, sturgeon, seals, whales, sea-horse;
(5) oil of sundry sorts, of whale, sea-horse, etc;
(6) pitch and tar, rosin and turpentine—having pines, spruce, and pitch trees in our country to make these on;
(7) hemp and flax;
(8) minerals discovered and proved, as of iron in sundry places, black lead (many other in hopes) for the improving of

which we are now about to carry over servants and instruments with us;

(9) besides many boats, shallops, hoys, lighters, pinnaces, we are in a way of building ships of an 100, 200, 300, 400 ton; five of them are already at sea, many more in hand at this present, we being much encouraged herein by reason of the plenty and excellence of our timber for that purpose and seeing all the materials will be had there in short time.

10. In giving of such magistrates, as are all of them godly men and members of our churches, who countenance those that be good and punish evil doers that a vile person dares not lift up his head, nor need a godly man to hang it down, that (to God's praise be it spoken) one may live there from year to year and not see a drunkard, hear an oath, or meet a beggar. Now, where sin is punished and judgment executed, God is wont to bless that place and protect it, Psal. 106:30; Jer. 5:1; Jos. 7:25, with 8:1, e contra Esa. 20:21.

11. In storing that place with very many of His own people, and divers of them eminent for godliness: now, where His people are there is His presence, and promise to be in the midst of them, a mighty God to save, and to joy over them with singing. Zeph. 3:17.

12. Above all our other blessings, in planting His own name and precious ordinances among us (we speak it humbly, and in His fear), our endeavor is to have all His own institutions, and no more than His own and all those in their native simplicity without any human dressings, having a liberty to enjoy all that God commands and yet urged to nothing more than He commands. Now, wheresoever He records His name, thither He will come and bless, Exod. 20:24, which promise He hath already performed to very many souls in their effectual conversion to Christ, and the edification of others in their holy faith who daily bless God that ever He carried them into those parts.

All which blessings named we look upon as an earnest-penny of more to come. If we seek His face and serve His providence, we have no cause to doubt that He for His part will fail to make seasonable supplies unto us:

1. By some means to carry on to their perfection our staple trades begun.
2. By additions of ammunition and powder.
3. By maintenance of schools of learning, especially the college, as also additions of building to it and furnishing the library.
4. By stirring up some well-minded to clothe and transport over poor children, boys and girls, which may be a great mercy to their bodies and souls and a help to us, they being super-abundant here, and we wanting hands to carry on our trades, manufacture, and husbandry there.
5. By stirring up some to show mercy to the Indians in affording maintenance to some of our godly, active young scholars, there to make it their work to study their language, converse with them, and carry light amongst them, that so the Gospel might be spread into those dark parts of the world.

Objection. But all your own cost and ours also will be lost, because there can be no subsistence there for any long time, for, 1. Your ground is barren.

Answer. 1. If you should see our goodly corn fields near harvest, you would answer this yourself. Secondly, how could it be thin that we should have English wheat at 4 shillings per bushel and Indian at 2.8, and this not only for ready money, but in way of exchange. Thirdly, that in a wilderness in so few years we should have corn enough for ourselves and our friends that come over, and much to spare.

2. *Objection.* Your ground will not continue above three or four years to bear corn.

Answer. Our ground hath been sown and planted with corn these seven, ten, twelve years already by ourselves, and (which is more than can be said here of English land) never yet summer tilled, but have borne corn every year since we first went, and the same ground planted as long by the Indians before, and yet have good crops upon it still and is like to continue as ever. But this is (as many other slanders against that good land) against all sense, reason, and experience.

3. *Objection.* But you have no money there.

Answer 1. It's true we have not much, though some there is, but we having those staple commodities named, they will (still as they are improved) fetch money from other parts. Ships, fish, iron, pipe-staves, corn, beaver, oil, etc., will help us with money and other things also.

2. Little money is raised in coin in England; how then comes it to abound but by this means?

3. We can trade amongst ourselves by way of exchange, one commodity for another, and so do usually.

4. *Objection.* You are like to want clothes hereafter.

Answer. 1. Linen fustians, dimities we are making already. Secondly, sheep are coming on for woolen cloth. Thirdly, in mean time we may be supplied by way of trade to other parts. Fourth, cordovan, deer, seal, and moose skins (which are beasts as big as oxen and their skins are buff) are there to be had plentifully, which will help this way, especially for servants' clothing.

5. *Objection.* Your winters are cold.

Answer. True, at sometimes when the wind blows strong at northwest, but it holds not long together and then it useth to be very moderate for a good space, the coldness being not natural (that place being 42 degrees) but accidental. Secondly, the cold there is no impediment to health, but very wholesome for our bodies, insomuch that all sorts generally—weak and strong—had scarce ever such measure of health in all their lives as there. Thirdly, it's not a moist and foggy cold, as in Holland and some parts of England, but bright, clear, and fair weather that men are seldom troubled in winter with coughs and rheums. Fourthly, it hinders not our employment, for people are able to work or travail usually all the winter long, so there is no loss of time simply in respect of the cold. Fifthly, good fires (wood being so plentiful) will make amends.

6. *Objection.* Many are grown weaker in their estates since they went over.

Answer. Are not divers in London broken in their estates? And many in England are grown poor, and thousands go a-begging (yet we never saw a beggar there) and will any tax the city or kingdom and say they are unsubsistable places?

Secondly, their estates now lie in houses, lands, horses, cattle, corn, etc., though they have not so much money as they had here, and so cannot make appearance of their wealth to those in England, yet they have it still so that their estates are not lost but changed.

3. Some men's estates may be weaker through great and vast common charges, which the first planters especially have been at in making the place subsistable and comfortable, which now others reap the fruit of. Unknown sums lie buried underground in such a work as that is.

4. Some may be poor (so we are sure), many are rich that carried nothing at all, that now have house, land, corn, cattle, etc., and such as carry something are much increased.

7. *Objection.* Many speak evil of the place.

Answer. Did not some do so of the Land of Canaan itself, yet Canaan was never the worse and themselves smarted for so doing. Secondly, some have been punished there for their delinquencies or restrained from their exorbitances, or discountenanced for their ill opinions and not suffered to vent their stuff, and hence being displeased take revenge by slanderous report. Thirdly, let such (if any such there be) as have ought to allege, deal fairly and above board and come and justify anything against the country to our faces while we are here to answer, but such never yet appeared in any of our presence to avouch anything of this kind, nor (we believe) dare do it without blushing.

8. *Objection.* Why do many come away from thence?

Answer. Do not many remove from one country to another, and yet none likes the country the less because some depart from it? Secondly, few that we know of intend to abide here but do come on some special business, and purpose to return. Thirdly, of them that are come hither to stay (on our knowledge), some of the wisest repent them already, and wish themselves there again. Fourthly, as some went thither upon sudden, undigested grounds, and saw not God leading them in their way but were carried by an unstayed spirit, so have they returned upon as slight, headless, unworthy reasons as they went. Fifthly, others must have elbow room, and cannot abide to be so pinioned with the strict government in the commonwealth, or discipline in the church. Now why should such live there? As Ireland will not brook venomous beasts, so will not that land vile persons and loose livers. Sixthly, though some few have removed from them, yet (we may truly say) thousands as wise as themselves would not change their place for any other in the world.

III

The New England Way

ONCE ESTABLISHED in New England, the Puritans were free to re-shape their religious institutions rather than abide the corruptions of the Church of England. Part of what would soon emerge as "the New England Way" could be taken for granted: there would be no lavish ceremonies, no garish vestments, no ornate chapels, no uneducated clergymen. Such matters had been clearly aired in England. But what of the more basic matters of the organization of churches, the relationship of church and state, the authority of the clergy, the doctrine of faith? On such fundamental matters, the English experience was not altogether clear. From 1616 to 1622, Henry Jacob had led a congregation in Southwark, England, that purported to be modeled on the precedents of the early Christians yet still within the Anglican fold (a stance later dubbed "non-separatist Congregationalism"), and many of the spokesmen among English Puritans—men like Preston and Perkins and Ames—had given careful attention to Biblical authority for forms of organization and worship, but there had been no application on a large scale. And the emigrants themselves were not one of mind on many matters. It therefore remained to be seen what shape theology and ecclesiology would take in "the free aire of the New World."

Initially it appeared unlikely that the Plymouth Church would serve as the model. Because Plymouth had been settled by separat-ists, though of a very moderate sort, the men who created Massa-chusetts Bay Colony viewed the Pilgrims with suspicion. Separatists to them seemed dangerous schismatics who were partly responsible for the Puritans' poor reputation among more orthodox Anglicans: Puritanism, many in England had charged, would inevitably lead to separatism. To a considerable extent it did. Despite John Cotton's claim that Puritans fled Anglican England not as "a separation from them as no churches; but rather a secession from the corrup-tions found amongst them . . .," the churches formed in the Massachusetts, Connecticut, and New Haven colonies were almost indistinguishable from those of Plymouth. Puritan spokesmen may have been sincere in their professions of loyalty to the Church of England, but their actions suggest otherwise. By moving to a place free from ecclesiastical supervision, and by creating a congregational system, the New Englanders were insuring that their wing of the Puritan heritage would grow increasingly away from the Anglican communion. Still, the exact form of the New England Way was as much the product of evolution as revolution, and it owed less to Plymouth's example than to the Reformed heritage it shared with the Separatist colony. Not until 1648 were its main doctrinal and ecclesiastical outlines clear, and even these were subject to change and open to dissent in the century that followed.

10. Setting Up the Churches of Christ

As New England settlers began the arduous task of creating organized societies in the wilderness, they gave high priority to the formation of Puritan churches. In some instances, leadership came from a clergyman who was part of the initial migration; in others, the people entered on church-founding with no guidance save their own religious convictions and the example of neighboring communities. In either event, a pattern rapidly emerged that was followed throughout the Puritan colonies: leaders among the settlers gathered voluntarily into a congregation, selected and installed a minister, and entered into a covenant with God. The sequence is well described by Edward Johnson (1598–1672) of Woburn, Massachusetts. Johnson migrated to New England in 1630, and after returning to England for several years, lived in Charlestown, Massachusetts, and then helped to found Woburn. There he served as selectman, militia captain, town clerk, and delegate to the General Court. In mid-century, Johnson also became a historian, writing his own version of the Puritan experiment.

Source: J. Franklin Jameson, ed., *Johnson's Wonderworking Providence . . .* , Original Narratives of Early American History (New York, 1910), 214–218.

Now to declare how this people [of Woburn] proceeded in religious matters, and so consequently all the Churches of Christ planted in New England: when they came once to hopes of being such a competent number of people as might be able to maintain a minister, they then surely seated themselves, and not before, it being as unnatural for a right New England man to live without an able ministry as for a smith to work his iron without a fire. Therefore this people that went about placing down a town began the foundation stone with earnest seeking of the Lord's assistance, by humbling of their souls before Him in days of prayer, and imploring His aid in so weighty a work. Then they address themselves to attend counsel of the most orthodox and ablest Christians, and more especially of such as the Lord had already placed in the ministry, not rashly running together themselves into a church before they had hopes of attaining an officer to preach the Word and administer the seals unto them, choosing rather to continue in fellowship with some other church for their Christian watch over them till the Lord would be pleased to provide.

They after some search meet with a young man named Mr. Thomas Carter, then belonging to the Church of Christ at Watertown, a reverend, godly man, apt to teach the sound and wholesome truths of Christ. Having attained their desires, in hopes of his coming unto them were they once joined in Church estate, he exercis[ed] his gifts of preaching and prayer among them in the meantime, and more especially in a day of fasting and prayer. Thus these godly people interest their affections one with the other, both minister and people. After this they make ready for the work, and the 24th of the 6th month, 1642, they assemble together in the morning about eight of the clock. After the reverend Mr. Syms had continued in preaching and prayer about the space of four or five hours, the persons that were to join in covenant, openly and professedly before the congregation and messengers of divers neighbor churches—among whom the reverend elder[s] of Boston, Mr. Cotton, Mr. Wilson; Mr. [Thomas] Allen of Charlestown; Mr. Shepard of Cambridge [and] Mr. Dunster; of Watertown, Mr. Knowles; of Dedham, Mr. [John] Allen; of Roxbury, Mr. Eliot; of Dorchester, Mr. Mather. As also it is the duty of the magistrates (in regard of the good and peace of the civil government) to be present, at least some one of them, not only to prevent the disturbance [that] might follow in the Commonwealth by any who under pretense of church covenant might bring in again those cursed opinions that caused such commotion in this and the other colony, to the great damage of the people, but also to countenance the people of God in so pious a work, that under them they may live a quiet and peaceable life, in all godliness and honesty. For this cause was present and honored Mr. Increase Nowell.

The persons stood forth and first confessed what the Lord had done for their poor souls, by the work of His Spirit in the preaching of His Word, and providences, one by one. And that all might know their faith in Christ was bottomed upon Him, as He is revealed in His Word, and that from their own knowledge, they also declare the same, according to that measure of understanding the Lord had given them. The elders, or any other messengers there present, question with them, for the better understanding of them in any points they doubt of, which being done, and all satisfied, they in the name of the churches to which they do belong hold out the right hand of fellowship unto them, they declaring their covenant in words expressed in writing to this purpose.

The Church Covenant

We that do assemble ourselves this day before God and His people, in an unfeigned desire to be accepted of Him as the Church of the Lord Jesus Christ, according to the rule of the New Testament, do acknowledge ourselves to be the most unworthy of all others, that we should attain such a high grace, and the most unable of ourselves to the performance of anything that is good, abhorring ourselves for all our former defilements in the worship of God, and other ways, and resting only upon the Lord Jesus Christ for atonement, and upon the power of His grace for the guidance of our whole after course, do here in the name of Christ Jesus, as in the presence of the Lord, from the bottom of our hearts agree together through His grace to give up ourselves, first unto the Lord Jesus as our only King, Priest, and Prophet, wholly to be subject unto Him in all things, and therewith one unto another, as in a church body, to walk together in all the ordinances of the Gospel, and in all such mutual love and offices thereof, as toward one another in the Lord. And all this, both according to the present light that the Lord hath given us, as also according to all further light, which He shall be pleased at any time to reach out unto us out of the Word by the goodness of His grace, renouncing also in the same covenant all errors and schisms, and whatsoever byways that are contrary to the blessed rules revealed in the Gospel, and in particular the inordinate love and seeking after the things of the world.

Every church hath not the same for words, for they are not for a form of words.

The 22nd of the 9th month following, Mr. Thomas Carter was ordained pastor in presence of the like assembly. After he had exercised in preaching and prayer the greater part of the day, two persons in the name of the church laid their hands upon his head and said, "We ordain thee Thomas Carter to be pastor unto this Church of Christ." Then one of the elders priest [present?], being desired of the church, continued in prayer unto the Lord for His more especial assistance of this His servant in His work, being a charge of such weighty importance, as is the glory of God and salvation of souls, that the very thought would make a man to tremble in the sense of his own inability to the work. The people having provided a dwelling house, built at the charge of the town in general, welcomed him unto them with joy that the Lord was pleased to give them such a blessing, that their eyes may see their Teacher's.

After this there were divers added to the church daily in this manner: the person desirous to join with the church cometh to the pastor and makes him acquainted therewith, declaring how the Lord hath been pleased to work his conversion, who discerning hopes of the person's faith in Christ, although weak, yet if any appear he is propounded to the church in general for their approbation, touching his godly life and conversation, and then by the pastor and some brethren heard again, who make report to the church of their charitable approving of the person. But before they come to join with the church, all persons within the town have public notice of it; then publicly he declares the manner of his conversion and how the Lord hath been pleased by the hearing of His Word preached, and the work of His Spirit in the inward parts of his soul, to bring him out of that natural darkness which all men are by nature in and under, as also the measure of knowledge the Lord hath been pleased to indue him withal. And because some men cannot speak publicly to edification through bashfulness, the less is required of such, and women speak not publicly at all, for all that is desired is to prevent the polluting [of] the blessed ordinances of Christ by such as walk scandalously, and that men and women do not eat and drink their own condemnation in not discerning the Lord's body.

After this manner were many added to the Church of Christ, and those seven that joined in church fellowship at first are now increased to seventy-four persons or thereabout, of which, according to their own confession, as is supposed, the greater part having been converted by the preaching of the Word in New England, by which may appear the powerful efficacy of the Word of Christ in the mouth of His ministers, and that this way of Christ in joining together in church covenant is not only for building up of souls in Christ, but also for converting of sinners and bringing them out of the natural condition to be ingrafted into Christ. For if this one church have so many, then assuredly there must be a great number comparatively throughout all the churches in the country. After this manner have the Churches of Christ had their beginning and progress hitherto. The Lord continue and increase them the world throughout.

11. Forms of Public Worship

In England, the Puritans had tried to ignore those parts of the Anglican service that they deemed offensive. But seldom could they with impunity conduct services exactly as they pleased, for complaints by orthodox clergymen or disgruntled parishioners often brought a speedy end to Puritan conventicles. Once in New England, however, the Puritans constructed forms of public worship that rapidly became hallmarks of the New England Way.

A. Church Services

Although individual churches exercised their right to worship God as they saw fit (within certain limitations), in practice the congregations followed very similar formats of public worship. Compared to Anglican procedures, they were drab, informal, and ascetic; according to Puritan adherents, they were beautiful in their simplicity, Biblically correct, and in keeping with the traditions of the original Christians. The author of the following description, Thomas Lechford (?–1644), did not like what he saw. He was one of scores, perhaps hundreds, who found the New England Way incompatible with their own convictions and returned to

England. Fortunately, Lechford took time upon his arrival in the mother country to write down his impressions of the New England Way and to vent his complaints against it.

Source: Thomas Lechford, *Plain Dealing or News from New England* [London, 1642], reprinted in Massachusetts Historical Society, *Collections*, 3 ser. III (1833), 76–79.

The public worship is in as fair a meeting house as they can provide, wherein in most places they have been at great charges. Every Sabbath or Lord's day they come together at Boston, by ringing of a bell, about nine of the clock or before. The pastor begins with solemn prayer continuing about a quarter of an hour. The teacher then readeth and expoundeth a chapter, then a psalm is sung, whichever one of the ruling elders dictates. After that the pastor preacheth a sermon, and sometimes *ex tempore* exhorts. Then the teacher concludes with prayer and a blessing.

Once a month is a sacrament of the Lord's Supper, whereof notice is given usually a fortnight before, and then all others departing save the church—which is a great deal less in number than those that go away—they receive the sacrament, the ministers and ruling elders sitting at the table, the rest in their seats, or upon forms. All cannot see the minister consecrating unless they stand up and make a narrow shift. The one of the teaching elders prays before and blesseth and consecrates the bread and wine, according to the words of institution; the other prays after the receiving of all the members; and next communion they change turns, he that began at that ends at this. And the ministers deliver the bread in a charger to some of the chief, and peradventure gives to a few the bread into their hands, and they deliver the charger from one to another till all have eaten; in like manner the cup, till all have drank, goes from one to another. Then a psalm is sung, and with a short blessing the congregation is dismissed. Anyone, though not of the church, may in Boston come in and see the sacrament administered if he will. [*Marginal note:* Once I stood without one of the doors, and looked in, and saw the administration. Besides I have had credible relation of all the particulars from some of the members.] But none of any church in the country may receive the sacrament there without leave of the congregation, for which pur-

pose he comes to one of the ruling elders who propounds his name
to the congregation before they go to the sacrament.

About two in the afternoon they repair to the meeting house
again, and then the pastor begins—as before noon—and a psalm
being sung, the teacher makes a sermon. He was wont, when I
came first, to read and expound a chapter also before his sermon in
the afternoon. After and before his sermon, he prayeth.

After that ensues baptism, if there be any, which is done by
either pastor or teacher in the deacon's seat, the most eminent
place in the church, next under the elder's seat. The pastor most
commonly makes a speech or exhortation to the church and parents concerning baptism, and then prayeth before and after. It is
done by washing or sprinkling. One of the parents being of the
church, the child may be baptized, and the baptism is into the
name of the Father, and of the Son, and of the Holy Ghost. No
sureties are required.

Which ended, follows the contribution, one of the deacons
saying, "Brethren of the congregation, now there is time left for
contribution, wherefore as God hath prospered you, so freely
offer." Upon some extraordinary occasions as building and repairing of churches or meeting houses, or other necessities, the ministers press a liberal contribution, with effectual exhortations out of
scripture. The magistrates and chief gentlemen first, and then the
elders, and all the congregation of men, and most of them that are
not of the church, all single persons, widows, and women in absence
of their husbands, come up one after another one way, and bring
their offerings to the deacon at his seat, and put it into a box of
wood for the purpose, if it be money or papers; if it be any other
chattel, they set it or lay it down before the deacons, and so pass
another way to their seats again. This contribution is of money, or
papers promising so much money (I have seen a fair gilt cup with a
cover, offered there by one, which is still used at the communion),
which monies and goods the deacons dispose towards the maintenance of the ministers and the poor of the church and the church's
occasions, without making account, ordinarily.

But in Salem church, those only that are of the church offer in
public; the rest are required to give to the ministry by collection at
their houses. At some other places they make a rate upon every
man, as well within as not of the church, residing with them, towards the church's occasions; and others are beholding now and

then to the General Court to study ways to enforce the maintenance of the ministry.

This done then follows the admission of members, or hearing matters of offense, or other things, sometimes till it be very late. If they have time, after this is sung a psalm, and then the pastor concludeth with a prayer and a blessing.

Upon the week days there are lectures in divers towns, and in Boston upon Thursdays, when Master Cotton teacheth out of the *Revelation*. There are days of fasting, thanksgiving, and prayers upon occasions,[1] but no holy days[2] except the Sunday.

In some churches nothing is read[3] on the first day of the week, or Lord's day, but a psalm dictated before or after the sermon, as at Hingham; there is no catechizing of children or others in any church (except in Concord church, and in other places, of those admitted, in their receiving), the reason given by some is because when people come to be admitted, the church hath trial of their knowledge, faith, and repentance, and they want a direct scripture for ministers' catechizing, as if, "Go teach all nations, and train up a child in the way he should go," did not reach to ministers' catechizings. But, God be thanked, the General Court was so wise in June last as to enjoin or take some course for such catechizing, as I am informed, but know not the way laid down in particular how it should be done.

1. And why not set fasting days and times, and set feasts, as well as set Synods in the Reformed Churches?
2. And why not holy days as well as the fifth of November, and the days of Purim among the Jews? Besides, the commemoration of the blessed and heavenly mysteries of our ever blessed Saviour, and the good examples and piety of the saints? What time is there for the moderate recreation of youth and servants but after divine services on most of those days, seeing that upon the Sunday it is justly held unlawful? And sure enough, at New England, the masters will and must hold their servants to their labor more than in other countries well planted is needful. Therefore I think even they should do well to admit of some holy days too, as not a few of the wiser sort among them hold necessary and expedient.
3. Whereas in England every Sunday are read in public chapters and psalms in every church, besides the eleven or twelve commandments, epistle and gospel, the Creed and other good forms and catechizings, and besides what is read upon holy days and other days both in the parish and Cathedral and collegiate churches and in the universities and other chapels, the benefit whereof, doubtless, as wise men will acknowledge to be exceeding great, as well as public preaching and expounding.

B. Puritan Preaching

In keeping with a church that had rebelled against ornate vestments and rote rituals, Puritan services stressed the reading of the Bible and, especially, sermons by the clergy. New England's was a preaching more than a praying clergy. Often long and dreary to the modern ear, Puritan sermons nonetheless held the key to the New England Way, for through the countless orations of New England divines the Puritan persuasion spread and reinforced itself among the people of New England. Drawing on their training at Cambridge, Oxford, or Harvard, as well as on the writings of masters of pulpit oratory such as William Perkins, the ministers sought to preach with a clarity or "plaine style" appropriate to their diverse audiences, yet with an intellectual sophistication appropriate to their complex theology.

While no single formula existed on which Puritan preachers modeled their discourses, the prevailing pattern owed much to "that great and famous Martyr of France" (Increase Mather's phrase), Petrus Ramus. One of the few Protestant martyrs—a victim of the St. Bartholomew massacre—he developed a comprehensive new logic of rhetoric that gained lasting favor among Calvinist scholars. A century after the founding of Massachusetts, a eulogist would praise a deceased minister as "well schooled in logic, Ramean discipline [and] Dr. Ames," a somewhat redundant listing, for it was through William Ames that most American Puritans encountered Ramus, and Ramean "discipline" amounted to a system of logic. Ramus stressed dichotomies: broad questions could be divided into alternative choices, each of which could in turn be further divided as the thesis systematically ascended from easily demonstrable arguments to the more elusive and intricate. Through their use of Ramist methodology, Puritan sermons were relatively easy to follow, and therefore more likely to be understood and, hopefully, acted upon.

Listeners in the congregation frequently took notes on sermons in order to preserve the essence of the preacher's message for future review and meditation. Unfortunately few of the notes survive, and those that do are often in a homemade shorthand hard to decipher. The examples presented below are typical. They were translated in the nineteenth century from the notebook of Henry Wolcott, Jr. (1610–1680), of Windsor, Connecticut, who outlined the sermons he heard, including the following two by Thomas Hooker (1586–1647), one of the leading clergymen of seventeenth-century New England and a founder of Connecticut. Hooker delivered the first of these sermons on a lecture day, at a time when the colony's Fundamental Orders (see document 16C below) were under consideration; the second he preached on the occasion of the first general election under the new frame of government. Hence both sermons stress political themes. They are, however, representative of Puritan pulpit rhetoric in their use of Biblical texts as points of departure and in their logical progression of argument, as is the sermon by Hooker that here follows Wolcott's notes. "The Application of Redemption," published posthumously in London, illustrates both Ramean method and Puritan sermon literature. Its theme is representative too: how the individual Christian must prepare his heart to receive God's saving grace, a crucial step in the morphology of conversion.

Source: "Abstracts of Two Sermons by Rev. Thomas Hooker," transcribed by J. H. Trumbull, Connecticut Historical Society, *Collections*, I (1860), 20–21; Thomas Hooker, *The Application of Redemption: The Ninth and Tenth Books* (London, 1656), 1–14.

BY MR. HOOKER, AT HARTFORD, MAY 31, 1638.

Text: Deut. i.:13. "Take you wise men, and understanding, and known among your tribes, and I will make them rulers over you." Captains over thousands, and captains over hundreds, over fifties, over tens, &c.

Doctrine. I. That the choice of public magistrates belongs unto the people, by God's own allowance.

II. The privilege of election, which belongs to the people, therefore must not be exercised according to their humors, but according to the blessed will and law of God.

III. They who have power to appoint officers and magistrates, it is in their power, also, to set the bounds and limitations of the power and place unto which they call them.

Reasons. 1. Because the foundation of authority is laid, firstly, in the free consent of the people.

2. Because, by a free choice, the hearts of the people will be more inclined to the love of the persons [chosen?] and more ready to yield [obedience?].

3. Because of that duty and engagement of the people.

Uses. The lesson taught is threefold:—

1st. There is matter of thankful acknowledgment in the [appreciation?] of God's faithfulness toward us, and the permission of these measures that God doth command and vouchsafe.

2dly. Of reproof—to dash the conceits of all those that shall oppose it.

3dly. Of exhortation—to persuade us as God hath given us liberty, to *take* it.

And lastly—as God hath spared our lives, and given us them in liberty, so to seek the guidance of God, and to choose *in* God and *for* God.

By Mr. Hooker, at Hartford, April 11th, 1639.

Text: Exodus xviii.: 17, 18. "And Moses' father-in-law said unto him, The thing that thou doest is not good. Thou wilt surely wear away, both those and this people that is with thee: for this thing is too heavy for thee; thou art not able to perform it thyself alone."

Doctrine. I. That in the very best of a man's performances there are, many times, more blemishes than a man is readily aware of.

Uses. 1. This should make us not to be confident in all those courses that we take up with most care and most [zeal?].

2. Matter of abasement and fear in our best [purposes?].

Doctrine. II. That the most conscientious governors or rulers may do some [——], and that when he is most [zealous?].

Uses. 1. We may therefore not think the worse of a governor because of some weakness.

2. To advise those that are in the place of government to seek to Heaven for help.

Doctrine. III. That a weaker man, in some affairs and at some times, may offer seasonable advice to one that is far wiser.

Use. To teach every one of us how to carry with us teachable hearts in [——] and [——].

Doctrine. IV. [Not intelligible.]

V. That government, it is heavy and burdensome.

Uses. 1. Of instruction: how to [honor?] our choice of magistrates.

2. Of exhortation: (1) to the people, how to carry themselves to governors: (2) to magistrates; they should look upon it as a burdensome thing.

"THE APPLICATION OF REDEMPTION, BY THE EFFECTUAL WORK OF THE WORD AND SPIRIT OF CHRIST, FOR THE BRINGING HOME OF LOST SINNERS TO GOD."

The Ninth Book.

Isaiah 57:15. *Thus saith He that is the high and the lofty One that inhabiteth eternity, whose name is Holy; I dwell in the high and the holy place, with him also that is of a contrite and humble spirit.*

The work of preparation having two parts: First, the Lord's manner of dispensation. He is pleased to deal with the soul, for the setting up the praise of His rich and glorious grace, and therefore with a holy kind of violence He plucks the sinner from his sins unto Himself and his Christ. This hath been dispatched already in the former discourse.

The second now follows: and that is the frame and disposition which is wrought in the hearts of such as the Lord hath purposed to save, and to whom He hath dispensed Himself in that gracious work of His.

This disposition consists especially in two things $\left\{\begin{array}{l}\text{contrition,}\\\text{humiliation.}\end{array}\right.$ That so I may follow the phrase of scripture and retain the Lord's own words in the text, where the Lord saith that he dwells with him that is "of an humble and contrite heart." To omit all manner of coherence and other circumstances, we will pass all the other specials in the verse and point at that particular which will suit our proceeding and may afford ground to the following discourse, that we may go no further than we see the pillar of fire, the Lord in His truth to go before us. We shall fasten then upon the last words only, as those that fit our intendment.

To make way for ourselves in short, there is one word alone to be opened, that so the point may be better fitted for our application; we must know what it is "to dwell" or how "God" is said to "dwell in a contrite and humble heart."

I answer, to dwell implies three things: First, that the Lord owns such as those in whom He hath an especial interest and claims a special propriety as though He left all the rest of mankind to lie waste as a common, that the world and the devil and sin may possess and use at their pleasure, reserving the honor of His justice, which by a strong hand He will exact as a tribute due to Himself out of all things in heaven and earth and hell and all; but persons whom He thus fits, He reserves for His own special improvement. As princes and persons of place and quality do lease out and let some forests and commons to the inhabitants bordering thereabout, reserving some acknowledgement of fealty and royalty to themselves, but the choice and best palaces or granges of greatest worth and profit, they reserve for their own peculiar to inhabit in. So here, the Lord leaseth out the world and the wicked in it to the devil and his angels and instruments, reserving a royalty and prerogative to Himself, as that He will have His homage and acknowledgement of dependence upon Himself; but His broken-hearted ones are His own for His own improvement. . . .

Secondly, where a man dwells, as he owns the house, so he takes up his abode there; it is the place of his residence. We say any may know where to seek men, or where to find them: at home, at their own house. That's the difference between inning and dwelling. We inn at a place in our passing by when we take repast only, and bait, but depart presently intending not to stay; but where we dwell we settle our abode, we take up our stand there and stir no further. So the Lord is said then to dwell in the soul when He vouchsafes the constant expression of His peculiar presence and assistance to the soul. . . .

[Thirdly] Dwelling, if it be attributed to the chiefest inhabitant and owner of the house, it implies also the ruling and ordering of the occasions that come under hand there, the exercising of the government of the house and family where the owner is and dwells. He that lodgeth at a house as a stranger, comes to an inn as a passenger, he takes what he finds, hath what he can receive of kindness and courtesy; but the owner is the commander of the house where he dwells and the orderer of all the affairs that appertain thereunto. So doth the Lord with a broken heart. Thus we are said to, "live in the spirit, and to walk in the spirit," Gal. 5:25. And it's that which follows by inference upon this ground, John 15:4,5: "If I abide in you and you abide in me, you shall bring forth much fruit." And therefore it's added also in this place, that the Lord dwells in the contrite and humble heart "to receive the spirit" of the contrite ones; they yield themselves to be acted by Him, and they shall be acted and quickened by Him to eternal life.

So that the full meaning is: the contrite and humble heart is such to whom the Lord vouchsafes acceptance, special presence and abode, and peculiar guidance; He owns him, abides with him, and rules in him forever. True, it is said Christ dwells in our hearts by faith, Eph. 3:17, and as many as believe in Him, they receive Him, John 1:12. That is done as by the next and immediate hand by which we lay hold on Christ and give entertainment to Him; but unless the heart be broken and humbled we cannot receive faith that we may receive Christ. . . .

Doctrine: *The heart must be broken and humbled before the Lord will own it as His, take up His abode with it, and rule in it.*

There must be contrition and humilition before the Lord comes to take possession; the house must be aired and fitted before it comes to be inhabited, swept by brokenness and emptiness of spirit before the Lord will come to set up His abode in it. This was typified in the passage of the children of Israel towards the promised land: they must come into and go through a vast and a roaring wilderness, where they must be bruised with many pressures, humbled under many overbearing difficulties they were to meet withal before they could possess that good land which abounded with all prosperity, flowed with milk and honey. The truth of this type, the prophet Hosea explains and expresseth at large in the Lord's dealing with His people in regard of their spiritual condition, Hos. 2:14,15, "I will lead her into the wilderness," and break her heart with many bruising miseries, and "then I will speak kindly to her heart, and will give her the Valley of Achor for a door of hope." The story you may recall out of Hos. 7:28 when Achan had offended in the execrable thing, and the hearts of the Israelites were discomfited and failed, like water spilt upon the ground, because they had caused the Lord to depart away from them. The text says, they having found out the offender by lot, they stoned him, and they said thou hast troubled Israel, we will trouble thee, and they called it the Valley of Achor; and after that God supported their hearts with hope and encouraged them with success, both in prevailing over their enemies and in possessing the land. So it shall be spiritually, the valley of consternation, perplexity of spirit, and brokenness of heart is the very gale and entrance of any sound hope and assured expectation of good. . . . And "an honest heart is a contrite and humble heart," so rightly prepared that faith is infused and the soul thereby carried unto Christ, and quickened with patience to persevere in good duties. As we say of grounds before we cast in seed, there is two things to be attended there: it must be a fit ground and a fat ground. The ground is fit when the weeds and greensward are plowed up, and the soil there and made mold. And this is done in contrition and humiliation. Then it must be a fat ground; the soil must have heart. We say the ground is plowed well and lies well, but it's worn out, it's out of heart. Now faith fats the soil, furnisheth the soul with ability to fasten upon Christ, and so to receive the seed of the Word and the graces of sanctification, and then it produceth good fruit in obedience. Upon this condition God's favor is promised . . . Psal. 55:17, "A broken and contrite heart, O God, thou wilt not despise," Nay, He will undoubtedly accept of it.

The reasons of the point are taken, partly in regard of the heart, which without these will neither be fitted nor enabled to act upon God in Christ for any good; partly in regard of God, all His ordinances and dispensations will be unprofitable and unable to do that good which He intends, and we need.

Reason 1. To the first in regard of our hearts: those lets and impediments which put a kind of incapability, yea, and impossibility upon the soul, whereby the coming of faith into the heart and so the entrance and residence of the spirit are hindered are by this disposition wrought and removed. These impediments are two: The first which stops the way and work of faith is a settled kind of contentedness in our corrupt condition, and the blind yet bold and presumptious confidence that a natural man hath and would maintain of his good condition. Each man sits down willingly, well apaid with his own estate and portion, sees no need of any change and therefore not willing to hear of it. Each man is so full of self-love that he is loath to pass a sentence against his own soul, to become a judge and self-condemner, and consequently an executioner of all his hopes and comforts at once, and so put his happiness and help out of his own hand. Besides, we are naturally afraid (out of the privy, yet direful guilt of our own consciences) to profess the wretchedness of our own miserable and damnable condition, as to put it upon a preemptory conclusion, and that beyond question—I am undone, I am a damned man—in the gall of bitterness, in the bonds of iniquity, lest they should stir such horrors which they are neither able to quiet, nor yet able to bear. And therefore out of the presumption of their own hearts, they would easily persuade and delude themselves they have no cause to alter their condition, and therefore they should not endeavor it.

Hence the carnal heart is said to bear up himself against all the assaults of the word, Deut. 29:19, "When all the curses of the law were denounced" with never so much evidence, yet the presumptuous sinner "blesseth himself," promiseth all good to himself, and secretly feeds himself with vain hopes that he shall attain it; therefore he will not stir to seek for a better estate, nor yet receive it if offered, Job 22:17, "They say unto the Almighty, depart from us, we desire not the knowledge of His ways." Do ministers press them, do others persuade them to a more serious and narrow search to get more grounded assurance of their estate in grace, they profess they bid them to their loss, they think they need not be better, nor do they desire to be other. It is impossible upon these terms that ever the soul should be carried by faith unto God.

For to be contented and quieted with our condition, as that which best pleaseth, and yet to seek out for another, are things contradictory. And yet this faith doth, for he that is in Christ is a new creature; behold all things are become new, 2 Cor. 5:17. He must have new comforts, new desires, new hopes; therefore the heart must be broken to pieces under the weight of the evil of sin and the curses due to the old condition before this will part. . . .

2. Be it granted that the soul finds sin as a plague, and therefore would be preserved from the evil of it. The second impediment which wholly keeps out faith is this: when the sinner expects supply and succor from its own sufficiency, either outward excellencies, abilities of nature, or common graces, or the beauty of some performances which issue from any of these, for this is natural to all men every since innocency, that since the staff was put into his own hand and then needed not, nay should not deny their own strength, therefore to this day this practice of old Adam remains still in all his posterity: they will scramble for their own comforts and try the utmost of their own strength to help themselves rather than be beholding to another to help them. Hence in cases of conscience and trouble men are so ready to resolve, so apt and free to promise and profess amendment what they will do, and others shall see it as well as they resolve it, and so alas it comes to nothing in conclusion: either they fall back unto their base courses when horror and fear is over, or else wasting away into a wearish formality and so perish in their hypocrisy. This is an apparent bar to faith, which is the going out of the soul to fetch all life and power from another. Now wholly to be in ourselves and to stay

upon our own ability, and yet to go out of himself to Christ and receive all from His sufficiency, are things which cannot stand together. "I came not to call the righteous," Math. 9:13, "while they sought to establish their own righteousness," they did not submit to the righteousness of God.

Hence therefore the second work of humiliation is required, whereby God plucks away all his props and emptieth him wholly of what he hath or seemeth to have. For pride (unto which humiliation is opposite) is but the rankness of praise, and praise is a fruit of a cause by counsel that hath power to do or not to do this or that, as he sees fit. Humiliation is the utter nothingness of the soul, that we have no power; it's not in our choice to dispose of ourselves, not yet to dispose of that which another gives, nor yet safe to repine at his dispose. In a word, as in a scion before it be ingrafted into another flock, it must be cut off from the old, and pared, and then implanted. In contrition we are cut off; in humiliation pared, and so fit to be implanted into Christ by faith.

Reason 2. In regard of God, without this disposition His Word will not, nay cannot, take any place in us, or prevail with us for our good. Counsels, and commands, and comforts, or whatever dispensations, they fall as water upon a rock when administered to a hard heart; they enter not, prevail not, profit not at all. As Christ told the Jews, John 8:37, "My Word takes no place in you," and Zach. 7:11,12, "They hardened their hearts as an adamant, etc."

Use 1: A word of terror to dash the hopes and sink the hearts of all haughty and hard hearted sinners: God owns not such, will never vouchsafe His gracious presence with them, or His blessing upon them for good; be where they will, dwell where they will, the Lord is not with them nor will dwell in them by His comforting, quickening, saving presence. Hear and fear then all you stout-hearted, stubborn, and rebellious creatures whose consciences can evidence that the day is yet to dawn, the hour yet to come, that ever you found your sins a pressure to you. They have been your pasttime and delight in which you have pleased yourselves, so far from being troubled for your evils that it is your only trouble you may not commit them with content; and without control you are troubled with admonitions, and counsels, and commands, and threatenings that cross you in your sins. You were never broken hearted here for your abominations; know assuredly that you will burn for them one day. Your proud hearts were never abased and laid in the dust; the Lord will ruinate both you and them. Never expect a good look from God, set your heart at rest for that; you may draw the eyes of others after you, make many of your deluded followers and favorites to look upon you, but the Lord will not come near nor once cast a loving look towards you, Psal. 138:6, "Though the Lord be high, He hath respect to the lowly, but he knows the proud afar off." Nay, the great God of heaven and earth is up in arms against thee, He is upon the march to work thy destruction, James 4:6, "The Lord resists the proud, but He gives grace to the humble." All grace is in His gift, and He doles it only to the bruised and abased . . .

Objection: But we do see our sins, and have had many girds and galls of conscience for them.

Answer: True, it may be there hath been some blows upon thine heart; conscience it hath smitten thee; the hammer of the word, it hath laid some strokes, but it hath not broken thy heart to this day, and that is thus discerned (to go no further now than the very expression of the text).

If thy soul be beaten to powder with this oppression of thy distempers (for so this brokenness of heart was opened before) then as it is with the hardest flints, when they are broken to dust, they are easily yielding and give way to take the impression of the hand, or whatever is laid upon them. The stone which out of its hardness before opposed and started aside from the strongest stroke that was laid now it's turned into dust. The least and easiest touch leaves a print and impression upon it; so it is expounded as appears in this opposition, 2 Chron. 30:8, "Be not stiff-necked, but yield yourselves." . . .

Pharaoh is the pattern of all proud hearts; he hardened himself in his wickedness against the word of the Lord. But a broken and humble heart either lies right or will come right; it will come to that bent of the rule that is revealed: hard things makes that which is most soft to assimilate to them; easy and yielding things assimilate to whatever they close; so water in a round vessel takes that form, in a three square vessel, takes that. So here.

Use 2: Instruction: To teach us to delight in such, to desire the society of such as are contrite and humble men, to dwell there where God dwells, seem their persons never so mean, their conditions never so base, their estates never so low, themselves never so despicable, yet if they be men of broken spirits, God is with them. Go into their societies as men that resolve to go to the court, for where the King is, the court is; and where God is, heaven is. The Lord hath two thrones, the one of glory in heaven, where He is all in all to His; another here on earth, an humble heart, where He doth all only of Himself, and for Himself. Therefore as they in Zachary 8, last, "Ten men shall lay hold on the skirt of a Jew, and they shall say, we will go with you, for we have heard God is with you." Much more here, for the Lord is not only with humble hearts, but He dwells in them. We should therefore entertain such servants into our families, such inhabitants into plantations, and such members into congregations for so you entertain God Himself. . . .

Use 3: *Exhortation:* To persuade us all, and to prevail with us to take the right way to enjoy God's presence, not only to seek for mercy, but seek it in God's order; not only to covet God's presence, but in God's manner. Labor to be humble and broken-hearted Christians, then expect we may that the Lord will manifest the presence of His grace and spirit with us, and in us, but not else. Every man catchest at Christ, and mercy, and comfort, but not in a right method, and therefore they lose Him, and their labor also. This is God's order: First, be humble and broken, and then He will revive your spirits with His presence, 2 Cor. 6:19, "Come out from among them, and touch no unclean thing; then I will receive you, and be a Father to you." In a word, strive to enter in at the straight gate of contrition and humiliation, and then you will hit the right way to Christ and eternal life.

12. Conversion Experience

As Edward Johnson pointed out in his description of the founding of the Woburn church, admission to full participation in a Puritan congregation was determined by vote of the membership. The principal criterion, besides an upright behavior, was evidence that God had chosen the candidate for eternal salvation, that he was a regenerate spirit rather than merely a man or woman who wanted to be picked for salvation. Here the New England Way departed from the practice of English Puritans and even for a time marked a distinction between separatist and nonseparatist Puritans in New England. All Puritan factions agreed that a person could not become a member of a church without some assurance that he was elect of God; only the congregations of Massachusetts, Connecticut, and New Haven (and subsequently Plymouth as well) insisted on public evidence of that assurance.

Such evidence was usually offered in open church session, where the candidate related his own religious wanderings and described the workings of Christ on his soul. The congregation was free to question the applicant—a procedure that may have discouraged some potential members. In most congregations, however, private recital before the pastor and sometimes the elders was acceptable for women, "who are usually more fearefull and bashfull"; other congregations permitted written confession. Few such recitations survive, but the substance of them is accurately preserved in the autobiographical writings that played an important role in Puritan literature. Typical is that of Thomas Shepard, emigrant to New England in 1635, and pastor of the First Church in Cambridge, Massachusetts, from then until his death in 1649.

Source: Colonial Society of Massachusetts, *Publications*, XXVII (1932), 360–365.

The first two years I spent in Cambridge was in studying and in my neglect of God and private prayer, which I had sometime used, and I did not regard the Lord at all unless it were at some fits. The third year, wherein I was sophister,* I began to be foolish and proud and to shew myself in the public schools,† and there to be a disputer about things which now I see I did not know then at all but only prated about them. And toward the end of this year when I was most vile (after I had been next unto the gates of death by the smallpox the year before) the Lord began to call me home to the fellowship of His grace, which was in this manner:

1. I do remember that I had many good affections (but blind and unconstant) often cast into me, since my father's sickness, by the spirit of God wrestling with me, and hence I would pray in secret. And hence when I was at Cambridge I heard old Dr. Chadderton,‡ the master of the college when I came and the first year I was there. To hear him upon a sacrament day my heart was much affected, but I did break loose from the Lord again; and half a year after, I heard Mr. Dickinson commonplace in the chapel upon those words "I will not destroy it for ten's sake." Gen. 19. And then again was much affected.

* Sophisters were university students who had demonstrated adequate mastery of logic; they could then participate in public disputations. [Editor]
† The public rooms in the University where disputations were held. [Editor]
‡ Laurence Chaderton, Master of Emmanuel College, 1584–1622. [Editor]

But I shook this off also and fell from God to loose and lewd company, to lust and pride and gaming and bowling and drinking. And yet the Lord left me not, but a godly scholar walking with me fell to discourse about the misery of every man out of Christianity, viz., that whatever they did was sin. And this did much affect me. And at another time when I did light in godly company I heard them discourse about the wrath of God, and the terror of it, and how intolerable it was, which they did present by fire, how intolerable the torment of that was for a time, what then would eternity be; and this did much awaken me. And I began to pray again, but then by loose company I came to dispute in the schools and there to join to loose scholars of other colleges and was fearfully left of God and fell to drink with them. And I drank so much one day that I was dead drunk and that upon a Saturday night, and so was carried from the place I had drink at and did feast at, unto a scholar's chamber, one Basset of Christ's College, and knew not where I was until I awakened late on that Sabbath and sick with my beastly carriage. And when I awakened I went from him in shame and confusion, and went out into the fields and there spent that Sabbath lying hid in the corn fields where the Lord who might justly have cut me off in the midst of my sin did meet me with much sadness of heart and troubled my soul, for this and other my sins which then I had cause and leisure to think of. And now when I was worst He began to be best unto me and made me resolve to set upon a course of daily meditation about the evil of sin and my own ways. Yet although I was troubled for this sin I did not know my sinful nature all this while.

2. The Lord therefore sent Dr. Preston* to be master of the college, and Mr. Stone and others commending his preaching to be most spiritual and excellent, I began to listen unto what he said, and the first sermon he preached was Rom. 12: be renewed in the spirit of your mind. In opening which point, viz., the change of heart in a Christian, the Lord so bored my ears as that I understood what he spake, and the secrets of my soul were laid upon before me—the hypocrisy of all my good things I thought I had in me, as if one had told him of all that ever I did, of all the turnings and deceits of my heart, insomuch as that I thought he was the most

* Master of Emmanuel College, 1622–1628, and a major influence on the many Emmanuel students who later migrated to New England. [Editor]

searching preacher in the world. And I began to love him much and to bless God I did see my frame and my hypocrisy and self and secret sins, although I found a hard heart and could not be affected with them.

3. I did therefore set more constantly (viz., 1624, May 3) upon the work of daily meditation, sometimes every morning, but constantly every evening before supper, and my chief meditation was about the evil of sin, the terror of God's wrath, day of death, beauty of Christ, the deceitfulness of the heart, etc. But principally I found this my misery: sin was not my greatest evil, did lie light upon me as yet, yet I was much afraid of death and the flames of God's wrath.

And this I remember, I never went out to meditate in the fields but I did find the Lord teaching me somewhat of myself or Himself or the vanity of the world I never saw before, and hence I took out a little book I have every day into the fields and writ down what God taught me, least I should forget them. And so the Lord encouraged me and I grew much.

But in my observation of myself I did see my atheism: I questioned whether there was a God, and my unbelief whether Christ was the Messiah, whether the scriptures were God's word or no. I felt all manner of temptations to all kind of religions, not knowing which I should choose, whether education might not make me believe what I had believed, and whether if I had been educated up among Papists I should not have been as verily persuaded that Popery is the truth, or Turkism is the truth. And at last I heard of Grindleton,* and I did question whether that glorious estate of perfection might not be the truth, and whether old Mr. Rogers' *Seven Treatises and the Practice of Christianity*, the book which did first work upon my heart, whether these men were not all legal men and their books so. But the Lord delivered me at last from them, and in the conclusion, after many prayers, meditations, [and] duties, the Lord let me see three main wounds in my soul: (1) I could not feel sin as my greatest evil; (2) I could do nothing but I did seek myself in it and was imprisoned there, and tho' I desired to be a preacher, yet it was honor I did look to, like a vile wretch, in the use of God's gifts I desired to have; (3) I felt a

---

* Grindleton was founder of a radical Protestant sect. [Editor]

depth of atheism and unbelief in the main matters of salvation and whether the scriptures were God's word.

These things did much trouble me, and in the conclusion did so far trouble me that I could not read the scriptures or hear them read without secret and hellish blasphemy calling all into question, and all Christ's miracles, and hereupon I fell to doubt whether I had not committed the impardonable sin; and because I did question whether Christ did not cast out devils from Beezlebub, etc., I did think and fear I had. And now the terrors of God began to break in like floods of fire into my soul. For three quarters of a year this temptation did last, and I had some strong temptations to run my head against walls and brain and kill myself. And so I did see as I thought God's eternal reprobation of me, a fruit of which was this dereliction to these doubts and darkness, and I did see a God like a consuming fire and an everlasting burning, and myself like a poor prisoner leading to that fire. And the thought of eternal reprobation and torment did amaze my spirits, especially at one time upon a Sabbath day at evening, and when I knew not what to do (for I went to no Christian and was ashamed to speak of these things) it came to my mind that I should do as Christ: when He was in agony He prayed earnestly, and so I fell down to prayer, and being in prayer I saw myself so unholy and God so holy that my spirits began to sink. Yet the Lord recovered me and poured out a spirit of prayer upon me for free mercy and pity, and in the conclusion of the prayer I found the Lord helping me to see my unworthiness of any mercy, and that I was worthy to be cast out of His sight, and to leave myself with Him to do with me what He would. And there, and never until then, I found rest, and so my heart was humbled and cast down, and I went with a stayed heart unto supper late that night and so rested here; and the terrors of the Lord began to assuage sweetly.

Yet when these were gone I felt my senselessness of sin and bondage to self, and unconstancy and loosing what the Lord had wrought, and my heartlessness to any good and loathing of God's ways. Whereupon walking in the fields, the Lord dropped this meditation into me: be not discouraged therefore because thou art so vile, but make this double use of it: (1) loathe thyself the more; (2) feel a greater need and put a greater price upon Jesus Christ who only can redeem thee from all sin. And this I found of wonderful use to me in all my course, whereby I was kept from sinkings of heart and did beat Satan, as it were, with his own weapons. And I saw Christ teaching me this before any man preached any such thing unto me, and so the Lord did help me to loathe myself in some measure and to say oft, "Why shall I seek the glory and good of myself who am the greatest enemy, worse than the devil can be, against myself, which self ruins me, and blinds me," etc. And thus God kept my heart exercised, and here I began to forsake my loose company wholly and to do what I could to work upon the hearts of other scholars, and to humble them, and to come into a way of holy walking in our speeches and otherwise; but yet I had no assurance Christ was mine.

4. The Lord therefore brought Dr. Preston to preach upon that text, 1 Cor. 1:30: Christ is made unto us wisdom, righteousness, sanctification, and redemption. And when he had opened how all the good I had, all the redemption I had, it was from Jesus Christ, I did then begin to prize Him, and He became very sweet unto me, although I had heard many a time Christ freely offered by his ministry, if I would come in and receive Him as Lord and Saviour and husband. But I found my heart ever unwilling to accept of Christ upon these terms; I found them impossible for me to keep that condition. And Christ was not so sweet as my lust, but now the Lord made Himself sweet to me and to embrace Him and to give up myself unto Him; but yet after this I had many fears and doubts.

5. I found therefore the Lord revealing free mercy and that all my help was in that to give me Christ and to enable me to believe in Christ and accept of Him, and here I did rest.

6. The Lord also letting me see my own constant vileness in everything put me to this question, "Why did the Lord Jesus keep the law, had no guile in His heart, had no unbrokenness but holiness there, was it not for them that did want it?" And here I saw Christ Jesus's righteousness for a poor sinner's ungodliness, but yet questioning whether ever the Lord would apply this and give this unto me.

7. The Lord made me see that so many as receive Him He gives power to be the sons of God, John 1:12, and I saw the Lord gave me a heart to receive Christ with a naked hand, even naked Christ, and so the Lord gave me peace. . . .

13. Church Polity

New England Puritans often claimed that their only disagreement with the Church of England lay in matters of form. This was substantially, though not entirely, true, for the origins of the Puritan revolt against the church had stemmed largely from matters of vestment, ceremony, and sacraments, and in England the Puritans' troubles with the hierarchy came most often from their refusal to carry out the traditional forms of worship. Inevitably, then, much of the debate among theologians in New England focused on procedural matters. And because each Puritan congregation was self-originating and independent, variation in standards of admission to church membership, baptism, and the serving of communion existed from the beginning, to the dismay of some spokesmen who favored more order and less option.

A. Principles of Congregationalism

At the request of several clergymen, the Massachusetts General Court in May, 1646, called for a meeting of representatives from the churches in Plymouth, Connecticut, New Haven, and Massachusetts to hammer out a platform of church organization drawn from Biblical authority and Puritan tradition. "Differences of opinion & practice of one church from another do already appear amongst us," the Court noted, "& others (if not timely prevented) are like speedily to ensue, & this not onely in lesser things, but even in pointes of no small consequence & very materiall." While some churches resisted the call out of fear that its results would be binding, and others questioned the right of the Court to call a conference on ecclesiastical affairs, by September, 1646, most congregations had acquiesced. The first session, lasting about two weeks, settled no substantive matters but did appoint three clergymen—Cotton of Boston, Richard Mather of Dorchester, and Ralph Partridge of Duxbury in Plymouth colony—each to draft a model of church government. A second session, in June of 1647, adjourned when "an epidemical sickness" hit New England, taking the lives of Thomas Hooker and Margaret Winthrop, among others. Finally in August, 1648, a third session completed the long-awaited statement of Congregational polity. The results of the synod, drafted largely by Richard Mather, with a preface by John Cotton, were promulgated in 1648 as the Cambridge Platform, a landmark in the evolution of New England Puritanism.

Source: Williston Walker, *Creeds and Platforms of Congregationalism* (New York, 1893), 203–207, 210–237.

Chapter I. Of the Form of Church Government; and That It Is One, Immutable, and Prescribed in the Word

Ecclesiastical polity, or church government or discipline, is nothing else but that form and order that is to be observed in the church of Christ upon earth. . . .

3. The parts of church government are all of them exactly described in the word of God (1 Tim. 3:15; 1 Chron. 15:13; Exod. 2:4; 1 Tim. 6:13, 16; Heb. 12:27, 28; 1 Cor. 15:24) being parts of means of instituted worship according to the Second Commandment, and therefore to continue one and the same unto the appearing of our Lord Jesus Christ, as a kingdom that cannot be shaken, until He shall deliver it up unto God, even to the Father (Deut. 12:32; Ezek. 45:8; 1 Kings 12:31, 32, 33). So that it is not left in the power of men, officers, churches, or any state in the world to add, or diminish, or alter anything in the least measure therein. . . .

Chapter II. Of the Nature of the Catholic* Church in General, and in Special of a Particular Visible Church

1. The catholic church is the whole company of those that are elected, redeemed, and in time effectually called from the state of sin and death unto a state of grace and salvation in Jesus Christ.

2. This church is either triumphant or militant. Triumphant, the number of them who are glorified in heaven; militant, the number of them who are conflicting with their enemies upon earth. . . .

6. A Congregational church is by the institution of Christ a part of the militant visible church, consisting of a company of saints by calling, united into one body by an holy covenant, for the public worship of God and the mutual edification of one another in the fellowship of the Lord Jesus (1 Cor. 14:23, 36; 1:2; 12:27; Exod. 19:5, 6; Deut. 29:1, 9–15; Acts 2:42; 1 Cor. 14:26).

* Note: Catholic here is used in the sense of universal, not Roman Catholic. [Editor]

Chapter III. Of the Matter of the Visible Church, Both in Respect of Quality and Quantity

1. The matter of the visible church are saints by calling.

2. By saints we understand: (1) Such as have not only attained the knowledge of the principles of religion, and are free from gross and open scandals, but also do, together with the profession of their faith and repentance, walk in blameless obedience to the word, so as that in charitable discretion they may be accounted saints by calling (though perhaps some or more of them be unsound and hypocrites inwardly) because the members of such particular churches are commonly by the Holy Ghost called saints and faithful brethren in Christ. . . . (2) The children of such who are also holy. . . .

4. The matter of the church, in respect of its quantity, ought not to be of greater number than may ordinarily meet together conveniently in one place (1 Cor. 14:21; Matth. 18:17), nor ordinarily fewer than may conveniently carry on church work. . . .

5. . . . Elders being appointed to feed not all flocks, but the particular flock of God over which the Holy Ghost had made them overseers (and that flock they must attend, even the whole flock), and one congregation being as much as any ordinary elders can attend, therefore there is no greater church than a congregation, which may ordinarily meet in one place. . . .

Chapter VI. Of the Officers of the Church, and Especially of Pastors and Teachers

1. A church being a company of people combined together by covenant for the worship of God, it appeareth thereby that there may be the essence and being of a church without any officers, seeing there is both the form and matter of a church, which is implied when it is said, "The apostles ordained elders in every church" (Acts 11:28).

2. Nevertheless, though officers be not absolutely necessary to the simple being of churches, when they be called, yet ordinarily to their calling they are, and to their well-being (Rom. 10:17; Lev. 3:15; 1 Cor. 12:28); and therefore the Lord Jesus Christ, out of His tender compassion, hath appointed and ordained officers, which He

would not have done if they had not been useful and needful to the church. . . .

3. These officers were either extraordinary or ordinary: extraordinary as apostles, prophets, evangelists; ordinary as elders and deacons. The apostles, prophets, and evangelists, as they were called extraordinary by Christ, so their office ended with themselves (1 Cor. 12:28; Eph. 4:11; Acts 8:6, 16, 19; 11:28; Rom. 11:13; 1 Cor. 4:9), whence it is that Paul directing Timothy how to carry along church administration, giveth no direction about the choice or course of apostles, prophets, or evangelists, but only of elders and deacons; and when Paul was to take his last leave of the church of Ephesus, he committed the care of feeding the church to no other but unto the elders of that church. The like charge does Peter commit to the elders (1 Tim. 3:1, 2, 8–13; Tit. 1:15; Acts 20:17, 28; 1 Pet. 5:1, 2, 3).

4. Of elders (who are also in scripture called bishops): some attend chiefly to the ministry of the word, as the pastors and teachers (1 Tim. 2:3; Phil. 1:1; Acts 20:17, 28); others attend especially unto rule, who are, therefore, called ruling elders (1 Tim. 5:17).

5. The office of pastor and teacher appears to be distinct. The pastor's special work is to attend to exhortation and therein to administer a word of wisdom (Eph. 4:11; Rom. 12:7, 8; 1 Cor. 12:3); the teacher is to attend to doctrine, and therein to administer a word of knowledge (1 Tim. 4:1, 2; Tit. 1:9), and either of them to administer the seals of that covenant unto the dispensation whereof they are alike called; as also to execute the censures, being but a kind of application of the word, the preaching of which, together with the application thereof, they are alike charged withal.

6. Forasmuch as both pastors and teachers are given by Christ for the perfecting of the saints and edifying of His body (Eph. 4:11, 12; 1:22, 23) . . . we account pastors and teachers to be both of them church officers, and not the pastor for the church and the teacher only for the schools (1 Sam. 10: 12, 19, 20), though this we gladly acknowledge, that schools are both lawful, profitable, and necessary for the training up of such in good literature or learning as may afterwards be called forth unto office of pastor or teacher in the church (2 Kings 2:3, 15).

Chapter VII. Of Ruling Elders and Deacons

[1] The ruling elder's office is distinct from the office of pastor and teacher (Rom. 12:7, 8, 9; 1 Tim. 5:17; 1 Cor. 12:28). The ruling elders are not so called to exclude the pastors and teachers from ruling, because ruling and governing is common to these with the other, whereas attending to teach and preach the word is peculiar unto the former (Heb. 13:17; 1 Tim. 5:17).

2. The ruling elder's work is to join with the pastor and teacher in those acts of spiritual rule which are distinct from the ministry of the word and sacraments committed to them (1 Tim. 5:17; 2 Chron. 23:19; Rev. 21:12; 1 Tim. 4:14; Matth. 18:17; 2 Cor. 2:7, 8; Acts 2:6; Acts 21:18, 22, 23), of which sort these be as followeth: (1) To open and shut the doors of God's house, by the admission of members approved by the church; by ordination of officers chosen by the church; by excommunication of notorious and obstinate offenders renounced by the church; and by restoring of penitents forgiven by the church. (2) To call the church together when there is occasion (Acts 6:2, 3; 13:15), and seasonably to dismiss them again. (3) To prepare matters in private that in public they may be carried [to] an end with less trouble and more speedy dispatch (2 Cor. 8:19; 16:5; 13:7, 17; 2 Thess. 2:10, 11, 12). (4) To moderate the carriage of all matters in the church assembled, as to propound matters to the church; to order the season of speech and silence; and to pronounce sentence according to the mind of Christ, with the consent of the church. (5) To be guides and leaders to the church in all matters whatsoever pertaining to church administrations and actions. (6) To see that none in the church live inordinately, out of rank and place without a calling, or idly in their calling (Acts 20:28, 32; 1 Thess. 5:12; Jam. 5:14; Acts 20:20). (7) To prevent and heal such offenses in life or in doctrine as might corrupt the church. (8) To feed the flock of God with a word of admonition. (9) And as they shall be sent for, to visit and pray over their sick brethren. (10) And at other times, as opportunity shall serve thereunto.

3. The office of a deacon is instituted in the church by the Lord Jesus (Acts 6:3, 6; Phil. 1:1; 1 Tim. 3:8; 1 Cor. 12:23; 9; Acts 4:35; 6:2, 3; Rom. 12:8). Sometimes they are called *helps*. The scripture telleth us how they should be qualified. "Grace, not double-

tongued, not given to much wine, not given to filthy lucre" (1 Tim. 3:8). They must first be proved, and then use the office of a deacon, being found blameless. The office and work of a deacon is to receive the offerings of the church, gifts given to the church, and to keep the treasury of the church, and therewith to serve the tables which the church is to provide for, as the Lord's table, the table of the ministers, and of such as are in necessity, to whom they are to distribute in simplicity. . . .

5. The ordinance of the apostle (1 Cor. 16:1, 2, 3), and practice of the church, commends the Lord's day as a fit time for the contributions of the saints.

6. The instituting of all these officers in the church is the work of God himself, of the Lord Jesus Christ, of the Holy Ghost (1 Cor. 12:28; Eph. 4:8, 11; Acts 20:28). And therefore such officers as He hath not appointed are altogether unlawful either to be placed in the church or to be retained therein, and are to be looked at as human creatures, mere inventions and appointments of man, to the great dishonor of Christ Jesus, the Lord of His, the King of His church, whether popes, cardinals, patriarchs, archbishops, lord-bishops, archdeacons, officials, commissaries, and the like. These and the rest of that hierarchy and retinue, not being plants of the Lord's planting, shall all be certainly rooted out and cast forth (Matth. 15:13).

7. The Lord hath appointed ancient widows (1 Tim. 5:9, 10) where they may be had to minister in the church, in giving attendance to the sick, and to give succor unto them, and others in the like necessities.

CHAPTER VIII. OF THE ELECTION OF CHURCH OFFICERS

[1] No man may take the honor of a church officer unto himself, but he that was called of God, as was Aaron (Heb. 5:4).

2. Calling unto office is either *immediate*, by Christ Himself; such was the call of the apostles and prophets (Gal. 1:1; Acts 14:23; 6:3). This manner of calling ended with them, as hath been said; or *mediate*, by the church.

3. It is meet that before any be ordained or chosen officers they should first be tried and proved, because hands are not suddenly to be laid upon any, and both elders and deacons must be of both honest and good report (1 Tim. 5:22; 7:10; Acts 16:2; 6:3). . . .

5. Officers are to be called by such churches whereunto they are to minister. Of such moment is the preservation of this power that the churches exercised it in the presence of the apostles (Acts 14:23; 1:23; 6:3, 4, 5).

6. A church being free cannot become subject to any but by a free election; yet when such a people do choose any to be over them in the Lord, then do they become subject and most willingly submit to their ministry in the Lord, whom they have so chosen (Gal. 5:13; Heb. 13:17).

7. And if the church have power to choose their officers and ministers (Rom. 16:17), then in case of manifest unworthiness and delinquency they have power also to depose them, for to open and shut, to choose and refuse, to constitute in office and to remove from office, are acts belonging to the same power. . . .

CHAPTER IX. OF ORDINATION AND IMPOSITION OF HANDS

1. Church officers are not only to be chosen by the church (Acts 13:3; 14:23), but also to be ordained by imposition of hands and prayer, with which at the ordination of elders fasting also is to be joined (1 Tim. 5:22).

2. This ordination (Numb. 8:10; Acts 6:5, 6; 13:2, 3), we account nothing else but the solemn putting a man into his place and office in the church, whereunto he had right before by election, being like the installing of a magistrate in the commonwealth. Ordination therefore is not to go before, but to follow election (Acts 6:5, 6; 14:23). The essence and substance of the outward calling of an ordinary officer in the church does not consist in his ordination but in his voluntary and free election by the church and his accepting of that election, whereupon is founded that relation between pastor and flock, between such a minister and such a people. . . .

3. In such churches where there are elders, imposition of hands in ordination is to be performed by those elders (1 Tim. 4:14; Acts 13:3; 1 Tim. 5:22).

4. In such churches where there are no elders (Numb. 3:10), imposition of hands may be performed by some of the brethren orderly chosen by the church thereunto. For, if the people may elect officers, which is the greater, and wherein the substance of the office doth consist, they may much more (occasion and need so

requiring) impose hands in ordination, which is less, and but the accomplishment of the other.

5. Nevertheless, in such churches where there are no elders, and the church so desire, we see not why imposition of hands may not be performed by the elders of other churches. Ordinary officers laid hands upon the officers of many churches: the presbytery at Ephesus laid hands upon Timothy an evangelist (1 Tim. 4:14; Acts 13:3); the presbytery at Antioch laid hands upon Paul and Barnabas. . . .

7. He that is clearly released from his office relation unto that church whereof he was a minister cannot be looked at as an officer, nor perform any act of office, in any other church, unless he be again orderly called unto office, which, when it shall be, we know nothing to hinder; but imposition of hands also in his ordination (Acts 20:28) ought to be used towards him again, for so Paul the apostle received imposition of hands twice at least from Ananias, Acts 9:17; 13:3.

CHAPTER X. OF THE POWER OF THE CHURCH AND ITS PRESBYTERY . . .

3. [The] government of the church (Rev. 3:7; 1 Cor. 5:12) is a mixed government (and so has been acknowledged long before the term of independency was heard of): in respect of Christ, the Head and King of the church, and the sovereign power residing in Him and exercised by Him, it is a monarchy; in respect of the holy brotherhood of the church, and power from Christ granted unto them (1 Tim. 5:27), it resembles a democracy; in respect of the presbytery and power committed unto them, it is an aristocracy. . . .

7. . . . The Holy Ghost frequently, yea, always, where it mentioneth church rule and church government, ascribeth it to elders, whereas the work and duty of the people is expressed in the phrase of "obeying their elders and submitting themselves unto them in the Lord." So as it is manifest that an organic or complete church is a body politic, consisting of some that are governors, and some that are governed in the Lord. . . .

10. This power of government in the elders doth not any wise prejudice the power of privilege in the brotherhood, as neither the power of privilege in the brethren doth prejudice the power of

government in the elders (Acts 14:15, 23: 6:2; 1 Cor. 5:4; 2 Cor. 2:6, 7), but they may sweetly agree together, as we may see in the example of the apostles, furnished with the greatest church power, who took in the concurrence and consent of the brethren in church administrations. . . .

Chapter XI. Of the Maintenance of Church Officers

1. The apostle concludes that necessary and sufficient maintenance is due unto the ministers of the word from the law of nature and nations, from the law of Moses, the equity thereof, as also the rule of common reason. Moreover, the scripture doth not only call elders *laborers* and *workmen* (Gal. 6:6), but also speaking of them doth say that the laborer is worthy of his hire. . . .

2. The scriptures . . . requiring this maintenance as a bounden duty and due debt, and not as a matter of alms and free gift, therefore people are not at liberty to do or not to do what and when they please in this matter, no more than in any other commanded duty and ordinance of the Lord. . . .

4. Not only members of churches but all that are taught in the word are to contribute unto him that teacheth in all good things. In case that congregations are defective in their contributions, the deacons are to call upon them to do their duty (Acts 6:3); if their call sufficeth not, the church by her power is to require it of their members; and where church power through the corruption of men doth not or cannot attain the end, the magistrate is to see that the ministry be duly provided for, as appears from the commended example of Nehemiah. . . .

Chapter XII. Of the Admission of Members into the Church

1. The doors of the churches of Christ upon earth do not by God's appointment stand so wide open that all sorts of people, good and bad, may freely enter therein at their pleasure (2 Chron. 29:19; Matth. 13:25; 22:12), but such as are admitted thereto, as members, ought to be examined and tried first, whether they be fit and meet to be received into church society or not. . . .

2. The things which are requisite to be found in all church members are repentance from sin and faith in Jesus Christ (Acts

2:38–42; 8:37), and therefore these are the things whereof men are to be examined at their admission into the church, and which then they must profess and hold forth in such sort as may satisfy rational charity that the things are indeed. . . .

3. The weakest measure of faith is to be accepted in those that desire to be admitted into the church (Rom. 14:1), if sincere. . . . Severity of examination is to be avoided.

4. In case any through excessive fear, or other infirmity, be unable to make their personal relation of their spiritual estate in public, it is sufficient that the elders having received private satisfaction make relation thereof in public before the church, they testifying their assents thereunto, this being the way that tendeth most to edification. But whereas persons are of greater abilities, there it is most expedient that they make their relations and confessions personally with their own mouth, as David professeth of himself (Psal. 66:6). . . .

6. This profession of faith and repentance, as it must be made by such at their admission that were never in church society before, so nothing hindereth but the same way also be performed by such as have formerly been members of some other church (Matth. 3:5, 6; Gal. 2:4; 1 Tim. 5:24), and the church to which they now join themselves as members may lawfully require the same. . . .

7. The like trial is to be required from such members of the church as were born in the same, or received their membership, or were baptized in their infancy or minority by virtue of the covenant of their parents, when being grown up into years of discretion they shall desire to be made partakers of the Lord's Supper; unto which because holy things must not be given unto the unworthy, therefore it is requisite (Matth. 7:6; 1 Cor. 11:27) that these as well as others should come to their trial and examination, and manifest their faith and repentance by an open profession thereof before they are received to the Lord's Supper, and otherwise not to be admitted thereunto. Yet these church members that were so born or received in their childhood, before they are capable of being made partakers of full communion, have many privileges which others (not church members) have not; they are in covenant with God, have the seal thereof upon them, viz., baptism; and so, if not regenerated, yet are in a more hopeful way of attaining regenerating grace and all the spiritual blessings both of the covenant and

seal; they are also under church watch and consequently subject to the reprehension, admonitions, and censures thereof, for their healing and amendment, as need shall require.

Chapter XIII. Of Church Members, Their Removal from One Church to Another, and of Recommendation and Dismission

1. Church members may not remove or depart from the church, and so one from another, as they please without just and weighty cause, but ought to live and dwell together (Heb. 10:25) for asmuch as they are commanded not to forsake the assembling of themselves together. Such departure tends to the dissolution and ruin of the body, as the pulling of stones and pieces of timber from the building and of members from the natural body tend to the destruction of the whole.

2. It is, therefore, the duty of church members in such times and places where counsel may be had to consult with the church whereof they are members (Prov. 11:16) about their removal, that accordingly they having their approbation may be encouraged, or otherwise desist. They who are joined with consent should not depart without consent, except forced thereunto.

3. If a member's departure be manifestly unsafe and sinful, the church may not consent thereunto; for in so doing (Rom. 14:23) they should not act in faith and should partake with him in his sin (1 Tim. 5:22). If the case be doubtful and the person not to be persuaded (Acts 21:14), it seemeth best to leave the matter unto God and not forcibly to detain him.

4. Just reasons for a member's removal of himself from the church are (1) If a man cannot continue without partaking in sin (Eph. 5:11). (2) In case of personal persecution (Acts 9:25, 29, 30; 8:1): so Paul departed from the disciples at Damascus; also in case of general persecution, when all are scattered. In case of real, and not only pretended, want of competent subsistence, a door being opened for better supply in another place (Neh. 13:20), together with the means of spiritual edification. In these, or like cases, a member may lawfully remove, and the church cannot lawfully detain him.

5. To separate from a church either out of contempt of their holy fellowship (2 Tim. 4:10), or out of covetousness, or for

greater enlargements, with just grief to the church, or out of schism, or want of love, and out of a spirit of contention in respect of some unkindness, or some evil only conceived or indeed in the church, which might and should be tolerated and healed with a spirit of meekness, and of which evil the church is not yet convinced (though perhaps himself be not admonished); for these or the like reasons to withdraw from public communion in word, or seals, or censures, is unlawful and sinful.

6. Such members as have orderly moved their habitation ought to join themselves unto the church in order (Isah. 56:8) where they do inhabit (Acts 9:26), if it may be; otherwise they can neither perform the duties nor receive the privileges of members. Such an example tolerated in some is apt to corrupt others, which if many should follow would threaten the dissolution and confusion of churches contrary to the scripture (1 Cor. 14:53).

7. Order requires that a member thus removing have letters testimonial and of dismission from the church (Acts 18:27) whereof he yet is unto the church whereunto he desireth to be joined, lest the church should be deluded, that the church may receive him in faith and not be corrupted in receiving deceivers and false brethren. Until the person dismissed be received unto another church, he ceaseth not by his letters of dismission to be a member of the church whereof he was. The church cannot make a member no member but by excommunication. . . .

CHAPTER XIV. OF EXCOMMUNICATION AND OTHER CENSURES

1. The censures of the church are appointed by Christ for the preventing, removing, and healing of offenses in the church (1 Tim. 5:20; Jude 19; Deut. 13:11; 1 Cor. 5:6; Rom. 2:24; Rev. 2:14, 15, 16, 20), for the reclaiming and gaining of offending brethren, for the deterring of others from the like offenses, for purging out the leaven which may infect the whole lump, for vindicating the honor of Christ and of His church and the holy profession of the gospel, and for preventing of the wrath of God that may justly fall upon the church if they should suffer His covenant and the seals thereof to be profaned by notorious and obstinate offenders.

2. If an offense be private (Matth. 5:23, 24) (one brother offending another), the offender is to go and acknowledge his repentance for it unto his offended brother, who is then to forgive

him; but if the offender neglect or refuse to do it, the brother offended is to go and convince and admonish him of it, between themselves privately. If therefore the offender be brought to repent of his offense, the admonisher has won his brother; but if the offender hear not his brother, the brother of the offended is to take with him one or two more (Verse 16), that in the mouth of two or three witnesses every word may be established. . . . If he refuse it (Verse 17), the offended brother is by the mouth of the elders to tell the church, and if he hear the church, and declare the same by penitent confession, he is recovered and gained. And if the church discern him to be willing to hear, yet not fully convinced of his offense, as in the case of heresy, they are to dispense to him a public admonition, which declaring the offender to lie under the public offense of the church doth thereby withhold or suspend him from the holy fellowship of the Lord's Supper till his offense be removed by penitent confession. If he still continue obstinate, they are to cast him out by excommunication.

3. But if the offense be more public at first, and of a more heinous and criminal nature (1 Cor. 5:4, 8, 11), to wit, such as are condemned by the light of nature, then the church without such gradual proceeding is to cast out the offender from their holy communion, for the further mortifying of his sin and the healing of his soul in the day of the Lord Jesus.

4. In dealing with an offender, great care is to be taken that we be neither over strict or rigorous, nor too indulgent or remiss; our proceeding herein ought to be with a spirit of meekness, considering ourselves, lest we also be tempted (Gal. 6:1), and that the best of us have need of much forgiveness from the Lord (Matth. 18:34, 35). Yet the winning and healing of the offender's soul being the end of these endeavors (Ezek. 13:10), we must not daub with untempered mortar, nor heal the wounds of our brethren slightly. On some have compassion, others save with fear.

5. While the offender remains excommunicate (Matth. 18:17), the church is to refrain from all member-like communion with him in spiritual things (1 Cor. 5:11), and also from all familiar communion with him in civil things (2 Thess. 3:6, 14) farther than the necessity of natural or domestical or civil relations require, and are therefore to forbear to eat and drink with him, that he may be ashamed.

6. Excommunication being a spiritual punishment, it doth not

prejudice the excommunicate in, or deprive him of, his civil rights, and therefore toucheth not princes or magistrates in respect of their civil dignity or authority (1 Cor. 14:24, 25), and the excommunicate being but as a publican and a heathen (2 Thess. 3:14), heathens being lawfully permitted to hear the word in church assemblies, we acknowledge therefore the like liberty of hearing the word may be permitted to persons excommunicate, that is permitted unto heathen. And because we are not without hope of his recovery, we are not to account him as an enemy, but to admonish him as a brother.

7. If the Lord sanctify the censure to the offender, so as by the grace of Christ he doth testify his repentance with humble confession of his sin, and judging of himself, giving glory unto God (2 Cor. 2:7, 8), the church is then to forgive him, and to comfort him, and to restore him to the wonted brotherly communion which formerly he enjoyed with them. . . .

CHAPTER XV. OF THE COMMUNION OF CHURCHES ONE WITH ANOTHER

[1.] Although churches be distinct, and therefore may not be confounded one with another, and equal, and therefore have not dominion one over another (Rev. 1:4; Cant. 8:8; Rom. 16:16; 1 Cor. 16:19; Acts 15:23; Rev. 2:1), yet all the churches ought to preserve church communion one with another, because they are all united unto Christ, not only as a mystical, but as a political head, whence is derived a communion suitable thereunto.

2. The communion of churches is exercised several ways (Cant. 8:8): (1) By way of mutual care in taking thought for one another's welfare. (2) By way of consultation one with another, when we have occasion to require the judgment and counsel of other churches touching any person or cause, wherewith they may be better acquainted than ourselves. . . . (3) A [third] way, then, of communion of churches is by way of admonition: to wit, in case any public offense be found in a church which they either discern not, or are slow in proceeding to use the means for the removing and healing of. . . . Though churches have no authority one over another, than one apostle had over another, yet as one apostle might admonish another, so may one church admonish another and yet without usurpation. . . . (4) A fourth way of

communion with churches is by way of participation: the members of one church occasionally coming to another, we willingly admit them to partake with them at the Lord's table (1 Cor. 12:13), it being the seal of our communion not only with Christ, not only with the members of our own church, but also of all the churches of the saints; in which regard we refuse not to baptize their children presented to us if either their own minister be absent or such a fruit of holy fellowship be desired with us. In like cases, such churches as are furnished with more ministers than one do willingly afford one of their own ministers to supply the absence or place of a sick minister of another church for a needful season. (5) A fifth way of church communion is by recommendation (Rom. 16:1): when the member of one church hath occasion to reside in another church, if but for a season, we commend him to their watchful fellowship by letters of recommendation. But if he be called to settle his abode there, we commit him according to his desire to the fellowship of their covenant by letters of dismission. (6) A sixth way of church communion (Acts 18:27) is in case of need to minister succor one unto another (Acts 11:22), either of able members to furnish them with officers or of outward support to the necessities of poorer churches (Verse 29), as did the churches of the Gentiles contribute liberally to the poor saints at Jerusalem (Rom. 13:26, 27).

3. When a company of believers purpose to gather into church fellowship, it is requisite for their safer proceeding and the mentioning of the communion of churches that they signify their intent unto the neighboring churches, walking according to the order of the gospel, and desire their presence and help and right hand of fellowship (Gal. 2:1, 2, 9, by proportion), which they ought readily to give unto them when there is no just cause to except against their proceedings.

4. Besides these several ways of communion, there is also a way of propagation of churches: when a church shall grow too numerous, it is a way and fit season to propagate one church out of another, by sending forth such of their members as are willing to remove, and to procure some officers to them (Isah. 40:20; Cant. 8:8, 9) as may enter with them into church estate among themselves, as bees when the hive is too full issue out by swarms and are gathered into other hives, so the churches of Christ may do the same upon the like necessity. . . .

Chapter XVI. Of Synods

1. Synods orderly assembled (Acts 15:2–15), and rightly proceeding according to the pattern (Acts 15), we acknowledge as the ordinance of Christ, and though not absolutely necessary to the being, yet many times, through the iniquity of men and perverseness of times, necessary to the well being of churches, for the establishment of truth and peace therein. . . .

3. Magistrates have power to call a synod by calling to the churches to send forth their elders and other messengers to counsel and assist them in matters of religion (2 Chron. 29:4, 5–11), but yet the constituting of a synod is a church act and may be transacted by the churches (Acts 15), even when civil magistrates may be enemies to churches and to church assemblies.

4. It belongeth unto synods and councils to debate and determine controversies of faith and cases of conscience (Acts 15:1, 2, 6, 7; 1 Chron. 15:13; 2 Chron. 29:6, 7; Acts 15:24, 28, 29); to clear from the word holy directions for the holy worship of God and good government of the church; to hear witness against maladministration and corruption for the reformation thereof; [but] not to exercise church censures in way of discipline, nor any other act of church authority or jurisdiction which that presidential synod did forbear.

5. The synod's directions and determinations, so far as consonant to the word of God, are to be received with reverence and submission, not only for their agreement therewith (Acts 15) (which is the principal ground thereof, and without which they bind not at all), but also secondarily, for the power, whereby they are made, as being an ordinance of God appointed thereunto in His word. . . .

Chapter XVII. Of the Civil Magistrates' Power in Matters Ecclesiastical

1. It is lawful, profitable, and necessary for Christians to gather themselves together into church estate and therein to exercise all the ordinances of Christ, according unto the word (Acts 2:41, 47; 4:1, 2, 3), although the consent of the magistrate could not be had thereunto, because the apostles and Christians in their time did frequently thus practice, when the magistrates being all of them

Jewish and pagan and most persecuting enemies would give no countenance or consent to such matters.

2. Church government stands in no opposition to civil government of commonwealths, nor any way intrencheth upon the authority of civil magistrates in their jurisdictions, nor any whit weakeneth their hands in governing, but rather strengtheneth them and furthereth the people in yielding more hearty and conscionable obedience to them. . . .

4. It is not in the power of magistrates to compel their subjects to become church members and to partake of the Lord's Supper (Ezek. 44:7, 9), for the priests are reproved that brought unworthy ones into the sanctuary (1 Cor. 5:11); then it was unlawful for the priests, so it is as unlawful to be done by civil magistrates. . . .

5. As it is unlawful for church officers to meddle with the sword of the magistrate (Matth. 2:25, 26), so it is unlawful for the magistrate to meddle with the work proper to church officers. The acts of Moses and David, who were not only princes but prophets, were extraordinary, therefore not inimitable. Against such usurpation the Lord witnessed by smiting Uzziah with leprosy for presuming to offer incense (2 Chron. 26:16, 17).

6. It is the duty of the magistrate to take care of matters of religion, and to improve his civil authority for the observing of the duties commanded in the first as well as for observing of the duties commanded in the second table. . . . The end of the magistrates' office is not only the quiet and peaceable life of the subject in matters of righteousness and honesty, but also in matters of godliness, yea of all godliness. . . .

8. Idolatry, blasphemy, heresy (Deut. 13; 1 Kings 20:28, 42), venting corrupt and pernicious opinions that destroy the foundation (Dan. 3:29), open contempt of the word preached (Zech. 13:3), profanation of the Lord's Day (Neh. 13:31), disturbing the peaceable administration and exercise of the worship and holy things of God (1 Tim. 2:2), and the like (Rom. 13:4) are to be restrained and punished by civil authority.

9. If any church, one or more, shall grow schismatical, rending itself from the communion of other churches, or shall walk incorrigibly and obstinately in any corrupt way of their own, contrary to the rule of the word, in such case the magistrate (Josh. 22) is to put forth his coercive power as the matter shall require. . . .

Although the Platform remained for more than a century the most comprehensive statement of the New England Way, it had taken shape amidst heated controversy and met with considerable resistance even after its publication and endorsement by leading ministers and laymen from the four Puritan colonies. Not until 1651 did it gain approval from the General Court of Massachusetts and then with a substantial dissenting vote. Still, with the issuance of the Platform the fundamental lines of Congregational polity became available for public scrutiny. And despite scattered resistance, the Platform clearly reflected a Puritan consensus on most matters of church structure.

B. Problems of Baptism and Membership

On two major matters, the Cambridge Platform said almost nothing—baptism of the children of morally upright but "non-regenerate" parents, and church membership for persons baptized as children who did not as adults have a conversion experience. The two problems were in fact two horns of a single dilemma: what qualifications must a person have to gain admission to the privileges of church membership, including the sacraments? The question most often arose over specific decisions on baptism: could the child of a church member have his own children baptized before he himself experienced regeneration and attained admission by the vote of his congregation? At the time of the Cambridge synod, at least three practices prevailed. A few churches baptized the children of all professing Christians, some churches baptized infants who had at least one grandparent in full communion, while most churches insisted that baptism be reserved for the children of full church members. A few New Englanders objected to infant baptism altogether.

No formal solution to the dilemma was reached until 1662. In the meantime, various alternatives were offered, and not a few practiced, so that the hoped-for unity of the New England Way had no application in matters of baptism. In 1657, a convention of Massachusetts and Connecticut ministers advocated a compromise that would preserve the high standards of admission to full church membership but accord partial membership to godly but unregenerate adults. Such adults could "own the covenant"—that is, subscribe to Puritan doctrine—as a sign of their good intentions and orthodoxy of belief. Their children could then receive baptism and be under the church's discipline, though the parents, because they had not yet felt God's hand on their hearts, would be barred from Holy Communion and from voting in church matters.

The ministers' answer to the ancient problem satisfied few and aroused many to vocal and pamphlet dispute. In order to settle the matter within its own jurisdiction, the Massachusetts General Court in 1662 sponsored another synod, held this time in Boston, of representatives of the Bay Colony congregations. There the opposition to the 1657 solution rallied under the leadership of President Charles Chauncy of Harvard and Increase and Eleazer Mather, sons of Richard Mather, the author of the 1657 report. But the advocates of the "Half-Way Covenant" won the day, led by Jonathan Mitchell of Cambridge, John Allen of Dedham, and the elder Mather. Theirs came close, however, to being a Pyrrhic victory: conformity to the new policy came slowly and bitterly as clergymen and parishioners wrangled over the decision well into the eighteenth century. As late as 1675 less than half the congregations in Massachusetts subscribed to the new doctrine, and even in the last quarter of the century when most churches at last gave formal assent to the half-way solution, few New Englanders took advantage of its provisions.

Source: Williston Walker, *Creeds and Platforms of Congregationalism* (New York, 1893), 313–314, 325–328, 330–331.

THE ANSWER
OF THE ELDERS AND OTHER
MESSENGERS
OF THE CHURCHES, ASSEMBLED AT BOSTON
IN THE YEAR 1662
TO
THE QUESTIONS PROPOUNDED TO THEM BY ORDER OF THE
HONORED GENERAL COURT

Question 1: Who are the subjects of baptism?
Answer: The answer may be given in the following propositions, briefly confirmed from the scriptures:

1. They that according to scripture are members of the visible church are the subjects of baptism.

2. The members of the visible church according to scripture are confederate visible believers, in particular churches, and their infant-seed, i.e., children in minority whose next parents, one or both, are in covenant.

3. The infant-seed of confederate visible believers are members of the same church with their parents, and when grown up are personally under the watch, discipline, and government of that church.

4. These adult persons are not therefore to be admitted to full communion merely because they are and continue members without such further qualifications as the word of God requireth thereunto.

5. Church members who were admitted in minority, understanding the doctrine of faith and publicly professing their assent thereunto, not scandalous in life, and solemnly owning the covenant before the church, wherein they give up themselves and their children to the Lord and subject themselves to the government of Christ in the church, their children are to be baptized.

6. Such church members who either by death or some other extraordinary providence have been inevitably hindered from public acting as aforesaid, yet have given the church cause in judgment of charity to look at them as so qualified, and such as had they been called thereunto, would have so acted, their children are to be baptized.

7. The members of orthodox churches, being sound in the faith and not scandalous in life, and presenting due testimony thereof; these occasionally coming from one church to another, may have their children baptized in the church whither they come, by virtue of communion of churches; but if they remove their habitation, they ought orderly to covenant and subject themselves to the government of Christ in the church where they settle their abode, and so their children to be baptized—it being the church's duty to receive such unto communion, so far as they are regularly fit for the same.

The confirmation of these propositions from the scripture followeth. . . .

Proposition Third

The infant-seed of confederate visible believers are members of the same church with their parents, and when grown up are personally under the watch, discipline, and government of that church.

1. That they are members of the same church with their parents appears: (1) Because so were Isaac and Ishmael of Abraham's family church and the children of the Jews and proselytes of Israel's national church, and there is the same reason for children now to be of the same Congregational Church with their parents. Christ's care for children, and the scope of the covenant as to obligation unto order and government, is as great now as then. (2) Either they are members of the same church with their parents, or

of some other church, or non-members; but neither of the latter, therefore the former. . . . (3) The same covenant act is accounted the act of parent and child, but the parent covenanting rendered himself a member of this particular church, therefore so it renders the child also. . . . (4) Children are in an orderly and regular state, for they are in that state wherein the order of God's covenant and His institution therein hath placed them, they being members by virtue of the covenant of God. To say their standing is disorderly would be to impute disorder to the order of God's covenant or irregularity to the rule. Now all will grant it to be most orderly and regular that every Christian be a member in some particular church and in that particular church where his regular habitation is, which to children usually is where their parents are. . . . Again, order requires that the child and the power of government over the child should go together. It would bring shame and confusion for the child to be from under government, Prov. 29:15, and parental and ecclesiastical government concurring, do mutually help and strengthen each other. Hence the parent and the child must be members of the same church. . . .

2. That when these children are grown up they are personally under the watch, discipline, and government of that church is manifest for: (1) Children were under patriarchal and mosaical discipline of old, Gen. 18:19, and 21:7, 10, 12; Gal. 5:3, and therefore under Congregational discipline now. (2) They are within the church, or members thereof (as hath been and after will be further proved) and therefore subject to church judicature, 1 Cor. 5:12. . . .

Proposition Fourth

These adult persons are not therefore to be admitted to full communion merely because they are and continue members without such further qualifications as the word of God requireth thereunto.

The truth hereof is plain: (1) From 1 Cor. 11:28, 29, where it is required that such as come to the Lord's Supper be able to examine themselves and to discern the Lord's body, else they will eat and drink unworthily, and eat and drink damnation or judgment to themselves when they partake of this ordinance. But mere membership is separable from such ability to examine oneself and discern the Lord's body, as in the children of the covenant that grow up to years is too often seen. (2) In the Old Testament, though men did continue members of the church, yet for ceremonial uncleanness they were to be kept from full communion in the holy things, Levit. 7:20, 21; Numb. 9:6, 7, and 19:13, 20. Yea and the priests and porters in the Old Testament had special charge committed to them that men should not partake in all the holy things unless duly qualified for the same, notwithstanding their membership, 2. Chron. 23:19; Ezekiel 22:26, and 44:7, 8, 9, 23, and therefore much more in these times where moral fitness and spiritual qualifications are wanting, membership alone is not sufficient for full communion. More was required to adult persons eating the Passover than mere membership; therefore so there is now to the Lord's Supper. . . . (3) Though all members of the Church are subjects of baptism, they and their children, yet all members may not partake of the Lord's Supper as is further manifest from the different nature of baptism and the Lord's Supper. Baptism firstly and properly seals covenant holiness as circumcision did, Gen. 17. Church membership, Rom. 15:8, planting into Christ, Rom. 6, and so members as such are the subjects of baptism, Matth. 28:19. But the Lord's Supper is the sacrament of growth in Christ and of special communion with Him, 1 Cor. 10:16, which supposeth a special renewal and exercise of faith and repentance in those that partake of that ordinance. Now if persons, even when adult, may be and continue members and yet be debarred from the Lord's Supper until meet qualifications for the same do appear in them, then may they also (until the qualifications) be debarred from that power of voting in the church which pertains to males in full communion. It seems not rational that those who are not themselves fit for all ordinances should have such an influence referring to all ordinances, as voting in election of officers, admission, and censure of members doth import. For how can they who are not able to examine and judge themselves be thought able and fit to discern and judge in the weighty affairs of the house of God? 1 Cor. 11:28, 31, with 1 Cor. 5:12.

Proposition Fifth

Church members who were admitted in minority, understanding the doctrine of faith and publicly professing their assent thereunto, not scandalous in life, and solemnly owning the covenant before the church, wherein they give up themselves and their children to the Lord and subject themselves to the government of Christ in the church, their children are to be baptized. This is evident from the arguments following:

Argument 1. These children are partakers of that which is the main ground of baptizing any children whatsoever, and neither the parents nor the children do put in any bar to hinder it. . . . (1) Interest in the covenant is the main ground of title to baptism, for so in the Old Testament this was the ground of title to circumcision, Gen. 17:7, 9, 10, 11, to which baptism now answers, Col. 2:11, 12, and in Acts 2:38, 39, they are on this ground exhorted to be baptized, because the promise or covenant was to them and to their children. . . .

Argument 5. The denial of baptism to the children in question hath a dangerous tendency to irreligion and apostasy because it denies them, and so the children of the church successively, to have any part in the Lord, which is the way to make them cease from fearing the Lord, Josh. 22:24, 25, 27. For if they have a part in the Lord, i.e., a portion in Israel and so in the Lord the God of Israel, then they are in the church, or members of it, and so to be baptized according to Proposition 1. The owning of the children of those that successively continue in covenant to be a part of the church is so far from being destructive to the purity and prosperity of the church, and of religion therein (as some conceive), that this imputation belongs to the contrary tenet. To seek to be more pure than the rule will ever end in impurity in the issue. God hath so framed His covenant, and consequently the constitution of His church thereby, as to design a continuation and propagation of His kingdom therein, from one generation to another. Hence the covenant runs to us and to our seed after us in their generations. To keep in the line and under the influence and efficacy of this covenant of God is the true way to the church's glory. To cut it off and disavow it cuts off the posterity of Zion and hinders it from being (as in the most glorious times it shall be) an eternal excellency, and the joy of many generations. . . .

14. Faith of the Puritan

The New England Puritans avoided setting down explicit statements of faith, partly because they shied away from formalized creeds, but largely because their English brethren provided them with a satisfactory document. The delegates to the Cambridge Synod of 1646–1648 had been directed by the Massachusetts General Court to "take some paines" to produce a confession of faith. Before the "reverend elders" could act, however, copies arrived from England of the Westminster Confession, drafted by leading English Puritans. The synod quickly endorsed it by proclaiming in the preface to the Cambridge Platform "our professed & hearty assent & attestation to the whole confession of faith. . . ." Slight changes were introduced in 1658 by a conference at the Savoy Palace in London; in 1680 a Massachusetts synod reissued the Savoy Declaration with minor modifications. Part of this document is reproduced here because it is the clearest and most thorough description of the New Englanders' theological beliefs; the fact that it originated in the mother country does not detract from its significance to the New England Way.

Source: Williston Walker, Creeds and Platforms of Congregationalism (New York, 1893), 374–380, 382–386.

Chapter VII. Of God's Covenant with Man

I. THE distance between God and the creature is so great that although reasonable creatures do owe obedience to Him as their Creator, yet they could never have attained the reward of life but by some voluntary condescension on God's part, which He hath been pleased to express by way of covenant.

II. The first covenant made with man was a covenant of works, wherein life was promised to Adam, and in him to his posterity, upon condition of perfect and personal obedience.

III. Man by his fall having made himself uncapable of life by that covenant, the Lord was pleased to make a second, commonly called the covenant of grace, wherein He freely offereth unto sinners life and salvation by Jesus Christ, requiring of them faith in Him, that they may be saved, and promising to give unto all those that are ordained unto life His holy Spirit to make them willing and able to believe. . . .

Chapter VIII. Of Christ the Mediator

I. It pleased God, in His eternal purpose, to choose and ordain the Lord Jesus, His only begotten Son, according to a covenant made between them both, to be the Mediator between God and man: the Prophet, Priest and King, the Head and Saviour of His Church, the Heir of all things, and Judge of the world, unto whom He did from all eternity give a people to be His seed, and to be by Him, in time, redeemed, called, justified, sanctified and glorified.

II. The Son of God, the second person in the Trinity, being very and eternal God, of one substance, and equal with the Father, did, when the fullness of time was come, take upon Him man's nature, with all the essential properties and common infirmities thereof, yet without sin, being conceived by the power of the Holy Ghost in the womb of the Virgin Mary of her substance, so that two whole perfect and distinct natures, the Godhead and the Manhood, were inseparably joined together in one person without conversion, composition or confusion; which person is very God and very man, yet one Christ, the only mediator between God and man. . . .

IV. This office the Lord Jesus Christ did most willingly undertake; which that He might discharge, He was made under the Law, and did perfectly fulfill it, and underwent the punishment due to us, which we should have borne and suffered, being made sin and a curse for us, enduring most grievous torments immediately from God in His soul, and most painful sufferings in His body, was crucified and died, was buried, and remained under the power of death, yet saw no corruption: on the third day He arose from the dead, with the same body in which He suffered, with which also He ascended into heaven, and there sitteth at the right hand of His Father, making intercession, and shall return to judge men and angels at the end of the world.

V. The Lord Jesus, by His perfect obedience and sacrifice of Himself, which He, through the Eternal Spirit, once offered up unto God, hath fully satisfied the justice of God, and purchased not only reconciliation but an everlasting inheritance in the kingdom of heaven, for all those whom the Father hath given unto Him.

VI. Although the work of Redemption was not actually wrought by Christ till after His incarnation, yet the virtue, efficacy and benefits thereof, were communicated unto the elect in all ages successively from the beginning of the world, in and by those promises, types and sacrifices, wherein He was revealed and signified to be the seed of the woman, which should bruise the serpent's head, and the Lamb slain from the beginning of the world, being yesterday and today the same, and forever. . . .

VIII. To all those for whom Christ has purchased redemption, He doth certainly and effectually apply and communicate the same, making intercession for them, and revealing unto them, in and by the word, the mysteries of salvation, effectually persuading them by His spirit to believe and obey, and governing their heart by His word and spirit, overcoming all their enemies by His almighty power and wisdom, in such manner and ways are are most consonant to His wonderful and unsearchable dispensation.

Chapter IX. Of Free-Will

I. GOD hath endued the will of man with that natural liberty and power of acting upon choice, that it is neither forced, nor, by any absolute necessity of nature, determined to do good or evil.

II. Man in his state of innocency had freedom and power to will and to do that which was well pleasing to God; but yet mutably, so that he might fall from it.

III. Man, by his fall into a state of sin, hath wholly lost all ability of will to any spiritual good, accompanying salvation, so as a natural man being altogether averse from that good, and dead in sin, is not able by his own strength to convert himself or to prepare himself thereunto.

IV. When God converts a sinner, and translates him into the state of grace, He freeth him from his natural bondage under sin, and by His grace alone enables him freely to will and to do that which is spiritually good; yet so as that, by reason of his remaining corruption, he doth not perfectly nor only will that which is good, but doth that which is also evil.

V. The will of man is made perfectly and immutably free to good alone in the state of glory only.

Chapter X. Of Effectual Calling

I. ALL those whom God hath predestinated unto life, and those only, He is pleased in His appointed and accepted time effectually to call by His word and spirit out of that state of sin and death in which they are by nature, to grace and salvation by Jesus Christ, enlightening their minds spiritually and savingly to understand the things of God, taking away their heart of stone and giving unto them an heart of flesh, renewing their wills, and by His Almighty power determining them to that which is good, and effectually drawing them to Jesus Christ; yet so as they come most freely, being made willing by His grace.

II. This effectual call is God's free and special grace alone, not from any thing at all foreseen in man, who is altogether passive therein, until being quickened and renewed by the Holy Spirit, he is thereby enabled to answer this call, and to embrace the grace offered and conveyed in it.

III. Elect infants, dying in infancy, are regenerated and saved by Christ, who worketh when and where and how He pleaseth; so also are all other elect persons who are uncapable of being outwardly called by the ministry of the word.

IV. Others not elected, although they may be called by the ministry of the word, and may have some common operations of the spirit, yet not being effectually drawn by their Father, they neither do nor can come unto Christ, and therefore cannot be saved; much less can men, not professing the Christian religion, be saved in any other way whatsoever, be they never so diligent to frame their lives according to the light of nature and the law of that religion they do profess; and to assert and maintain that they may is very pernicious, and to be detested.

Chapter XI. Of Justification

I. THOSE whom God effectually calleth, He also freely justifieth, not by infusing righteousness into them, but by pardoning their sins, and by accounting and accepting their persons as righteous, not for any thing wrought in them or done by them, but for Christ's sake alone. . . .

II. Faith thus receiving and resting on Christ and His righteousness is the alone instrument of justification; yet it is not alone in the person justified, but is ever accompanied with all other saving graces, and is no dead faith, but worketh by love.

III. Christ, by his obedience and death, did fully discharge the debt of all those that are justified, and did, by the sacrifice of

Himself in the blood of His cross, undergoing in their stead the penalty due unto them, make a proper, real, and full satisfaction to God's justice in their behalf. Yet, inasmuch as He was given by the Father for them, and His obedience and satisfaction accepted in their stead, and both freely, not for any thing in them, their justification is only of free grace, that both the exact justice and rich grace of God might be glorified in the justification of sinners.

IV. God did from all eternity decree to justify all the elect, and Christ did in the fullness of time die for their sins, and rise again for their justification. Nevertheless, they are not justified personally until the Holy Spirit doth in due time actually apply Christ unto them.

V. God doth continue to forgive the sins of those that are justified, and although they can never fall from the state of justification, yet they may by their sins fall under God's fatherly displeasure. And, in that condition, they have not usually the light of His countenance restored unto them until they humble themselves, confess their sins, beg pardon, and renew their faith and repentance.

VI. The justification of believers under the Old Testament was, in all these respects, one and the same with the justification of believers under the New Testament. . . .

Chapter XIII. Of Sanctification

I. THEY that are effectually called and regenerated, being united to Christ, having a new heart, and a new spirit created in them, through the virtue of Christ's death and resurrection, are also further sanctified really and personally, through the same virtue, by His word and spirit dwelling in them, the dominion of the whole body of sin is destroyed, and the several lusts thereof are more and more weakened and mortified, and they more and more quickened and strengthened in all saving graces, to the practice of all true holiness, without which no man shall see the Lord.

II. This sanctification is throughout in the whole man, yet imperfect in this life; there abide still some remnants of corruption in every part, whence ariseth a continual and irreconcilable war, the flesh lusting against the spirit, and the spirit against the flesh.

III. In which war, although the remaining corruption, for a time, may much prevail, yet through the continual supply of strength from the sanctifying spirit of Christ, the regenerate part doth overcome, and so the saints grow in grace, perfecting holiness in the fear of God. . . .

Chapter XV. Of Repentance Unto Life and Salvation . . .

V. Such is the provision which God hath made, through Christ, in the covenant of grace, for the preservation of believers unto salvation, that although there is no sin so small but it deserves damnation; yet there is no sin so great, that it shall bring damnation on them who truly repent; which makes the constant preaching of repentance necessary.

Chapter XVI. Of Good Works

I. GOOD works are only such as God hath commanded in His holy word, and not such as, without the warrant thereof, are devised by men out of blind zeal, or upon any pretense of good intentions.

II. These good works, done in obedience to God's commandments, are the fruits and evidences of a true and lively faith, and by them believers manifest their thankfulness, strengthen their assurance, edify their brethren, adorn the profession of the gospel, stop the mouths of the adversaries, and glorify God, whose workmanship they are created in Christ Jesus thereunto, that having their fruit unto holiness, they may have the end, eternal life.

III. Their ability to do good works is not at all of themselves, but wholly from the spirit of Christ. And that they may be enabled thereunto, besides the graces they have already received, there is required an actual influence of the same Holy Spirit, to work in them to will and to do of His good pleasure; yet are they not hereupon to grow negligent, as if they were not bound to perform any duty, unless upon a special motion of the spirit, but they ought to be diligent in stirring up the grace of God that is in them. . . .

VII. Works done by unregenerate men, although, for the matter of them, they may be things which God commands, and of good use both to themselves and to others: yet because they proceed not from an heart purified by faith, nor are done in a right manner according to the word, nor to a right end, the glory of God, they are therefore sinful, and cannot please God, nor make a man meet to receive grace from God; and yet their neglect of them is more sinful and displeasing to God.

Chapter XVII. Of the Perseverance of the Saints

I. THEY whom God hath accepted in His beloved, effectually called and sanctified by His spirit, can neither totally nor finally fall away from the state of grace, but shall certainly persevere therein to the end, and be eternally saved.

II. This perseverance of the saints depends not upon their own free will, but upon the immutability of the decree of election, from the free and unchangeable love of God the Father upon the efficacy of the merit and intercession of Jesus Christ, and union with Him, the oath of God, the abiding of His spirit, and the seed of God within them, and the nature of the covenant of grace; from all which ariseth also the certainty and infallibility thereof.

III. And although they may, through the temptation of Satan, and of the world, the prevalency of corruption remaining in them, and the neglect of the means of their preservation, fall into grievous sins, and for a time continue therein, whereby they incur God's displeasure, and grieve His Holy Spirit, come to have their graces and comforts impaired, have their hearts hardened, and their consciences wounded, hurt and scandalize others, and bring temporal judgments upon themselves; yet they are and shall be kept by the power of God through faith unto salvation.

Chapter XVIII. Of the Assurance of Grace and Salvation

I. ALTHOUGH temporary believers and other unregenerate men may vainly deceive themselves with false hopes, and carnal presumptions of being in the favor of God, and state of salvation, which hope of theirs shall perish, yet such as truly believe in the Lord Jesus, and love Him in sincerity, endeavoring to walk in good conscience before Him, may, in this life, be certainly assured that they are in the state of grace, and may rejoice in the hope of the glory of God, which hope shall never make them ashamed.

II. This certainty is not a bare conjectural and probable persuasion, grounded upon a fallible hope, but an infallible assurance of faith, founded on the blood and righteousnes of Christ, revealed in the gospel; and also upon the inward evidence of those graces; unto which promises are made, and on the immediate witness of the Spirit, testifying our adoption, and as a fruit thereof, leaving the heart more humble and holy.

III. This infallible assurance doth not so belong to the essence of faith, but that a true believer may wait long, and conflict with many difficulties before he be partaker of it; yet being enabled by the Spirit to know the things which are freely given him of God, he may without extraordinary revelation, in the right use of ordinary means, attain thereunto: And therefore it is the duty of everyone to give all diligence to make his calling and election sure, that thereby his heart may be enlarged in peace and joy in the Holy Ghost, in love and thankfulness to God, and in strength and cheerfulness in the duties of obedience, the proper fruits of this assurance; so far is it from inclining men to looseness.

IV. True believers may have the assurance of their salvation divers ways shaken, diminished and intermitted, as by negligence in preserving of it, by falling into some special sin which woundeth the conscience and grieveth the spirit by some sudden or vehement temptation, by God's withdrawing the light of His countenance, suffering even such as fear Him to walk in the darkness and to have no light; yet are they neither utterly destitute of that seed of God and life of faith that love of Christ and the brethren, that sincerity of heart, and conscience of duty, out of which, by the operation of the spirit, this assurance may in due time be revived, and by the which, in the meantime, they are supported from utter despair.

IV

The Proper Ordering of Society

THE CORE of Puritan New England was its Congregational polity. But Puritanism had political, economic, and social manifestations as well, for it required of its adherents a number of convictions about the role of government, about the nature of work, and about family relationships which in both tangible and intangible ways reshaped their lives. Subscription to Puritan theology imposed upon the believer an obligation to live all parts of his life in accordance with Holy Writ, and Holy Writ, if carefully searched, would be found sufficient for most occasions. And what was true for the individual Puritan was assumed true of a Puritan (they would have said "Christian") society.

The seventeenth-century mind, both Anglican and Puritan, placed good order among the *sine qua non* of Christian society. "Orderly comlinesse is a part of the goodnesse of a thing," wrote William Perkins, "but disorder is the effect of sin," and few orthodox members of the Church of England would have disagreed. They did differ however over the forms that order should take and over who should determine the nature of good order. Anglicans looked to the past, to traditional forms and traditional authorities, especially the King and the hierarchy of the church. Puritans, on the other hand, looked to the Bible and to the concepts of a new society based on God's intentions rather than man's inventions. Hence the institutions of society must be recast whenever they failed to meet the Puritans' test of proper order. By the time of the great migration the Puritans felt they had little chance of reforming the social and political evils of England; they blanched at arbitrary rule by the King, persecutions by Bishop Laud, widespread disruption in the English economy, and a seemingly pervasive deterioration in public and private morals. It was when England seemed on the verge of total disorder that Puritans by the thousands sought refuge in America. There the Puritans could create a society in which their own version of right order prevailed. And among the premises in the new arrangement of society was the belief that while each Christian must exercise constant and strict control over himself, the whole society, because of its collective covenant with God, must exercise rigorous discipline and mutual surveillance, lest the weaker strands cause the fabric to tear, and encourage God to punish the community for not living up to its side of the bargain. Good order thus imposed upon the leaders of society an obligation to exhort their followers and to restrict them by law when the common welfare seemed imperiled.

From such premises came a rash of Puritan literature, ranging from cautionary advice to formal frames of government. Much of it was aimed at the godly: even visible saints needed occasional restraints and reminders. More immediately in need of regulation were those who could not be counted on to heed the word of God or of His earthly agents in church and state. Hence the Puritans shaped their political, economic, and social institutions much as they had their religious polity, allowing room for local variations and individual differences, but imposing general restraints in the interest of an orderly, tranquil, and godly society. And as with their religious polity, the Puritan colonies' rules often failed to be flexible enough for all of the people.

15. Theoretical Foundations

Puritan concepts of an orderly and godly society leaned heavily on English tradition. Spurred by the turmoil that seemed endemic to England, American Puritans modeled their society in large part on sixteenth-century notions of political and economic stability and social inequality, while at the same time attempting reformation of those aspects they deemed out of tune with God's plan. Thus the Puritans of New England drew freely on Biblical injunctions to support or modify precepts they had inherited from Old England, yet they accepted almost instinctively much of the political and social framework of Elizabethan England.

A. "General and Particular Callings"

Helping to keep their commonwealths outwardly content and, for the most part, humbly submissive to their leaders, was the doctrine of calling: God assigned to each person his several roles in life. To challenge one's lot or to alter one's station smacked of rebellion against divine will. This applied not only to vocational roles such as carpenter or merchant, but equally to broader roles such as husband, servant, or subject. The classic explanation of callings came from William Perkins (1558–1602), an English divine who shared with William Ames the New Englanders' highest esteem.

Source: William Perkins, "A Treatise of the Vocations, Or Callings of Men, with the Sorts and Kinds of Them and the Right Use Thereof," *The Workes of That Famous and Worthy Minister of Christ in the University of Cambridge, Mr. William Perkins* (3 vols., London, 1612–1637) I, 750–752, 754–758.

. . . *A vocation or calling, is a certain kind of life, ordained and imposed on man by God, for the common good.* First of all I say, it is a certain condition or kind of life: that is, a certain manner of leading our lives in this world. For example, the life of a king is to spend his time in the governing of his subjects, and that is his calling; and the life of a subject is to live in obedience to the magistrate, and that is his calling. The state and condition of a minister is to lead his life in preaching of the gospel and word of God, and that is his calling. A master of a family is to lead his life in the government of his family, and that is his calling. In a word, that particular and honest manner of conversation whereunto every man is called and set apart, that is (I say) his calling.

Now in every calling we must consider two causes. First, the efficient and author thereof. Secondly, the final and proper end. The author of every calling is God himself, and therefore Paul saith; *As God hath called every man, let him walk,* vers. 17. And for this cause, the order and manner of living in this world is called a vocation, because every man is to live as he is called of God. For look as in the camp, the general appointeth to every man his place and standing: one place for the horseman, and another for the footman, and to every particular soldier likewise his office and standing in which he is to abide against the enemy and therein to live and die. Even so it is in human societies: God is the general, appointing to every man his particular calling and as it were his standing, and in that calling he assigns unto him his particular office in performance whereof he is to live and die. And as in a camp, no soldier can depart his standing without the leave of the general, no more may any man leave his calling except he receive liberty from God. Again, in a clock made by the art and handiwork of man, there be many wheels and every one hath his several motion, some turn this way, some that way, some go softly, some apace, and they are all ordered by the motion of the watch. Behold here a notable resemblance of God's special providence over mankind, which is the watch of the great world, allotting to every man his motion and calling, and in that calling, his particular office and function. Therefore it is true that I say, that God himself is the author and beginning of callings.

This overthroweth the heathenish opinion of men which think that the particular condition and state of man in this life comes by chance or by the bare will and pleasure of man himself. Secondly, by this which hath been said, we learn that many persuading themselves of their callings have for all this no calling at all. As for example, such as live by usury, by carding and dicing, by maintaining houses of gaming, by plays and such like. For God is the author of every lawful calling, but these and such miserable courses of living are either against the word of God or else are not grounded thereupon, and therefore are no callings or vocations but avocations from God and his ways. . . .

The final cause or end of every calling I note in the last words of the description: *for the common good*, that is, for the benefit and good estate of mankind. In man's body there be sundry parts and members, and every one hath his several use and office which it performeth not for itself, but for the good of the whole body, as the office of the eye is to see, of the ear to hear, and the foot to go. Now all societies of men are bodies, a family is a body, and so is every particular church a body, and the commonwealth also; and in these bodies there be several members which are men walking in several callings and offices, the execution whereof must tend to the happy and good estate of the rest; yea of all men every where, as much as possible is. The common good of men stands in this, not only that they live, but that they live well, in righteousness and holiness and consequently in true happiness. And for the attainment hereunto, God hath ordained and disposed all callings and in his providence designed the persons to bear them. Here then we must in general know that he abuseth his calling, whosoever he be, that against the end thereof employs it for himself, seeking wholly his own and not the common good. And that common saying, *Every man for himself, and God for us all*, is wicked, and is directly against the end of every calling or honest kind of life.

Thus much of the description of vocation in general. Now before I come particularly to entreat of the special kinds of callings, there are two general rules to be learned of all, which belong to every calling.

The first: whatsoever any man enterpriseth or doth, either in word or deed, he must do it by virtue of his calling, and he must keep himself within the compass, limits, or precincts thereof. This rule is laid down in these words of the Apostles: *Let every man abide in that calling wherein he was called.* The drift whereof is to bind men to their calling and to teach them to perform all their actions by warrant thereof. It is said, Hebr. 11:6, *Without faith it is impossible to please God; and Whatsoever is not of faith, is sin.* Whatsoever is not done within the compass of a calling is not of faith, because a man must first have some warrant and word of God to assure him of his calling, to do this or that thing, before he can do it in faith. . . .

The second general rule which must be remembered is this: That every man must do the duties of his calling with diligence, and therefore Solomon saith, Eccl. 9:10, *Whatsoever is in thine hand to do, do it with all thy power.* St. Paul bids him that ruleth, rule with diligence, and every man to wait on his office, Rom. 12:8. And Jeremy saith, Jer. 48:10, *Cursed is he that doth the work of the Lord negligently.* . . . To them which employ their gifts more is given, and from them which employ them not is taken that which they have; and labor in a calling is as precious as gold or silver. Hereupon he that maims a man, and disables him to do the work of his calling, by God's law is bound to give him the value of his labor, Exod. 21:19. And to like purpose our people have a common saying that an occupation is as good as land, because land may be lost but skill and labor in a good occupation is profitable to the end because it will help at need, when land and all things fail. And on the other side, we must take heed of two damnable sins that are contrary to this diligence. The first is idleness, whereby the duties of our callings and the occasions of glorifying God are neglected or omitted. The second is slothfulness, whereby they are performed slackly and carelessly. God in the parable of the husbandman calls them that are idle into his vineyard, saying, *Why stand ye idle all the day?* Mat. 20:6. And the servant that had received but one talent is called an evil servant because he was slothful in the use of it, for so it is said, *Thou evil servant and slothful,* Mat. 25:26. St. Paul gives this rule to the Thessalonians, *He that would not labor, must not eat;* yet such a one he would have to be noted by a letter, as [one who] walked inordinately. And this he sheweth, that sloth and negligence in the duties of our callings are a disorder against that comely order which God hath set in the societies of mankind, both in church and commonwealth. And indeed, idleness and sloth are the causes of many damnable sins. The idle body and the idle brain is the shop of the devil. The sea, if it moved not, could not but putrify, and the body, if it be not stirred and moved, breedeth diseases. Now the idle and slothful person is a sea of corruption, and when he is most idle, Satan is least idle, for then is he most busy to draw him to manifold sins.

Thus much of the two general rules. Now follow the parts and kinds of vocations. And they are of two sorts: general, or particular. The general calling is the calling of Christianity, which is common to all that live in the Church of God. The particular is that special calling that belongs to some particular men, as the calling of a magistrate, the calling of a minister, the calling of a master, of a father, of a child, of a servant, of a subject, or any other calling that is common to all. And Paul acknowledg[ed] this distinction of callings when he saith, *Let every man abide in that calling, wherein he is called;* that is, in that particular and personal calling in which he was called to be a Christian. Of these two in order.

The general calling is that whereby a man is called out of the world to be a child of God, a member of Christ, and heir of the kingdom of heaven. This calling belongs to every one within the compass of the church, not any one accepted. Here I have just occasion to make a long discourse touching the calling of men to Christ and Christian Religion, but I will only touch the main duties thereof. . . .

. . . Now followeth the second kind of calling, and that is personal. A personal calling is the execution of some particular office arising of that distinction which God makes between man and man in every society. First, I say, it is the execution of some particular office, as for example the calling of a magistrate is to execute the office of government over his subjects, the office of a minister is to execute the duty of teaching his people, the calling of a master is to execute the office of authority and government over his servants, the office of a physician is to put in practice the good means whereby life and health are preserved. In a word, in every estate the practice and execution of that particular office wherein any man is placed is his personal calling.

Secondly, I add, that it ariseth from that distinction which God maketh between man and man in every society to shew what is the foundation and ground of all personal callings. And it is a point to be considered of us, which I thus explain: God in his word hath ordained the society of man with man, partly in the commonwealth, partly in the church, and partly in the family; and it is not the will of God that man should live and converse alone by himself. Now for the maintaining of society, he hath ordained a certain bond to link men together, which St. Paul calleth the bond of peace, and the bond of perfection, namely, love. And howsoever he hath ordained societies, and the bond of them all, yet hath he appointed that there should still remain a distinction between man and man, not only in regard of person, but also in other respects. . . . First, in regard of the inward gifts which God bestowed on every man, giving to several men several gifts according to His good pleasure. . . . Secondly, persons are distinguished by order, whereby God hath appointed that in every society one person should be above or under another, not making all equal, as though the body should be all head and nothing else. But even in degree and order He hath set a distinction, that one should be above another. And by reason of this distinction of men, partly in respect of gifts, partly in respect of order, come personal callings. For if all men had the same gifts, and all were in the same degree and order, then should all have one and the same calling; but inasmuch as God giveth diversity of gifts inwardly, and distinction of order outwardly, hence proceed diversity of personal callings, and therefore I added, that personal callings arise from that distinction which God maketh between man and man in every society. And thus we see what is a personal calling. Now before I come to entreat of the parts thereof, there be other general rules to be learned which concern all personal callings whatsoever.

I. Rule. Every person of every degree, state, sex, or condition without exception, must have some personal and particular calling to walk in. . . .

Hence we may learne sundry points of instruction: first of all, that it is a foul disorder in any commonwealth that there should be suffered rogues, beggars, vagabonds; for such kind of persons commonly are of no civil society or corporation, nor of any particular church, and are as rotten legs and arms that drop from the body. Again, to wander up and down from year to year to this end, to seek and procure bodily maintenance, is no calling, but the life of a beast, and consequently a condition or state of life flat against the rule that every one must have a particular calling. And therefore the statute made the last Parliament for the restraining of beggars and rogues is an excellent statute, and being in substance the very law of God, is never to be repealed.

Again, hereby is otherthrown the condition of monks and friars who challenge to themselves that they live in a state of perfection because they live apart from the societies of men in fasting and prayer. But contrariwise, this monkish kind of living is damnable, for besides the general duties of fasting and prayer, which appertain to all Christians, every man must have a particular and personal calling that he may be a good and profitable member of some society and body. And the ancient church condemned all monks for thieves and robbers that besides the general duties of prayer and fasting did not withal employ themselves in some other calling for their better maintenance.

Thirdly, we learn by this that miserable and damnable is the estate of those that being enriched with great livings and revenues do spend their days in eating and drinking, in sports and pastimes, not employing themselves in service for church or commonwealth. It may be happily thought that such gentlemen have happy lives, but it is far otherwise, considering every one, rich or poor, man or woman, is bound to have a personal calling in which they must perform some duties for the common good, according to the measure of the gifts that God hath bestowed upon them.

Fourthly, hereby also it is required that such as we commonly call serving men should have, beside the office of waiting, some other particular calling, unless they tend on men of great place and state: for only to wait and give attendance is not a sufficient calling, as common experience telleth. For waiting servants, by reason they spend the most of their time in eating and drinking, sleeping and gaming after dinner and after supper, do prove the most unprofitable members both in church and commonwealth. . . .

II. *Rule.* Every man must judge that particular calling in which

God hath placed him to be the best of all callings for him. I say not simply best, but best for him. This rule is set forth unto us in the example of Paul, *I have learned* (saith he) *in whatsoever state I am, to be content and well pleased.* The practice of this duty is the stay and foundation of the good estate both of church and commonwealth, for it maketh every man to keep his own standing and to employ himself painfully within his calling; but when we begin to mislike the wise disposition of God, and to think other men's callings better for us than our own, then follows confusion and disorder in every society. When Absalom, a child and subject of king David, was not content with his estate, but sought his father's kingdom and said, *O that I were judge among you,* many contentions and hurlyburlies followed in the commonwealth of the Jews all his days. . . . And from time to time, the greatest discords that have fallen out in the Church of God have issued from this fountain. And the same is also true in the commonwealth: hence come treacheries, treasons, and seditions, when men, not content with their own estate and honors, seek higher places, and being disappointed grow to discontentments and so forward to all mischief. Therefore in a word, the good estate of the church and commonwealth is when every person keeps himself to his own calling. And this will undoubtedly come to pass, if we consider what be our callings; and that we are placed in them of God; and therefore judge them to be the best callings of all for us.

III. Rule. Every man must join the practice of his personal calling with the practice of the general calling of Christianity, before described. More plainly: every particular calling must be practiced in and with the general calling of a Christian. It is not sufficient for a man in the congregation, and in common conversation, to be a Christian, but in his very personal calling he must shew himself to be so. As for example, a magistrate must not only in general be a Christian, as every man is, but he must be a Christian magistrate in executing the office of a magistrate, in bearing the sword. A master of a family must not only be a Christian abroad in the town and in the congregation, in the sight of strangers, but also in the administration and regiment of his particular family, towards wife, children, and servants. It is not enough for a woman to be virtuous openly to strangers, but her virtue must privately shew itself in her subjection and obedience to her own husband. A schoolmaster must not only be a Christian in the assembly, when he heareth the word and receiveth the sacraments, but he must also shew himself to be a Christian in the office of teaching. . . .

V. *Rule.* A particular calling must give place to the general calling of a Christian when they cannot both stand together. As for example: a servant is bound to his master to obey him, either because he is a vassal, or at the least because he is hired to serve for wages. The said master being a zealous Papist, threateneth his servant, being a Protestant, that unless he condescend to hear Mass, he shall either burn at a stake or carry a fagot. Now the servant seeing the malicious purpose of his master, and not finding himself able to bear the brunt of a trial in this case, he departs and withdraws himself for a time. And the question is, whether he doth well or no? The answer is, he doth, and in such a case he may lawfully fly from his master, for a servant that by personal calling is bound to an earthly master is further by a general calling bound unto God. And the particular calling of any man is inferior to the general calling of a Christian. And when they cannot both stand together, the particular calling must give place because we are bound unto God in the first place, and unto man, under God: and so far only as we may withal, keep our bond with God. . . .

In addition to the two kinds of calling elaborated by Perkins, the Puritans observed a third: the call to do—or not to do—a specific act. Before making any major decision such as marriage, a long journey, or even a business transaction, the Puritan searched his soul for evidence of what God intended, so that man's action would reflect the Lord's decision. Thus it was that Michael Wigglesworth, who had long been concerned about his sexual impulses, decided upon matrimony only after concluding "It [is] pretty clear to me that god calleth to a speedy change of my condition." The Puritans' orderly society, then, rested not only on the broad implications for social control implied in Perkins' two categories, but also on a self-discipline rooted in the desire to do God's will, which, in turn, fostered both a dependence on the superior Biblical knowledge of the clergy and a tendency toward excessive introspection.

B. "A Modell of Christian Charity"

The broad outlines of New England's experiment in Christian living took form before settlement was well under way. Although in 1630 the Pilgrim colony at Plymouth was a decade old and clusters of Englishmen dotted the Massachusetts coast, the total English population north of the Hudson River had yet to reach five hundred, and no organization or doctrine provided a common focus for the scattered settlements. With the arrival of the Winthrop fleet in 1630—seventeen ships and nearly a thousand colonists—came not only a sharp increase in population but the first public guidelines by which the Puritans would shape and measure their experiment. The most comprehensive statement of Puritan social, political, and economic intensions was offered on board the Arabella by John Winthrop in a lay sermon on the eve of the voyage.

Source: Massachusetts Historical Society, *Collections*, 3d ser. VII (1838), 33–38, 40, 44–48.

CHRISTIAN CHARITY
A MODEL HEREOF

God Almighty in His most holy and wise providence hath so disposed of the condition of mankind as in all times some must be rich, some poor, some high and eminent in power and dignity, other mean and in subjection.

THE REASON HEREOF

1. *Reason:* First, to hold conformity with the rest of His works, being delighted to show forth the glory of His wisdom in the variety and difference of the creatures and the glory of His power, in ordering all these differences for the preservation and good of the whole and the glory of His greatness; that as it is the glory of princes to have many officers, so This Great King will have many stewards, counting Himself more honored in dispensing His gifts to man by man, than if He did it by His own immediate hand.

2. *Reason:* Secondly, that He might have the more occasion to manifest the work of His spirit: first, upon the wicked in moderating and restraining them, so that the rich and mighty should not eat up the poor, nor the poor and despised rise up against their superiors and shake off their yoke; secondly, in the regenerate in exercising His graces in them, as in the great ones, their love, mercy, gentleness, temperance, etc., in the poor and inferior sort, their faith, patience, obedience, etc.

3. *Reason:* Thirdly, that every man might have need of other, and from hence they might be all knit more nearly together in the bond of brotherly affection; from hence it appears plainly that no man is made more honorable than another or more wealthy, etc.,

out of any particular and singular respect to himself but for the glory of his Creator and the common good of the creature, man. Therefore God still reserves the property of these gifts to Himself, as Ezeckiel 16:17. He there calls wealth his gold and his silver, etc. Proverbs 3:9. He claims their service as His due—*honor the Lord with thy riches*, etc.—all men being thus (by divine providence) ranked into two sorts, rich and poor. Under the first are comprehended all such as are able to live comfortably by their own means duly improved, and all others are poor according to the former distribution. There are two rules whereby we are to walk one towards another: justice and mercy. These are always distinguished in their act and in their object, yet may they both concur in the same subject in each respect—as sometimes there may be an occasion of showing mercy to a rich man, in some sudden danger of distress, and also doing of mere justice to a poor man in regard of some particular contract, etc. There is likewise a double law by which we are regulated in our conversation one towards another: in both the former respects, the law of nature and the law of grace, or the moral law or the law of the gospel, to omit the rule of justice as not properly belonging to this purpose otherwise than it may fall into consideration in some particular cases. By the first of these laws, man as he was enabled so withal [is] commanded to love his neighbor as himself. Upon this ground stands all the precepts of the moral law which concerns our dealings with men. To apply this to the works of mercy, this law requires two things: first, that every man afford his help to another in every want or distress; secondly, that he perform this out of the same affection which makes him careful of his own good according to that of our Saviour, Matthew [7:12]. *Whatsoever ye would that men should do to you. . . .* This was practiced by Abraham and Lot in entertaining the angels and the old man of Gibea.

The law of grace or the gospel hath some difference from the former as in these respects: first, the law of nature was given to man in the estate of innocency, this of the gospel in the estate of regeneracy; secondly, the former propounds one man to another, as the same flesh and image of God, this as a brother in Christ also and in the communion of the same spirit, and so teacheth us to put a difference between Christians and others. *Do good to all especially to the household of faith.* [Galatians 6:10.] Upon this ground the Israelites were to put a difference between the brethren of such as were strangers, though not of the Canaanites. Thirdly, the law of nature could give no rules for dealing with enemies for all are to be considered as friends in the estate of innocency, but the gospel commands love to an enemy. Proof: *if thine enemy hunger, feed him; love your enemies, do good to them that hate you.* Matthew 5:44.

This law of the gospel propounds likewise a difference of seasons and occasions: there is a time when a Christian must sell all and give to the poor as they did in the Apostles' times. There is a time also when Christians (though they give not all yet) must give beyond their ability, as they of Macedonia. Corinthians 2:6. Likewise community of perils calls for extraordinary liberality and so doth community in some special service for the church. Lastly, when there is no other means whereby our Christian brother may be relieved in this distress, we must help him beyond our ability, rather than tempt God in putting him upon help by miraculous or extraordinary means. . . .

This duty of mercy is exercised in three kinds: giving, lending, and forgiving.

Question: What rule shall a man observe in giving in respect of the measure?

Answer: If the time and occasion be ordinary, he is to give out of his abundance—let him lay aside as God hath blessed him. If the time and occasion be extraordinary, he must be ruled by them, taking this withal, that then a man cannot likely do too much, especially if he may leave himself and his family under probable means of comfortable subsistence. . . .

Question: What rule must we observe in lending?

Answer: Thou must observe whether thy brother hath present or probable or possible means of repaying thee. If there be none of these, thou must give him according to his necessity rather than lend him as he requires. If he hath present means of repaying thee, thou art to look at him not as an act of mercy but by way of commerce, wherein thou art to walk by the rule of justice. But, if his means of repaying thee be only probable or possible, then is he an object of thy mercy. Thou must lend him, though there be danger of losing it, Deuteronomy 15:7. If any of thy brethren be poor, etc., thou shalt lend him sufficient. That men might not shift off this duty by the apparent hazard, he tells them that though the Year of Jubilee were at hand (when he must remit it, if he were not able to repay it before) yet he must lend him, and that cheerfully. It may not grieve thee to give him (saith he); and because some might object—why so I should soon impoverish myself and my family—he adds, with all they work, etc., for our Saviour. Matth. 5:42. *From him that would borrow of thee turn not away.*

Question: What rule must we observe in forgiving?

Answer: Whether thou didst lend by way of commerce or in mercy, if he have nothing to pay thee, [thou] must forgive him (except in cause where thou hast a surety or a lawful pledge). Deuteronomy 15:2. Every seventh year the creditor was to quit that which he lent to his brother if he were poor, as appears verse 8:[4], save when there shall be no poor with thee. In all these and like cases Christ was a general rule, Matthew 7:22. *Whatsoever ye would that men should do to you do ye the same to them also.*

Question: What rule must we observe and walk by in cause of community of peril?

Answer: The same as before, but with more enlargement towards others and less respect towards ourselves and our own right. Hence it was that in the primitive church they sold all, had all things in common, neither did any man say that that which he possessed was his own. Likewise in their return out of the captivity, because the work was great for the restoring of the church and the danger of enemies was common to all, Nehemiah exhorts the Jews to liberality and readiness in remitting their debts to their brethren, and disposes liberally of his own to such as wanted and stands not upon his own due—which he might have demanded of them. Thus did some of our forefathers in times of persecution here in England, and so did many of the faithful in other churches whereof we keep an honorable remembrance of them. And it is to be observed that both in scriptures and later stories of the churches that such as have been most bountiful to the poor saints, especially in these extraordinary times and occasions, God hath left them highly commended to posterity. . . .

The definition which the scripture gives us of love is this: love is the bond of perfection. First, it is a bond or ligament. Secondly, it makes the work perfect. There is no body but consists of parts, and that which knits these parts together gives the body its perfection because it makes each part so contiguous to other as thereby they do mutually participate with each other—both in strength and infirmity, in pleasure and pain. To instance in the most perfect of all bodies, Christ and His church make one body. The several parts of this body considered apart before they were united were as disproportionate and as much disordering as so many contrary qualities or elements. But when Christ comes and by his spirit and love knits all these parts to Himself and each to other, it is become the most perfect and best proportioned body in the world. Ephesians 4:16. Christ, by whom all the body being knit together by every joint for the furniture thereof (according to the effectual power which is in the measure of every perfection or parts, [is] a glorious body without spot or wrinkle, the ligaments hereof being Christ, or his love, for Christ is love. 1 John 4:8. So this definition is right: Love is the bond of perfection.

From hence we may frame these conclusions:

1. First, all true Christians are of one body in Christ. 1 Corinthians 12:12–13, 17. Ye are the body of Christ and members of their part.

Secondly. The ligaments of this body which [is] knit together are love.

Thirdly. No body can be perfect which wants its proper ligaments.

Fourthly. All the parts of this body being thus united are made so contiguous in a special relation as they must needs partake of each other's strength and infirmity, joy, sorrow, weal and woe. 1 Corinthians 12:26. If one member suffers, all suffer with it; if one be in honor, all rejoice with it.

Fifthly. This sensibleness and sympathy of each other's conditions will necessarily infuse into each part a native desire and endeavor to strengthen, defend, preserve, and comfort the other. . . .

It rests now to make some application of this discourse by the present design, which gave the occasion of writing of it. Herein are four things to be propounded: first, the persons; secondly, the work; thirdly, the end; fourthly, the means.

1. For the persons, we are a company professing ourselves fellow members of Christ. In which respect only, though we were absent from each other many miles, and had our employments as far distant, yet we ought to account ourselves knit together by this

bond of love, and live in the exercise of it, if we would have comfort of our being in Christ. This was notorious in the practice of the Christians in former times, as is testified of the Waldenses from the mouth of one of the adversaries, Aeneas Sylvius, *mutuo* [blank] *penè antequam norint:* they used to love any of their own religion even before they were acquainted with them.

Secondly. For the work we have in hand, it is by a mutual consent through a special overruling providence, and a more than ordinary approbation of the churches of Christ, to seek out a place of cohabitation and consortship under a due form of government, both civil and ecclesiastical. In such cases as this the care of the public must oversway all private respects, by which not only conscience, but mere civil policy doth bind us; for it is a true rule that particular estates cannot subsist in the ruin of the public.

Thirdly. The end is to improve our lives to do more service to the Lord, the comfort and increase of the body of Christ whereof we are members, that ourselves and posterity may be the better preserved from the common corruptions of this evil world, to serve the Lord and work out our salvation under the power and purity of his holy ordinances.

Fourthly. For the means whereby this must be effected, they are twofold: a conformity with the work and end we aim at. These we see are extraordinary. Therefore we must not content ourselves with usual, ordinary means. Whatsoever we did or ought to have done when we lived in England, the same must we do and more also where we go. That which the most in their churches maintain as a truth in profession only, we must bring into familiar and constant practice, as in this duty of love we must love brotherly without dissimulation. We must love one another with a pure heart, fervently; we must bear one another's burdens; we must not look only on our own things, but also on the things of our brethren. Neither must we think that the Lord will bear with such failings at our hands as he doth from those among whom we have lived, and that for three reasons:

1. In regard of the more near bond of marriage between Him and us, wherein He hath taken us to be His after a most strict and peculiar manner which will make Him the more jealous of our love and obedience. So He tells the people of Israel: *you only have I*

known of all the families of the earth, therefore will I punish you for your transgressions.

Secondly, because the Lord will be sanctified in them that come near Him. We know that there were many that corrupted the service of the Lord, some setting up altars before His own, others offering both strange fire and strange sacrifices also. Yet there came no fire from Heaven, or other sudden judgment upon them as did upon Nadab and Abihu, who yet we may think did not sin presumptuously.

Thirdly, when God gives a special commission, He looks to have it strictly observed in every article. When He gave Saul a commission to destroy Amalech, He indented with him upon certain articles, and because he failed in one of the least, and that upon a fair pretense, it lost him the kingdom which should have been his reward if he had observed his commission. Thus stands the cause between God and us. We are entered into covenant with Him for this work; we have taken out a commission. The Lord hath given us leave to draw our own articles. We have professed to enterprise these actions upon thcsc and these ends. We have hereupon besought Him of favor and blessing. Now if the Lord shall please to hear us, and bring us in peace to the place we desire, then hath He ratified this covenant and sealed our commission, and will expect a strict performance of the articles contained in it. But if we shall neglect the observation of these articles, which are the ends we have propounded, and dissembling with our God shall fall to embrace this present world and prosecute our carnal intentions—seeking great things for ourselves and our posterity—the Lord will surely break out in wrath against us, be revenged of such a perjured people, and make us know the price of the breach of such a covenant.

Now the only way to avoid this shipwreck and to provide for our posterity is to follow the counsel of Micah: to do justly, to love mercy, to walk humbly with our God. For this end we must be knit together in this work as one man; we must entertain each other in brotherly affection; we must be willing to abridge ourselves of our superfluities for the supply of others' necessities; we must uphold a familiar commerce together in all meekness, gentleness, patience, and liberality; we must delight in each other, make others' conditions our own, rejoice together, mourn together, labor and suffer together always having before our eyes our commission and community in the work, our community as members of the same body, so shall we keep the unity of the spirit in the bond of peace. The Lord will be our God and delight to dwell among us as His own people and will command a blessing upon us in all our ways, so that we shall see much more of His wisdom, power, goodness, and truth than formerly we have been acquainted with. We shall find that the God of Israel is among us when ten of us shall be able to resist a thousand of our enemies; when He shall make us a praise and glory, that men shall say of succeeding plantations: the Lord make it like that of New England. For we must consider that we shall be as a city upon a hill, the eyes of all people are upon us; so that if we shall deal falsely with our God in this work we have undertaken and so cause Him to withdraw His present help from us, we shall be made a story and a byword through the world. We shall open the mouths of enemies to speak evil of the ways of God and all professors for God's sake. We shall shame the faces of many of God's worthy servants and cause their prayers to be turned into curses upon us, till we be consumed out of the good land whither we are going; and to shut up this discourse with that exhortation of Moses—that faithful servant of the Lord—in his last farewell to Israel (Deuteronomy 30): Beloved, there is now set before us life and good, death and evil, in that we are commanded this day to love the Lord our God and to love one another, to walk in His ways and to keep His commandments and His ordinances and His laws, and the articles of our covenant with Him, that we may live and be multiplied, and that the Lord our God may bless us in the land whither we go to possess it. But if our hearts shall turn away so that we will not obey, but shall be seduced and worship other gods, our pleasures and profits, and serve them, it is propounded unto us this day, we shall surely perish out of the good land whither we pass over this vast sea to possess it.

Therefore let us choose life,
that we, and our seed,
may live by obeying His
voice, and cleaving to Him,
for He is our life, and
our prosperity.

16. Political Order

Winthrop's emphasis on natural order, holy precepts, and Christian love had at least indirect application to political order, for the spirit of his message is evident in the shaping of early New England government. Society must be stable and effective; it must also be humane and suited to the realities of human character. Hence much of Puritan political writing is an attempt to define limits of authority and to establish institutions that encourage men—both rulers and the ruled—to act orderly and with Christian forbearance.

A. Boundaries of Church and State

Because of the profoundly religious quality of his world view, the Puritan had many temptations to turn theocratic. Clergymen bulked large in early New England, and the church claimed a central role in the corporate society as well as in individual lives. But there were limits. Civil society had its own prerogatives, for as Winthrop pointed out in 1637, Christ not only created the church but "he hath sett up another kingdome in this worlde, wherein magistrates are his officers, and they are to be accountable to him. . . ." The New England colonies were thus more truly Bible commonwealths than theocracies; the church did not dictate to the state nor did clergymen hold political office; yet because most officeholders, as an explicit or implicit requirement for election, maintained good standing in the church, because clergymen advised the magistrates on most important matters of state, and because by law the state had responsibility for encouragement and defense of orthodoxy, early New England from the hindsight of the twentieth century appears theocentric if not theocratic. On the other hand, unlike old England and most other European nations, the Puritan outposts in America witnessed no ecclesiastical courts, and according to Massachusetts law, censure of a church could not "degrade or depose any man from any Civill dignitie, office, or Authoritie he shall have in the Commonwealth." Thus church and state functioned in separate but overlapping domains, staffed for the most part by men in comfortable accord with both branches of society.

The most candid and thorough statements of civil and ecclesiastical bounds came from John Cotton (1584–1652) of Boston, the outstanding clergyman of the first generation in New England, who not surprisingly leaned somewhat more favorably toward clerical authority than did Winthrop and other lay leaders. The following explanation of New England's church-state theory appeared in a letter to Lord Saye and Sele, who had inquired about the Bay Colony's political structure.

Source: Thomas Hutchinson, The History of the Colony of Massachusetts Bay . . . (Boston, 1764), 496–500.

. . . It is very suitable to God's all sufficient wisdom and to the fullness and perfection of Holy Scriptures, not only to prescribe perfect rules for the right ordering of a private man's soul to everlasting blessedness with Himself, but also for the right ordering of a man's family, yea, of the commonwealth too, so far as both of them are subordinate to spiritual ends, and yet avoid both the church's usurpation upon civil jurisdictions, *in ordine ad spirtualia*, and the commonwealth's invasion upon ecclesiastical administrations, *in ordine* to civil peace and conformity to the civil state. God's institutions (such as the government of church and of commonwealth be) may be close and compact, and co-ordinate one to another, and yet not confounded. God hath so framed the state of church government and ordinances that they may be compatible to any commonwealth, though never so much disordered in His frame. But yet when a commonwealth hath liberty to mold His own frame (*scripture plenitudinem adoro*) I conceive the scripture hath given full direction for the right ordering of the same, and that, in such sort as may best maintain the *euexia* of the church.

Mr. Hooker doth often quote a saying out of Mr. Cartwright (though I have not read it in him) that no man fashioneth his house to his hangings, but his hangings to his house. It is better that the commonwealth be fashioned to the setting forth of God's house, which is His church, than to accommodate the church frame to the civil state. Democracy I do not conceive that ever God did ordain as a fit government either for church or commonwealth. If the people be governors, who shall be governed? As for monarchy and aristocracy, they are both of them clearly approved, and directed in scripture, yet so as referreth the sovereignty to Himself, and setteth up theocracy in both, as the best form of government in the commonwealth, as well as in the church.

The law, which your Lordship instanceth in (that none shall be chosen to magistracy among us but a church member) was made and enacted before I came into the country; but I have hitherto wanted sufficient light to plead against it. First, the rule that directeth the choice of supreme governors is of like equity and weight in all magistrates, that one of their brethren (not a stranger) should be set over them, Deuteronomy 17:15, and Jethro's counsel to Moses was approved of God, that the judges, and officers to be set over the people, should be men fearing God, Exodus 18:21, and Solomon maketh it the joy of a commonwealth when the righteous are in authority, and their mourning when the wicked rule, Proverbs 29:21; Job 34:30.

Your Lordship's fear that this will bring in papal excommunication is just and pious, but let your Lordship be pleased again to consider whether the consequence be necessary. *Turpius ejicitur quam non admittitur*: non-membership may be a just cause of non-admission to the place of magistracy, but yet ejection out of his membership will not be a just cause of ejecting him out of his magistracy. A godly woman, being to make a choice of a husband, may justly refuse a man that is either cast out of church fellowship, or is not yet received into it, but yet when she is once given to him, she may not reject him then for such defect. Mr. Humphrey was chosen for an assistant (as I hear) before the colony came over hither, and though he be not as yet joined into church fellowship (by reason of the unsettledness of the congregation where he liveth), yet the commonwealth does still continue his magistracy to him, as knowing he waiteth for opportunity of enjoying church fellowship shortly.

When your Lordship doubteth that this course will draw all things under the determination of the church, *in ordine ad spiritualia* (seeing the church is to determine who shall be members, and none but a member may have to do in the government of a commonwealth), be pleased (I pray you) to conceive that magistrates are neither chosen to office in the church, nor do govern by directions from the church, but by civil laws, and those enacted in general courts and executed in courts of justice by the governors and assistants. In all which the church (as the church) hath nothing to do, only it prepareth fit instruments both to rule and to choose rulers, which is no ambition in the church, nor dishonor to the commonwealth. The apostle, on the contrary, thought it a great dishonor and reproach to the church of Christ if it were not able to yield able judges to hear and determine all causes among their brethren, 1 Corinthians 6:1–5, which place alone seemeth to me fully to decide this question. For it plainly holdeth forth this argument: it is a shame to the church to want able judges of civil matters (as v. 5) and an audacious act in any church member voluntarily to go for judgment otherwhere than before the saints (as v. 1), then it will be no arrogance nor folly in church members, nor prejudice to the commonwealth, if voluntarily they never choose any civil judges but from amongst the saints, such as church members are called to be. But the former is clear, and how then can the latter be avoided? If this therefore be (as your Lordship rightly conceiveth) one of the main objections if not the only one which hindereth this commonwealth from the entertainment of the propositions of those worthy gentlemen, we entreat them, in the name of the Lord Jesus, to consider in meekness of wisdom it is not any conceit or will of ours, but the holy counsel and will of the Lord Jesus (whom they seek to serve as well as we) that overruleth us in this case, and we trust will overrule them also, that the Lord only may be exalted amongst all his servants. What pity and grief were it that the observance of the will of Christ should hinder good things from us!

But your Lordship doubteth that if such a rule were necessary then the church estate and the best ordered commonwealth in the world were not compatible. But let not your Lordship so conceive. For the church submitteth itself to all the laws and ordinances of men, in what commonwealth soever they come to dwell. But it is one thing to submit into what they have no calling to reform, another thing voluntarily to ordain a form of government, which to the best discerning of many of us (for I speak not of myself) is expressly contrary to rule. Nor need your Lordship fear (which yet I speak with submission to your Lordship's better judgment) that this course will lay such a foundation as nothing but a mere democracy can be built upon it. Bodin confesseth that though it be *status popul aris*, where a people choose their own governors, yet the government is not a democracy if it be administered not by the people, but by the governors, whether one (for then it is a monarchy, though elective) or by many, for then (as you know) it is aristocracy. In which respect it is that church government is justly denied (even by Mr. Robinson) to be democratical, though the people choose their own officers and rulers.

Nor need we fear that this course will in time cast the commonwealth into distractions, and popular confusions. For (under correction) these three things do not undermine, but do mutually and strongly maintain one another (even those three which we principally aim at): authority in magistrates, liberty in people, purity in the church. Purity, preserved in the church, will preserve well ordered liberty in the people, and both of them establish well balanced authority in the magistrates. God is the author of all these three, and neither is Himself the God of confusion, nor are His ways the ways of confusion, but of peace. . . .

B. Evolution of Government

Although the Massachusetts Bay Company's charter set forth the essentials of the colony's government, it left much unsaid. Details had to be worked out, and even the letter of the charter was at times overlooked by those entrusted with its application, for they feared that the experiment might succumb to a hasty distribution of power. Thus government evolved slowly and erratically—as can be seen in Governor Winthrop's Journal, where he reveals not only the gradual progress toward political stability but also the persistence of dissent, debate, and even bitter controversy. Christian charity was often put to severe test. The following letter from Captain Israel Stoughton (d.1645 ?) to his brother reveals, more clearly than does Winthrop's account, the tensions and conflicts that accompanied the search for political order in Massachusetts Bay. Israel Stoughton, wealthy political and military figure, had settled in Dorchester in 1630.

Source: Massachusetts Historical Society, Proceedings, V (1860–1862), 136–141.

Here hath been somewhat to do too about a negative voice, for the magistrates would that no law nor act of court should be current and established (excepting choice of magistrates) unless the greater number of magistrates present do also approve and consent to it, though all [the] country and three of seven of the magistrates do like and desire it, and they plead the patent allows them this power and some also have well liked it. Others have not liked it, and [they are] now the greater number by far, I suppose five or ten for one, and of the ministers, too, [many] are of an other mind. I know none that have read the patent (excepting magistrates) that esteem it their due, but yet many more willing to have condescended to it at the first, whose minds are now changed. The conclusion of that business is: it sleeps in silence, and is so like. For it is concluded by some that the magistrates hereafter will never ask it, nor the people never give it, but only thus, that whereas now our courts for making laws consist of the body of magistrates, and three committees [i.e., representatives] chosen by every town to join with them, that there shall be power of suspension or either party in cases where they agree not, until the mind of the whole body of the country may conveniently be known, and then the issue to be on the major part's side according to the patent, and so both tumultuousness and many mischiefs may be prevented. This was at first proposed and approved by ministers and country, but not by magistrates. . . .

When I came into the country, for one whole year after the government was solely in the hands of the assistants. The people chose them magistrates, and then they made laws, disposed lands, raised monies, punished offenders, etc., at their discretion. Neither did the people know the patent nor what prerogative and liberty they had by the same. But, there being some sums of money raised, and a speech of more, it made some inquisitive into matters, and particularly after the patent. About which time Mr. Winthrop, Governor, having the patent did give way to the country upon their motion to see it, and all the magistrates (as in charity I must say) were willing to admit the people to join with themselves in the governance of the state, by three deputies for each town. So in May last year there was a General Court, wherein things were so agitated. In which court I was by our town chosen a committee, and by the committees chosen the chief speaker on the country's behalf (there being three speakers). And indeed such was their good opinion of me (unworthy I confess) that they would have chosen me into an assistant's place but that they said they needed me more there for the present. So that court passed and though there was a little opposition in one particular case, yet all ended in peace with manifestations of great love and the magistrates' good approbation of us that had in some points opposed and crossed them, at least some of Boston, where Mr. Winthrop dwells.

Then there was a second court about August last, not for choice of magistrates but for making laws etc., where I was also both a committee and speaker (as before). In that court there were some more straight passages, and specially about the negative voice which fell to be my portion much to oppose, though not alone. In which court time, Mr. Winthrop and myself had accidentally some private discourse about the patent and the power of assistants and governor. So likewise had one Mr. Ludlow, an assistant, and dwelling in Dorchester where I live, but the conclusion of the court was all peace and love, and no manifestations of anything to the contrary. Nay, Mr. Winthrop, having somewhat harshly and unadvisedly taken up a young man, a committee, came after in private to me, and excused himself, and professed to me that for that young man's part and mine, though we had much opposed him, yet the more he honored us both in his very heart, adding that he saw our aims and ends were good. So that court finished.

Then there was again a third court that year, in March last, chiefly called about Captain Endecott, his fact about the cross,* where I was again a committee, and a speaker, but not the chief, because Mr. Bellingham, a great man and a lawyer, was then a committee, and he was chief speaker. Now after I was chosen, great probability there was that the negative voice would be questioned, whereupon many lay hard upon me to give them my reasons in writing why I refused to yield it so as they had desired it. Well, I utterly refused a good while, till at length three men of our church came to me in the name of Mr. Warham (our pastor) to entreat it of me, saying that the ministers were to meet about it and he much desired my reasons before they met. And they pressed my conscience that I sinned if I refused. Hereupon having but now half a day's time to do it in, I notwithstanding condescended and gave (it being one sheet of paper) twelve reasons of my refusal to give them such a negative as they challenged. Now no sooner had Mr. Warham the thing, but he (without my privity) carries it to the ministers, presents it at their meeting, which for aught I ever heard was well approved by every man of them. Sure I am, four of them did come to me and give me large thanks and applause for the thing, and Mr. Cotton that had preached at first for the magistrates having a negative (though afterward yielded to a stopping voice only such as before I expressed) desired the paper, took it home, and finding some of the reasons to be grounded upon the patent, did (as he professed to me) in the simplicity of his heart send them to Mr. Winthrop to be resolved in some points of the patent, who as it seems by the sequel took such distaste at them and me for them that moved him to what follows.

The day of the court coming (for I knew not a tittle of aught until the minute of time that I was accused), in the morning he

---

* In 1634, John Endecott publicly cut the red cross from the English flag, on the grounds that it smacked of idolatry. [Editor]

possesseth the governor with my book and so soon as ever we were met, all the country being put out, save magistrates, committees, and ministers. The governor and some of the magistrates charged me for writing a book against the magistrates and so fell into such bitter terms against me as was much, if it had been proved. For Mr. Winthrop said of me, this is the man that had been the troubler of Israel, and that I was a worm (such an one as Mr. Hooker had spoke of in his sermon) and an underminer of the state. . . .

But now to the point. They charged my book for this and that. One thing was that I should say in it that I, by my fact, had freed the state so and so. Now this I utterly denied, [arguing] that [I] had not so written, and the book was read and so read as that it did expressly so speak. At which I was amazed and desired to see it myself, and I confess there wanted a comma, but that being added they all confessed the sense was quite otherwise and so were silenced in that point. And it was so plain without a comma that no man excepted at it till Mr. Winthrop, nor did any make such sense of it but he, and such as he had possessed. But then the main accusation which they stuck to was that I denied the assistants to be magistrates, and made them but ministers of justice etc., which charge I denied and affirmed I never did deny them to be magistrates, though I also did say they were ministers of justice and might without dishonor be called ministers as well as magistrates, both by the rule of the word, Romans 13:2, and the custom of London whose printed oath for all freemen styles the aldermen by that term and title; thus, "the mayor and all other ministers of the city," and so comprehends the aldermen. Third, "and by the rule of the patent," and "with respect to the patent," and "to General Courts assembled," for I had written thus in it (the reasons against the negative) "the patent makes their power ministerial according to the greater vote of the General Courts and not magisterial according to their own discretion." These were my very expressions, whereby I intended and meant that their power, call it ministerial or magisterial or magistratical (which you will), was not so great that they could do ought or hinder ought simply according to their own wills, but they must air and respect General Courts, which by patent consist of the whole company of freemen. And this is in very deed the magistrates' own judgment and the judgment of every man in the land that hath expressed himself, and yet for this, my expression, they would have me to affirm they were no magi-

strates, and these my words should be a proof of it. Other words
they took great offense at, but instances in no other but these two. I
confess there were some others that were very plain English, such
as to some is offensive, but I know little reason it should be to any,
sure I am it was not other than such as I would allow and most
desire from my meanest servant in any cause wherein he hath to
deal with me.

But much ado there was, and because it was adjudged by some it
would much please and pacify them if I would desire that it might
be burnt, at length for peace's sake, and to show how little I esteem
ought of mine, I said let the book be burnt if it please them, to give
them content I regarded it not. So that business ended, yet so that
they caused it to be recorded that such a thing was burnt as weak
and offensive.

But still they were not pacified towards me, but would have it be
that I denied them to be magistrates, and for the further proof of
that point Mr. Winthrop and Mr. Ludlow, of whom I spoke
before, did affirm to the court upon their credit (without oath)
that I had in the time of the last court (before when I had some
conference with them as I told you before about their power and
authority) said to them that the assistants were not magistrates. So
that though I had constantly denied it, and had also unknown to
me then a witness that can upon oath testify that my words to Mr.
Winthrop did not so import, nor were they any affirmation at all,
but merely thus: in answer to something he had said, which was
that assistants had power simply by their places over our persons,
goods, and lives, without any law of ours, I replied, "What, is it so?
I had thought your power had been so and not so."

The same witness also being an ear witness of my words to Mr.
Ludlow, and a very wise and godly young man (the same that I
spoke of before that Mr. Winthrop snubbed but after did somewhat recant) he being a brother of our church, suspecting that Mr.
Ludlow had forsworn himself (for he was not now a committee to
hear) did go in private (before our two ministers, myself, and
another) to this Mr. Ludlow and begin to deal with him for what
he had done, until that he purged himself, thus, by saying he did
not give in his witness upon oath.

And so, the conclusion of the matter was that I by way of
punishment of that whereof they charged me must be dissolved for
bearing any office within this jurisdiction for three years. . . .

Now followed the great General Court in May which continued two days for the whole body, and is not yet ended (though prorogued) for magistrates and committees. This General Court, one Mr. Haynes was chosen governor, a very godly man of Mr. Hooker's charge. Captain Endecott is left out partly for his business in the cross, and partly for other matters. So also our Mr. Ludlow is now no magistrate, though within six days before it was most probable and almost past question that he would be chosen governor (for we desire to change year by year the governorship, but the assistants more rarely, yet sometimes lest it be esteemed hereditary). Now he is neither governor nor assistant; so did Divine Providence dispose it. And I question whether he will ever be magistrate more, for many have taken great offense at him. The causes I forbear to relate, but they are both wise and godly men that are offended, and not many much sorry.

And to tell you the truth (for it is like you may hear of it from others), Mr. Winthrop had very many hands against him for being either governor (which some attempted) or assistant. The cause, it is like[ly] they know best that put in blanks. I suppose they were not his enemies nor none of the most simple. He hath lost much of that applause that he hath had (for indeed he was highly magnified) and I heard some say they put in blanks not simply because they would not have him a magistrate, but because they would admonish him thereby to look a little more circumspectly to himself. He is indeed a man of man, but he is but a man, and some say they have idolized him and do now confess their error. My opinion is that God will do him good by some, as also He hath done good to some by him, and that he is a godly man, and a worthy magistrate, notwithstanding some few passages at which some have stumbled. . . .

C. Format of a New Colony

The migration in the mid-1630s of several hundred settlers from the Bay Colony to the Connecticut River Valley marked New England's first major internal expansion. It also served as the Puritans' first opportunity to fashion a political structure entirely of their own making and based on the lessons of more than a decade in the American wilderness. Long deliberations resulted in the Fundamental Orders of Connecticut, completed in 1639, which served as the colony's constitution until 1662. Little is known about the drafting of the Orders, but it seems likely that among those who exerted an important influence were clergyman Thomas Hooker, magistrate John Haynes, and lawyer Roger Ludlow, with Ludlow probably responsible for the final version.

To a large extent, the Fundamental Orders paraphrased the basic political structure set forth in the Massachusetts charter. But it did more. Its opening paragraph stressed the holy purpose to which the drafters were committing themselves, and they made sure that their government would continue to reflect that purpose by requiring that the governor "be always a member of some approved congregation," and that freemanship be limited to those "having been admitted inhabitants of the town wherein they live"—a virtual guarantee that all voters would be of orthodox and upright character.

Source: Francis N. Thorpe, ed., *The Federal and State Constitution, Colonial Charters, and Other Organic Laws* (7 vols., Washington, 1909), I, 519–522.

Forasmuch as it hath pleased the Almighty God by the wise disposition of His divine providence so to order and dispose of things that we, the inhabitants and residents of Windsor, Hartford, and Wethersfield, are now cohabiting and dwelling in and upon the river of Connecticut and the lands thereunto adjoining; And well knowing where a people are gathered together the word of God requires that to maintain the peace and union of such a people there should be an orderly and decent government established according to God, to order and dispose of the affairs of the people at all seasons as occasion shall require; Do therefore associate and conjoin ourselves to be as one public state or commonwealth; And do for ourselves and our successors, and such as shall be adjoined to us at any time hereafter, enter into combination and confederation together to maintain and preserve the liberty and purity of the gospel of our Lord Jesus which we now profess, as also the discipline of the churches, which according to the truth of said gospel is now practiced among us; As also in other civil affairs to be guided and governed according to such laws, rules, orders, and decrees as shall be made, ordered, and decreed, as follows:

1. It is ordered, sentenced, and decreed that there shall be yearly two General Assemblies or Courts, the one the second Thursday in April, the other the second Thursday in September following. The first shall be called the Court of Election, wherein shall be yearly chosen from time to time so many magistrates and other public

officers as shall be found requisite. Whereof one to be chosen governor for the year ensuing and until another be chosen, and no other magistrate to be chosen for more than one year; provided always there be six chosen besides the governor, which being chosen and sworn according to an oath recorded for that purpose shall have power to administer justice according to the laws here established, and for want thereof according to the rule of the word of God; which choice shall be made by all that are admitted freemen and have taken the Oath of Fidelity, and do cohabit within this jurisdiction (having been admitted inhabitants by the major part of the town wherein they live) or the major part of such as shall be then present.

2. It is ordered, sentenced, and decreed that the election of the aforesaid magistrates shall be on this manner: every person present and qualified for choice shall bring in (to the persons deputized to receive them) one single paper with the name of him written in it whom he desires to have governor, and he that hath the greatest number of papers shall be governor for that year. And the rest of the magistrates or public officers to be chosen in this manner: the secretary for the time being shall first read the names of all that are to be put to choice and then shall severally nominate them distinctly, and everyone that would have the person nominated to be chosen shall bring in one single paper written upon, and he that would not have him chosen shall bring in a blank, and everyone that hath more written papers than blanks shall be a magistrate for that year, which papers shall be received and told by one or more that shall be then chosen by the Court and sworn to be faithful therein; but in case there should not be six chosen as aforesaid, besides the governor, out of those which are nominated, then he or they which have the most written papers shall be a magistrate or magistrates for the ensuing year, to make the foresaid number.

3. It is ordered, sentenced, and decreed that the secretary shall not nominate any person, nor shall any person be chosen newly into the magistracy which was not propounded in some General Court before, to be nominated the next election; and to that end it shall be lawful for each of the towns aforesaid by their deputies to nominate any two whom they conceive fit to be put to election; and the Court may add so many more as they judge requisite.

4. It is ordered, sentenced, and decreed that no person be chosen governor above once in two years, and that the governor be

always a member of some approved congregation, and formerly of the magistracy within this jurisdiction; and all the magistrates freemen of this commonwealth, and that no magistrate or other public officer shall execute any part of his or their office before they are severally sworn, which shall be done in the face of the Court, if they be present, and in case of absence by some, deputized for that purpose.

5. It is ordered, sentenced, and decreed that to the aforesaid Court of Election the several towns shall send their deputies, and when the elections are ended they may proceed in any public service, as at other Courts. Also the other General Court in September shall be for making of laws, and any other public occasion, which concerns the good of the commonwealth.

6. It is ordered, sentenced, and decreed that the governor shall either by himself or by the secretary, send out summons to the constables of every town for the calling of these two standing Courts, one month at least before their several times. And also if the governor and the greatest part of the magistrates see cause upon any special occasion to call a General Court, they may give order to the secretary so to do within fourteen days' warning, and if urgent necessity so require, upon a shorter notice, giving sufficient grounds for it to the deputies when they meet, or else be questioned for the same. And if the governor and major part of magistrates shall either neglect or refuse to call the two general standing Courts or either of them, as also at other times when the occasions of the commonwealth require, the freemen thereof, or the major part of them, shall petition to them so to do. If then it be either denied or neglected, the said freemen, or the major part of them, shall have power to give order to the constables of the several towns to do the same, and so may meet together and choose to themselves a moderator, and may proceed to do any act of power which any other General Court may.

7. It is ordered, sentenced, and decreed that after there are warrants given out for any of the said General Courts, the constable or constables of each town shall forthwith give notice distinctly to the inhabitants of the same, in some public assembly, or by going or sending from house to house, that at a place and time by him or them limited and set, they meet and assemble themselves together to elect and choose certain deputies to be at the General Court then following, to agitate the affairs of the

commonwealth; which said deputies shall be chosen by all that are admitted inhabitants in the several towns and have taken the Oath of Fidelity, provided that none be chosen a deputy for any General Court which is not a freeman of the commonwealth.

The foresaid deputies shall be chosen in the manner following: every person that is present and qualified as before expressed shall bring the names of such, written in several papers, as they desire to have chosen for that employment, and these three or four, more or less, being the number agreed on to be chosen for that time, that have the greatest number of papers written for them shall be deputies for that court, whose names shall be endorsed on the back side of the warrant and returned into the court, with the constable's or constables' hand unto the same.

8. It is ordered, sentenced, and decreed that Windsor, Hartford, and Wethersfield shall have power, each town, to send four of their freemen as deputies to every General Court, and whatsoever other towns shall be hereafter added to this jurisdiction, they shall send so many deputies as the Court shall judge meet, a reasonable proportion to the number of freemen that are in the said towns being to be attended therein; which deputies shall have the power of the whole town to give their votes and allowance to all such laws and orders as may be for the public good, and unto which the said towns are to be bound.

9. It is ordered and decreed that the deputies thus chosen shall have power and liberty to appoint a time and a place of meeting together before any General Court, to advise and consult of all such things as may concern the good of the public as also to examine their own elections, whether according to the order, and if they or the greatest part of them find any election to be illegal, they may seclude such for present from their meeting, and return the same and their reasons to the Court. And if it prove true, the Court may find the party or parties so intruding and the town, if they see cause, and give out a warrant to go to a new election in a legal way, either in part or in whole. Also the said deputies shall have power to find any that shall be disorderly at their meetings, or for not coming in due time or place according to appointment; and they may return the said fines into the Court if it be refused to be paid, and the treasurer to take notice of it, and to estreat or levy the same as he does other fines.

10. It is ordered, sentenced, and decreed that every General

Court, except such as through neglect of the governor and the greatest part of magistrates the freemen themselves do call, shall consist of the governor, or someone chosen to moderate the Court, and four other magistrates at least, with the major part of the deputies of the several towns legally chosen; and in case the freemen, or major part of them, through neglect or refusal of the governor and major part of the magistrates, shall call a Court, it shall consist of the major part of freemen that are present or their deputies, with a moderator chosen by them. In which said General Courts shall consist the supreme power of the commonwealth, and they only shall have power to make laws or repeal them, to grant levies, to admit of freemen, dispose of lands undisposed of to several towns or persons, and also shall have power to call either Court or magistrate or any other person whatsoever into question for any misdemeanor, and may for just causes displace or deal otherwise according to the nature of the offense; and also may deal in any other matter that concerns the good of this commonwealth, except election of magistates, which shall be done by the whole body of freemen.

In which Court the governor or moderator shall have power to order the Court to give liberty of speech, and silence unseasonable and disorderly speakings, to put all things to vote, and in case the vote be equal, to have the casting voice. But none of these Courts shall be adjourned or dissolved without the consent of the major part of the Court.

11. It is ordered, sentenced, and decreed that when any General Court upon the occasions of the commonwealth have agreed upon any sum or sums of money to be levied upon the several towns within this jurisdiction, that a committee be chosen to set out and appoint what shall be the proportion of every town to pay of the said levy, provided the committees be made up of an equal number out of each town.

D. Fundamentals of Law

At almost the same time that the colonies of Connecticut and New Haven were fashioning new frames of civil government, Massachusetts began to create an orderly legal code, which in turn would influence the other Puritan colonies. In March, 1635 John Winthrop noted in his Journal that "the deputies having conceived great danger to our estate, in regard that our magistrates, for want of positive laws, in many cases, might proceed according to their discretions, it was agreed that some men should be appointed to frame a body of laws, in resemblance to a Magna Charta. . . ." The committee formed in 1635 made little headway, but in the following year a second committee consisting of five magistrates and three clergymen produced a draft for consideration by the General Court.

Composed by John Cotton, "Moses his Judicialls" failed to gain official sanction; it proved too severe in its list of crimes, too aristocratic in its call for counselors with life tenure, and too Biblical in its overwhelming reliance on the Old Testament. Yet it was adopted for a time in New Haven, and many of its provisions found their way into subsequent Massachusetts codifications. Along with the Plymouth codification of 1636, "Moses his Judicialls" serves as a landmark in early Puritan efforts to spell out the political and legal guidelines of reformed societies.

It fell to Nathaniel Ward (1578–1652), an Ipswich clergyman with legal training in England, to produce the first acceptable formulation on Massachusetts law. Adopted in 1641, his Body of Liberties was less a codification of existing law than a bill of rights for citizens of Massachusetts. Among the "Rites, liberties, and priveledges" guaranteed in the document were many in advance of prevailing English law. Yet from the outset Ward's compilation was intended only as a temporary statement; the General Court soon appointed new committees to reconsider existing laws and to propose new ones "whereby we may manifest our utter disaffection to arbitrary government, & so all relations [may] be safely & sweetly directed & perfected. . . ." Not until 1648 could such a tall order be met.

In an important respect The Book of the Laws and Liberties Concerning the Inhabitants of the Massachusetts of 1648 served as a secular counterpart to the Cambridge Platform of the same year, for between them they showed to the world and to the settlers themselves what Winthrop had meant aboard the Arbella by "a due forme of Government both civill and ecclesiasticall." In the Cambridge Platform both lay and clerical architects had drawn up the New Zion's ecclesiastical blueprints; in the Laws and Liberties a very similar group had made major additions to the secular edifice originally framed by the colonial charter. Yet the drafters of the code—among them former lawyers such as John Winthrop, Nathaniel Ward, and Richard Bellingham, and prominent clergymen such as John Cotton, Thomas Shepard, and Richard Mather—proved amazingly flexible, for they produced a document that has won high praise from legal scholars for its improvement on English law and its willingness to overlook Biblical precedent for the sake of a workable set of laws.

Extracted below are the preface, in which the purpose of the code is expounded, the section on capital laws, which differs significantly from English provisions, and the section dealing with the church, which clearly reveals, as did the final section of the Cambridge Platform, the close partnership of church and state in the Puritan construct.

Source: *The Laws and Liberties of Massachusetts, Reprinted from the Copy of the 1648 Edition in the Henry E. Huntington Library* (Cambridge, Mass., 1929), A2f, 5–6, 18–20.

To Our Beloved Brethren and Neighbors
The Inhabitants of the Massachusetts, the Governor, Assistants and Deputies Assembled in the General Court of that
Jurisdiction with Grace and Peace in our
Lord Jesus Christ.

So soon as God had set political government among His people, Israel, He gave them a body of laws for judgment both in civil and criminal causes. These were brief and fundamental principles, yet withal so full and comprehensive as out of them clear deductions were to be drawn to all particular cases in future times. For a commonwealth without laws is like a ship without rigging and steerage. Nor is it sufficient to have principles or fundamentals, but these are to be drawn out into so many of their deductions as the time and condition of that people may have use of. And it is very unsafe and injurious to the body of the people to put them to learn their duty and liberty from general rules; nor is it enough to have laws except they be also just. Therefore among other privileges which the Lord bestowed upon His peculiar people, these He calls them specially to consider of, that God was nearer to them and their laws were more righteous than other nations. . . . [O]ur churches and civil state have been planted and grown up (like two twins) together, like that of Israel in the wilderness, by which we were put in mind (and had opportunity put into our hands) not only to gather our churches and set up the ordinances of Christ Jesus in them, according to the Apostolic pattern, by such light as the Lord graciously afforded us, but also withal to frame our civil polity and laws according to the rules of His most Holy Word, whereby each do help and strengthen other (the churches the civil authority, and the civil authority the churches) and so both prosper the better without such emulation and contention for privileges or priority as have proved misery (if not ruin) of both in some other places.

For this end about nine years since we used the help of some of the elders of our churches to compose a model of the judicial laws of Moses, with such other cases as might be referred to them, with intent to make use of them in composing our laws, but not to have them published as the laws of this jurisdiction; nor were they voted in Court. For that book entitled, *The Liberties Etc.*, published about seven years since (which contains also many laws and orders both for civil and criminal causes) and is commonly, though without ground, reported to be our fundamentals that we own as established by authority of this Court, and that after three years' experience and general approbation. And accordingly we have inserted them into this volume under the several heads to which they belong, yet not as fundamentals for divers of them have since been repealed or altered and more may justly be (at least) amended hereafter as further experience shall discover defects or inconveniences, for *Nihil simul natum et perfectum*. The same must we say of the present volume; we have not published it as a perfect body of laws sufficient to carry on the government established for future times, nor could it be expected that we should promise such a thing. For if it be no disparagement to the wisdom of that High Court of Parliament in England that in four hundred years they could not so compile their laws and regulate proceedings in courts of justice etc., but that they had still new work to do of the same kind almost every Parliament, there can be no just cause to blame a poor colony (being unfurnished of lawyers and statesmen) that in eighteen years hath produced no more nor better rules for a good and settled government than this book holds forth. Nor have you (our brethren and neighbors) any cause, whether you look back upon our native country or take your observation by other states and commonwealths in Europe, to complain of such as you have employed in this service, for the time which hath been spent in making laws and repealing and altering them so often, nor of the charge which the country hath been put to for those occasions, the civilian gives you a satisfactory reason of such continual alterations, additions etc. *Crescit in Orbe dolus*.

These laws, which were made successively in divers former years we have reduced under several heads in an alphabetical method that so they might the more readily be found, and that the divers laws concerning one matter being placed together, the scope and intent of the whole and of every of them might the more easily be apprehended. We must confess we have not been so exact in placing every law under its most proper title as we might and would have been. The reason was our hasty endeavor to satisfy your longing expectation, and frequent complaints for want of such a volume to be published in print wherein (upon every occasion) you might readily see the rule which you ought to walk by. And in this (we hope) you will find satisfaction, by the help of the references under the several heads, and the table which we have added in the end. For such laws and orders as are not of general concernment we have not put them into this book, but they remain still in force and are to be seen in the book of the Records of the Court, but all general laws not here inserted nor mentioned to be still of force are to be accounted repealed.

You have called us from amongst the rest of our brethren and given us power to make these laws. We must now call upon you to see them executed, remembering that old and true proverb, "The execution of the law is the life of the law." If one sort of you, viz., non-freemen, should object that you had no hand in calling us to this work and therefore think yourselves not bound to obedience, etc., we answer that a subsequent or implicit consent is of like force in this case, as an expressed precedent power: for in putting your persons and estates into the protection and way of subsistance held forth and exercised within this jurisdiction, you do tacitly submit to this government and to all the wholesome laws thereof, and so is the common repute in all nations, and that upon this maxim: *Qui sentit commodum sentire debet et onus.*

If any of you meet with some law that seems not to tend to your particular benefit, you must consider that laws are made with respect to the whole people and not to each particular person, and obedience to them must be yielded with respect to the common welfare, not to thy private advantage. And as thou yieldest obedience to the law for common good, but to thy disadvantage, so another must observe some other law for thy good, though to his own damage. Thus must we be content to bear another's burden and so fulfill the law of Christ.

That distinction which is put between the laws of God and the laws of men becomes a snare to many as it is misapplied in the ordering of their obedience to civil authority, for when the authority is of God and that in way of an ordinance, Romans 13:1, and when the administration of it is according to deductions and rules gathered from the Word of God and the clear light of nature in civil nations, surely there is no human law that tendeth to common good (according to those principles) but the same is mediately a law of God, and that in way of an ordinance which all are to submit unto and that for conscicncc sakc. Romans 13:5.

By order of the General Court,

INCREASE NOWELL, Secretary . . .

CAPITAL LAWS

1 If any man after legal conviction shall have or worship any other God but the Lord God, he shall be put to death. Exodus 22:20; Deuteronomy 13:6, and 10; Deuteronomy 17:2, 6.

2 If any man or woman be a witch, that is, hath or consulteth with a familiar spirit, they shall be put to death. Exodus 22:18; Leviticus 20:27; Deuteronomy 18:10, 11.

3 If any person within this jurisdiction, whether Christian or pagan, shall wittingly and willingly presume to blaspheme the Holy name of God, Father, Son, or Holy Ghost, with direct, express, presumptious, or high-handed blasphemy, either by willful or obstinate denying the true God, or His Creation, or government of the world, or shall curse God in like manner or reproach the Holy religion of God as if it were but a politic device to keep ignorant men in awe, or shall utter any other kind of blasphemy of the like nature and degree, they shall be put to death. Leviticus 24:15, 16.

4 If any person shall commit any willful murther, which is man-slaughter, committed upon premeditate malice, hatred, or cruelty not in a man's necessary and just defense, nor by mere casualty against his will, he shall be put to death. Exodus 21:12, 13; Numbers 35:31.

5 If any person slayeth another suddenly in his anger, or cruelty of passion, he shall be put to death. Leviticus 24:17; Numbers 35:20, 21.

6 If any person shall slay another through guile, either by poisoning or other such devilish practice, he shall be put to death. Exodus 21:14.

7 If any man or woman shall lie with any beast, or brute creature, by carnal copulation, they shall surely be put to death; and the

beast shall be slain and buried, and not eaten. Leviticus 20:15, 16.

8 If any man lieth with mankind as he lieth with a woman, both of them have committed abomination; they both shall surely be put to death, unless the one party were forced or be under fourteen years of age, in which case he shall be severely punished. Leviticus 20:13.

9 If any person commit adultery with a married or espoused wife, the adulterer and adulteress shall surely be put to death. Leviticus 20:19 and 18:20; Deuteronomy 22:23, 27.

10 If any man stealeth a man or mankind, he shall surely be put to death. Exodus 21:16.

11 If any man rise up by false witness wittingly and of purpose to take away any man's life, he shall be put to death. Deuteronomy 19:16, 18:16.

12 If any man shall conspire and attempt any invasion, insurrection, or public rebellion against our commonwealth, or shall endeavor to surprise any town or towns, fort or forts therein, or shall treacherously and perfidiously attempt the alteration and subversion of our frame of polity or government fundamentally, he shall be put to death. Numbers 16; 2 Samuel 3:2; 2 Samuel 18; 2 Samuel 20.

13 If any child or children above sixteen years old and of sufficient understanding shall curse or smite their natural father or mother, he or they shall be put to death, unless it can be sufficiently testified that the parents have been very unchristianly negligent in the education of such children, or so provoked them by extreme and cruel correction that they have been forced thereunto to preserve themselves from death or maiming. Exodus 21:17; Leviticus 20:9; Exodus 21:15.

14 If a man have a stubborn or rebellious son of sufficient years and understanding, viz., sixteen years of age, which will not obey the voice of his father or the voice of his mother, and that when they have chastened him will not harken unto them, then shall his father and mother, being his natural parents, lay hold on him and bring him to the Magistrates assembled in Court, and testify unto them that their son is stubborn and rebellious and will not obey their voice and chastisement, but lives in sundry notorious crimes; such a son shall be put to death. Deuteronomy 21:20, 21.

15 If any man shall ravish any maid or single woman, committing carnal copulation with her by force, against her own will, that is above the age of ten years, he shall be punished either with death or with some other grievous punishment, according to circumstances as the judges or General Court shall determine. [1641] . . .

ECCLESIASTICALS

1 All the people of God within this jurisdiction who are not in a church way, and be orthodox in judgment and not scandalous in life, shall have full liberty to gather themselves into a church estate, provided they do it in a Christian way with due observation of the rules of Christ revealed in His word, provided also that the General Court doth not, nor will hereafter, approve of any such companies of men as shall join in any pretended way of church fellowship unless they shall acquaint the magistrates and the elders of the neighbor churches where they intend to join, and have their approbation therein.

2 And it is farther ordered that no person being a member of any church which shall be gathered without the approbation of the Magistrates and the said churches shall be admitted to the freedom of this commonwealth.

3 Every church hath free liberty to exercise all the ordinances of God according to the rules of the scripture.

4 Every church hath free liberty of election and ordination of all her officers from time to time, provided they be able, pious, and orthodox.

5 Every church hath also free liberty of admission, recommendation, dismission, and expulsion or deposal of their officers and members upon due cause, with free exercise of the discipline and censures of Christ according to the rules of His word.

6 No injunction shall be put upon any church, church officer, or member in point of doctrine, worship, or discipline, whether for substance or circumstance besides the institutions of the Lord.

7 Every church of Christ hath freedom to celebrate days of fasting and prayer and of thanksgiving according to the word of God.

8 The elders of churches also have liberty to meet monthly, quarterly, or otherwise in convenient numbers and places, for

conference and consultations about Christian and church questions and occasions.

9 All churches also have liberty to deal with any their members in a church way that are in the hands of justice, so it be not to retard and hinder the course thereof.

10 Every church hath liberty to deal with any Magistrate, Deputy of Court, or other officer whatsoever that is a member of theirs in a church way, in case of apparent and just offense, given in their places, so it be done with due observance and respect.

11 We also allow private meetings for edification in religion amongst Christians of all sorts of people, so it be without just offense, both for number, time, place, and other circumstances.

12 For the preventing and removing of error and offense that may grow and spread in any of the churches in this jurisdiction, and for the preserving of truth and peace in the several churches within themselves, and for the maintenance and exercise of brotherly communion amongst all churches in the country: It is allowed and ratified by the authority of this Court as a lawful liberty of the Churches of Christ that once in every month of the year (when the season will bear it) it shall be lawful for the Ministers and Elders of the churches near adjoining, together with any other of the brethren, with the consent of the churches, to assemble by course in every several church one after another to the intent that after the preaching of the word by such a Minister as shall be requested thereto by the Elders of the church where the assembly is held, the rest of the day may be spent in public Christian conference about the discussing and resolving of any such doubts and cases of conscience concerning matter of doctrine, or worship, or government of the church as shall be propounded by any of the brethren of that church; with leave also to any other brother to propound his objections or answers for further satisfaction according to the word of God, provided that the whole action be guided and moderated by the Elders of the church where the assembly is held, or by such others as they shall appoint. And that nothing be concluded and imposed by way of authority from one or more churches upon another, but only by way of brotherly conference and consultations, that the truth may be searched out to the satisfying of every man's conscience in the sight of God according to

His word; and because such an assembly and the work thereof cannot be duly attended if other lectures be held the same week, it is therefore agreed with the consent of the churches, that in what week such an assembly is held all the lectures in all the neighboring churches for the week days shall be forborne, that so the public service of Christ in this assembly may be transacted with greater diligence and attention. [1641]

13 Forasmuch as the open contempt of God's word and messengers thereof is the desolating sin of civil states and churches, and that the preaching of the word by those whom God doth send is the chief ordinary means ordained of God for the converting, edifying, and saving the souls of the elect through the presence and power of the Holy Ghost thereunto promised, and that the ministry of the word is set up by God in His churches for those holy ends, and according to the respect or contempt of the same and of those whom God hath set apart for His own work and employment, the weal or woe of all Christian states is much furthered and promoted, it is therefore ordered and decreed: That if any Christian (so called) within this jurisdiction shall contemptuously behave himself toward the word preached or the messengers thereof called to dispense the same in any congregation, when he doth faithfully execute his service and office therein according to the will and word of God, either by interrupting him in his preaching or by charging him falsely with any error which he hath not taught in the open face of the church, or like a son of Korah cast upon his true doctrine or himself any reproach, to the dishonour of the Lord Jesus who hath sent him and to the disparagement of that His Holy ordinance, and making God's ways contemptible and ridiculous; that every such person or persons (whatsoever censure the Church may pass) shall for the first scandal be convented and reproved openly by the Magistrate at some lecture, and bound to their good behavior. And if a second time they break forth into the like contemptuous carriages, they shall either pay five pounds to the public treasury, or stand two hours openly upon a block or stool four foot high on a lecture day with a paper fixed on his breast, written in capital letters, "AN OPEN AND OBSTINATE CONTEMNER OF GOD'S HOLY ORDINANCES," that others may fear and be ashamed of breaking out into the like wickedness. [1646]

14 It is ordered and decreed by this Court and authority thereof that wheresoever the ministry of the word is established according to the order of the Gospel throughout this jurisdiction every person shall duly resort and attend thereunto respectively upon the Lord's day and upon such public fast days and days of thanksgiving as are to be generally kept by the appointment of authority. And if any person within this jurisdiction shall without just and necessary cause withdraw himself from hearing the public ministry of the word after due means of conviction used, he shall forfeit for his absence from every such public meeting five shillings. All such offenses to be heard and determined by any one Magistrate or more from time to time. [1646]

15 Forasmuch as the peace and prosperity of churches and members thereof, as well as civil rights and liberties are carefully to be maintained, it is ordered by this Court and decreed: that the civil authority here established hath power and liberty to see the peace, ordinances, and rules of Christ be observed in every church according to His word. As also to deal with any church member in a way of civil justice notwithstanding any church relation, office, or interest, so it be done in a civil and not in an ecclesiastical way. Nor shall any church censure, degrade, or depose any man from any civil dignity, office, or authority he shall have in the commonwealth. [1641]

16 Forasmuch as there are many inhabitants in divers towns who leave their several habitations and thereby draw much of the income of their estates into other towns, whereby the ministry is much neglected, it is therefore ordered by this Court and the authority thereof: that from henceforth all lands, cattle, and other estates of any kind whatsoever shall be liable to be rated to all common charges whatsoever, either for the church, town, or commonwealth in the same place where the estate is from time to time. And to the end there may be a convenient habitation for the use of the ministry in every town in this jurisdiction to remain to posterity, it is decreed by the authority of this Court that where the major part of the inhabitants (according to the order of regulating valid town acts) shall grant, build, or purchase such habitation, it shall be good in law and the particular sum upon each person assessed by just rate shall be duly paid according as in other cases of town rates; provided always that such grant, deed of purchase, and the deed of gift there-

upon to the use of a present preaching Elder and his next successor, and so from time to time to his successors, be entered in the town book and acknowledged before a Magistrate and recorded in the Shire court. [1647]

17. Economic Order

During the reigns of Elizabeth and the first two Stuarts, England suffered from widespread economic unrest, which hit some areas with particular severity in the years of Puritan migration. Depressions came with sickening frequency: from 1619 to 1624, 1629 to 1631, and again from 1637 to 1640. In between there were local depressions which heightened unemployment, famine, and beggary. But until the 1630s Englishmen had little opportunity to escape; migration to the continent meant severing most ties with their homeland, while Ireland and Virginia appeared too primitive or hazardous to justify taking women and children. A new alternative appeared when the small colony at Plymouth demonstrated the viability of life in New England.

Although modern scholars are reluctant to explain the settlement of New England on primarily economic grounds, there is no doubt that declining wages, increasing costs, and unstable incomes encouraged many devout Puritans, and many non-Puritans, to believe that God meant them to join the experiment in the New World. The autobiographical writings of New Englanders invariably mention economic distress as an impetus to migration, and there seems little doubt that in their land-hunger England's yeoman class seized avidly the opportunity to gain freehold title to handsome tracts of land that much resembled their homeland. Many also jumped at the chance to earn high wages or set up shops of their own in the rapidly expanding colonies. It is therefore not surprising that Winthrop gave attention to economic matters in his "A Modell of Christian Charity," or that he and other leaders of early New England took steps to curb threats to New England's economic stability.

A. A Breach of Economic Ethics

In an attempt to prevent inflation and to limit profit to seemly levels in a society beset with shortages of labor and goods, the Puritan colonies passed frequent restrictions on prices, wages, and conditions of commerce. Some regulations promoted business development, such as temporary monopolies to encourage certain kinds of trade, or tax exemptions to encourage the building of mills, mines, and tanneries.

Other regulations limited economic development—at least from a laissez-faire perspective—such as price and wage ceilings, and limitations on the sale of luxury items. There were also unwritten rules, ethical standards to be adhered to by all who feared the censure of church and state. Governor Winthrop described in his Journal the fate of a man who ignored, perhaps unwittingly, the community's economic precepts.

Source: James K. Hosmer, ed. *Winthrop's Journal "History of New England," 1630–1649* (2 vols., New York, 1908), I, 315–318.

[9 November 1639] At a general court holden at Boston, great complaint was made of the oppression used in the country in sale of foreign commodities; and Mr. Robert Keayne, who kept a shop in Boston, was notoriously above others observed and complained of. And, being convented, he was charged with many particulars; in some, for taking above six-pence in the shilling profit; in some above eight-pence; and, in some small things, above two for one; and being hereof convict (as appears by the records), he was fined £200, which came thus to pass. The deputies considered, apart, of his fine, and set it at £200; the magistrates agreed but to £100. So, the court being divided, at length it was agreed that his fine should be £200, but he should pay but £100, and the other should be respited to the further consideration of the next General Court. By this means the magistrates and deputies were brought to an accord which otherwise had not been likely, and so much trouble might have grown and the offender escaped censure. For the cry of the country was so great against oppression, and some of the elders and magistrates had declared such detestation of the corrupt practice of this man (which was the more observable because he was wealthy and sold dearer than most other tradesmen, and for that he was of ill report for the like covetous practice in England, that incensed the deputies very much against him). And sure the course was very evil, especial circumstances considered: (1) he being an ancient professor of the gospel; (2) a man of eminent parts; (3) wealthy, and having but one child; (4) having come over for conscience' sake and for the advancement of the gospel here; (5) having been formerly dealt with and admonished, both by private friends and also by some of the magistrates and elders, and having promised reformation, being a member of a church and commonwealth now in their infancy and under the curious observation of all churches and civil states in the world.

These added much aggravation to his sin in the judgment of all men of understanding. Yet most of the magistrates (though they discerned of the offense clothed with all these circumstances) would have been more moderate in their censure: (1) because there was no law in force to limit or direct men in point of profit in their trade; (2) because it is the common practice in all countries for men to make use of advantages for raising the prices of their commodities; (3) because, though he were chiefly aimed at, yet he was not alone in this fault; (4) because all men through the country, in sale of cattle, corn, labor, etc., were guilty of the like excess in prices; (5) because a certain rule could not be found out for an equal rate between buyer and seller, though much labor had been bestowed in it, and divers laws had been made, which, upon experience, were repealed, as being neither safe nor equal. Lastly, and especially, because the law of God appoints no other punishment but double restitution; and, in some cases, as where the offender freely confesseth and brings his offering, only half added to the principal. After the court had censured him, the church of Boston called him also in question, where (as before he had done in the court) he did, with tears, acknowledge and bewail his covetous and corrupt heart, yet making some excuse for many of the particulars which were charged upon him, as partly by pretense of ignorance of the true price of some wares, and chiefly by being misled by some false principles, as (1) that if a man lost in one commodity he might help himself in the price of another; (2) that if, through want of skill or other occasion, his commodity cost him more than the price of the market in England, he might then sell it for more than the price of the market in New England, etc. These things gave occasion to Mr. Cotton, in his public exercise the next lecture day, to lay open the error of such false principles, and to give some rules of direction in the case.

Some false principles were these:

1. That a man might sell as dear as he can, and buy as cheap as he can.

2. If a man lose by casualty of sea, etc., in some of his commodities, he may raise the price of the rest.

3. That he may sell as he bought, though he paid too dear, etc., and though the commodity be fallen, etc.

4. That, as a man may take the advantage of his own skill or ability, so he may of another's ignorance or necessity.

5. Where one gives time for payment, he is to take like recompense of one as of another.

The rules for trading were these:

1. A man may not sell above the current price, i.e., such a price as is usual in the time and place, and as another (who knows the worth of the commodity) would give for it, if he had occasion to use it; as that is called current money, which every man will take, etc.

2. When a man loseth in his commodity for want of skill, etc., he must look at it as his own fault or cross, and therefore must not lay it upon another.

3. Where a man loseth by casualty of sea, or, etc., it is a loss cast upon himself by providence, and he may not ease himself of it by casting it upon another; for so a man should seem to provide against all providences, etc., that he should never lose. But where there is a scarcity of the commodity, there men may raise their price, for now it is a hand of God upon the commodity and not the person.

4. A man may not ask any more for his commodity than his selling price, as Ephron to Abraham, the land is worth thus much.

The cause being debated by the church, some were earnest to have him excommunicated; but the most thought an admonition would be sufficient. Mr. Cotton opened the causes, which required excommunication, out of that in 1 Cor. 5:11. The point now in question was whether these actions did declare him to be such a covetous person, etc. Upon which he showed that it is neither the habit of covetousness (which is in every man in some degree) nor simply the act that declares a man to be such, but when it appears that a man sins against his conscience, or the very light of nature, and when it appears in a man's whole conversation. But Mr. Keayne did not appear to be such, but rather upon an error in his judgment, being led by false principles; and, beside, he is otherwise liberal, as in his hospitality, and in church communion, etc. So, in the end, the church consented to an admonition.

B. Apologia

In his "Last Will and Testament of Me . . ." Robert Keayne (c. 1595–1656) gave his version of the episode that had cast so dark a cloud over his life. Keayne's side of the story reveals not only the coercive tendencies of the Puritan church and state but also the tensions generated in the economic sphere by the Puritan tradition. A desire to keep the economy well ordered had run headlong into the individual's need to make sufficient profit, and into his responsibility to follow a civil calling with vigor and dedication. Keayne's story reflects as well the difficulty of enforcing economic order in a frontier society where goods and services could hardly be measured by ordinary standards.

Source: [Tenth] Report of the Record Commissioners of the City of Boston, [Miscellaneous Papers] (Boston, 1886), 30–31.

I did not then nor dare not now go about to justify all my actions. I know God is righteous and doth all upon just grounds, though men may mistake in their grounds and proceedings, counsel have erred, and courts may err, and a faction may be too hard and outvote the better or more discerning part. I know the errors of my life. The failings in my trade and otherwise have been many. Therefore from God it [censure by the court] was most just. Though it had been much more severe I dare not so open my mouth against it, nor never did as I remember, but to justify Him. Yet I dare not say, nor did I ever think (as far as I can call to mind), that the censure was just and righteous from men. Was the price of a bridle, not for taking but only asking, 2 s. for it which cost here 20 d. such a heinous sin, which have since been commonly sold and still are for 2 s. 6 d. and 3 s. or more, though worse in kind? Was it such a heinous sin to sell 2 or 3 dozen of great gold buttons for 2 s. 10 d. per dozen that cost 2 s. 2 d. ready money in London and bought at the best hand, such a heinous sin, as I showed to many by my invoice (though I could not find it at that instant when the Court desired to see it) and since was confirmed by special testimony from London? And yet the buttons [were] not paid for when the complaint was made, nor I think not yet; neither did the complaint come from him that bought and owed them, nor with

his knowledge or consent, as he hath since affirmed, but merely
from the spleen and envy of another, whom it did nothing concern.
Was this so great an offense? Indeed, that it might be made so,
some out of their ignorance would needs say they were copper and
not worth 9 d. per dozen. But these were weak grounds to pass
heavy censures upon.

Was the selling of 6 d. nails for 8 d. per lb. and 8 d. nails for 10
d. per lb. such a crying and oppressing sin? Though as I remember
it was above two years before he that bought them paid me for
them (and not paid for if I forgot not) when he made that quarreling exception and unrighteous complaint in the Court against me
(he then being of the Court himself) as if I had altered and corrupted my book in adding more to the price than I had set down
for them at first delivery, which if I had set down 8 d. for that after
2 years' forbearance, which I would have sold for 7 d. if he had paid
me presently. I think it had been a more honest act in me than it
was in him that promised or at least pretended to pay me presently
that he might get them at a lower price than a man could well live
upon, and when he had got my goods into his hands to keep me 2
or 3 years without my money. And though all that while there was
no fault found at the prices, but when he could for shame keep the
money no longer, yet he will requite it with a censure in the Court.
For my own part, as I did ever think it an ungodly act in him, so I
do think in my conscience that it had been more just in the Court
to have censured him than me for this thing, though this was the
chiefest crime alleged and most powerfully carried against me, and
other things drawn in to make this the more probable and to help
to make up a censure, as some farthing skeins of thread, etc.

But the truth of the thing was this: This man sent unto me for 2
or three thousand of 6 d. nails. I sent to him a bag full of that sort,
just as them came to me from Mr. Foote's in London, never
opened nor altered by me. These I entered into my book at 8 d. per
lb., thinking he would have paid me in a very short time. It fell out
that these nails proved somewhat too little for his work. He sent
them again and desired me to let him have bigger for them. I took
them and sent him a bag of 8 d. nails of the same quantity at 10 d.
per lb. Now because I was loath to alter my book and to make a
new charge I only altered the figures in my book and made the
figure of 6 a figure of 8 for 8 d. nails and the figure of 8 that
before stood for 8 d. a lb. I made 10 d. Now though he knew of the

change of these 6 d. nails for 8 d. (which I had quite forgot through my many other occasions and the length of time that they had stood in the book unpaid) yet this he concealed from me and from the Court also. But to make the matter more odious he challenged me and my book of falsehood, supposing that because he had kept me so long from my money therefore I had made the price higher by altering the figures than at first I had charged them down, and that I required 10 d. per lb. for 6 d. nails. And so [he] carried it in the Court, where he was the more easily believed because he was a magistrate and of esteem therein, though it was a most unjust and untrue charge, and only from his own imagination, till I cleared it by good testimony from an honest man in his own town whom he sent for the first nails and did so bring them back and received the bigger nails for them. [This man] came to me of his own accord and told me he heard there was a difference between such a man and I, which he said he could clear, and related the matter fully to me, which I was very glad to hear, which brought all things to my mind: what was the ground of altering the figures in the book, which before I had forgot though I saw it was done with my own hand. And this was the very truth of the thing.

I presently acquainted our honored governor Mr. John Winthrop and some others who were very glad that the truth of that reproach was so unexpectedly discovered and cleared. Many if not most of the Court was satisfied with it, and saw the thing to be very plain in my debt book. But the party himself would not be satisfied, but [claimed] they were 6 d. nails set down at 10 d. per lb., though himself saw the figure of 8 as plain as the figure of 10.

Now I leave it to the world to judge, or to any impartial man, or any that hath understanding in trade, whether this was a just offense or so crying a sin that I had such cause to be so penitent for (this being the chief, and pressed on with so great aggravation by my opposers) except it should be that my actions, innocent in themselves, were misconstrued. And I knew not how to help myself, especially considering it was no oppressing price but usual with others at that time to sell the like so, and since for almost half as much more, frequently as I think all know, and yet both given and taken without exception, or at least without public complaint. Yea, and the same gentleman himself, since he hath turned merchant and trader, seems to have lost his former tenderness of

conscience that he had when he [was] a buyer and not to be
so scrupulous in his own gains. . . .

18. Social Order

The Puritan tradition that originated in England and found full expression in America went far beyond political and economic regulation. It
went also into personal behavior of many kinds, for every sinner
threatened the whole society: God's wrath could be unleashed at communities as well as individuals; the community's covenant with God
made each member responsible for the purity of the whole. Social regulation was not, of course, a uniquely Puritan formulation. Even without
Puritan prodding, England's Crown and Parliament had often taken it
upon themselves to outlaw certain kinds of social behavior (drunken-
ness and prostitution for example) and encourage others (family responsibility and vocational diligence); the Puritan differed from his
fellow countrymen in intensity and scope, not in principle. As a
contemporary poet put it:

> A Puritan, is he . . . that doth the selfe-accusing Oath refuse:
>   that hates the Ale-house, and a Stage, and Stews.
> A Puritan, is he, whose austere life,
>   will not admit a Mistress and a Wife.
> That when his betters sweares, doth bite the lip;
>   nor wilbe drunken for good fellowship.
> That wisheth for the amendment of the best:
>   blames the least ill, and doth the worst detest.

This characteristic of Puritanism—of condemning minor infractions of
social decorum—may have been the surface reflection of the Puritans'
more profound emphasis on reformation of the individual soul. In any
event, when given a chance in the New England colonies to practice
what they could only preach in the mother country, the Puritans
showed a vigor in social restrictions that finds only weak parallels in the
other British colonies and in England.

A. Social Restrictions

Drawing in many cases upon English examples, in other instances upon
Biblical precedent, the governments of the Puritan colonies passed
scores of restrictions on the daily habits of their citizens. Some of the
laws, such as those limiting finery and hair styles, seem to have been
ignored by both the magistrates and the public, even by the elders'
wives. Other laws, such as those restricting the sale and consumption of

alcoholic beverages, were frequently violated but not with impunity, as abundant court entries testify. The following regulations are representative of Puritan society's efforts to regulate the daily habits of its saints and sinners alike.

Source: Nathaniel B. Shurtleff, ed., *Records of the Governor and Company of the Massachusetts Bay in New England* (5 vols., Boston, 1853–1854), I, 84, 126; V, 240–241; J. Hammond Trumbull, ed., *Public Records of the Colony of Connecticut* (15 vols., Hartford, 1850), I, 8, 47–48, 78; Nathaniel B. Shurtleff and David Pulsifer, eds., *Records of the Colony of New Plymouth* (12 vols., Boston, 1855–1861), X, 53; Charles J. Hoadly, ed., *Records of the Colony . . . of New Haven* (2 vols., Hartford, 1857–1858), II, 596–597, 605.

It is . . . ordered that all persons whatsoever that have cards, dice, or tables in their houses shall make away with them before the next Court, under pain of punishment.

(Massachusetts Bay, 22 March 1631)

The Court, taking into consideration the great, superfluous, and unnecessary expenses occasioned by reason of some new and immodest fashions, as also the ordinary wearing of silver, gold, and silk laces, girdles, hatbands, etc., hath therefore ordered that no person, either man or woman, shall hereafter make or buy any apparel, either woolen, silk, or linen, with any lace on it, silver, gold, silk, or thread, under the penalty of forfeiture of such clothes, etc.

Also, that no person, either man or woman, shall make or buy any slashed clothes, other than one slash in each sleeve, and another in the back; also, all cutworks, embroidered or needlework caps, bands, and rayles are forbidden hereafter to be made and worn, under the aforesaid penalty; also, all gold or silver girdles, hatbands, belts, beaver hats are prohibited to be bought and worn hereafter, under the aforesaid penalty, etc.

Moreover, it is agreed, if any man shall judge the wearing of any the forenamed particulars, new fashions, or long hair, or anything of the like nature, to be uncomely, or prejudicial to the common good, and the party offending reform not the same upon notice given him, that then the next Assistant, being informed thereof, shall have power to bind the party so offending to answer it at the next Court, if the case so requires; provided, and it is the meaning of the Court, that men and women shall have liberty to wear out such apparel as they are now provided of (except the immoderate great sleeves, slashed apparel, immoderate great rayles, long wings, etc.); this order to take place a fortnight after the publishing thereof.   (Massachusetts Bay, 3 September 1634)

It is ordered that no young man that is neither married nor hath any servant and be no public officer shall keep house by himself, without consent of the town where he lives first had, under pain of 20s per week.

It is ordered that no master of a family shall give habitation or entertainment to any young man to sojourn in his family but by the allowance of the inhabitants of the said town where he dwells, under the like penalty of 20s per week.

(Connecticut, 21 February 1637)

Forasmuch as many persons intangle themselves by rash and inconsiderate contracts for their future joining in marriage covenant, to the great trouble and grief of themselves and their friends; for the avoiding whereof it is ordered that whosoever intend to join themselves in marriage covenant shall cause that their purpose of contract to be published in some public place and at some public meeting in the several towns where such persons dwell, at the least eight days before they enter into such contract. . . .

(Connecticut, 10 April 1640)

Whereas divers persons depart from amongst us and take up their abode with the Indians in a profane course of life; for the preventing whereof it is ordered that whatsoever person or persons that now inhabiteth or shall inhabit within this jurisdiction and shall depart from us and settle or join with the Indians, that they shall suffer three years' imprisonment at least in the house of correction and undergo such further censure by fine or corporal punishment as the particular Court shall judge meet to inflict in such cases.   (Connecticut, 1 December 1642)

Whereas there is great abuse in taking of tobacco in very uncivil manner in the streets and dangerously in outhouses, as barns, stalls, about haystacks, corn stacks, and other places, it is therefore enacted by this Court that if any person or persons shall be found or seen hereafter taking tobacco publicly in the open streets of any town (unless it be soldiers in the time of their training), or in and about barns, stalls, haystacks, cornstacks, hay yards, or other such places or outhouses, that every such person or persons so offending shall forfeit and pay to the town's use for the first default 12d, for the second 2s, and so for every such default afterwards 2s. . . .

(Plymouth, 20 October 1646)

And it is further ordered that every person so licensed to draw and sell strong beer, ale, wine, or strong liquor do see and take care that good order and all rules of sobriety be duly attended in his course, and house, and about the same; and that he neither see nor suffer any to be drunken or to drink excessively, or to continue tipling above the space of an hour, or at unseasonable times, or after nine of the clock at night without weighty cause; nor that any children or servants without the consent of parents or governors be permitted to sit or stay there drinking or unnecessarily to spend their time there, especially at late or unseasonable hours; but that he duly complain to authority, that all such disorders may be seasonably suppressed, under the penalty of five shillings for the first offense, with such increase of fine for a continued slightness or neglect as the Court shall determine.

Provided notwithstanding, that such licensed persons may entertain strangers, land travelers, seafaring men, lodgers, or others for their necessary occasions, refreshment, or during meals, when they come from their journeys or voyages, or when they prepare for their journey or voyage in the night, or next day early, or such, may continue in such houses of common entertainment as their business and lawful occasions may require, so that there be no disorder among them.

But every person found drunken, namely so that he be thereby for the present bereaved or disabled in the use of his understanding, appearing in his speech, gesture, or carriage, in any of the said houses or elsewhere, shall forfeit for the first time ten shillings; and for excess of drinking, or continuing in any such place unnecessarily at unseasonable times, or after nine of the clock at night, five shillings, and for continuing tipling there above the space of an hour, two shillings sixpence for the first offense, and for the second offense in each kind, and for all further disorder, quarreling, or disturbance, whether a first or second time, such further fine or punishment as the Court shall determine. (New Haven, ca.1656)

Whosoever shall profane the Lord's day, or any part of it, either by sinful servile work, or by unlawful sport, recreation, or otherwise, whether willfully, or in a careless neglect, shall be duly punished by fine, imprisonment, or corporally according to the nature and measure of the sin and offense. But if the Court upon examination, by clear and satisfying evidence, find that the sin was proudly, presumptuously, and with a high hand committed against the known command and authority of the blessed God, such a person therein despising and reproaching the Lord shall be put to death, that all others may fear and shun such provoking rebellious courses. Numbers 15:30–36. (New Haven, ca.1656)

It is ordered by this Court and the authority thereof that henceforth the selectmen of each town take care that tithing men be annually chosen in their several precincts of their most prudent and discreet inhabitants, and sworn to the faithful discharge of their trust (where no magistrate or commissioners are) before the said selectmen of the place. And the said tithing men are required diligently to inspect all houses, licensed or unlicensed, where they have notice or have ground to suspect that any person or persons do spend their time or estates, by night or by day, in tipling, gaming, or otherwise unprofitably, or do sell by retail, within doors or without, strong drink, wine, ale, cider, rum, brandy, perry, metheglin, and without license. . . .

Also, the tithing men are required diligently to inspect the manners of all disorderly persons, and where by more private admonitions they will not be reclaimed, they are, from time to time, to present their names to the next magistrate or commissioner invested with magistratical power, who shall proceed against them as the law directs; as also they are, in like manner, to present the names of all single persons that live from under family government, stubborn and disorderly children and servants, nightwalkers, tipplers, Sabbath breakers, by night or by day, and such as absent themselves from the public worship of God on the Lord's days, or whatever the course or practice of any person or persons whatsoever tending to debauchery, irreligion, profaneness, and atheism among us, wherein by omission of family government, nurture, and religious duties, and instruction of children and servants, or idleness, profligate, uncivil, or rude practices of any sort; the names of all which persons, with the fact whereof they are accused, and witnesses thereof, they shall present to the next magistrate or commissioner where any are in the said town invested with magistratical power, who shall proceed against and punish all such misdemeanors by fine, imprisonment, or binding over to the County Court, as the law directs.   (Massachusetts Bay, 15 October 1679)

B. The Well-Ordered Family

Although some legislation in the Puritan colonies concerned obligations within the family, that institution more frequently took its guidance from sermons, clerical counseling, and admonitory publications. Such guidance was meant to be taken seriously, for as Cotton Mather pointed out in A Family Well-Ordered, or an Essay to Render Parents and Children Happy in One Another . . . , "well-ordered families naturally produce a good order in other societies." A contemporary of Mather's, Rev. Benjamin Wadsworth of Boston, made the same point at greater length in a collection of sermons entitled, "The Well-Ordered Family," in which he gave detailed advice on the proper relationship between the several members of a family, including a master and his servant (an integral part of the colonial family).

As with other forms of social regulation, the difference between Puritan and non-Puritan attitudes toward family order lay less in kind than in the energy with which they were advocated and applied. Especially evident in the following excerpt is the heavy Puritan emphasis on the religious duties of both parties.

Source: Benjamin Wadsworth, *The Well-Ordered Family* . . .
    (Boston, 1712), 1–2, 103–106, 108–112, 114–121.

PREFACE

Good order in any society renders it beautiful and lovely. The upholding of Good Order in it tends to promote the benefit and comfort of all the members of it. This is true of families as well as of other societies. A family wherein the true worship of God, good pious instruction and government are upheld is beautiful in the eyes of God himself; he delights to bless such. *He blesseth the habitation of the just.* Every Christian (every Gospel minister especially) should do all he can to promote the glory of God and the welfare of those about him, and the well ordering [of] matters in particular families tends to promote these things. I believe the ignorance, wickedness (and consequent judgments) that have prevailed, and still are prevailing among us, are not more plainly owing to any one thing than to the neglect of family religion, instruction, and government; and the reviving of these things would yield as comfortable a prospect of our future good as almost any one thing I can think of. . . .

IV. To say something about the duties of masters and servants. Under the title of masters, mistresses also may be comprehended; for they are to be submitted to, Genesis 16:9. They are to have an hand in guiding the house and governing the family, 1 Timothy 5:14. And by servants we may understand male and female, both menservants and maidservants; for both the one and the other should be under government, and in subjection, Exodus 20:10. Under this last head therefore I shall say something about (1) the duties of masters to their servants; (2) the duties of servants to their masters.

About the duties of masters to their servants. Here I shall say,

1. Masters should suitably provide for the bodily support and comfort of their servants. Servants are of their household, and if they provide not for such, they're worse than infidels and have denied the faith. 1 Timothy 5:8. The virtuous woman allows to her household both food and raiment. Proverbs 31:15, 21. It's true sometimes, by bargain or agreement, the servants themselves (or their parents or guardians) are to provide them clothes; when 'tis so, then the master is free from that care and charge. But when servants are wholly at the finding and allowance of their masters, then their masters should provide them suitable food, raiment, lodging such as may be for their health and comfort. And in case of sickness or lameness, such physic and careful tendance as are needful should be granted to them. When the good centurion had a servant sick, he besought the Lord Jesus (the best physician for soul and body) to heal him. Matthew 8:5, 6. He did not treat his sick servant like a worthless dog (or as the barbarous Amalekite left his sick servant to perish, 1 Samuels 30:13), but shewed a tender care of and concern for him, and the same is the undeniable duty

of all masters and mistresses, in the like case of sickness on their servants. For any to pinch their servants (though Negroes, Indians, or any slaves), not allowing them such food, raiment, sleep (and careful tendance in case of sickness) as are needful for them, is an unmerciful, wicked, and abominable thing.

2. Masters should keep their servants diligently employed. Indeed they should allow them sufficient time to eat, drink, sleep; and on proper occasions some short space for relaxation and diversion may doubtless be very advisable. To be sure, servants should be allowed time for secret prayer, learning their catechism, reading the Bible, and other good books for the spiritual benefit. Those masters don't show much religion who won't allow their servants time for such things as these. But though time should be allowed for these things, yet we may say in general servants should be kept diligently employed in business. 'Tis said of the virtuous woman, Proverbs 31:27, she looketh well to the ways of her household, and eateth not the bread of idleness. She won't be idle herself, nor suffer her household to be so neither; she'll keep them well to their business. She shewed her virtue in this; all masters and mistresses should imitate her herein. Idleness is the devil's school; Satan finds work for those who are not employed for God. No good comes of idleness. Don't suffer your servants to be idle; oversee them carefully and inspect their carriage to prevent their unfaithfulness. On the other hand, don't be Egyptian taskmasters to them; don't put them on work beyond their power and ability (nor on work improper and unsuitable for that sort of service they engaged for) and don't require an unreasonable measure of work from them.

3. Masters should defend and protect their servants. Since their servants are under their care, and employed in their business, if any would wrong or injure them, they should endeavor to protect and defend them. This is just and equal, right and reason require it; now masters should do for their servants that which is just and equal. Colossians 4:1. Masters themselves should not abuse their servants, nor suffer (if they can prevent it) others to injure them.

4. Masters should govern their servants well. They should charge them to obey God's commands, to live soberly, righteously, and godly. They should use their authority in furthering their servants in a blameless behavior and in restraining them from sin. They should not suffer manservant nor maidservant to profane the

Sabbath, Exodus 10:10. By the same rule, they should restrain them from all other sin as far as they possibly can. Therefore they should chasten and correct them if need so require. Judgments are prepared for scorners, and stripes for the back of fools, Proverbs 19:29. A servant will not be corrected by words, for though he understand he will not answer, Proverbs 29:19. If he's so foolhardy, high, and stout as not to be mended by words, then correction should be used for his reformation. Yet you should not correct them (as we said before of children) in rage and passion; nor upon uncertainties, unless you are sure of their faults; nor should your corrections be cruel and unmerciful; if milder ones will do, more severe ones should ever be avoided. Masters should not be tyrannical to their servants, nor act as though they had an arbitrary unlimited power over them. They should not oppress them, Deuteronomy 24:14. Nor rule them with rigor, Leviticus 25:43. The Apostle says to masters concerning their servants, Ephesians 6:9, forbearing threatening. . . .

. . . We should give to servants (as well as others) what's their right and due. If we keep back the wages of hirelings, or defraud them of their due, their cries will enter into the ears of the Lord of Sabaoth (the Lord of hosts) and great will our guilt and danger be. Samuels 5:3, 4. At his day thou shall give him his hire—lest he cry against thee to the Lord, and it be sin unto thee. Deuteronomy 24:15. The wages of him that is hired shall not abide with thee all night, until the morning. Leviticus 19:13. No, it should be paid presently. This indeed seems to refer to day laborers, but the law in proportion may extend to servants hired for some longer time; wages should be paid them as soon as they are due. God says, Malachi 3:5, I will be a swift witness against those that oppress the hireling in his wages. Let those conscientiously consider this text who are backward to pay those whom they hire to work for them.

5. Masters should teach and instruct their servants well. When masters take apprentices, to teach them some particular trade or occupation, they ought in duty and conscience to give them all the skill and insight they can in such their occupation. . . . Masters should communicate to their servants all the honest skill to be used in their trade, but no ill tricks or cheating fallacious practices. Well, but should not masters take care of the souls of the servants and teach them the truths and duties of religion? Yes indeed they

should, 'tis their indispensable duty so to do; but this was spoken to before, under the head of parents bringing up their children religiously. The things there offered should direct and move masters to bring up their servants in the knowledge, fear, and service of God. If you suffer your servants to be ignorant, irreligious, vicious, they may do unspeakable mischief to the souls of your young children, if you have such in the family. . . .

. . . Having thus hinted at the duty of masters to their servants, we may say something about the duty of servants to their masters. And here I might say,

1. Servants should fear their masters. God says, Malachi 1:6, If I be a master where is my fear? This plainly intimates that servants should fear their masters; yea, they're bid to obey them with fear and trembling, Ephesians 6:5. To be subject to them with all fear, 1 Peter 2:18. They should therefore stand in awe of their masters and mistresses and be afraid justly to offend them in anything.

2. Servants should honor their masters. 1 Timothy 6:1. Let as many servants as are under the yoke count their own masters worthy of all honor; that the name of God and His doctrine be not blasphemed. Servants are bid, Timothy 2:9, not to answer again; the word signifies not contradicting. Servants should in their words and actions put respect and honor on their masters; they must not give saucy, impudent, contradicting answers to them. If those servants who pretend and profess to be Christians are rude and unmannerly to their masters, carry it as though they were their equals; if they are sullen, surly, humorsome so as scarce to give an answer when spoken to, or if they give ill language, cross, provoking impudent words, I say if they do thus, then they expose the Christian religion (which they profess) to be blasphemed and ill spoken of. Those who don't honor their masters, they dishonor God by breaking his plain commands.

3. Servants should obey their masters, diligent and faithful in their service and to their interest. The word of God is very plain and express for this. Colossians 3:22, 23. Servants, obey in all things (that is, all lawful things, as was before hinted about children obeying their parents). . . . Though when you think they act unreasonably, you may sometimes humbly and modestly suggest your thoughts in the matter, as Naaman's servants did, 2

Kings 5:13, yet their lawful commands you ought to obey. You therefore that are servants, take heed,

(1) To obey all the lawful commands of your masters and mistresses. Art thou a servant, and art thou set about some mean, servile laborious work? Then remember, 'tis God set thee about it, for God bids thee obey thy master. Don't scornfully think that that work is below or beneath thee which God sets thee about. When thou disobeyeth the lawful commands of thy master, thou disobeyeth God himself, and despiseth his authority; that's vile indeed.

(2) Obey your masters willingly, heartily, cheerfully. God bids you obey your masters with the heart, and with good will, Ephesians 6:6, 7. If therefore you mutter, grumble, find fault, are sullen, and show a backward unwilling mind to do what you're set about, you then break the plain commands of the great God: you rebel against and dishonor him. Therefore be hearty, cheerful, willing in obeying your masters and mistresses; endeavor to please them well in all things. God bids you do so.

(3) Obey God in obeying your masters. That is, obey your masters for this reason, because God bids you obey them. If this principle prevails (as it should) in your hearts and consciences, it will prompt you to obey all the lawful commands of your masters; and to be as diligent and faithful in their absence as in their presence, behind their backs as before their faces. The Scriptures but now mentioned show that you should obey your masters in singleness of heart, not with eye service as men pleasers, you should do it heartily as to the Lord and not to men; you should do it as unto Christ. When your master or mistress bids you do this or that, Christ bids you do it, because He bids you obey them; therefore do what's out of obedience to Christ as to Him and for Him. If you act from this principle you may really please and honor Christ, while you're doing the meanest work you are set about. It may be you sometimes think that magistrates and ministers and those in public stations have an opportunity to bring much honor to God ('tis true, they have so) but as for you poor underling servants, you can do little or nothing for God's honor; but this is your mistake. If you obey your masters, are faithful in their service, and that out of obedience to God (as has been said), you then honor and glorify God; He's as well and really pleased with what you thus do as with

anything that's done by those in public stations. . . . Having thus shewed that servants should honor and obey their masters and be faithful to their interest, we may (before we proceed to other distinct heads) draw a few inferences from these things.

(1) Servants act very wickedly when they dishonor and disobey their masters. It may be some servants, by telling false tales and stories out of the house, do greatly hurt their masters and mistresses in their credit, reputation, and business; such are wicked servants; they disobey and dishonor God, in thus dishonoring those that are over them. Possibly some servants are very high, proud, stout; they'll scarce bear to be commanded or restrained: they are for much liberty. They must have liberty for their tongues to speak almost what and when they please; liberty to give or receive visits of their own accord, and when they will; liberty to keep what company they please; liberty to be out late on nights, to go and come almost when they will, without telling why or wherefore; such liberty they contend for; they won't be ruled, governed, restrained; or it may be the work they are set about, they reckon 'tis beneath and below them, they won't stoop to do it, but will rather disobey masters or mistresses. Such servants are very wicked. They are daring in their plain disobedience to God, their abominable rebellion against Him; they trample God's laws, His authority, under their feet.

(2) Servants are very wicked when they are lazy and idle in their masters' service. The slothful servant is justly called wicked, Matthew 25:26. When Abraham sent a faithful servant about a weighty affair, that servant being arrived at the place designed, he would not so much as eat till he had told his errand; and having finished his business, he was for hastening home as soon as might be, Genesis 24:33, 35. He was not for loitering and playing by the way, as many servants are. . . .

(3) Servants are very wicked when they cheat their masters or hurt them in their estate or interest. When servants will take money, victuals, drink, clothes, or any goods, anything belonging to their masters or mistresses, and will sell them, give them away, or employ them in junkets and merry meetings, they do very wickedly therein. This is theft, this is purloining, and not showing as good fidelity as they should. Titus 2:10. Those also do very wickedly who will entertain or encourage servants in such vile practices.

(4) Servants do very wickedly when they run away from their masters. When servants run away from their masters or mistresses, and quit and forsake their service, this must needs be a very great wickedness; for it's directly contrary to those commands of God before mentioned. . . . So when upon the beating of a drum servants will list themselves volunteers and quit their masters' service, without the knowledge or consent of their masters, therein they do very wickedly. They rebel against God's authority which requires them to be faithful and obedient to their masters. Indeed if servants are impressed to go into the war, the case is quite different; that power which does impress them is superior to the power of their masters, and they ought to submit to it; but for them of their own accord to list volunteers and quit their masters' service is plain disobedience to God. God has set up authority and government in families; those who throw it off or run from it rebel against Him. Servants are not proper judges who is fit to go into public service; others are more proper than they to determine in such a case. 'Tis not true courage or public-spiritedness that makes servants (ordinarily) list volunteers, but 'tis a loose humor, a refractory spirit; they would be from under the yoke of family government. Those servants who have thus quitted their masters' service should be deeply humbled before God for their great wickedness; they should heartily repent of it. Having thus shewed that servants should honor and obey their masters, and having mentioned a few inferences therefrom, we may proceed to say,

4. Servants should patiently bear any deserved chastisements their masters inflict on them. When they are justly chastened for a fault, they should bear it patiently and should reform. Nay, if their masters through mistake or passion sometimes chasten them wrongfully, they should yet strive to bear it as patiently as they can. The Apostle says, 1 Peter 2:19, 20: For this is thankworthy, if a person for conscience towards God endure grief, suffering wrongfully. For what glory is it if when you are buffeted for your faults, ye shall take it patiently? But if when you do well and suffer for it, you take it patiently, this is acceptable with God. If such patience should be shown under undeserved punishments, then surely those that are deserved should be borne with great patience indeed. 'Tis true, if masters make a trade of being cruel or unreasonable in

inflicting groundless punishments on their servants, 'tis fit such servants should be relieved and helped by civil authority, and that their masters should be punished by the same.

5. Servants should pray for God's blessing on their masters' affairs. Abraham's pious, faithful servant did so, Genesis 24:12, and obtained success in the business his master set him about. The example of this praying servant is fit to be imitated by all servants. . . .

19. Microcosm: The Puritan Village

As generations of students of Puritan New England have pointed out, for most early settlers the town rather than the colony embodied the heart of social, economic, and political order. Most New Englanders seldom strayed far from their home towns; the regulations passed in town meeting, enforced by selectmen and constables, and reinforced by the pervasive authority of the village church served as codes of behavior from cradle to grave. The early regulations of Springfield, Massachusetts, are typical.

Source: Henry Morris, *Early History of Springfield* (Springfield, Mass., 1876), 51–52, 58–63.

May the 14th, 1636.

We whose names are underwritten, being by God's providence engaged together to make a plantation, at and over against Agawam on Connecticut, do mutually agree to certain articles and orders to be observed and kept by us and by our successors, except we and every of us, for ourselves and in our persons, shall think meet upon better reasons to alter our present resolutions.

Firstly. We intend by God's grace, as soon as we can with all convenient speed, to procure some godly and faithful minister with whom we purpose to join in church covenant to walk in all the ways of Christ.

Secondly. We intend that our town shall be composed of forty families, or if we think meet after to alter our purpose, yet not to exceed the number of fifty families, rich and poor.

Thirdly. That every inhabitant shall have a convenient proportion for a house lot, as we shall see meet for everyone's quality and estate.

Fourthly. That everyone that hath a house lot shall have a proportion of the cow pasture to the north of End Brook, lying northward from the town; and also that everyone shall have a share of the Hasseky Marsh, over against his lot if it be to be had, and everyone to have his proportionable share of all the woodland.

Fifthly. That everyone shall have a share of the meadow or planting ground, over against them as nigh as may be, on Agawam side.

Sixthly. That the Longmeadow, called Masacksick, lying in the way to Dorchester, shall be distributed to every man as we shall think meet, except we shall find other conveniences for some, for their milch cattle and other cattle also.

Seventhly. That the meadow and pasture called Nayas, towards Pawtucket on the side of Agawam lying about four miles above in the ridge, shall be distributed [six and a half lines erased] as above said in the former order, and this was altered and with consent before the hands were set to it.

Eighthly. That all rates that shall arise upon the town shall be laid upon lands according to everyone's proportion, acre for acre of house lots, and acre for acre of meadow, both alike on this side and both alike on the other side; and for farms that shall lie farther off, a less proportion as we shall after agree, except we shall see meet to remit one half of the rate from land to other estate.

Ninthly. That whereas Mr. William Pynchon, Jehu Burr, and Henry Smith have constantly continued to prosecute the same, at great charges and at great personal adventure, therefore, it is mutually agreed that forty acres of meadow lying on the south of End Brook under a hillside shall belong to the said parties free from all charges forever. That is to say, twenty acres to Mr. William Pynchon and his heirs and assigns forever, and ten acres to Jehu Burr, and ten acres to Henry Smith and to their heirs and assigns forever, which said forty acres is not disposed to them as any allotment of town lands, but they are to have their accommodations in all other places notwithstanding.

Tenthly. That whereas a house was built at a common charge which cost £6 and also the Indians demand a great sum to buy their right in the said lands, and also a great shallop which was requisite for the first planting, the value of such engagements is to be borne by each inhabitant at their first entrance as they shall be rated by us till the said disbursements shall be satisfied, or else in case the said house and boat be not so satisfied for, then so much meadow to be set out about the said house as may countervail the said extraordinary charge.

Eleventhly. It is agreed that no man except Mr. William Pynchon shall have above ten acres for his house lot. . . .

[Bylaws of the Town, adopted 5 February 1649]

6. For the prevention of sundry evils that may befall this township through ill-disposed persons that may thrust themselves in amongst us against the liking and consent of the generality of the inhabitants or select townsmen by purchasing a lot or place of habitation, etc., it is therefore ordered and declared that no inhabitant shall sell or in any kind pass away his house lot or any part of it or any other of his allotments to any stranger before he have made the select townsmen acquainted who his chapman is and they accordingly allow of his admission, under penalty of paying twenty shillings for every parcel of land so sold or forfeiting his land so sold or passed away. But if the select townsmen see ground to disallow of the admission of the said chapman, then the town or inhabitants shall have thirty days' time to resolve whether they will buy the said allotments, which said allotments they may buy as indifferent parties shall apprise them. But in case the inhabitants shall delay to make a purchase of the said lands above thirty days after the propounding of it to the select townsmen, then the said seller shall have his liberty to take his chapman, and such chapman or stranger shall be esteemed as entertained and allowed of by the town as an inhabitant.

7. It is ordered that if any man of this township or any proprietor of land here or any that shall or may dispose of land here shall under the color of friendship, or any other ways, entertain any person or persons here to abide as inmates or shall subdivide their house lots to entertain them as tenants or other ways for a longer time than one month, or thirty days, without the consent or allowance of the select townsmen (children or servants of the family that remain single persons excepted), [he] shall forfeit for the first

default twenty shillings to the town and also he shall forfeit twenty shillings per month for every month that any such person or persons shall so continue in this township without the consent of the select townsmen; and if in time of their abode after the limitation above said they shall need relief, not being able to maintain themselves, then he or they that entertained such persons shall be liable to be rated by the selectmen for the relief and maintenance of the said party or parties so entertained, as they in their discretion shall judge meet.

8. For the regulating of workmen's and laborers' wages, it is ordered: (1) That all workmen shall work the whole day allowing convenient time for food and rest. (2) That all husbandmen and ordinary laborers from the first day of November to the first of March shall not take above sixteen pence by the day wages; for the other eight months they shall not take above twenty pence by the day, except in time of harvest for reaping and mowing or for other extraordinary work such as are sufficient workmen are allowed two shillings per day. (3) That all carpenters, joiners, sawyers, wheelwrights, or such like artificers, from the first day of November to the first of March, shall not take above twenty pence per day wages, and for the other eight months not above two shillings per day. Tailors not to exceed twelve pence per day throughout the year. (4) That all teams consisting of four cattle with one man shall not take above six shillings a day wages; from May till October to work eight hours and the other part of the year six hours for their day's work.

And it is further ordered that whosoever shall either by giving or taking exceed these rates, he shall be liable to be punished by the magistrate according to the quality and nature of the offense. . . .

12. Whereas there is observation taken of the scarcity of timber about the town for building, sawing, shingles, and such like, it is therefore ordered that no person shall henceforth transport out of the town to other places any building timber, board logs, or sawn boards, or planks, or shingle timber, or pipe staves which shall be growing in the town commons; viz., from Chicopee River to Freshwater Brook and six miles east from the great river; and if any man shall be found to transgress this order, he shall be liable to a fine of twenty shillings for every freight, or load, of such timber, boards, shingle, or such like, by him so transported. . . .

14. Whereas it is judged offensive and noisome for flax and hemp to be watered or washed in or by the brook before men's doors which is for ordinary use for dressing meat, therefore it is ordered that no person henceforth shall water or wash any flax or hemp in the said brook, either on the east or west side of the street or anywhere near adjoining to it, and if any person shall be found transgressing herein, he shall be liable to a fine of six shillings eight pence for every such default. . . .

16. Whereas it is judged needful in sundry respects that each inhabitant should have the several parcels of his land recorded, therefore for prevention of future inconveniences it is ordered that every particular inhabitant of this township shall repay to the recorder that is chosen and appointed by the town for that purpose, who, upon information given him by each person of his several parcels of land, the number of acres, with the length and breadth of the said allotments, and who are bordering on each side of him, shall by virtue of his office fairly record each parcel of land within the limits, bounds, and situation thereof in a book for that purpose, for which his pains the owner of said lands shall pay unto the recorder two pence for every parcel of his land so recorded. And if any person shall neglect the recording of his lands longer than six months after the grant of it, he shall be liable to a fine of three shillings for every parcel of his land that is not then recorded; and if after that he shall neglect to record it he shall pay twelve pence per month for every month's neglect of any parcel. And ancient grants are all to be recorded by the last of May next upon like penalty. . . .

20. For the better carrying on of town meetings it is ordered that whensoever there shall any public notice be given to the inhabitants by the select townsmen, or any other in their behalf, of some necessary occasion wherein the selectmen desire to advise with the inhabitants, and the day, time, and place of meeting be appointed, it is expected that all the inhabitants attend personally such meeting so appointed. And in case the time and hour of meeting be come, though there be but nine of the inhabitants assembled, it shall be lawful for them to proceed in agitation of whatever business is there propounded to them; and what the major part of the assembly there met shall agree upon, it shall be taken as the act of the whole town and binding to all.

21. The first Tuesday in November yearly is mutually agreed on and appointed to be a general town meeting for the choice of town officers, making, continuing, and publishing of orders, etc., on which day it is more especially expected that each inhabitant give his personal attendance, and if any shall be absent at the time of calling, or absent himself without consent of the major part, he shall be liable to a fine of two shillings sixpence.

22. It is also ordered that on the first Tuesday in November there shall be yearly chosen by the inhabitants two wise, discreet men who shall by virtue of an oath imposed on them by the magistrate for that purpose faithfully present on the court days all such breaches of court or town orders or any other misdemeanors as shall come to their knowledge, either by their own observation or by credible information of others, and shall take out process for the appearance of such as are delinquents or witnesses to appear the said day, when all such presentments by the said parties shall be judicially heard and examined by the magistrate, and warrants for distresses granted for the levying of such fines or penalties as are annexed to the orders violated or which shall seem meet and reasonable to the magistrate to impose or inflict according to the nature of the offense. These to stand in this office for a year or till others be chosen in their room.

23. It is ordered and declared that when any man shall be fairly and clearly chosen to any office or place of service in and to the town, if he shall refuse to accept the place, or shall afterwards neglect to serve in that office to which he shall be chosen, every such person shall pay twenty shillings fine for refusal to the town treasurer, unless he has served in that office the year before; no person being, to be compelled to serve two years together in the same office, except selectmen, two whereof, if chosen again, are to stand two years together; that so there may be always some of the old selectmen who are acquainted with the town affairs joining with the new. . . .

25. To the end that the common highways of the town may be laid out where they may be most convenient and advantageous for the general use of the town, it is therefore ordered that the select townsmen shall have full power and authority to lay out all common highways for the town where and how they shall judge most convenient and useful for the inhabitants, though it be through or

at the end of men's lots. Provided they give them reasonable satisfaction according to equity, but if the party like not thereof then it shall be referred to the judgment of indifferent parties mutually chosen by the party and the select townsmen; and if those two indifferent parties do not agree they shall pitch upon a third person to join with them and determine it. . . .

V

Troublers in Zion

IT WAS one thing to advocate, even decree, an orderly society, quite another to make it so. Every law had a lawbreaker, every doctrine a heretic. Much, therefore, of the New England Puritan's time and talent focused on eradicating whatever the Puritan authorities viewed as dangerous nonconformity in church or state. Perhaps posterity has exaggerated the enthusiasm with which the Puritans purged their ranks, but it seems certain that the expulsion of overt dissenters to New England's religious and social mores played an important role in the Puritan colonies, where the identification and punishment, or ejection, of "dangerous heretics" and other trouble-makers occurred with more vigor and frequency than in the rest of British America.

20. Puritan Theory of Exclusion

The Puritans believed that a society living in accordance with God's will had a right and an obligation to punish or expel anyone who strayed too far from holy precepts, since God would hold the whole community responsible for individual transgressions. One way to avoid divine punishment was to exclude from their colonies all who did not share the Puritans' basic premises. Presumably such persons would not come to New England in the first place or would leave willingly if requested to; as Nathaniel Ward announced in his oft-quoted Simple Cobler of Aggawam in America (1647), "All Familists, Antinomians, Anabaptists, and other Enthusiasts, shall have free Liberty to keep away from us, and such as will come to be gone as fast as they can, the sooner the better." But laws insuring an uncontaminated society were deemed necessary as early as 1637. John Winthrop nicely summarized the Puritan theory of exclusion in his defense of a law requiring newcomers to gain permission of the magistrates before settling in Massachusetts: "If we heere be a corporation established by free consent, if the place of our co-habitation be our owne, then no man hath right to come into us . . . without our consent."

With the concept of exclusion, as voiced by Ward and Winthrop, the seventeenth-century mind took little exception, at least until later in the century. What bridled non-Puritans was the conformity forced on persons already in New England, even on those—such as orthodox Anglicans—who held views that enjoyed complete freedom in the mother country. The rights of an Englishman, it appeared, meant one thing in old England, quite another in New England.

From the beginning of Puritan settlement, there were a few rugged souls ready to challenge the assumption that the saints' way was the only way, or even that the saints were correctly identified. There were outside critics too, men who watched from old England the developments in the New World and who, especially after 1640, viewed with alarm the relative rigidity of American Puritanism at a time when its English counterpart was beginning to lean toward religious toleration. The circumstances were, of course, quite different. English Puritans had to compromise in order to survive; American Puritans still thought they could show the world a Bible commonwealth undefiled by heterodox beliefs or behavior. Time would eventually prove the Americans wrong.

Meanwhile, the growing divergence between the English and the American wings of the Puritan movement gave each side an opportunity to present its case. Nathaniel Ward's pamphlet was a part of that debate, as were the writings of Roger Williams on toleration, especially his exchanges with John Cotton. But Williams expressed himself in an idiom that is difficult for modern readers to unravel. More clear and concise statements of the opposing cases are found in Cotton's exchange of letters with Sir Richard Saltonstall, former resident of New England, who in approximately 1650 sent the following letter to "my reverend and worthyly much esteemed friends Mr. Cotton and Mr. Wilson, preachers to the church which is at Boston in New-England."

Source: The Prince Society, *Hutchinson Papers* (2 vols., Albany, N.Y., 1865), II, 127–134.

Reverend and dear friends, whom I unfeignedly love and respect:

It doth not a little grieve my spirit to hear what sad things are reported daily of your tyranny and persecutions in New England, as that you fine, whip, and imprison men for their consciences. First, you compel such to come into your assemblies as you know will not join with you in your worship, and when they shew their dislike thereof or witness against it, then you stir up your magistrates to punish them for such (as you conceive) their public affronts. Truly, friends, this your practice of compelling any in matters of worship to do that whereof they are not fully persuaded is to make them sin, for so the Apostle (Rom. 14 and 23) tells us, and many are made hypocrites thereby, conforming in their outward man for fear of punishment. We pray for you and wish you prosperity every way, hoped the Lord would have given you so much light and love there that you might have been eyes to God's people here, and not to practice those courses in a wilderness which you went so far to prevent. These rigid ways have laid you very low in the hearts of the saints. I do assure you I have heard them pray in the public assemblies that the Lord would give you meek and humble spirits, not to strive so much for uniformity as to keep the unity of the spirit in the bond of peace.

When I was in Holland about the beginning of our wars, I remember some Christians there that then had serious thoughts of planting in New England desired me to write to the governor thereof to know if those that differ from you in opinion, yet holding the same foundation in religion, as Anabaptists, Seekers, Antinomians, and the like, might be permitted to live among you, to which I received this short answer from your then governor, Mr. Dudley: God forbid (said he) our love for the truth should be grown so cold that we should tolerate errors. And when (for satisfaction of myself and others) I desired to know your grounds, he referred me to the books written here between the Presbyterians and Independents, which if that had been sufficient, I needed not have sent so far to understand the reasons of your practice. I hope you do not assume to yourselves infallibility of judgment when the most learned of the Apostles confesseth he knew but in part and saw but darkly as through a glass. For God is light, and no further than he doth illuminate us can we see, be our parts and learning never so great. Oh that all those who are brethren, though yet they cannot think and speak the same things, might be of one accord in the Lord. Now the God of patience and consolation grant you to be thus minded towards one another, after the example of Jesus Christ our blessed Saviour, in whose everlasting arms of protection he leaves you who will never leave to be

Your truly and much affectionate friend in the nearest union,

RICHARD SALTONSTALL

[Cotton's Answer]

Honored and dear Sir:

My brother Wilson and self do both of us acknowledge your love . . . in the late lines we received from you. . . . [As to] the complaints you hear . . . against our tyranny and persecutions in fining, whipping, and imprisoning men for their consciences, be pleased to understand we look at such complaints as altogether injurious in respect of ourselves, who had no hand or tongue at all to promote either the coming of the persons you aim at into our assemblies, or their punishment for their carriage there. Righteous judgment will not take up reports, much less reproaches, against the innocent. The cry of the sins of Sodom was great and loud and reached up to heaven, yet the righteous God (giving us an example what to do in the like case), He would first go down to see whether their crime were altogether according to the cry before He would proceed to judgment (Gen. 18:20, 21), and when He did find the truth of the cry, He did not wrap up all alike promiscuously in the judgment, but spared such as He found innocent. We are amongst those whom (if you knew us better) you would account of (as the matron of Abel spake of herself) peaceable in Israel, 2 Sam. 20:19.

Yet neither are we so vast in our indulgence or toleration as to think the men you speak of suffered an unjust censure. For one of them (Obadiah Holmes) being an excommunicate person himself, out of a church in Plymouth patent, came into this jurisdiction and took upon him to baptize, which I think himself will not say he was compelled here to perform. And he was not ignorant that the rebaptizing of an elder person, and that by a private person out of [church] office and under excommunication, are all of them manifest contestations against the order and government of our churches established (we know) by God's law, and (he knoweth) by the laws of the country. And we conceive we may safely appeal to the ingenuity of your own judgment whether it would be tolerated in any civil state for a stranger to come and practice contrary to the known principles of their church-estate? As for his whipping, it was more voluntarily chosen by him than inflicted on him. His censure by the court was to have paid (as I know) thirty pounds or else to be whipped. His fine was offered to be paid by friends for him freely, but he chose rather to be whipped; in which case, if his suffering of stripes was any worship of God at all, surely it could be accounted no better than will-worship. The other (Mr. Clarke) was wiser in that point, and his offense was less, so was his fine less, and himself (as I hear) was contented to have it paid for him, whereupon he was released. The imprisonment of either of them was no detriment. I believe they fared neither of them better at home, and I am sure Holmes had not been so well clad of many years before.*

But be pleased to consider this point a little further. You think to compel men in matter of worship is to make men sin, according to Rom. 14:23. If the worship be lawful in itself, the magistrate compelling him to come to it compelleth him not to sin, but the sin is in his will that needs to be compelled to a Christian duty. Josiah compelled all Israel, or (which is all one) made to serve the Lord their God, 2 Chron. 34:33, yet his act herein was not blamed but recorded amongst his virtuous actions. For a governor to suffer any within his gates to profane the Sabbath is a sin against the fourth commandment, both in the private householder and in the magistrate; and if he requires them to present themselves before the Lord, the magistrate sinneth not, nor doth the subject sin so great a sin as if he did refrain to come. If the magistrate connive at his absenting himself from Sabbath duties, the sin will be greater in the magistrate than can be in the other's passive coming. Naaman's passive going into the house of Rimmon did not violate the peace of his conscience, 2 Kings 5:18, 19. Bodily presence in a stewes, forced to behold the lewdness of whoredoms there committed, is no whoredom at all. No more is it spiritual whoredom to be compelled by force to go to mass.

But (say you) it doth but make men hypocrites to compel men to conform the outward man for fear of punishment. If it did so, yet better to be hypocrites than profane persons. Hypocrites give God part of his due, the outward man, but the profane person giveth God neither outward nor inward man.

Your prayers for us we thankfully accept, and we hope God hath given us so much light and love (which you think we want) that if our native country were more zealous against horrid blasphemies and heresies than we be, we believe the Lord would look at it as a better improvement of all the great salvations he hath wrought for them than to set open a wide door to all abominations in religion. Do you think the Lord hath crowned the state with so many victories that they should suffer so many miscreants to pluck the crown of sovereignty from Christ's head? Some to deny his Godhead, some his manhood; some to acknowledge no Christ, nor heaven, nor hell, but what is in a man's self? Some to deny all

* For a different view of this episode, see document 25 below. [Editor]

churches and ordinances, and so to leave Christ no visible kingdom upon earth? And thus Christ by easing England of the yoke of a kingdom shall forfeit His own kingdom among the people of England. Now God forbid, God from heaven forbid, that the people and state of England should so ill requite the Lord Jesus. You know not if you think we came into this wilderness to practice those courses here which we fled from in England. We believe there is a vast difference between men's inventions and God's institutions. We fled from men's inventions, to which we else should have been compelled; we compel none to men's inventions.

If our ways (rigid ways as you call them) have laid us low in the hearts of God's people, yea and of the saints (as you style them), we do not believe it is any part of their saintship. Michal had a low esteem of David's zeal, but he was never a whit lower in the sight of God, nor she higher.

What you wrote out of Holland to our then governor, Mr. Dudley, in behalf of Anabaptists, Antinomians, Seekers, and the like, it seemeth met with a short answer from him, but zealous, for zeal will not bear such mixtures as coldness or lukewarmness will, Rev. 2:2, 14, 15, 20. Nevertheless, I tell you the truth, we have tolerated in our church some Anabaptists, some Antinomians, and some Seekers, and do so still at this day, though Seekers of all others have less reason to desire toleration in church fellowship. For they that deny all churches and church ordinances since the apostasy of Antichrist, they cannot continue in church fellowship but against their own judgment and conscience. And therefore four or five of them who openly renounced the church fellowship which they had long enjoyed, the church said amen to their act, and (after serious debate with them till they had nothing to answer) they were removed from their fellowship. Others carry their dissent more privately and inoffensively, and so are borne withal in much meekness. We are far from arrogating infallibility of judgment to ourselves or affecting uniformity; uniformity God never required, infallibility He never granted us. We content ourselves with unity in the foundation of religion and of church order. Superstructures we suffer to vary; we have here Presbyterian churches as well as Congregational, and have learned (through grace) to keep the unity of the spirit in the bond of peace. Only we are loath to be blown up and down (like chaff) by every wind of new notions.

You see how desirous we are to give you what satisfaction we may to your loving expostulation, which we pray you to accept with the same spirit of love wherewith it is indited. The Lord Jesus guide and keep your heart forever in the ways of His truth and peace. So humbly commending our due respect and hearty affection to your worship, we take leave and rest.

21. Morton of Merrymount

The most famous of New England's dissenters found themselves at theological loggerheads with the Puritan tradition: Roger Williams objected to several Congregational premises, Anne Hutchinson to the Puritans' Biblical interpretation, the Anabaptists to their application of the first sacrament to infants. But earlier and more colorful was the purely secular case of Thomas Morton, amateur poet, frontier freebooter, and wilderness bon vivant.

Not much is known of Morton except that he settled in Mount Wollaston (now Quincy) in 1625, gathered around him an assortment of ex-servants, lighthearted traders, and Indian maids, and proceeded so to annoy the Puritans that they ousted him from the Bay not once but thrice. That he was nominally Anglican seems to have been of small significance; Morton's faults, in the eyes of the Puritans, lay in general with his disorderly conduct ("riotous prodigallitie and profuse excess," according to William Bradford) and in particular in his selling guns to the Indians. In 1628, several small New England plantations contributed to a fund for the removal of "Mine-Host of Merrymount," as he styled himself. After summarily shipping Morton to England, Bradford wrote an explanation to Sir Ferdinando Gorges of the Council for New England.

Source: Massachusetts Historical Society, *Collections*, 1 ser. III (1794), 63–64.

Honorable Sir:

As you have ever been not only a favorer but also a most special beginner and furtherer of the good of this country, to your great cost and no less honor, we whose names are underwritten, being some of every plantation in the land, deputed for the rest, do humbly crave your worship's help and best assistance in the speedy (if not too late) redress of our almost desperate state and condition in this place, expecting daily to be overrun and spoiled by the savages, who are already abundantly furnished with pieces, powder and shot, swords, rapiers and faslings—all of which arms and munition is this year plentifully and publicly sold unto them by our own countrymen who, under the pretense of fishing, come atrading amongst them; yea, one of them (as your worships may further understand by our particular informations) hath for his part sold twenty or twenty-one pieces and one hundred weight of powder, by which you may conceive of the rest; for we hear the savages have above sixty pieces amongst them, besides other arms. In a word, there is now almost nothing vendible amongst them but such munition, so they have spoiled the trade in all other things. And as vice is always fruitful, so from the greedy covetousness of the fishermen, and their evil example, the like hath began to grow amongst some who pretend themselves to be planters, though indeed they intend nothing less but to take opportunity of the time and provide themselves and begone, and leave others to quench the fire which they have kindled. Of which number Mr. Thomas Morton is one, being of late a dweller in the Massachusetts Bay, and the head of a turbulent and seditious crew, which he had gathered unto him, who, dwelling in the midst of us, hath set up the like practice in these parts and hath sold sundry pieces to the natives, who can use them with great dexterity, excelling our English therein, and have been vaunting with them at Sowams, Narragansett, and many other places, so as they are spread both north and south all the land over, to the great peril of all our lives.

In the beginning of this mischief we sought friendly to dissuade him from it, but he scorned us therein and prosecuted it the more, so as we were constrained for the safety of ourselves, our wives and innocent children, to apprehend him by force (though with some peril) and now have sent him to the Council of New England to receive according to his demerits and be disposed of as their honors shall think fit, for the preventing of further mischief, the safety of our lives, and the terror of all other delinquents in the same kind. Now our hope and humble request is that your worship, and those honorable of his majesty's council for New England, will commiserate our case, tender our lives, and pity our infants, and consider the great charges and expenses that we and our assistants and associates have been at, besides all the miseries and hardships that we have broken through in these beginnings which have hitherto happily succeeded for the planting of this country, which

is hopeful if it be cherished and protected against the cankered covetousness of these licentious men. If not, we must return and quit the country. Wherefore we beseech your worship to afford us your favorable assistance and direction in bringing this man to his answer before those whom it may concern, and to credit our true informations, sent by this bearer, lest by his audacious and colored pretenses he deceive you, which know not things as we do. . . .
June 9, Anno 1628.   At your service, etc.

Morton escaped punishment in England and was back at Merry-mount before the end of 1629. By that time, settlement of the Massachusetts colony was well under way, and Morton now had to contend with more formidable opponents. In 1631, he was again shipped to England, this time for seizing an Indian canoe. He later returned but was harried by the Puritans until he eventually fled to the coast of Maine —where at that time the long arm of Puritan law seldom reached.

But Morton may have had the last word. In 1637, he published New English Canaan, a satirical narrative of his running battle with Puritan authority, an account that continues to be read with amusement and sympathy. Part of its longevity stems from clever parodies of Myles Standish ("Captain Shrimp"), John Endecott ("Captain Littleworth"), and John Winthrop ("Joshua Temperwell").

22. Defection in the Clergy

Rogers Williams was neither the first Puritan nor the first clergyman to be banished from a New England colony. But he was the first cause célèbre, for at the time of his expulsion from Massachusetts, Williams was widely known and respected; he also had enough toughness and talent to outlive and outargue most of his former persecutors.

The reasons for Williams's banishment are complex, as a close reading of the following extract from Winthrop's Journal will make clear. And there is little else from which to judge, for other contemporary sources are frustratingly silent about the man Governor Winthrop first mentions as "a godly minister." At any rate, we know that as early as April, 1631, Williams was in trouble with the Bay Colony authorities for insisting on overt separatism from the Church of England, among other reasons. The next year, after serving briefly as a clergyman in Plymouth, Williams accepted a call to the Congregational church at Salem. Soon he was in trouble again.

Source: James K. Hosmer, ed., Winthrop's Journal "History of New England," 1630–1649 (2 vols., New York, 1908), I, 116–119, 142, 149, 154–155, 157, 162–163, 168.

[December 27, 1633.] The governor [John Winthrop] and assistants met at Boston, and took into consideration a treatise, which Mr. Williams (then of Salem) had sent to them, and which he had formerly written to the governor and council of Plymouth, wherein, among other things, he disputes their right to the lands they possessed here, and concluded that, claiming by the King's grant, they could have no title, nor otherwise, except they compounded with the natives. For this, taking advice with some of the most judicious ministers (who much condemned Mr. Williams' error and presumption), they gave order that he should be convented at the next Court, to be censured, etc. There were three passages chiefly whereat they were much offended: (1) for he charged King James to have told a solemn public lie because in his patent [to the Massachusetts Bay Company] he blessed God that he was the first Christian prince that had discovered this land; (2) for that he charged him and others with blasphemy for calling Europe Christendom, or the Christian world; (3) for that he did personally apply to our present King Charles these three places in the Revelations, viz., [blank].

Mr. Endecott being absent, the governor wrote to him to let him know what was done, and withal added divers arguments to confute the said errors, wishing him to deal with Mr. Williams to retract the same, etc. Whereto he returned a very modest and discreet answer. Mr. Williams also wrote to the governor, and also to him and the rest of the council, very submissively, professing his intent to have been only to have written for the private satisfaction of the governor, etc., of Plymouth, without any purpose to have stirred any further in it, if the governor here had not required a copy of him; withal offering his book, or any part of it, to be burned.

At the next Court he appeared penitently, and gave satisfaction of his intention and loyalty. So it was left, and nothing done in it. . . .

[January 24, 1634.] The governor and council met again at Boston to consider of Mr. Williams' letter, etc., when, with the advice of Mr. Cotton and Mr. Wilson, and weighing his letter, and further considering of the aforesaid offensive passages in his book (which being written in very obscure and implicative phrases might well admit of doubtful interpretation), they found the matters not to be so evil as at first they seemed. Whereupon they agreed that upon his retraction, etc., or taking an oath of allegiance to the King, etc., it should be passed over. . . .

[November 27, 1634.] [The Court was] informed that Mr. Williams of Salem had broken his promise to us, in teaching publicly against the King's patent, and our great sin in claiming right thereby to this country, etc., and for usual terming the churches of England anti-Christian. We granted summons to him for his appearance at the next Court. . . .

[April 30, 1635.] The governor [Thomas Dudley] and assistants sent for Mr. Williams. The occasion was for that he had taught publicly that a magistrate ought not to tender an oath to an unregenerate man, for that we thereby have communion with a wicked man in the worship of God and cause him to take the name of God in vain. He was heard before all the ministers and very clearly confuted. Mr. Endecott was at first of the same opinion, but he gave place to the truth. . . .

[July 8, 1635.] At the General Court, Mr. Williams of Salem was summoned, and did appear. It was laid to his charge, that being under question before the magistracy and churches for divers dangerous opinions, viz. (1) that the magistrate ought not to punish the breach of the first table [of the Ten Commandments] otherwise than in such cases as did disturb the civil peace; (2) that he ought not to tender an oath to an unregenerate man; (3) that a man ought not to pray with such, though wife, child, etc.; (4) that a man ought not to give thanks after the sacrament nor after meat, etc.; and that the other churches were about to write to the church of Salem to admonish him of these errors; notwithstanding the church had since called him to [the] office of a teacher. Much debate was about these things. The said opinions were adjudged by all, magistrates and ministers (who were desired to be present), to be erroneous and very dangerous, and the calling of him to office, at that time, was judged a great contempt of authority. So, in fine, time was given to him and the church of Salem to consider of these things till the next General Court, and then either to give satisfaction to the Court or else to expect the sentence—it being professedly declared by the ministers (at the request of the court to give their advice) that he who should obstinately maintain such opinions (whereby a church might run into heresy, apostasy, or tyranny, and yet the civil magistrate could not intermeddle) were to be removed, and that the other churches ought to request the magistrates so to do. . . .

[July 12, 1635.] Salem men had proffered a petition, at the last General Court, for some land in Marblehead Neck, which they did challenge as belonging to their town; but, because they had chosen Mr. Williams their teacher while he stood under question of authority, and so offered contempt to the magistrates, etc., their petition was refused till, etc. Upon this the church of Salem wrote to other churches, to admonish the magistrates of this as a heinous sin, and likewise the deputies; for which, at the next General Court, their deputies were not received until they should give satisfaction about the letter. . . .

[August 16, 1635.] Mr. Williams, pastor of Salem, being sick and not able to speak, wrote to his church a protestation, that he could not communicate with the churches in the Bay; neither would he communicate with them except they would refuse communion with the rest; but the whole church was grieved herewith. . . .

[October 7, 1635.] At this General Court, Mr. Williams, the teacher at Salem, was again convented, and all the ministers in the Bay being desired to be present, he was charged with the said two letters—that to the churches, complaining of the magistrates for injustice, extreme oppression, etc., and the other to his own church, to persuade them to renounce communion with all the churches in the Bay as full of anti-Christian pollution, etc. He justified both these letters and maintained all his opinions; and being offered further conference or disputation, and a month's respite, he chose to dispute presently. So Mr. Hooker was appointed to dispute with him, but could not reduce him from any of his errors. So the next morning the Court sentenced him to depart out of our jurisdiction within six weeks, all the ministers, save one, approving the sentence; and his own church had him under question also for the same cause; and he, at his return home, refused communion with his own church, who openly disclaimed his errors and wrote an humble submission to the magistrates, acknowledging their fault in joining with Mr. Williams in that letter to the churches against them, etc. . . .

[January, 1636.] The governor [John Haynes] and assistants met at Boston to consider about Mr. Williams, for that they were credibly informed, that, notwithstanding the injunction laid upon him (upon the liberty granted him to stay [in Massachusetts] till the spring) not to go about to draw others to his opinions, he did use to entertain company in his house, and to preach to them, even of such points as he had been censured for; and it was agreed to send him into England by a ship then ready to depart. The reason was because he had drawn above twenty persons to his opinion, and they were intended to erect a plantation about the Narragansett Bay, from whence the infection would easily spread into these churches (the people being, many of them, much taken with the apprehension of his godliness). Whereupon a warrant was sent to him to come presently to Boston, to be shipped, etc. He returned answer (and divers of Salem came with it), that he could not come without hazard of his life, etc. Whereupon a pinnace was sent with commission to Captain Underhill, etc., to apprehend him, and carry him aboard the ship (which then rode at Natascutt), but when they came at his house they found he had been gone three days before; but whither they could not learn.

He had so far prevailed at Salem as many there (especially of devout women) did embrace his opinions, and separated from the churches, for this cause, that some of their members, going into England, did hear the ministers there, and when they came home the churches here held communion with them. . . .

Winthrop makes no explanation for Williams' nicely timed disappearance so close to Underhill's arrival. Fortunately, Williams himself provided a clue many years later in a letter to Major John Mason of Connecticut: "When I was unkindly and unchristianly (as I believe) driven from my howse and land, and wife and children . . . that ever honoured Governour Mr. Wintrop, privately wrote to me to steer my Course to Nahigonset Bay. . . . I tooke his prudent Motion as an Hint and Voice from God, and (Waving all other Thoughts and Motions) I steerd my Course from Salem (though in Winter snow, which I feel yet) unto these parts. . . ." Williams and Winthrop remained good friends— even bought an island together in Narragansett Bay—until the latter's death in 1649. In many respects, then, the expulsion of Williams was a family quarrel: the well-ordered Puritans pushed to the outskirts of their experiment one of their brethren who, as William Bradford had observed earlier, was "a man godly and zealous, having many precious parts, but very unsettled in judgmente."

23. The Trial of Anne Hutchinson

No sooner was Roger Williams on his way to Providence than a more serious threat to the Puritan experiment emerged. By 1637, noted John Winthrop, it was "as common here to distinguish between men, by [their] being under a covenant of grace or a covenant of works, as in other countries between Protestants and papists." The instigator, in the government's eyes, was Anne Hutchinson, who had arrived in Massachusetts only two years earlier, accompanied by her merchant husband and eleven children. She became anathema to orthodox Puritans for interpreting rigidly and publicly the doctrine that Christians could do nothing about their own salvation. Anne Hutchinson, her brother-inlaw John Wheelwright, and their followers, held that God determined all; many New England clergymen preached that potential converts could effect a state of "preparative sorrow" — as a matter of readiness, the clergy insisted, not of "works." Further, Mrs. Hutchinson proclaimed that those who were truly saved need not concern themselves with human law; their salvation transcended anything their mortal bodies might do. She was no libertine, but the implications of her interpretation frightened the leaders of a society concerned about the behavior of all its members. She offended the authorities, too, by purporting to know who was and who was not saved — hardly an acceptable role for anyone in Puritan society, least of all a housewife. In 1644, Thomas Welde (c. 1590–1662) castigated Hutchinson in the preface to an equally harsh diatribe by Winthrop. But the transcript of the civil trial (followed by one in Hutchinson's congregation that led to her excommunication) reveals her keen mind and her opponents' confusion.

Source: Thomas Hutchinson, *The History of the Colony of Massachusetts-Bay* (3 vols., Boston, 1767), II, 482–520.

    Mr. Winthrop, governor.   Mrs. Hutchinson, you are called here as one of those that have troubled the peace of the commonwealth and the churches here. You are known to me a woman that hath had a great share in the promoting and divulging of those opinions that are causes of this trouble and to be nearly joined not only in affinity and affection with some of those the court had taken notice of and passed censure upon, but you have spoken diverse things, as we have been informed, very prejudicial to the honor of the churches and ministers thereof, and you have maintained a meeting and an assembly in your house that hath been condemned by the general assembly as a thing not tolerable nor comely in the sight of God nor fitting for your sex. And notwithstanding that was cried down, you have continued the same; therefore we have thought good to send for you to understand how things are, that if you be in an erroneous way we may reduce you that so you may become a profitable member here among us; otherwise, if you be obstinate in your course, that then the court may take such course that you may trouble us no further. Therefore I would intreat you to express whether you do not hold and assent in practice to those opinions and factions that have been handled in court already, that is to say, whether you do not justify Mr. Wheelwrights' sermon and the petition.

Mrs. Hutchinson. I am called here to answer before you, but I hear no things laid to my charge.

Gov. I have told you some already, and more I can tell you.

[Mrs. H.] Name one, sir.

Gov. Have I not named some already?

Mrs. H. What have I said or done?

Gov. Why for your doings, this you did harbor and countenance those that are parties in this faction that you have heard of.

[Mrs. H.] That's a matter of conscience, sir.

Gov. Your conscience you must keep or it must be kept for you. . . .

Gov. Why do you keep such a meeting at your house as you do every week upon a set day?

Mrs. H. It is lawful for me to do so, as it is all your practices, and can you find a warrant for yourself and condemn me for the same thing? The ground of my taking it up was, when I first came to this land—because I did not go to such meetings as those were—it was presently reported that I did not allow of such meetings but held them them unlawful, and therefore in that regard they said I was proud and did despise all ordinances. Upon that, a friend came unto me and told me of it, and I to prevent such aspersions took it up, but it was in practice before I came, therefore I was not the first.

Gov. For this, that you appeal to our practice, you need no confutation. If you meeting had answered to the former, it had not been offensive, but I will say that there was no meeting of women alone, but you meeting is of another sort; for there are sometimes men among you.

Mrs. H. There was never any man with us.

Gov. Well, admit there was no man at your meeting and that you was sorry for it, there is no warrant for your doings. And by what warrant do you continue such a course?

Mrs. H. I conceive there lies a clear rule in Titus, that the elder women should instruct the younger, and then I must have a time wherein I must do it.

Gov. All this I grant you, I grant you a time for it, but what is this to the purpose that you, Mrs. Hutchinson, must call a company together from their callings to come to be taught of you?

Mrs. H. Will it please you to answer me this and to give me a rule, for then I will willingly submit to any truth. If any come to my house to be instructed in the ways of God, what rule have to put them away?

Gov. But suppose that a hundred men come unto you to be instructed, will you forbear to instruct them?

Mrs. H. As far as I conceive I cross a rule in it.

Gov. Very well, and do you not so here?

Mrs. H. No, sir, for my ground is, they are men.

Gov. Men and women, all is one for that, but suppose that a man should come and say "Mrs. Hutchinson, I hear that you are a woman that God hath given his grace unto and you have knowledge in the word of God, I pray instruct me a little." Ought you not to instruct this man?

Mrs. H. I think I may. Do you think it not lawful for me to teach women, and why do you call me to teach the court?

Gov. We do not call you to teach the court but to lay open yourself. . . .

Dep. gov. [Thomas Dudley] I would go a little higher with Mrs. Hutchinson. About three years ago we were all in peace. Mrs. Hutchinson, from that time she came, hath made a disturbance, and some that came over with her in the ship did inform me what she was as soon as she was landed. I being then in place [as governor], dealt with the pastor and teacher of Boston and desired them to enquire of her, and then I was satisfied that she held nothing different from us. But within half a year after, she had vented diverse of her strange opinions and had made parties in the country, and at length it comes that Mr. Cotton and Mr. Vane were of her judgment, but Mr. Cotton hath cleared himself that he not of that mind. But now it appears by this woman's meeting that Mrs. Hutchinson hath so forestalled the minds of many by their resort to her meeting that now she hath a potent party in the country. Now if all these things have endangered us as from that foundation, and if she in particular hath disparaged all our ministers in the land that they have preached a covenant of works, and only Mr. Cotton a covenant of grace, why this is not to be suffered, and therefore being driven to the foundation and it being found that Mrs. Hutchinson is she that hath depraved all the ministers and hath been the cause of what is fallen out, why we must take away the foundation and the building will fall.

Mrs. H.   I pray, sir, prove it that I said they preached nothing but a covenant of works.

Dep. Gov.   "Nothing but a covenant of works," why a Jesuit may preach truth sometimes.

Mrs. H.   Did I ever say they preached a covenant of works then?

Dep. Gov.   If they do not preach a covenant of grace, clearly then, they preach a covenant of works.

Mrs. H.   No, sir, one may preach a covenant of grace more clearly than another, so I said . . . .

[The court heard testimony from six clergymen about Mrs. Hutchinson's earlier statements on doctrine.]

Dep. Gov.   I called these witnesses and you deny them. You see they have proved this and you deny this, but it is clear. You say they preached a covenant of works and that they were not able ministers of the new testament. Now there are two other things that you did affirm, which were that the scriptures in the letter of them held forth nothing but a covenant of works, and likewise that those that were under a covenant of works cannot be saved.

Mr.s H.   Prove that I said so.

[Gov.]   Did you say so?

Mrs. H.   No, sir, it is your conclusion. . . .

Gov.   Mrs. Hutchinson, the court you see hath labored to bring you to acknowledge the error of your way that so you might be reduced. The time now grows late; we shall therefore give you a little more time to consider of it and therefore desire that you attend the court again in the morning.

The next morning.

Gov.   We proceeded the last night as far as we could in hearing of this cause of Mrs. Hutchinson. There were diverse things laid to her charge: her ordinary meetings about religious exercises, her speeches in derogation of the ministers among us, and the weakening of the hands and hearts of the people towards them. Here was sufficient proof made of that which she was accused of in that point concerning the ministers and their ministry, as that they did preach a covenant of works when others did preach a covenant of grace, and that they were not able ministers of the new testament, and that they had not the seal of the spirit. And this was spoken not as was pretended out of private conference, but out of conscience and warrant from scripture alledg[ing] the fear of man is a snare, and seeing God hath given her a calling to it she would freely speak. Some other speeches she used, as that the letter of the scripture held forth a covenant of works, and this is offered to be proved by probable grounds. . . .

Mrs. H. If you please to give me leave I shall give you the ground of what I know to be true. Being much troubled to see the falseness of the constitution of the Church of England, I had like to have turned separatist; whereupon I kept a day of solemn humiliation and pondering of the thing. This scripture was brought unto me—he that denies Jesus Christ to be come in the flesh is antichrist. This I considered of, and in considering found that the papists did not deny Him to be come in the flesh, nor we did not deny Him, Who then was antichrist? Was the Turk antichrist only? The Lord knows that I could not open scripture; He must by His prophetical office open it unto me. So after that being unsatisfied in the thing, the Lord was pleased to bring this scripture out of the Hebrews: "He that denies the testament denies the testator," and in this did open unto me and give me to see that those which did not teach the new covenant had the spirit of antichrist, and upon this He did discover the ministry unto me and ever since. I bless the Lord, He hath let me see which was the clear ministry and which the wrong. Since that time I confess I have been more choice and He hath let me to distinguish between the voice of my beloved and the voice of Moses, the voice of John Baptist and the voice of antichrist, for all those voices are spoken of in scripture. Now if you do condemn me for speaking what in my conscience I know to be truth I must commit myself unto the Lord.

Mr. Nowell. How do know that that was the Spirit?

Mrs. H. How did Abraham know that it was God that bid him offer his son, being a breach of the sixth commandment?

Dep. Gov. By an immediate voice.

Mrs. H. So to me by an immediate revelation.

Dep. Gov. How! an immediate revelation?

Mrs. H. By the voice of His own Spirit to my soul. I will give you another scripture, Jer. 46. 27, 28—out of which the Lord shewed me what He would do for me and the rest of His servants.—But after He was pleased to reveal Himself to me, I did presently like Abraham run to Hagar. And after that He did let me see the atheism of my own heart, for which I begged of the Lord that it might not remain in my heart, and being thus, He did shew me this (a twelvemonth after) which I told you of before. Ever since that time I have been confident of what He hath revealed unto me. . . .

When our teacher [John Cotton] came to New England it was a great trouble unto me, my brother Wheelwright being put by also. I was then much troubled concerning the ministry under which I lived, and then that place in the 30th of Isaiah was brought to my mind: "Though the Lord give thee bread of adversity and water of affliction yet shall not thy teachers be removed into corners any more, but thine eyes shall see thy teachers." The Lord giving me this promise, and they being gone, there was none then left that I was able to hear, and I could not be at rest but I must come hither. Yet that place of Isaiah did much follow me — though the Lord give thee the bread of adversity and water of affliction. This place lying I say upon me, then this place in Daniel was brought unto me and did shew me that "though I should meet with affliction yet I am the same God that delivered Daniel out of the lion's den, I will also deliver thee." Therefore I desire you to look to it, for you see this scripture fulfilled this day, and therefore I desire you that as you tender the Lord and the church and commonwealth to consider and look what you do. You have power over my body, but the Lord Jesus hath power over my body and soul, and assure yourselves thus much: you do as much as in you lies to put the Lord Jesus Christ from you, and if you go on in this course you begin you will bring a curse upon you and your posterity, and the mouth of the Lord hath spoken it. . . .

Mrs. H. But now having seen Him which is invisible, I fear not what man can do unto me.

Gov. Daniel was delivered by a miracle; do you think to be delivered so too?

Mrs. H. I do here speak it before the court. I look that the Lord should deliver me by His providence. . . .

Dep. Gov. These disturbances that have come among the Germans have all been grounded upon revelations, and so they that have vented them have stirred up their hearers to take up arms against their prince and to cut the throats one of another, and these have been the fruits of them. And whether the devil may inspire the same into their hearts here I know not, for I am fully persuaded that Mrs. Hutchinson is deluded by the devil, because the spirit of God speaks truth in all His servants.

Gov. I am persuaded that the revelation she brings forth is delusion.

All the court but some two or three ministers cry out, "We all believe it — we all believe it. . . ."

Gov. The court hath already declared themselves satisfied concerning the things you hear, and concerning the troublesomeness of her spirit and the danger of her course amongst us, which is not to be suffered. Therefore if it be the mind of the court that Mrs. Hutchinson, for these things that appear before us, is unfit for our society, and if it be the mind of the court that she shall be banished out of our liberties and imprisoned till she be sent away, let them hold up their hands.

All but three.

Those that are contrary minded hold up yours.

Mr. Coddington and Mr. Colborn, only.

Mr. Jennison.   I cannot hold up my hand one way or the other, and I shall give my reason if the court require it.

Gov.   Mrs. Hutchinson, the sentence of the court you hear is that you are banished from our jurisdiction as being a woman not fit for our society, and are to be imprisoned till the court shall send you away.

Mrs. H.   I desire to know wherefore I am banished?

Gov.   Say no more. The court knows wherefore and is satisfied.

24. A Challenge to Puritan Political Control

The challenge of Anne Hutchinson and her followers led not only to her expulsion but to new efforts among the Puritans to clarify and codify their own doctrines. Indirectly at least, the Hutchinsonian uprising led to the Cambridge Platform. Similarly, an uprising of a different kind in 1646 may have spurred completion of the Bay Colony's first comprehensive code of laws.

Robert Child (c. 1613–1654), a physician and scientific jack-of-all-trades, arrived in Massachusetts in the late 1630s but returned to England after touring the Puritan colonies. Perhaps in an attempt to avoid the political turmoil of the mother country, he moved to Massachusetts in 1645—a time when the flow of Englishmen went largely in the other direction. Almost immediately he embroiled himself in New England's politics, then in somewhat of a turmoil themselves. As principal signer of the following petition to the Massachusetts General Court, Dr. Child allied himself with a curious assortment of gentle rebels against the Puritan monopoly on political power. Of the seven petitioners, at least one was an Anglican (yet a voter, having been admitted to freemanship before the imposition of religious restriction); another was a church member but not a freeman; the rest were respectable citizens, though neither communicants nor freemen. Child himself was a Puritan of Presbyterian inclination—which is to say that he shared most of the New England Puritans' theological assumptions but preferred the Presbyterian polity then in official favor with Parliament.

After some opening felicities, the remonstrants insisted that the Bay Colony had abridged their rights as Englishmen.

Source: The Prince Society, Hutchinson Papers (2 vols., Albany, N.Y., 1865), I, 214–223.

We who in behalf of ourselves and diverse of our countrymen, laying our hands upon our breasts and seriously considering that the hand of our good God, who through His goodness hath safely brought us and ours through the great ocean and planted us here, seems not now to be with us, yea rather against us, blasting all our designs—though contrived with much deliberation, undertaken with great care, and proceeding with more than ordinary probability of successful events—by which many of good estates are brought to the brink of extreme poverty, yea at this time laying His just hand upon our families, taking many away to Himself, striking others with unwanted malignant sicknesses, and with some shameful diseases, have thought it convenient with all respectiveness to present these our sincere requests and remonstrances to this honored court. . . .

1. Whereas this place hath been planted by the encouragement, next under God, of letters patents given and granted by His Majesty of England to the inhabitants thereof, with many privileges and immunities, viz.: incorporation into a company, liberty of choosing governors, settling government, making laws not repugnant to the laws of England, power of administering the oath of allegiance to all, etc., as by the said letters patents more largely appeareth. Notwithstanding, we cannot according to our judgments discern a settled form of government according to the laws of England, which may seem strange to our countrymen, yea to the whole world, especially considering we are all English. Neither do we so understand and perceive our own laws or liberties, or any body of laws here so established, as that thereby there may be a sure and comfortable enjoyment of our lives, liberties, and estates, according to our due and natural rights as freeborn subjects of the English nation. By which many inconveniences flow into plantations, viz. jealousies of introducing arbitrary government—which many are prone to believe, construing the procrastination of such settled laws, to proceed from an overgreedy spirit of arbitrary power (which it may be is their weakness), such proceedings being detestable to our English nation and to all good men, and at present a chief cause of the intestine war in our dear country. Further, it gives cause to many to think themselves hardly dealt with, others too much favored, and the scale of justice too much bowed and unequally balanced. From when also proceedeth fears and jealousies of illegal commitments, unjust imprisonments, taxes, rates, customs, levies of ungrounded and undoing assessments, unjustifiable presses, undue fines, unmeasurable expenses and charges, of unconceivable dangers through a negative or destructive vote unduly placed and not well regulated, in a word, of a non-certainty of all things we enjoy, whether lives, liberties, or estates; and also of undue oaths, being subject to exposition according to the will of him or them that gives them, and not according to a due and unbowed rule of law, which is the true interpreter of all oaths to all men, whether judge or judged.

Wherefore our humble desire and request is that you would be pleased to consider of our present condition and upon what foundation we stand, and unanimously concur to establish the fundamental and wholesome laws of our native country, and such others as are no ways repugnant to them, unto which all of us are most accustomed. . . .

2. Whereas there are many thousands in these plantations, of the English nation, freeborn, quiet, and peaceable men, righteous in their dealings, forward with hand, heart, and purse to advance the public good, known friends to the honorable and victorious Houses of Parliament, lovers of their nation, etc., who are debarred from all civil employments (without any just cause that we know), not being permitted to bear the least office (though it cannot be denied but some are well qualified), no not so much as to have any vote in choosing magistrates, captains, or other civil and military officers, notwithstanding they have here expended their youth, born the burthen of the day, wasted much of their estates for the subsistence of these poor plantations, paid all assessments, taxes, rates at least equal if not exceeding others. Yea when the late war was denounced against the Narragansett Indians without their consent, their goods were seized on for the service, themselves and servants especially forced and impressed to serve in that war, to the hazarding of all things most dear and near unto them, whence issue forth many great inconveniences, secret discontents, murmurings, rents in the plantations, discouragements in their callings, unsettledness in their minds, strife, contention, and the Lord only knows to what a flame in time it may kindle; also jealousies of too much unwarranted power and dominion on the one side and of perpetual slavery and bondage on the other, and—which is intolerable—even by those who ought to love and respect them as brethren.

We therefore desire that civil liberty and freedom be forthwith granted to all truly English, equal to the rest of their countrymen, as in all plantations is accustomed to be done and as all freeborn enjoy in our native country (we hoping here in some things to enjoy greater liberties than elsewhere, counting it no small loss of liberty to be as it were banished from our native home and enforced to lay our bones in a strange wilderness), without imposing any oaths or covenant on them, which we suppose cannot be warranted by the letters patent and seem not to concur with the oath of allegiance formerly enforced on all and later covenants lately imposed on many here present by the honorable Houses of

Parliament, or at least to detract from our native country and laws—which by some are styled foreign and this place termed rather a free state than a colony or corporation of England. All of us [are] very willing to take such oaths and covenants as are expressions of our desires of advancing the glory of God and good of this place and of our duties to the state of England and love to our nation, being composed according to the laws and customs of other corporations of England. But all of us are exceeding unwilling by any policies whatsoever to be rent from our native country, though far distant from it, valuing our free derivations, the immunities and privileges which we and our posterity do and we hope shall always enjoy above the greatest honors of this country, not cemented to the state of England, and [we] glory to be accounted, though but as rushes of that land, yet that we may continue to write that we and ours are English; or lest we entreat that the bodies of us and ours (English subjects possessing here no privileges) may not be impressed, nor goods forcibly taken away, lest we, not knowing the justice of this war, may be ignorantly and unwillingly enforced upon our own destruction, and that all assessment, taxes, impositions—which are many and grievous (if civil liberty be not granted)—may be taken off, that in all things we may be strangers, otherwise we suppose ourselves in a worse case here and less free than the natives amongst whom we live, or any aliens. Further, that none of the English nation, who at this time are too forward to be gone and very backward to come hither, be banished, unless they break the known laws of England in so high a measure as to deserve so high a punishment, and that those few that come over may settle here without having two magistrates' hands, which sometimes not being possible to obtain hath procured a kind of banishment to some who might have been serviceable to this place, as they have been to the state of England, etc. And we likewise desire that no greater punishments be inflicted upon offenders than are allowed and set by the laws of our native country.

3. Whereas there are divers sober, righteous, and godly men, eminent for knowledge and other gracious gifts of the holy spirit, no ways scandalous in their lives and conversation, members of the Church of England (in all ages famous for piety and learning) not dissenting from the latest and best reformation of England, Scotland, etc., yet they and their posterity are detained from the seals of the covenant of free grace because, as it is supposed, they will

not take these churches' covenants, for which as yet they see no light in God's word. Neither can they clearly perceive what they are, every church having their covenant differing from another's, at least in words—yea, some churches sometime adding, sometime detracting, calling it sometimes the covenant of grace, sometimes a branch of it, sometimes a profession of the free covenant, etc.— notwithstanding, they are compelled under a severe fine every Lord's day to appear at the congregation, and notice is taken of such who stay not till baptism be administered to other men's children, though denied to their own, and in some places forced to contribute to the maintenance of those ministers who vouchsafe not to take them into their flock, though desirous of the ordinances of God, etc., yet they are not accounted so much as brethren nor publicly so called, nor is Christian vigilancy (commanded to all) any way exercised to them. Whence, as we conceive, do abound an ocean of inconveniences, dishonor to God and to his ordinances, little profit by the ministry, increase of Anabaptism and of those that totally contemn all ordinances as vain, fading of Christian graces, decrease of brotherly love, heresies, schisms, etc., the whole body of the members of the Church of England, like sheep scattered in the wilderness, without a shepherd, in a forlorn condition.

We therefore humbly entreat you, in whose hands it is to help and whose judicious eyes discern these great inconveniences, for the glory of God and the comfort of your brethren and countrymen, to give liberty to the members of the Church of England not scandalous in their lives and conversations (as members of these churches) to be taken into your congregation and to enjoy with you all those liberties and ordinances Christ hath purchased for them and into whose name they are baptized, that the Lord may be one and His name one amongst us in this place; that the seals of the covenant may be applied to them and their posterity, as we conceive they ought to be, till inconveniences hereby be found prejudicial to the churches and colony (which we hope shall never be), not doubting but the same Christian favor will be shewed to all its members of these churches when they shall retire to our dear native country (if their conversations be righteous and holy), or otherwise to grant liberty to settle themselves here in a church way, according to the best reformations of England and Scotland. If not, we and they shall be necessitated to apply our humble desires to the honorable Houses of Parliament, who we hope will take our sad conditions into their serious considerations, to provide able ministers for us (this place not being so well provided as to spare any), or else out of their charity—many estates being wasted—to transport us to some other place where we may live like Christians and not be accounted burthens, but serviceable both to church and state.

These things being granted, by the blessing of God to us in Christ, we hope to see the now contemned ordinances of God highly prized; the gospel much darkened break forth as the sun at noonday; Christian charity and brotherly love, almost frozen, wax warm; zeal and holy emulation more fervent; jealousy of arbitrary government (the bane of all commonwealths) quite banished; the wicked, if any such be found, in their courses disheartened; the righteous actors in their ways encouraged; secret discontents, fretting like cankers, remedied; merchandising and shipping, by special providence wasted, speedily increased; mines undertaken with more cheerfulness; fishing with more forwardness; husbandry, now withering, forthwith flourishing; villages and plantations, much deserted presently, more populous; all mechanical trades, the great enriching of all commonwealths, heartily going on; staple commodities, the life of trade, presently raised; our almost lost credit regained; our brethren of England's just indignation, and their force as a post flying from us, turned to embrace us; the honorable Houses of Parliament, patrons of piety, under their wings in these dangerous times with alacrity shrouding us; the privileges and immunities which we and ours enjoy in our native land more firmly settled; foreign enemies, daily threatening, totally discouraged; unsettled men, now abounding, firmly planted; that the prosperity of England may not be the ruin of this plantation but the contrary: hands, hearts, and purses, now straitened, freely opened for public and honorable services; strife and contention, now rife, abated; taxes and sesses lightened; the burthens of the state but pleasure, etc. . . .

Subscribed,

ROBERT CHILD	THOMAS FOWLE	SAMUEL MAVERICK
THOMAS BURTON	DAVID YALE	JOHN DAUD
JOHN SMITH		

The response of the Massachusetts authorities came at the next session of the General Court, in the form of a declaration in which the petitioners' claim met unsympathetic rebuttal. Moreover, Child and his associates were fined and admonished. When they tried to sail for England to appeal directly to Parliament, they were again seized and fined more heavily under the recent law that permitted the death penalty for anyone who "shall treachorously or perfidiously attempt the alteration of our frame of Polity or Government fundamentally." Yet in the end the impact of the Child petitioners bore importantly on the evolution of the Puritan tradition in America: partly as a result of the ruckus they raised, a law of 1647 permitted nonfreemen to participate in town politics, including the right to vote for local officials. The following year saw the publication of "the Book of the General Laws and Libertyes concerning the inhabitants of the Massachusetts." These offered no relief to Anglicans and Presbyterians in church or state, but at least all residents of the colony now had access to written laws. By their outspoken insistence on a public statement of the colony's laws, Dr. Child and his friends had helped to bring one forth.

25. Baptists

During the 1640s, the disparity between English and American views of religious toleration widened. After a visit to the British West Indies in 1645, a relative of the younger John Winthrop advised him that "the law of banishing for conscience . . . makes us stinke every wheare." Part of the New Englanders' unsavory reputation stemmed from their treatment of the Baptists—or Anabaptists, as they were often called. Their principal theological innovation lay in rejection of infant baptism; only a mature mind, they held, could grasp the import and majesty of the sacrament. Hence infant baptism was meaningless. The corollary held that the Congregationalists were misinterpreting the Bible and indulging in a faulty administration of the sacraments. For such contentions the Baptists felt the brunt of Puritan repression, a fact they soon broadcast to the world in pamphlets of the sort that follows, this one by Dr. John Clark (1609–1676), under the subtitle "A Faithfull and True Relation of the Prosecution of Obediah Holmes, John Crandall, and John Clarke, Meerly for Conscience Toward God. . . ."

Source: John Clark, "Ill Newes from New-England," Massachusetts Historical Society, Collections, 4 ser. II (1854), 27–33.

It came to pass that we three, by the good hand of our God, came into the Massachusetts Bay upon the 16th day of the 5th month, 1651; and upon the 19th of the same, upon occasion of business, we came unto a town in the same Bay called Lynn, where we lodged at a blind man's house near two miles out of this town, by the name of William Witter, who being baptized into Christ waits— as we also do—for the Kingdom of God and the full consolation of the Israel of God. Upon the 20th day, being the first day of the week, not having freedom in our spirits for want of a clear call from God to go unto the public assembly to declare there what was the mind and counsel of God concerning them, I judged it was a thing suitable to consider what the counsel of God was concerning our-selves; and finding by sad experience that the hour of temptation spoken of was coming upon all the world (in a more eminent way) to try them that are upon the earth, I fell upon the consideration of that word of promise, made to those that keep the word of His patience, which present thoughts, while in conscience towards God and good will unto His saints, I was imparting to my companions in the house where I lodged, and to four or five strangers that came in unexpected after I had begun, opening and proving what is meant by the hour of temptation, what by the word of His patience, and their keeping it, and how He that hath the key of David (being the promiser) will keep those that keep the word of His patience from the hour of temptation; while I say I was yet speaking, there comes into the house where we were two con-stables, who with their clamorous tongues made an interruption in my discourse, and more uncivilly disturbed us than the pursuivants of the old English bishops were wont to do, telling us that they were come with authority from the magistrate to apprehend us. I then desired to see the authority by which they thus proceeded, whereupon they plucked forth their warrant, and one of them with a trembling hand (as conscious he might have been better em-ployed) read it to us, the substance whereof was as followeth:

> By virtue hereof, you are required to go to the house of William Witter, and so to search from house to house for certain erroneous persons, being strangers, and them to apprehend, and in safe custody to keep, and tomorrow morning by eight of the clock to bring before me,
>
> Robert Bridges.

When he had read the warrant, I told them, "Friends, there shall not be (I trust) the least appearance of a resisting of that authority by which you come unto us; yet I tell you, that by virtue hereof you are not strictly tied, but if you please you may suffer us to make an end of what we have begun, so may you be witnesses either to or against the faith and order which we hold"; to which they answered they could not. . . .

. . . They apprehended us and carried us away to the alehouse, or ordinary, where after dinner one of them said unto us, "Gentlemen, if you be free I will carry you to the meeting"; to whom was replied, "Friend, had we been free thereunto we had prevented all this. Nevertheless, we are in thy hand, and if thou wilt carry us to the meeting, thither will we go"; to which he answered, "Then will I carry you to the meeting." To this we replied, "Because we perceive thou hast not long been employed in thine office, and that may follow hereupon which thou expectest not, we will inform thee that if thou forcest us unto your assembly, then shall we be constrained to declare ourselves that we cannot hold communion with them." The constable answered, "That is nothing to me, I have not power to command you to speak when you come there, or to be silent." To this I again replied, "Friend, know a little further: since we have heard the word of salvation by Jesus Christ, we have been taught as those that first trusted in Christ to be obedient unto Him both by word and deed; wherefore if we be forced to your meeting we shall declare our dissent from you both by word and gesture."

After all this, when he had consulted with the man of the house, he told us he would carry us to the meeting, so to their meeting were we brought while they were at their prayers and uncovered. And at my first stepping over the threshold I unveiled myself, civilly saluted them, turned in to the seat I was appointed to, put on my hat again, and so sat down, opened my book, and fell to reading. Here upon Mr. Bridges being troubled, commanded the constable to pluck off our hats, which he did, and where he laid mine, there I let it lie until their prayer, singing, and preaching was over. After this I stood up and uttered myself in these words following: "I desire as a stranger, if I may, to propose a few things to this congregation, hoping in the proposal thereof I shall commend myself to your consciences to be guided by that wisdom that is from above, which being pure is also peaceable, gentle, and easy to be entreated," and therewith I made a stop, expecting if the Prince of Peace had been among them, I should have had a suitable answer of peace from them; but no other voice I heard but of their pastor, as he is called, and their magistrate.

Their pastor answered by way of query, whether I was a member of a church? etc. Before I could give an answer, Mr. Bridges spake, saying, "If the congregation please to give you leave, well; if not, I shall require your silence, for," said he, "we will have no objections made against what is delivered," etc. To which I answered, "I am not about for present to make objections against what is delivered, but as by my gesture at my coming into your assembly I declared my dissent from you, so lest that should prove offensive unto some whom I would not offend, I would now by word of mouth declare the grounds, which are these: first, from the consideration we are strangers each to other, and so strangers to each other's inward standing with respect to God, and so cannot conjoin and act in faith, and what is not of faith is sin; and in the second place, I could not judge that you are gathered together and walk according to the visible order of our Lord"; which when I had declared, Mr. Bridges told me I done and spoke that for which I must answer, and so commanded me silence. When their meeting was done, the officer carried us again to the ordinary, where—being watched over that night as thieves and robbers—we were the next morning carried before Mr. Bridges, who made our *mittimus* and sent us to the prison at Boston. . . .

. . . Upon the 5th day sevennight after [we] were brought to our trial, in the forenoon we were examined; in the afternoon, without producing either accuser, witness, jury, law of God or man, we were sentenced. In our examination the Governor upbraided us with the name of Anabaptists. To whom I answered, "I disown the name. I an neither an Anabaptist, nor a Pedobaptist, nor a Catabaptist." He told me in haste I was all. I told him he could not prove us to be either of them. He said, "Yes, you have re-baptized"; I denied it, saying, "I have baptized many, but I never re-baptized any." Then said he, "You deny the former baptism and make all our worship a nullity." I told him he said it; moreover I said unto them (for therefore do I conceive I was brought before them to be a testimony against them), "If the testimony which I hold forth be true and according to the mind of God, which I undoubtedly affirm it is, then it concerns you to look to your standing." The like to this affirmed the other two; so after much discourse we were committed again to prison, and in the afternoon towards night we were called forth again, and immediately after the court was set my sentence was read, which was as followeth:

The Sentence of John Clarke of Rhode Island. 31. 5. 51.

Forasmuch as you John Clarke, being come into this jurisdiction about the 20th of July, did meet at one William Witter's house at Lynn, upon the Lord's day, and there did take upon you to preach to some other of the inhabitants of the same town, and being there taken by the constable, and coming afterwards into the assembly at Lynn, did in disrespect of the ordinances of God and His worship keep on your hat (the pastor being then in prayer), insomuch you would not give reverence in valing your hat till it was forced off your head, to the disturbance of the congregation, and professing against the institution of the church as not being according to the gospel of Jesus Christ; and that you the said John Clarke did upon the day following meet again at the said Witter's, and in contempt to authority, you being then in the custody of the law, and did there administer the Sacrament of the Supper to one excommunicate person, to another under admonition, and to another that was an inhabitant of Lynn and not in fellowship with any church; and upon your answer in open court, you affirmed that you did never rebaptize any, yet did acknowledge you did baptize such as were baptized before, and thereby did necessarily deny the baptism that was before to be baptism, the churches no churches, and also all other ordinances, and ministers, as if all were a nullity; and also did in the court deny the lawfulness of baptizing of infants, and all this tends to the dishonor of God, the despising the ordinances of God among us, the peace of the churches, and seducing the subjects of this commonwealth from the truth of the gospel of Jesus Christ, and perverting the straight ways of the Lord; therefore the court doth fine you twenty pounds to be paid, or sufficient sureties that the said sum shall be paid, by the first day of the next court of assistants, or else to be well whipped, and that you shall remain in prison till it be paid or security given in for it.

By the court,

INCREASE NOWELL.

After my sentence was read, the sentences of the other two were likewise pronounced: the sentence of Obadiah Holmes was to pay by the aforesaid time thirty pounds or be well whipped; and the sentence of John Crandall was to pay five pounds, or be well whipped. This being done, I desired to know whether I might not speak a few things to the court, to which the Governor replied,

"Your sentence is passed." I told him that which I was to speak was in reference unto a promise that was made us by Mr. Bridges when we were first apprehended and brought before him. "Then," said the Governor, "speak on." "When we were at first apprehended, and brought before Mr. Bridges," said I, "I said unto him, 'We are strangers, and strangers to your laws, and may be transgressors of them before we are aware, we would therefore desire this courtesy of you as strangers, that you would shew us the law by which we are transgressors.' But then no other answer could we have from him than this, 'When you come to the court you shall know the law.' Now we have been before the court in the forenoon upon examination, this afternoon we have heard our sentence read, yet have we not heard the law produced by which we are condemned. We therefore now desire to see the law in which our sentence may be read, and the rather, because we find in the beginning of your laws this provision for the security of your own (and we hope you are not less regardful of strangers), viz.: that no man shall be molested, but by a law made by the General Court, and lawfully published, or in defect of a law in a particular case, by the word of God."

When this was spoken, Mr. Bridges could easily turn to the law by which we might be freed, but none were able to turn to the law of God or man by which we were condemned. At length the Governor stepped up and told us we had denied infants' baptism, and being somewhat transported, broke forth and told me I had deserved death, and said he would not have such trash brought into their jurisdiction. Moreover, he said, "You go up and down and secretly insinuate into those that are weak, but you cannot maintain it before our ministers, you may try, and discourse or dispute with them," etc. To this I had much to reply, but that he commanded the jailer to take us away. . . .

26. Quakers

More persistent and more outspoken than the Baptists were members of a sect that emerged in England in the mid-seventeenth century as the Society of Friends, commonly known as Quakers. Despite a Massachusetts day of public humiliation to implore God's aid against "the

Ranters and Quakers," by the fall of 1656 several had managed to evade laws against their entry into New England. The early Quakers exhibited remarkably aggressive ways: disruption of church services and repudiation of civil authority, for example, and a host of lesser irritants such as refusal to doff hats in church or court. In Massachusetts, Deborah Wilson walked naked through the streets of Salem, Lydia Wardell went unclothed into the church at Newbury, and Thomas Newhouse dramatically smashed two bottles in front of the Boston congregation with a warning that "thus will the Lord break you in pieces." Every New England colony save Rhode Island legislated against the Friends. New Haven's enactment was typical.

Source: Charles J. Hoadly, ed., Records of the Colony . . . of New Haven (2 vols., Hartford, 1857–1858), II, 238–241.

Whereas there is a cursed sect of heretics lately risen up in the world, which are commonly called Quakers, who take upon them that they are immediately sent of God and infallibly assisted by the spirit, who yet speak and write blasphemous opinions, despise government and the order of God in church and commonwealth, speaking evil of dignities, reproaching and reviling magistrates and ministers, seeking to turn the people from the faith and to gain proselytes to their pernicious ways; this court taking into serious consideration the premises and to prevent (as much as in them lies) the like mischief as by their means is wrought in our native country, do hereby order and declare:

That whosoever shall hereafter bring or cause to be brought, directly or indirectly, any known Quaker or Quakers, or other blasphemous heretics, into this jurisdiction, every such person shall forfeit the sum of £50 to the jurisdiction, except it appear that he wanted true knowledge or information of their being such, and in that case he hath liberty to clear himself by his oath, when sufficient proof to the contrary is wanting. And for default of payment or satisfying security, [he] shall be committed to prison, there to remain till the said sum be satisfied to the jurisdiction treasurer.
. . .

And it is hereby further ordered that what Quaker or Quakers soever shall come into this jurisdiction from foreign parts or places adjacent, if it be about their civil lawful occasions to be quickly dispatched among us, which time of stay shall be limited by the civil authority in each plantation, and that they shall not use any

means, by words, writings, books, or any other way go about to
corrupt or seduce others, nor revile or reproach, or any other way
make disturbance or offend; they shall upon their first arrival, or
coming in, appear or be brought before the authority of the place,
and from them have license to pass about and issue their lawful
occasions, and shall (for the better prevention of hurt to the
people) have one or more to attend upon them at their charge till
such occasions of theirs be dispatched and they returned out of the
jurisdiction, which if they refuse to do, they shall then be denied
such free passage and commerce, and be caused to return back
again. But if at this first time they shall offend in any of the ways as
is before expressed, and contrary to the intent of this law, they
shall be committed to prison, severely whipped, kept to work, and
none suffered to converse with them during their imprisonment,
which shall be no longer than necessity requires, and at their own
charge sent out of the jurisdiction.

And if after they have once suffered the law as before and shall
presume to come into this jurisdiction again, every such male
Quaker shall for the second offense be branded on the hand with
the letter H, be committed to prison and kept to work till he can
be sent away at his own charge; and for a third offense shall be
branded on the other hand, committed to prison, and kept to work
as aforesaid. And every woman Quaker that hath suffered the law
here, and shall presume to come into this jurisdiction again, shall
be severely whipped, committed to prison, and kept to work till she
can be sent away at her own charge, and so also for her coming
again she shall be alike used as aforesaid. And for every Quaker, he
or she, that shall a fourth time herein again offend, they shall
have their tongues bored through with a hot iron, committed to
prison, and kept at work till they be sent away at their own charge.
And all and every Quaker arising from among ourselves shall be
dealt with and suffer the like punishment as the law provides
against foreign Quakers.

And it is further ordered that if any person shall knowingly bring
into this jurisdiction any Quakers' books, papers, or writings concerning their devilish opinions, [he] shall pay for every such book
or writing, being legally proved against him or them, the sum of
£5. And whosoever shall disperse or conceal any such book, paper,
or writing, and shall not immediately deliver in the same to the
magistrate in the place, or to the deputies or constables where

there is no magistrate, and it be after found with him or her, or in his or her house, or otherwise fully proved that they had such book or writing in their custody, shall pay £5 for the disposing or concealing of every such book or writing. And when any such books or writings are brought or come into the hands of any of the magistrates, deputies, or constables in any plantation, they shall with the advice and approbation of the minister of the place keep them in safe custody, that none may come to see and read them and so receive hurt by them, which this court leaves to their discretion to order. And being so kept, they shall be brought to New Haven and presented to the next General Court, unless they shall see cause to send them before, or that the governor and magistrates shall call for them upon any occasion that may concern the jurisdiction.

And if any person or persons in this jurisdiction shall henceforth entertain and conceal any such Quaker or Quakers, or other blasphemous heretics (knowing them so to be), every such person shall forfeit to the jurisdiction 20 shillings for every hour's entertainment and concealment of any Quaker or Quakers, etc., as aforesaid, and shall be committed to prison till the forfeiture be fully paid or satisfying security given for the same.

And it is by this court further ordered that if any person within this colony shall take upon them to defend the heretical opinions of the said Quakers, or any of the said books or papers aforesaid, ex animo, or so as may corrupt the minds of the weak hearers (if legally proved), shall be fined for the first time 40 shillings. If they shall persist in the same, and shall so again defend it the second time, £4. If still notwithstanding, they shall again so defend and maintain the said Quakers' heretical opinions, they shall be committed to prison, there to remain till there be convenient passage for them to be sent away, being sentenced by the court of magistrates to banishment.

Lastly, it is hereby ordered that what person or persons soever shall revile the office or person of magistrates or ministers, as it is usual with the Quakers, such person or persons shall be severely whipped, or pay the sum £5.

No laws could thwart the determination of the early Quakers. When imprisonment and fines proved ineffective, Massachusetts threatened any who reentered the colony after banishment with the cropping of an ear, and in 1658 this barbarous penalty was performed on three men who had twice returned after expulsion. In the following June Massa-

chusetts banished three Quakers with the threat of death if they returned. All did come back, whereupon the General Court meted out full measure: in October 1659 two were hanged on the Boston Common. The third, a former disciple of Anne Hutchinson named Mary Dyer, received a gallows reprieve—partly because of her sex, partly in order to demonstrate the Court's contention that "wee desire theire life absent rather then theire death present." But Mrs. Dyer returned to Boston the following spring and was executed, as was a fourth Quaker in 1661. That put an end to capital punishment for heretics, though not to the persecution of Quakers. Throughout the rest of the century, Friends remained unwelcome troublers of Zion, but a revulsion among the people and magistrates of Massachusetts combined with directives from London to halt further application of the supreme penalty. Within another generation the Quakers and many other sects openly observed their religious services in Boston and elsewhere in the Puritan colonies, a sign that the Puritan monopoly on the religious life of New England had ended. The execution of the Quakers had marked the illogical conclusion of the theory of exclusion; from that point on the theory eroded reluctantly but inexorably as more liberal concepts of toleration seeped into New England from England and from neighboring colonies.

VI

Propagating the Heritage

SINCE ONE of the Puritans' motives for setting up a New Zion in America had been to promote the eventual reformation of all mankind, Puritan New England took steps to spread its message to friend and foe alike. The latter would learn primarily from the Puritans' example; as Winthrop had pointed out in his "A Modell of Christian Charity," "the eies of all people are uppon us." To those who watched from afar, the example of Christian living and the reading of Puritan tracts would have to suffice. At the same time, the Puritans of New England had a more immediate task: to spread among the non-believers of New England a veneration for Puritan convictions and Puritan mores. Included among the non-believers, in a special way, were the children of the saints themselves, for they would soon inherit the reins of New Zion; they and their contemporaries whose parents had somehow failed to find signs of saving grace must be subjected to a Puritan version of Christian education—in both the narrow sense of learning catechisms and the broad sense of learning arts and sciences.

27. Schools in the Wilderness

In the cultural baggage they brought to America as part of the Puritan tradition, the early New Englanders included a high regard for formal education. In large measure their motivation was religious: to permit everyman to read the Bible and thus be able to obey God's laws and perhaps find eternal salvation. In part, also, it was humanistic: to help every citizen acquire the knowledge and skill to be a happy and productive member of society—though of course the end purpose of society was the glorification of God and therefore in itself a religious aim. Whatever the aim, it called for a system of universal education.

A. Schools Ordered

Prior to 1635, whatever schooling took place in New England was of an informal sort: parents and occasionally clergymen held privately arranged sessions for individuals or small groups of youngsters. In 1635, Boston hired a schoolmaster; Charlestown followed suit the next year and Dorchester three years after that. New Haven, not founded until 1638, voted in 1641 that "a free school shall be set up in this town." But because in a frontier society not all parents and not all towns could be counted on to accept in full their educational responsibilities, the Massachusetts legislature in the 1640s took steps to insure at least minimum schooling for all children. Connecticut adopted the Bay Colony's regulations almost verbatim, and New Haven accepted them in spirit, if not in letter. Plymouth and Rhode Island lagged behind for most of the seventeenth century.

Source: Nathaniel B. Shurtleff, ed., Records of the Governor and Company of the Massachusetts Bay in New England (5 vols., Boston, 1853–1854) II, 8–9, 203.

14 June 1642

This [General] Court [of Massachusetts] taking into consideration the great neglect in many parents and masters in training up their children in learning and labor, and other employments which may be profitable to the commonwealth, do hereupon order and decree that in every town the chosen men appointed for managing the prudential affairs of the same shall henceforth stand charged with the care of the redress of this evil, so as they shall be liable to be punished or fined for the neglect thereof, upon any presentment of the grand jurors, or other information or complaint in any plantations in this jurisdiction; and for this end they, or the greater part of them, shall have power to take account from time to time of their parents and masters, and of their children, concerning their calling and employment of their children, especially of their ability to read and understand the principles of religion and the capital laws of the country, and to impose fines upon all those who refuse to render such account to them when required; and they shall have power (with consent of any court or magistrates) to put forth apprentice the children of such as shall not be able and fit to employ and bring them up, nor shall take course to dispose of them themselves; and they are to take care that such as are set to keep cattle be set to some other employment withal as spinning upon the rock, knitting, weaving tape, etc.; and that boys and girls be not suffered to converse together so as may occasion any wanton, dishonest, or immodest behavior; and for their better performance of this trust committed to them, they may divide the town amongst them, appointing to every of the said townsmen a certain number of families to have special oversight of; they are also to provide that a sufficient quantity of materials as hemp, flax, etc., may be raised in their several towns, and tools and implements provided for working out the same; and for their assistance in this so needful and beneficial employment, if they meet with any difficulty or opposition which they cannot well master by their own power, they may have recourse to some of the magistrates, who shall take such course for their help and encouragement as the occasion shall require, according to justice; and the said townsmen, at the next court in those limits, after the end of their year, shall give a brief account in writing of their proceedings herein; provided that they have been so required by some court or magistrate a month at least before; and this order to continue for two years, and till the court shall take further order.

11 November 1647

It being one chief project of that old deluder, Satan, to keep men from the knowledge of the scriptures, as in former times by keeping them in an unknown tongue, so in these latter times by persuading from the use of tongues, that so at least the true sense and meaning of the original might be clouded by false glosses of saint-seeming deceivers, that learning may not be buried in the grave of our fathers in the church and commonwealth, the Lord assisting our endeavors.

It is therefore ordered that every township in this jurisdiction, after the Lord hath increased them to the number of fifty householders, shall then forthwith appoint one within their town to teach all such children as shall resort to him to write and read, whose wages shall be paid either by the parents or masters of such children, or by the inhabitants in general, by way of supply, as the major part of those that order the prudentials of the town shall appoint; provided those that send their children be not oppressed by paying much more than they can have them taught for in other towns; and it is further ordered that where any town shall increase to the number of 100 families or householders, they shall set up a grammar school, the master thereof being able to instruct youth so far as they may be fitted for the university, provided that if any town neglect the performance hereof above one year, that every such town shall pay £5 to the next school till they shall perform this order.

B. Schools Established

Not all Puritan communities complied with the Court's directives (as records of punitive action against them make clear), but the majority did. Typical was the town of Dorchester, on the southern side of Boston Harbor, which in 1645 set up a regular procedure for the administration of its educational endeavors. A crucial part of those procedures enjoined the school wardens and schoolmaster to make sure their young scholars ingested "dutifull behavior" and "the principles of Christian religion," as well as the usual academic fare.

Source: *Fourth Report of the [Boston] Record Commissioners* (Boston, 1880), 54–57.

Upon a general and lawful warning of all the inhabitants, the 14th of the 1st month, 1645, these rules and orders presented to the town concerning the school of Dorchester are confirmed by the major part of the inhabitants then present.

First, it is ordered that three able and sufficient men of the plantation shall be chosen to be wardens or overseers of the school above mentioned, who shall have the charge, oversight, and ordering thereof, and of all things concerning the same in such manner as is hereafter expressed, and shall continue in their office and place for term of their lives respectively, unless by reason of any of them removing his habitation out of the town, or for any other weighty reason the inhabitants shall see cause to elect or choose others in their room, in which cases, and upon the death of any of the said wardens, the inhabitants shall make a new election and choice of others.

And Mr. Haward, Deacon Wiswall, Mr. Atherton are elected to be the first wardens or overseers.

Secondly, the said wardens shall have full power to dispose of the school stock, whether the same be in hand or otherwise, both such as is already in being and such as may by any good means hereafter be added; and shall collect and receive the rents, issues, and profits arising and growing of and from the said stock. And the said rents, issues, and profits [they] shall employ and lay out only for the best behoof and advantage of the said school, and the furtherance of learning thereby, and shall give a faithful and true account of their receipts and disbursements so often as they shall be thereunto required by the inhabitants or the major part of them.

Thirdly, the said wardens shall take care and do their utmost and best endeavor that the said school may from time to time be supplied with an able and sufficient schoolmaster, who nevertheless is not to be admitted into the place of schoolmaster without the general consent of the inhabitants or the major part of them.

Fourthly, so often as the said school shall be supplied with a schoolmaster so provided and admitted as aforesaid, the wardens shall from time to time pay or cause to be paid unto the said schoolmaster such wages out of the rents, issues, and profits of the school stock as shall of right come due to be paid.

Fifthly, the said wardens shall from time to time see that the schoolhouse be kept in good and sufficient repair, the charges of which reparation shall be defrayed and paid out of such rents, issues, and profits of the school stock, if there be sufficient, or else of such rents as shall arise and grow in the time of the vacancy of the schoolmaster—if there be any such—and in defect of such vacancy the wardens shall repair to the seven men of the town for the time being, who shall have power to tax the town with such sum, or sums, as shall be requisite for the repairing of the schoolhouse as aforesaid.

Sixthly, the said wardens shall take care that every year at or before the end of the 9th month there be brought to the schoolhouse 12 sufficient cart or wain loads of wood for fuel, to be for the use of the schoolmaster and the scholars in winter, the cost and charges of which said wood to be borne by the scholars for the time being, who shall be taxed for the purpose at the discretion of the said wardens.

Lastly, the said wardens shall take care that the schoolmaster for the time being do faithfully perform his duty in his place, as schoolmasters ought to do, as well as in other things as in these which are hereafter expressed, viz.:

First, that the schoolmaster shall diligently attend his school and do his utmost endeavor for benefiting his scholars according to his best discretion, without unnecessarily absenting himself to the prejudice of his scholars and hindering their learning.

Secondly, that from the beginning of the 1st month until the end of the 7th he shall every day begin to teach at seven of the clock in the morning and dismiss his scholars at five in the afternoon. And for the other five months, that is from the beginning of the 8th month until the end of the 12th month, it shall every day begin at eight of the clock in the morning and [end] at four in the afternoon.

Thirdly, every day in the year the usual time of dismissing at noon shall be at eleven and to begin at one, except that

Fourthly, every second day in the week he shall call his scholars together between twelve and one of the clock to examine them what they have learned on the Sabbath day preceding, at which time also he shall take notice of any misdemeanor or disorder that any of his scholars shall have committed on the Sabbath, to the end that at some convenient time due admonition and correction may be administered by him according as the nature and quality of the offense shall require. At which said examination any of the elders or other inhabitants that please may be present to behold his religious care herein and to give their countenance and approbation of the same.

Fifthly, he shall equally and impartially receive and instruct such as shall be sent and committed to him for that end, whether their parents be poor or rich, not refusing any who have right and interest in the school.

Sixthly, such as shall be committed to him, he shall diligently instruct as they shall be able to learn, both in humane learning and good literature, and likewise in point of good manners and dutiful behavior towards all, specially their superiors as they shall have occasion to be in their presence, whether by meeting them in the street or otherwise.

Seventhly, every 6th day of the week at two of the clock in the afternoon, he shall catechize his scholars in the principles of Christian religion, either in some catechism which the wardens shall provide and present, or in defect thereof in some other.

Eighthly, and because all man's endeavors without the blessing of God must needs be fruitless and unsuccessful, therefore it is to be a chief part of the schoolmaster's religious care to commend his scholars and his labors amongst them unto God by prayer, morning and evening, taking care that his scholars do reverently attend during the same.

Ninthly, and because the rod of correction is an ordinance of God necessary sometimes to be dispensed unto children, but such as may easily be abused by overmuch severity and rigor on the one hand, or by overmuch indulgence and lenity on the other, it is therefore ordered and agreed that the schoolmaster for the time being shall have full power to minister correction to all or any of his scholars, without respect of persons, according as the nature and quality of the offense shall require; whereto all his scholars must be duly subject and no parent or other of the inhabitants shall hinder or go about to hinder the master therein. Nevertheless, if any parent or others shall think there is just cause of complaint against the master for too much severity, such shall have liberty friendly and lovingly to expostulate with the master about the same, and if they shall not attain to satisfaction, the matter is then to be referred to the wardens, who shall impartially judge betwixt the master and such complainants. And if it shall appear to them that any parent shall make causeless complaints against the master in this behalf, and shall persist and continue so doing, in such case the wardens shall have power to discharge the master of the care and charge of the children of such parents. But if the thing complained of be true, and that the master have indeed been guilty of ministering excessive correction, and shall appear to them to continue therein notwithstanding that they have advised him otherwise, in such case—as also in the case of too much lenity or any other great neglect of duty in his place, persisted in it—it shall be in the power of the wardens to call the inhabitants together to consider whether it were not meet to discharge the master of his place that so some other more desirable may be provided.

And because it is difficult if not impossible to give particular rules that shall reach all cases which may fall out, therefore for a conclusion it is ordered and agreed, in general, that where particular rules are wanting there, it shall be a part of the office and duty of the wardens to order and dispose of all things that concern the school, in such sort as in their wisdom and discretion they shall judge most conducible for the glory of God and the training up of the children of the town in religion, learning, and civility.

And these orders to be continued till the major part of the town shall see cause to alter any part thereof.

C. Schoolbooks

More important to Puritan education than the physical structure of the schoolhouse or perhaps even than the character of the schoolmaster were the books put into young hands. A standard speller came off the Cambridge Press in 1643, and somewhat later a catechism by John Cotton entitled Spiritual Milk for Boston Babes in Either England, Drawn out of the Breasts of Both Testaments; both books were widely used. But the core of youthful studies was the primer, at first imported from England but after the 1680s written and published in New England. Authors of the primers seized every opportunity to promote moral and religious precepts, even while ostensibly teaching the alphabet.

Source: Paul Leicester Ford, ed., The New-England Primer (New York, 1897), 65–72.

A   In Adam's fall
    We sinned all.

B   Thy life to mend
    This Book attend.

C   The Cat doth play
    And after stay.

D   A Dog will bite
    A thief at night.

E   An Eagle's flight
    Is out of sight.

F   The idle Fool
    Is whipped at school.

G   As runs the Glass
    Man's life doth pass.

H   My book and Heart
    Shall never part.

J   Job feels the rod
    Yet blesses God.

K   Our King the good
    No man of blood.

L   The Lion bold
    The lamb doth hold.

M   The Moon gives light
    In time of night.

N   Nightingales sing
    In time of Spring.

O   The royal Oak
    it was the tree
    That saved His
    Royal Majesty.

P   Peter denies
    His Lord and cries.

Q   Queen Esther comes
    in royal state
    To save the Jews
    from dismal fate.

R   Rachel doth mourn
    For her first-born.

S   Samuel anoints
    Whom God appoints.

T   Time cuts down all
    Both great and small.

U   Uriah's beauteous wife
    Made David seek his life.

W   Whales in the sea
    God's voice obey.

X   Xerxes the great did die
    And so must you and I.

Y   Youth forward slips
    Death soonest nips.

Z   Zacheus he did climb the tree
    His Lord to see.

Now the child being entered in his letters and spelling, let him learn these and such like sentences by heart, whereby he will be both instructed in his duty, and encouraged in his learning:

THE DUTIFUL CHILD'S PROMISES

I will fear God, and honor the King.
I will honor my father and mother.
I will obey my superiors.
I will submit to my elders.
I will love my friends.
I will hate no man.
I will forgive my enemies, and pray to God for them.
I will as much as in me lies keep all God's Holy Commandments.
I will learn my catechism.
I will keep the Lord's day holy.
I will reverence God's sanctuary,
    For our God is a consuming fire.

AN ALPHABET OF LESSONS FOR YOUTH

A wise son makes a glad father, but a foolish son is the heaviness of his mother.

Better is a little with the fear of the Lord, than great treasure and trouble therewith.

Come unto Christ all ye that labor and are heavy laden, and He will give you rest.

Do not the abominable thing which I hate, saith the Lord.

Except a man be born again, he cannot see the kingdom of God.

Foolishness is bound up in the heart of a child, but the rod of correction shall drive it far from him.

Grieve not the Holy Spirit.

Holiness becomes God's house forever.

It is good for me to draw near unto God.

Keep thy heart with all diligence, for out of it are the issues of life.

Liars shall have their part in the lake which burns with fire and brimstone.

Many are the afflictions of the righteous, but the Lord delivers them out of them all.

Now is the accepted time, now is the day of salvation.

Out of the abundance of the heart the mouth speaketh.

Pray to thy Father which is in secret, and thy Father which sees in secret shall reward thee openly.

Quit you like men, be strong, stand fast in the faith.

Remember thy Creator in the days of thy youth.

Salvation belongeth to the Lord.

Trust in God at all times ye people, pour out your hearts before Him.

Upon the wicked God shall rain an horrible tempest.

Woe to the wicked, it shall be ill with him, for the reward of his hands shall be given him.

EXhort one another daily while it is called today, lest any of you be hardened through the deceitfulness of sin.

Young men ye have overcome the wicked one.

Zeal hath consumed me, because thy enemies have forgotten the words of God.

Choice Sentences

1. Praying will make thee leave sinning or sinning will make thee leave praying.

2. Our weakness and inabilities break not the bond of our duties.

3. What we are afraid to speak before men, we should be afraid to think before God.

28. Collegiate Education

Elementary and grammar schools formed the base of Puritan formal education; at the apex sat collegiate institutions. From the outset, the colonists realized that some graduates of the grammar schools might journey to England to attend Oxford or Cambridge. But the trip would be dangerous, costly, and perhaps fruitless, for the university as well as the church felt Archbishop Laud's purge of Puritan influence. The solution lay in creating new colleges in America, a formidable task for a frontier society. Yet the need for a trained ministry and an enlightened magistracy could not be denied if the Puritan experiment in Christian living were to survive the first generation.

A. Founding of Harvard

A surprisingly large number—one hundred thirty or more—of the early settlers of New England had attended English or Continental universities, and a great many of them had studied at Emmanuel College, Cambridge. With Emmanuel as a model, the Puritan settlers moved speedily to establish collegiate education in New England. In October, 1636, the Massachusetts legislature voted to appropriate £400 "towards a schoale or colledge." Two years later, John Harvard of Charlestown (B.A. Emmanuel, 1632; M.A. 1635) willed to the fledgling institution a library of nearly four hundred volumes and a legacy of almost £800. Soon New Englanders were boasting of their "colledge" in a pamphlet published in London in 1643.

Source: *New England's First Fruits: With Divers Other Special Matters Concerning That Country* (London, 1643; reprinted New York, 1865), 23–30.

After God had carried us safe to New England, and we had builded our houses, provided necessaries for our livelihood, reared convenient places for God's worship, and settled the civil government, one of the next things we longed for and looked after was to advance learning and perpetuate it to posterity, dreading to leave an illiterate ministry to the churches when our present ministers shall lie in the dust. And as we were thinking and consulting how to effect this great work, it pleased God to stir up the heart of one Mr. Harvard (a godly gentleman and a lover of learning, there living amongst us) to give the one half of his estate (it being in all about £1,700) towards erecting of a college, and all his library. After him another gave £300, others after them cast in more, and the public hand of the state added the rest. The college was by common consent appointed to be at Cambridge (a place very pleasant and accommodate) and is called, according to the name of the first founder, Harvard College.

The edifice is very fair and comely within and without, having in it a spacious hall where they daily meet at commons, lectures, exercises, and a large library with some books to it, the gifts of divers of our friends, their chambers and studies also fitted for and possessed by the students, and all other rooms of office necessary and convenient, with all needful offices thereto belonging. And by the side of the college a fair grammar school for the training up of young scholars and fitting of them for academical learning, that still as they are judged ripe they may be received into the college of this school. Master Corlet is the master, who hath very well approved himself for his abilities, dexterity, and painfulness in teaching and education of the youth under him.

Over the college is Master Dunster placed as President, a learned, conscionable, and industrious man, who hath so trained up his pupils in the tongues and arts, and so seasoned them with the principles of divinity and Christianity, that we have to our great comfort, and in truth beyond our hopes, beheld their progress in learning and godliness also. The former of these hath appeared in their public declamations in Latin and Greek and disputations logical and philosophical, which they have been wonted (besides their ordinary exercises in the college hall) in the audience of the magistrates, ministers, and other scholars, for the probation of their growth in learning, upon set days, constantly once every month to make and uphold. The latter hath been manifested in sundry of them by the savory breathings of their spirits in their godly conversation. Insomuch that we are confident, if these early blossoms may be cherished and warmed with the influence of the friends of learning and lovers of this pious work, they will by the help of God come to happy maturity in a short time.

Over the college are twelve overseers chosen by the General Court, six of them are of the magistrates, the other six of the ministers, who are to promote the best good of it and (having a power of influence into all persons in it) are to see that everyone be diligent and proficient in his proper place. . . .

The times and order of their studies unless experience shall shew cause to alter:

The second and third day of the week, read lectures as followeth:

To the first year at eighth of the clock in the morning, logic the first three quarters, physics the last quarter.

To the second year at the ninth hour, ethics and politics at convenient distances of time.

To the third year at the tenth, arithmetic and geometry the three first quarters, astronomy the last.

Afternoon,

The first year disputes at the second hour.

The second year at the third hour.

The third year at the fourth, every one in his art.

The fourth day reads Greek.

To the first year, the etymology and syntax at the eighth hour.

To the second at the ninth hour, prosody and dialects.

Afternoon,

The first year at second hour, practice the precepts of grammar in such authors as have variety of words.

The second year at third hour, practice in poesy, Nonnus, Duport, or the like.

The third year, perfect their theory before noon and exercise style, composition, imitation, epitome, both in prose and verse, afternoon.

The fifth day reads Hebrew and the Eastern tongues.

Grammar to the first year, hour the eighth.

To the second, Chaldee at the ninth hour.

To the third, Syriac at the tenth hour.

Afternoon,

The first year practice in the Bible at the second hour.

The second in Ezra and Daniel at the third hour.

The third at the fourth hour in Trostius New Testament.

The sixth day reads rhetoric to all at the eighth hour.

Declamations at the ninth. So ordered that every scholar may declaim once a month. The rest of the day *vacat rhetoricis studiis.*

The seventh day reads divinity catechetical at the eighth hour, commonplaces at the ninth hour.

Afternoon,

The first hour reads history in the winter.

The nature of plants in the summer.

The sum of every lecture shall be examined before the new lecture be read.

B. Laws, Liberties, and Orders of Harvard

The governing board of the new college set standards of admission and decorum considered appropriate for the young men who aspired to become Bachelors or Masters of Arts.

Source: Colonial Society of Massachusetts, *Collections,* XV (1925), 24–27.

THE LAWS, LIBERTIES, AND ORDERS OF HARVARD COLLEGE
CONFIRMED BY THE OVERSEERS AND PRESIDENT OF THE
COLLEGE IN THE YEARS 1642, 1643, 1644, 1645,
AND 1646, AND PUBLISHED TO THE SCHOLARS FOR
THE PERPETUAL PRESERVATION OF THEIR WELFARE
AND GOVERNMENT

1. When any scholar is able to read Tully or such like classical Latin author *ex tempore,* and make and speak true Latin in verse and prose *suo* (*ut aiunt*) *Marte,* and decline perfectly the paradigms of nouns and verbs in the Greek tongue, then may be he admitted into the College, nor shall any claim admission before such qualifications.

2. Everyone shall consider the main end of his life and studies, to know God and Jesus Christ which is Eternal Life, John 17:3.

3. Seeing the Lord giveth wisdom, everyone shall seriously by prayer in secret seek wisdom of Him. Prov. 2:2, 3, etc.

4. Everyone shall so exercise himself in reading the scriptures twice a day that they be ready to give an account of their proficiency therein, both in theoretical observations of language and logic, and in practical and spiritual truths as their tutor shall require, according to their several abilities respectively, seeing the entrance of the word giveth light, etc., Psal. 119:130.

5. In the public church assembly, they shall carefully shun all gestures that shew any contempt or neglect of God's ordinances and be ready to give an account to their tutors of their profiting, and to use the helps of storing themselves with knowledge as their tutors shall direct them. And all sophisters and bachelors (until themselves make commonplace) shall publicly repeat sermons in the hall whenever they are called forth.

6. They shall eschew all profanation of God's holy name, attri-

butes, word, ordinances, and times of worship, and study with reverence and love carefully to retain God and His truth in their minds.

7. They shall honor as their parents, magistrates, elders, tutors, and aged persons, by being silent in their presence (except they be called on to answer), not gainsaying, shewing all those laudable expressions of honor and reverence in their presence that are in use, as bowing before them, standing uncovered, or the like.

8. They shall be slow to speak, and eschew not only oaths, lies, and uncertain rumors, but likewise all idle, foolish, bitter scoffing, frothy, wanton words, and offensive gestures.

9. None shall pragmatically intrude or intermeddle in other men's affairs.

10. During their residence, they shall studiously redeem their time, observe the general hours appointed for all the scholars, and the special hour for their own lecture, and then diligently attend the lectures without any disturbance by word or gesture. And if of anything they doubt, they shall inquire as of their fellows, so in case of non-resolution modestly of their tutors.

11. None shall under any pretense whatsoever frequent the company and society of such men as lead an ungirt and dissolute life.

Neither shall any without license of the overseers of the college be of the artillery or trainband.

Nor shall any without license of the overseers of the college, his tutor's leave, or in his absence the call of parents or guardians go out to another town.

12. No scholar shall buy, sell, or exchange anything to the value of sixpence without the allowance of his parents, guardians, or tutors. And whosoever is found to have sold or bought any such thing without acquainting their tutor or parents, shall forfeit the value of the commodity or the restoring of it, according to the discretion of the president.

13. The scholars shall never use their mother tongue except tha[t] in public exercises of oratory or such like they be called to make them in English.

14. If any scholar being in health shall be absent from prayer or lectures, except in case of urgent necessity or by the leave of his tutor, he shall be liable to admonition (or such punishment as the president shall think meet) if he offend above once a week.

15. Every scholar shall be called by his surname only till he be invested with his first degree, except he be fellow-commoner or a Knight's eldest son, or of superior nobility.

16. No scholars shall under any pretense of recreation or other cause whatever (unless foreshewed and allowed by the president or his tutor) be absent from his studies or appointed exercises above an hour at morning-bever, half an hour at afternoon-bever, an hour and an half at dinner, and so long at supper.

17. If any scholar shall transgress any of the laws of God or the house out of perverseness or apparent negligence, after twice admonition he shall be liable if not *adultus* to correction. If *adultus*, his name shall be given up to the overseers of the college that he may be publicly dealt with after the desert of his [fau]lt, but in [gros]ser offenses such gradual proceeding shall not be ex[pected].

18. Every scholar that on proof is found able to read the original of the Old and New Testament into the Latin tongue, and to resolve them logically, withal being of honest life and conversation, and at any public act hath the approbation of the overseers and master of the college, may be invested with his first degree [of Bachelor of Arts].

19. Every scholar that giveth up in writing a synopsis or *summa* of logic, natural and moral philosophy, arithmethic, geometry, and astronomy, and is ready to defend his theses or positions, withal skilled in the originals as aforesaid, and still continues honest and studious, at any public act after trial he shall be capable of the second degree of Master of Arts.

C. A Second Puritan College

Despite frequent shortages of funds, occasional internal dissensions, and distractions from the English Civil War, Indian uprisings, and other external crises, Harvard flourished. Students came from all over New England and not a few also from the other British colonies and from England. By the third quarter of the seventeenth century, Harvard graduates staffed most of the important positions in church and state throughout the Puritan colonies; by 1700, a total of 465 young men had graduated from the college at Cambridge.

But increasingly it seemed to residents of the Connecticut Valley that Harvard was unduly expensive ("it being so very remote from us"); some also expressed concern over Harvard's gradual but perceptible drift from the serious and purposeful atmosphere of the early years ("Places of Learning should not be Places of Riot and Pride"); and beginning in the 1690s some of the more conservative supporters of Harvard took alarm at the growing influence of liberals such as tutors John Leverett and William Brattle. (In 1707, over the strenuous opposition of the Mathers, Leverett became the first non-cleric to gain the presidency of Harvard.) In any event, in 1701 a group of Congregational clergymen, mostly Harvard graduates, met to found a new college. It went by the title "Collegiate School" until renamed for a generous benefactor.

The new college, like Harvard, had early difficulties with paucity of income, frequent changes in staff, and rebellious students. Within a few years of its opening, Samuel Johnson—later president of King's College—reported that the students were finding fault with their tutors and that "the Unruly & Ungoverned Schollars [were] advanced to a Great height . . . by some Gentlemen up on Connecticut River. . . ." The roots of that episode and most of the other difficulties of the Collegiate School lay in finding a satisfactory location: Saybrook, Hartford, and New Haven all vied vigorously for the honor of housing the second Puritan college. Saybrook, at the mouth of the Connecticut River, held the early lead, and it was there that the first degrees were awarded in 1702. But after long and acrimonious debate, New Haven won out, and the college moved there in 1716. Or at least part of it did, for dissent continued and that year three campuses existed—at Saybrook, Wethersfield, and New Haven. Even after New Haven won backing from the state legislature, where in the lower house "there was great throws & pangs & Controversy & mighty Struglings," Wethersfield held a rump commencement. That proved the last gasp of the dissidents, however, for in 1718 Elihu Yale's handsome donation provided the college with an adequate endowment and a permanent name. Until then, as the following letter to Jeremiah Dummer, Connecticut's agent in London, illustrates, the trustees had their hands full providing shelter, books, and a modicum of stability.

Source: Franklin B. Dexter, ed., *Documentary History of Yale* (New Haven, 1916), 146–148.

Right Worshipful Sir:

We have remaining grateful resentments* of your generous donation of an handsome number of books to furnish our library, indeed not yet prepared. We are in hopes of having shortly perfected our splendid collegiate house, which was raised on the eighth instant. We behold its fair aspect in the marketplace of New Haven, mounted in an eminent place thereof, in length ten rods, in breadth twenty-one foot, and near thirty foot upright, a

* "Resentments" is here used in the antiquated sense of "appreciation." [Editor]

spacious hall and an equally spacious library, all in a little time to be splendily completed. It was some months past far from our thoughts that the house would have been built in any other town than Saybrook, but great dissatisfaction taken by some of our own number hath occasioned a dark cloud of reflection on that place as unfit for the school, by whom also vigorous endeavors have been used that Hartford or some place near it might be the seat of literature in our colony—which all of us underwritten could not admit as convenient for the so great distance from the seaside.

Wherefore necessity obliging us to remove it from Saybrook, the greater part by far of our number have agreed upon the large and pleasant town of New Haven to be the kind alumna to bear in her arms and cherish in her bosom the infant nursery of learning in our government.

We easily persuade ourselves [that] the design of your liberal donation was to lend a generous hand to advance the interest of learning in our colony, and particularly to brighten the countenances of the trustees under whose oversight the school hath flourished, and we hope yet will, [and] not to furnish many illiterate families in Saybrook with a stock of books each, as we have heard the uneasy spirits of that town incline and seem resolved from an opinion that your donation, right worshipful sir, is the propriety of the school in that place—which if your intention justify, we are sorry that your shelves of our famous library should appear ashamed for want of your books further to beautify them.

The affair of our school hath been in a condition of pregnancy; painful with a witness have been the throes thereof in this General Assembly. But we just now hear that after the violent pangs threatening the very life of the babe, divine providence as a kind obstetrix hath mercifully brought the babe into the world, and behold a manchild is born, whereat we all rejoice. And when Your Honor heareth the same, we are persuaded that Your Honor will bear a part in our joy that, with the countenance and concurrence of the General Assembly, both of the upper and lower house, the carrying on of the collegiate house in this celebrated town of New Haven be proceeded on and forwarded and finished by the care of the trustees with all convenient speed. Now we rejoice that our settling the Collegiate School at New Haven is favored with so ample approbation as that of the two houses, and now there is an hopeful prospect of the peace of the colony, which hath been so threatened on said settlement. We shall also rejoice to understand by a line from Your Honor that we have not mistaken your donation to be made unto the trustees for the use of the Collegiate School, wherever the same were finally settled, and particularly at New Haven, the place of the remains of an assured friend of Your Honor, the Reverend Mr. Pierpont, a most obliging, capable, and industrious undertaker for the school, deceased, whose great serviceableness we cannot lose the sense of. We cheerfully and gratefully acknowledge the many kind offices of the liberal benefactors of our school and shall with all thankfulness receive further donations of such generous gentlemen, who through the influence of heaven may cast a smiling aspect upon our nursery. We shall not give further trouble now after unfeigned wishes of Your Honor's prosperity, and acknowledgment that we are

Right Worshipful Sir

Your most obliged and humble servants,

JAMES NOYES

SAMUEL ANDREW

SAMUEL RUSSELL

JOSEPH WEBB

JOHN DAVENPORT

New Haven, October 31, 1717.

29. The Uses of History and Biography

There were several ways a Puritan could proselytize his heritage: by living an exemplary life, by preserving for his children and others a record of his own psychic pilgrimage, and by actively attempting to convince others that they should forgo sin and embrace right ways of civil and religious behavior. Because seventeenth-century New England was a relatively literate society—perhaps fifty to sixty percent of the white males could read—it is thus not surprising that clerical and secular writings played an important role in the transmission of the Puritan heritage to outsiders and to new generations of insiders.

A. An Elegy on John Cotton

The apotheosis of the first founders, especially the first ministers, rapidly became a Puritan pastime. Even such secular writers as William Bradford and Edward Johnson succumbed. More often, however, the clergy-

men paid tribute to each other, as in John Norton's elegy upon the death of John Cotton in 1652.

Source: Massachusetts Historical Society, *Collections*, 4 ser. IV (1858), 331–332.

A FUNERAL
ELEGY,

Upon the Death of the Truly Reverend
MR. JOHN COTTON
Late Teacher of a Church of Christ at Boston
in New England: Who Died the Twenty-third,
Was Buried the Twenty-ninth of December, 1652.

And after Winthrop, Hooker, Shepard's hearse,
Doth Cotton's death call for a mourning verse.
Thy will be done, yet Lord who dealeth thus,
Make this great death expedient for us.
Luther pulled down the Pope, Calvin the prelate slew,
Of Calvin's lapse, chief cure to Cotton's due.
Cotton whose learning, temper, godliness,
The German Phoenix lively did express.
Melanchthon's all, may Luther's word but pass
Melanchthon's all in our great Cotton was.
Then him in flesh scarce dwelt a better one,
So great's our loss when such a spirit's gone.
Whilst he was here, life was more life to me,
Now he is not, death hence less death to me.
That comets great men's death do oft forego,
This present comet doth too sadly show,
This prophet's dead, yet must in's doctrine speak,
This comet saith, else must New England break.
What e're it be, the heavens avert it far,
That meteors should succeed our greatest star.
In Boston's orb Winthrop and Cotton were,
These lights extinct, dark is our hemisphere.
In Boston once how much shined of our glory,
We now lament, posterity will story.
Let Boston live, who had and saw their worth,

And did them honor, both in life and death.
To him New England trust in this distress,
Who will not leave his exiles comfortless.

B. Life of Theophilus Eaton

*While most Puritan writing had strong tinges of hagiography, it re-
mained for Cotton Mather to achieve the epitome in that realm as in so
much of Puritan life. Mather's grandiose Magnalia Christi Americana,
written in the 1690s and published in 1702, attempted to summarize
in one large volume the achievements and aspirations of the settlers in
New England, or, as his title proclaims, "the greatness of Christ in
America." His uncritical emphasis on the virtues of the leading figures
and his unabashed contention that God was on the side of the New
Englanders makes the Magnalia a curiosity to the modern reader. Yet
no other product of the Puritan mind reveals so clearly the function of
historical biography among the American Puritans. A case in point is the
following sketch of Theophilus Eaton, governor of New Haven colony
from 1639 to 1658.*

*During the quarter century of New Haven's existence as a separate
colony, Eaton's counterpart in ecclesiastical leadership was John Davenport, "the strictest man for the church covenant, and admitting of
members in N. England." Between them, Eaton and Davenport gave
their colony even more a sense of Puritan influence on the total society
than had been achieved in Massachusetts.*

Source: Cotton Mather, *Magnalia Christi Americana* (2 vols., London, 1702; reprinted Hartford, 1852), I, 149–155.

HUMILITAS HONORATA[1]

THE LIFE OF THEOPHILUS EATON, ESQ., GOVERNOUR OF NEW
HAVEN COLONY
*Justitiæ Cultor, Rigidi Servator Honesti,
In Commune Bonum.*[2]

1. It has been enquired why the Evangelist Luke, in the first
sacred history which he addressed unto his fellow-citizen, gave him
the title of "The most excellent Theophilus," but in the next he
used no higher a style than plain Theophilus! And though several
other answers might be given to that enquiry, 'tis enough to say
that neither the civility of Luke, nor nobility of Theophilus were

1. Humility in honor.
2. Exact in justice—honest, humble, plain—
   His private virtues were the public's gain.

by age abated; but Luke herein considered the disposition of Theophilus, as well as his own, with whom a reduced age had rendered all titles of honour mere disagreeable superfluities. Indeed, nothing would have been more unacceptable to the governour of our New Haven colony, all the time of his being so, than to have been advanced and applauded above the rest of mankind, yet it must be now published unto the knowledge of mankind that New England could not of his quality show a more excellent person, and this was Theophilus Eaton, Esq., the first governour of that colony. Humility is a virtue whereof Amyraldus observes, "There is not so much as a shadow of commendation in all the pagan writers." But the reader is now concerned with writings which will commend a person for humility; and therefore our Eaton, in whom the shine of every virtue was particularly set off with a more than ordinary degree of humility, must now be proposed as commendable.

2. 'Tis reported that the earth taken from the banks of Nilus will very strangely sympathize with the place from whence it was taken, and grow moist or dry according to the increase and the decrease of the river. And in spite of that Popish lie which pretends to observe the contrary, this thing has been signally moralized in the daily observation, that the sons of ministers, though betaking themselves to other employments, do ordinarily carry about with them an holy and happy savor of their ministerial education. 'Twas remarkably exemplified in our Theophilus Eaton, who was born at Stony Stratford in Oxfordshire, the eldest son to the faithful and famous minister of the place. But the words of old used by Philostratus concerning the son of a great man, "As for his son, I have nothing else to say, but that he was his son," they could not be used concerning our Theophilus, who, having received a good education from his pious parents, did live many years to answer that education in his own piety and usefulness.

3. His father being removed unto Coventry, he there at school fell into the intimate acquaintance of that worthy John Davenport, with whom the providence of God many years after united in the great undertaking of settling a colony of Christian and reformed churches on the American strand. Here his ingenuity and proficiency rendered him notable; and so vast was his memory that although he wrote not at the church, yet when he came home he would, at his father's call, repeat unto those that met in his father's

house the sermons which had been publickly preached by others, as well as his own father, with such exactness as astonished all the neighborhood. . . .

4. During the time of his hard apprenticeship he behaved himself wisely; and his wisdom, with God's favor, particularly appeared in his chaste escape from the snares of a young woman in the house where he lived, who would fain have taken him in the pits by the wise man cautioned against, and who was herself so taken only with his most comely person, that she died for the love of him when she saw him gone too far to be obtained; whereas, by the like snares, the apprentice that next succeeded him was undone for ever. But being a person herewithal most signally diligent in his business, it was not long before the maxim of the wise man was most literally accomplished in his coming to "stand before princes," for being made a freeman of London he applied himself unto the East Country trade and was publickly chosen the deputy-governor of the company, wherein he so acquitted himself as to become considerable. And afterwards going himself into the East Country, he not only became so well acquainted with the affairs of the Baltic Sea, but also became so well improved in the accomplishments of a man of business, that the King of England employed him as an agent unto the King of Denmark. The concerns of his agency he so discreetly managed that as he much obliged and engaged the East Land company (who in token thereof presented his wife with a basin and ewer double gilt, and curiously wrought with gold, and weighing above sixty pound), so he found much acceptance with the King of Denmark and was afterwards used by that prince to do him no little services. Nevertheless, he kept his integrity amongst the temptations of that court, whereat he was now a resident; and not seldom had he most eminent cause to acknowledge the benignity and interposal of Heaven for his preservations. Once particularly, when the King of Denmark was beginning the King of England's health while Mr. Eaton, who disliked such health-drinking, was in his presence, the King fell down in a sort of a fit, with the cup in his hand, whereat all the nobles and courtiers wholly applied themselves to convey the King into his chamber, and there was no notice taken who was to pledge his health; whereby Mr. Eaton was the more easily delivered from any share in the debauch.

5. Having arrived unto a fair estate (which he was first willing to

do), he married a most virtuous gentlewoman, to whom he had first espoused himself after he had spent three years in an absence from her in the East Country. But this dearest and greatest of his temporal enjoyments proved but a temporal one; for living no longer with him than to render him the father of two children, she almost killed him with her own death; and yet at her death she expressed herself wondrous willing "to be dissolved, and to be with Christ, from whom," she said, "I would not be detained one hour for all the enjoyments upon earth." He afterwards married a prudent and pious widow, the daughter of the bishop of Chester; unto the three former children of which widow he became a most exemplary, loving and faithful father, as well as a most worthy husband unto herself, by whom he afterwards had five children, two sons and three daughters. But the second of his children by his latter wife dying some while before, it was not long before his two children by his former wife were smitten with the plague, whereof the elder died, and his house thereupon shut up with a "Lord, have mercy!" However, the Lord had this mercy on the family, to let the distemper spread no further; and so Mr. Eaton spent many years a merchant of great credit and fashion in the city of London.

6. At length conformity to ceremonies humanely invented and imposed in the worship of God was urged in the Church of England with so much rigor that Mr. Davenport was thereby driven to seek a refuge from the storm in the cold and rude corners of America. Mr. Eaton had already assisted the new Massachusetts colony as being one of the patentees for it, but had no purpose of removing thither himself until Mr. Davenport, under whose excellent ministry he lived, was compelled unto a share in this removal. However, being fully satisfied in his own conscience that unlawful things were now violently demanded of him, he was willing to accompany his persecuted pastor in the retreat from violence now endeavored, and many eminent Londoners cheerfully engaged with him in this undertaking. Unto New England this company of good men came in the year 1637, where, choosing to be a distinct colony by themselves, more accommodated unto the designs of merchandise than of husbandry, they sought and bought a large territory in the southern parts of the country for their habitations. In the prosecution hereof, the chief care was devolved upon Mr. Eaton, who, with an unexampled patience, took many tedious and hazardous journeys through a desolate wilderness full of barbarous

Indians, until upon mature deliberation he pitched upon a place now called New Haven, where they soon formed a very regular town; and a number of other towns along the seaside were quickly added thereunto. . . .

7. Mr. Eaton and Mr. Davenport were the Moses and Aaron of the Christian colony now erected in the south-west parts of New England; and Mr. Eaton being yearly and ever chosen their governor, it was the admiration of all spectators to behold the discretion, the gravity, the equity with which he still managed all their public affairs. . . . As in his government of the commonwealth, so in the government of his family, he was prudent, serious, happy to a wonder; and albeit he sometimes had a large family, consisting of no less than thirty persons, yet he managed them with such an even temper that observers have affirmed, "They never saw an house ordered with more wisdom!" He kept an honorable and hospitable table, but one thing that still made the entertainment thereof the better was the continual presence of his aged mother, by feeding of whom with an exemplary piety till she died, he ensured his own prosperity as long as he lived. His children and servants he would mightily encourage unto the study of the Scriptures and countenance their addresses unto himself with any of their enquiries; but when he discerned any of them sinfully negligent about the concerns either of their general or particular callings, he would admonish them with such a penetrating efficacy, that they could scarce forbear falling down at his feet with tears. A word of his was enough to steer them!

8. So exemplary was he for a Christian that one who had been a servant unto him could many years after say, "Whatever difficulty in my daily walk I now meet withal, still something that I either saw or heard in my blessed master Eaton's conversation helps me through it all; I have reason to bless God that ever I knew him!" It was his custom when he first rose in a morning to repair unto his study, a study well perfumed with the meditations and supplications of an holy soul. After this, calling his family together, he would then read a portion of the Scripture among them, and after some devout and useful reflections upon it, he would make a prayer, not long, but extraordinarily pertinent and reverent; and in the evening some of the same exercises were again attended. On the Saturday morning he would still take notice of the approaching Sabbath in his prayer, and ask the grace to be remembering of it

and preparing for it; and when the evening arrived, he, besides this, not only repeated a sermon, but also instructed his people, with putting of questions referring to the points of religion, which would oblige them to study for an answer; and if their answer were at any time insufficient, he would wisely and gently enlighten their understandings, all which he concluded with singing of a psalm. When the Lord's day came, he called his family together at the time for the ringing of the first bell and repeated a sermon, whereunto he added a fervent prayer, especially tending unto the sanctification of the day. At noon he sang a psalm, and at night he retired an hour into his closet, advising those in his house to improve the same time for the good of their own souls. He then called his family together again, and in an obliging manner conferred with them about the things with which they had been entertained in the house of God, shutting up all with a prayer for the blessing of God upon them all. For solemn days of humiliation or of thanksgiving, he took the same course and endeavored still to make those that belonged unto him understand the meaning of the services before them. He seldom used any recreations, but being a great reader, all the time he could spare from company and business he commonly spent in his beloved study, so that he merited the name which was once given to a learned ruler of the English nation, the name of Beauclerk. In conversing with his friends, he was affable, courteous, and generally pleasant, but grave perpetually; and so cautelous and circumspect in his discourses, and so modest in his expressions, that it became a proverb for incontestable truth, "Governor Eaton said it." . . . .

10. Thus continually he, for about a score of years, was the glory and pillar of New Haven colony. He would often say, "Some count it a great matter to die well, but I am sure 'tis a great matter to live well. All our care should be while we have our life to use it well, and so when death puts an end unto that, it will put an end unto all our cares." But having excellently managed his care to live well, God would have him to die well, without any room or time then given to take any care at all; for he enjoyed a death sudden to everyone but himself! Having worshipped God with his family after his usual manner, and upon some occasion with much solemnity charged all the family to carry it well unto their mistress who was now confined by sickness, he supped, and then took a turn or two abroad for his meditations. After that he came in to bid his

wife good-night before he left her with her watchers, which when he did, she said, "Methinks you look sad!" Whereto he replied, "The differences risen in the church of Hartford make me so"; she then added, "Let us even go back to our native country again"; to which he answered, "You may (and so she did), but I shall die here." This was the last word that ever she heard him speak, for, now retiring unto his lodging in another chamber, he was overheard about midnight fetching a groan; and unto one sent in presently to enquire how he did, he answered the enquiry with only saying, "Very ill!" and without saying any more, he fell "asleep in Jesus," in the year 1657, loosing anchor from New Haven for the better;

Sedes, ubi Fata, Quietas Ostendunt.[3]

Now let his gravestone wear at least the following epitaph:

New England's glory, full of warmth and light,
Stole away (and said nothing) in the night.

30. Attempts to Puritanize the Heathen

By mid-seventeenth century most colonists of New England stemmed from English stock and therefore enjoyed a common cultural heritage. New England's schools and colleges, sermons and eulogies, laws and civil institutions were thus designed for a relatively homogeneous population in the attempt to foster Puritan beliefs. But there were also non-Englishmen in New England, most notably the thousands of American Indians who had lived there long before the white man intruded, and a small but growing number of black Africans. To the Puritan these cultural "strangers" posed a double challenge. The heathens, the Puritans believed, must be converted to Reformed Protestantism; they must also take on the social and political habits of the true Christian. In short, they had to become dark-hued Puritans.

A. Eliot Among the Indians

Although one of the oft-stated purposes of Puritan colonization was the conversion of the Indians, little was done to make this a reality until mid-century. Differences in language, resistance by Indian civil and religious leaders (sachems and powwows) who saw in the new faith a

3. Where Destiny points out eternal rest.

challenge to their own authority, and the rigours social and theological demands made of the converts to Puritanism—Indian or white—made large-
scale conversion of the natives unlikely. So too did Puritan church
polity, which made each clergyman the servant of an individual congregation; there were no religious orders or ministers-at-large to proselytize
the heathen on behalf of the collective congregations. Still, throughout
the seventeenth and early eighteenth centuries, the conversion of their
Indian neighbors was a cherished Puritan project, and one that reveals
much about the objectives and outlook of Puritan society. John Eliot,
pastor of the First Church of Roxbury, studied the native dialect and by
1646 could preach with some effectiveness to Indian audiences. He also
took the lead in creating "praying towns," where Christianized Indians
could live apart from their unconverted brethren and where the missionaries could inculcate English mores as well as Puritan theology. The
early successes of Eliot and others were publicized in England in hopes
that funds might be contributed to further the missionary effort.

The following account was probably written by Thomas Shepard or
by John Wilson (c. 1591–1667), pastor of the First Church of Boston,
who accompanied Eliot on several visits to tribes in eastern Massachusetts.

Source: Massachusetts Historical Society, Collections, 3 ser. IV
(1834), 3–4, 8–9, 13–14, 17, 20–22.

Upon October 28, 1646, four of us (having sought God) went
unto the Indians inhabiting within our bounds, with desire to
make known the things of their peace to them. A little before we
came to their wigwams,[1] five or six of the chief of them met us
with English salutations, bidding us much welcome; who leading
us into the principal wigwam of Waaubon,[2] we found many more
Indians—men, women, children—gathered together from all
quarters round about, according to appointment, to meet with us
and learn of us. Waaubon, the chief minister of justice among
them, exhorting and inviting them before thereunto, being one
who gives more grounded hopes of serious respect to the things of
God than any that as yet I have known of that forlorn generation,
and therefore since we first began to deal seriously with him hath
voluntarily offered his eldest son to be educated and trained up in
the knowledge of God, hoping, as he told us, that he might come
to know Him although he despaired much concerning himself.
And accordingly his son was accepted and is now at school in

1. Indian houses or tents made of barks or mats.
2. The name of an Indian.

Dedham, whom we found at this time standing by his father among the rest of his Indian brethren, in English clothes.

They being all there assembled, we began with prayer, which now was in English, being not so far acquainted with the Indian language as to express our hearts herein before God or them, but we hope it will be done ere long. . . .

When prayer was ended, it was a glorious affecting spectacle to see a company of perishing, forlorn outcasts diligently attending to the blessed word of salvation then delivered, professing they understood all that which was then taught them in their own tongue. It much affected us that they should smell some things of the alabaster box broken up in that dark and gloomy habitation of filthiness and unclean spirits. For about an hour and a quarter the sermon continued, wherein one of our company ran through all the principal matter of religion, beginning first with a repetition of the Ten Commandments and brief explication of them, then shewing the curse and dreadful wrath of God against all those who break them, or any one of them, or the least title of them, and so applied it unto the condition of the Indians present with much sweet affection; and then preached Jesus Christ to them, the only means of recovery from sin and wrath and eternal death, and what Christ was and whether He was not gone, and how He will one day come again to judge the world in flaming fire; and of the blessed estate of all those that by faith believe in Christ and know Him feelingly. He spake to them also (observing his own method as he saw most fit to edify them) about the creation and fall of man, about the greatness and infinite being of God, the maker of all things, about the joys of heaven, and the terrors and horrors of wicked men in hell, persuading them to repentance for several sins which they live in, and many things of the like nature, not meddling with any matters more difficult, and which to such weak ones might at first seem ridiculous until they had tasted and believed more plain and familiar truths. . . .

A True Relation of Our Coming to the Indians the Second Time

Upon November 11, 1646, we came the second time unto the same wigwam of Waaubon, where we found many more Indians met together than the first time we came to them. And having seats provided for us by themselves, and being sat down awhile, we began again with prayer in the English tongue; our beginning this time was with the younger sort of Indian children in catechizing of them, which being the first time of instructing them we thought meet to ask them but only three questions in their own language, that we might not clog their minds or memories with too much at first. The questions asked and answered in the Indian tongue were these three: 1. *Question:* who made you and all the world? *Answer:* God. 2. *Question:* who do you look should save you and redeem you from sin and hell? *Answer:* Jesus Christ. 3. *Question:* how many commandments hath God given you to keep? *Answer:* ten. These questions being propounded to the children severally and one by one, and the answers being short and easy, hence it came to pass that before we went through all, those who were last catechized had more readily learned to answer to them by hearing the same question so oft propounded and answered before by their fellows. And the other Indians who were grown up to more years had perfectly learned them, whom we therefore desired to teach their children again when we were absent, that so when we came again we might see their profiting, the better to encourage them hereunto; we therefore gave something to every child. . . .

Thus having spent some hours with them, we propounded two questions: what do you remember of what was taught you since the last time we were here? After they had spoken one to another for some time, one of them returned this answer, that they did much thank God for our coming, and for what they heard; they were wonderful things unto them.

Do you believe the things that are told you, viz., that God is *musquantum,* i.e., very angry, for the least sin in your thoughts or words or works? They said yes, and hereupon we set forth the terror of God against sinners, and mercy of God to the penitent and to such as sought to know Jesus Christ, and that as sinners should be after death *chechainuppan,* i.e., tormented alive (for we know no other word in the tongue to express extreme torture by), so believers should after death *wowein wicke Jehovah,* i.e., live in all bliss with Jehovah the blessed God, and so we concluded conference.

Having thus spent the whole afternoon, and night being almost come upon us, considering that the Indians formerly desired to know how to pray and did think that Jesus Christ did not understand Indian language, one of us therefore prepared to pray in their own language, and did so for above a quarter of an hour together, wherein divers of them held up eyes and hands to heaven, all of them (as we understood afterwards) understanding the same; but one of them I cast my eye upon was hanging down his head with his rag before his eyes weeping. At first I feared it was some soreness of his eyes, but lifting up his head again, having wiped his eyes (as not desirous to be seen), I easily perceived his eyes were not sore, yet somewhat red with crying, and so held up his head for a while; yet such was the presence and mighty power of the Lord Jesus on his heart, that he hung down his head again and covered his eyes again and so fell wiping and wiping of them weeping abundantly, continuing thus till prayer was ended, after which he presently turns from us and turns his face to a side and corner of the wigwam, and there falls aweeping more abundantly by himself. Which one of us perceiving, went to him and spake to him encouraging words, at the hearing of which he fell aweeping more and more; so leaving of him, he who spake to him came unto me (being newly gone out of the wigwam) and told me of his tears. So we resolved to go again both of us to him, and speak to him again, and we met him coming out of the wigwam and there we spake again to him, and he there fell into a more abundant renewed weeping, like one deeply and inwardly affected indeed, which forced us also to such bowels of compassion that we could not forbear weeping over him also. And so we parted greatly rejoicing for such sorrowing. . . .

A Third Meeting with the Indians

November 26. I could not go myself, but heard from those who went of a third meeting, the Indians having built more wigwams in the wonted place of meeting to attend upon the word the more readily. The preacher understanding how many of the Indians discouraged their fellows in this work, and threatening death to some if they heard any more, spake therefore unto them about temptations of the devil, how he tempted to all manner of sin, and how the evil heart closed with them, and how a good heart abhorred them. The Indians were this day more serious than ever before and propounded divers questions again, as: (1) Because some Indians say that we must pray to the devil for all good, and some to God, they would know whether they might pray to the devil or no? (2) They said they heard the word humiliation oft used in our churches and they would know what that meant? (3) Why the English call them Indians, because before they came they had another name? (4) What a spirit is? (5) Whether they should believe dreams? (6) How the English come to know God so much and they so little? To all which they had fit answers, but being not present I shall not set them down. Only their great desire this time was to have a place for a town and to learn to spin. . . .

We have cause to be very thankful to God, who hath moved the hearts of the General Court to purchase so much land for them to make their town in which the Indians are much taken with,[3] and it is somewhat observable that while the Court were considering where to lay out their town, the Indians (not knowing of anything) were about that time consulting about laws for themselves and their company who sit down with Waaubon. There were ten of them, two of them are forgotten. Their laws were these:

1. That if any man be idle a week, at most a fortnight, he shall pay five shillings.

2. If any unmarried man shall lie with a young woman unmarried, he shall pay twenty shillings.

3. If any man shall beat his wife, his hands shall be tied behind him and carried to the place of justice to be severely punished.

4. Every young man if not another's servant, and if unmarried, he shall be compelled to set up a wigwam and plant for himself, and not live shifting up and down to other wigwams.

5. If any woman shall not have her hair tied up but hang loose or be cut as men's hair, she shall pay five shillings.

6. If any woman shall go with naked breasts, they shall pay two shillings six pence.

7. All those men that wear long locks shall pay five shillings.

8. If any shall kill their lice between their teeth, they shall pay five shillings. This law though ridiculous to English ears, yet tends to preserve cleanliness among Indians. . . .

3. This town the Indians did desire to know what name it should have, and it was told them it should be called Noonatomen, which signifies in English rejoicing, because they hearing the word and seeking to know God, the English did rejoice at it, and God did rejoice at it, which pleased them much; and therefore that is to be the name of their town.

A Fourth Meeting with the Indians

This day being December 9, the children being catechized, and that place of Ezekiel touching the dry bones being opened and applied to their condition, the Indians offered all their children to us to be educated amongst us, and instructed by us, complaining to us that they were not able to give anything to the English for their education. For this reason there are therefore preparations made towards the schooling of them, and setting up a school among them or very near unto them. . . . [One Indian] complained of other Indians that did revile them and call them rogues and such like speeches for cutting off their locks, and for cutting their hair in a modest manner as the New English generally do. For since the word hath begun to work upon their hearts, they have discerned the vanity and pride which they placed in their hair, and have therefore of their own accord (none speaking to them that we know of) cut it modestly. They were therefore encouraged by some there present of chief place and account with us not to fear the reproaches of wicked Indians, nor their witchcraft and powwows and poisonings, but let them know that if they did not dissemble but would seek God unfeignedly, that they would stand by them and that God also would be with them. . . .

B. "The Negro Christianized"

The first blacks probably arrived in New England in 1638, when, as Governor Winthrop noted laconically in his Journal, the Desire arrived from the West Indies with "some cotton, and tobacco, and negroes, etc." These first blacks had been acquired in exchange for Indian captives taken in the Pequot War of 1637, and undoubtedly were held for long terms of servitude, perhaps for life. By 1700 the black population of New England numbered about one thousand, some of them free but most held as permanent bond servants.

The Puritans shared with other British Americans an ethnocentricity that allowed them to prate endlessly on freedom for themselves, while holding people of darker skins as personal property. The Puritan differed from his white countrymen only in his relatively lenient treatment of free blacks and slaves (which may merely have reflected the relative paucity of blacks in New England), and in a somewhat greater attention to the religious condition of their bondsmen. But of efforts toward the liberation of slaves, the Puritan record before 1730 reads as poorly as that of the other British colonies. Samuel Sewall's The Selling of Joseph (1700) appears to have been a solitary and ineffective protest against human bondage, even though it cited the venerable William Ames in arguing that the enslavement of humans violates both moral and biblical law. More representative of Puritan thinking was Cotton Mather, who accepted the institution of slavery as divinely established and shared the prevailing low opinion of the Negro's intellectual capacity, but who insisted on the parity of white men and blacks in the eyes of God.

Source: Cotton Mather, The Negro Christianized: An Essay to Excite and Assist that Good Work, the Instruction of Negro-Servants in Christianity (Boston, 1706), 3–6, 23–25, 28–29.

It is a golden sentence that has been sometimes quoted from Chrysostom: that for a man to know the art of alms is more than for a man to be crowned with the diadem of kings, but to convert one soul unto God is more than to pour out ten thousand talents into the basket of the poor. Truly, to raise a soul from a dark state of ignorance and wickedness to the knowledge of God and the belief of Christ and the practice of our holy and lovely religion, 'tis the noblest work that ever was undertaken among the children of men. . . .

It is come to pass by the providence of God, without which there comes nothing to pass, that poor Negroes are cast under your government and protection. You take them into your families; you look on them as part of your possessions; and you expect from their service a support, and perhaps an increase, of your other possessions. How agreeable it would be if a religious master or mistress thus attended would now think with themselves, "Who can tell but that this poor creature may belong to the election of God! Who can tell but that God may have sent this poor creature into my hands that so one of the elect may by my means be called and by my instruction be made wise unto salvation. The glorious God will put an unspeakable glory upon me if it may be so!" The considerations that would move you to teach your Negroes the truths of the glorious gospel as far as you can, and bring them, if it may be, to live according to those truths a sober, and a righteous, and a godly life; they are innumerable. And if you would after a reasonable manner consider the pleas which we have to make on the behalf of God, and of the souls which He has made, one would wonder that they should not be irresistible. Show yourselves men, and let rational arguments have their force upon you to make you treat not as brutes but as men, those rational creatures whom God has made your servants. . . .

. . . [I]t is just and equal that your servants be not overwrought, and that while they work for you you should feed them, and cloth them, and afford convenient rest unto them, and make their lives comfortable. So it is just and equal that you should acquaint them, as far as you can, with the way to salvation by Jesus Christ. You deny your Master in Heaven if you do nothing to bring your servants unto the knowledge and service of that glorious Master. One table of the Ten Commandments has this for the sum of it: "Thou shalt love thy neighbor as thyself." Man, thy Negro is thy neighbor. T'were an ignorance, unworthy of a man, to imagine otherwise. Yea, if thou dost grant, "That God hath made of one blood all nations of men," he is thy brother too. Now canst thou love thy Negro and be willing to see him lie under the rage of sin and the wrath of God? Canst thou love him and yet refuse to do anything that his miserable soul may be rescued from eternal miseries? Oh, let thy love to that poor soul appear in thy concern to make it, if thou canst, as happy as thy own! We are commanded, Gal. 6:10: "As we have opportunity let us do good unto all men, especially unto them who are of the household of faith." Certainly we have opportunity to do good unto our servants who are of our own household; certainly we may do something to make them good, and bring them to be of the household of faith. In a word, all the commandments in the Bible which bespeak our charity to the souls of others, and our endeavor that the souls of others may be delivered from the snares of death, every one of these do oblige us to do what we can for the souls of our Negroes. They are more nearly related to us than many others are; we are more fully capable to do for them than for many others. . . .

It has been cavilled by some that it is questionable whether the Negroes have rational souls or no. But let that brutish insinuation be never whispered any more. Certainly their discourse will abundantly prove that they have reason. Reason shows itself in the design which they daily act upon. The vast improvement that education has made upon some of them argues that there is a reasonable soul in all of them. An old Roman and pagan would call upon the owner of such servants, "Homines tamen esse memento." They are men and not beasts that you have bought, and they must be used accordingly. 'Tis true, they are barbarous; but so were our own ancestors. The Britons were in many things as barbarous, but a little before our Savior's nativity, as the Negroes are at this time if there be any credit in Caesar's *Commentaries*. Christianity will be the best cure for this barbarity.

Their complexion sometimes is made an argument why nothing should be done for them. A gay sort of argument! As if the great God went by the complexion of men in His favors to them! As if none but whites might hope to be favored and accepted with God! Whereas it is well known that the whites are the least part of mankind. The biggest part of mankind, perhaps, are copper colored, a sort of tawnies. And our English that inhabit some climates do seem growing apace to be not much unlike unto them. As if because a people from the long force of the African sun and soil upon them (improved perhaps to further degrees by maternal imaginations and other accidents) are come at length to have the small fibres of their veins and the blood in them a little more interspersed through their skin than other people, this must render them less valuable to heaven than the rest of mankind? Away with such trifles! The God who looks on the heart is not moved by the color of the skin, is not more propitious to one color than another. Say rather, with the Apostle, Acts 10:34, 35: "Of a truth I perceive that God is no respecter of persons; but in every nation he that feareth Him and worketh righteousness is accepted with him."

Indeed their stupidity is a discouragement. It may seem unto as little purpose to teach as to wash an Ethiopian. But the greater their stupidity the greater must be our application. If we can't learn them so much as we would, let us learn them as much as we can. A little divine light and grace infused into them will be of great account. And the more difficult it is to fetch such forlorn things up out of the perdition whereinto they are fallen, the more laudable is the undertaking. There will be the more of a triumph if we prosper in the undertaking. Let us encourage ourselves from that word, Matth. 3:9, "God is able of these stones to raise up children unto Abraham." . . .

. . . They who cannot themselves personally so well attend the instruction of the Negroes may employ and reward those that shall do it for them. In many families the children may help the Negroes to learn the catechism, or their well instructed and well disposed English servants may do it. And they should be rewarded by the masters when they do it. In a plantation of many Negroes, why should not a teacher be hired on purpose, to instill into them the principles of the catechism? Or, if the overseers are once catechised themselves, they may soon do the office of catechisers unto those that are under them. However, 'tis fit for the master also personally to enquire into the progress which his Negroes make in Christianity and not leave it entirely to the management of others. . . .

Despite Mather's exhortations, Puritan congregations admitted few black communicants. In 1641, long before Mather's birth, a Negro maid of Israel Stoughton joined the Dorchester church, an event that received considerable publicity. But there are few other recorded instances of black church members during New England's first century. Nor did the Puritan emphasis on education lead to widespread efforts on behalf of black scholars. Even Mather's own school in Boston closed after a brief career because of public apathy and the reluctance of slave owners to let their servants imbibe the heady wine of spiritual equalitarianism. And so it remained for Mather, John Eliot (who did achieve modest success in educating Indians along Puritan lines), Samuel Willard, and a few others to champion the cause of converting and "civilizing" the heathen while their fellow New Englanders increasingly turned Puritanism into a tribalistic ritual for the descendants of the founding fathers. The heathen, it seemed, was not keen on becoming a Puritan; and the Puritan heritage—except in the hands of a few self-appointed missionaries—had proved half-hearted in its attempts to make the New England Zion a multi-racial affair.

VII

Attitudes Toward the Natural and Supernatural

IN MANY WAYS, the Puritan mind was paradoxical, and not least so in its attitude toward natural phenomena and the events of human life. Convinced that an omnipotent creator controlled the destiny of everybody, the Puritan sought constantly to understand God's motives: why should a storm wreak havoc in Boston, a child die, a drought descend? Invariably the event was believed to harbor its own answer: God's lesson could be gleaned from the signs He placed for all to see.

Some men, of course, would be too obtuse, others too indifferent to profit from the lesson, but it behooved God-fearing folk to read the signs carefully. Thus in 1640 John Endecott could clearly see, if others could not, the "extraordinary Judgment" that caused the ship *Mary Rose* to explode in Charlestown Harbor: the captain and crew "would constantlie Jeere at the holie brethren of New England" and had spent the previous Lord's day drinking, singing, and reading the Anglican Book of Common Prayer. And Simon Bradstreet in 1664 noted that close on the heels of a "great blazing starre" came a plague in London, an Anglo-Dutch War, and, two years later, the great London fire. Among other examples to be found among Puritan writings, surely the most famous is John Winthrop's account of the final session of the synod at which the Cambridge Platform was composed. A snake had slithered into the meetinghouse, Winthrop reported, "but Mr. Thompson, one of the elders of Braintree (a man of much faith), trode upon the head of it, and so held it with his foot and staff . . . until it was killed. This being so remarkable, and nothing falling out but by divine providence, it is out of doubt, the Lord discovered somewhat of his mind in it. The serpent is the devil; the synod the representative of the churches of Christ in New England. The devil had formerly and lately attempted their disturbance and dissolution; but their faith in the seed of the woman overcame him and crushed his head."

It was a short step from such explanations to what later generations would call superstition. If the devil could assume any shape, and if he held particular malice toward the churches of Christ, no doubt he would enlist some unwary souls in his crusade; in order to defeat him, his accomplices must be discovered and crushed. Hence the arrest, trial, and execution of witches.

This is not to say that the Puritans were slaves to superstition. Seeds of scientific thought had been planted in many Puritan minds at Cambridge and Oxford; indeed the late sixteenth and seventeenth centuries were alert to advances in scientific thought, and by the early eighteenth century a scientific revolution was under way that could not help but influence any intelligent mind. The problem for the Puritan was not to resist the new trend but to fit it into his theological framework. For most Puritans, this was not too difficult. It was axiomatic with them that God worked in many wonderful ways, and new scientific findings merely added to the evidence. Were not the circulation of the blood, the movement of celestial bodies, the infinite pattern and variety in flora and fauna further signs of His remarkable power and love? Then study nature, accept its truths, and give full credit to the Lord. Still, some Puritans, oblivious to the spirit of scientific thought, clung tenaciously to simplistic explanations of natural phenomena and human behavior.

Throughout the seventeenth and eighteenth centuries, science battled superstition for control of the Puritan mind. By 1735, eight of New England's citizens had been elected to the Royal Society of London for impressive work in scientific reportage or experimentation, but New England had also witnessed the worst persecution of witches in the New World. Approximately thirty-five persons lost their lives because of Satan's wiles, far more than in all the other British colonies together, though far less than in England or on the Continent. In its attitudes toward the wonders of the world, Puritan society revealed the strange diversity of its heritage.

31. Remarkable Salvations

Cotton Mather (1663–1728) did not differ significantly from his fellow Puritans in his beliefs about God's guiding hand. Where he did differ was in his insatiable urge to record every example, a habit perhaps inherited from his father, whose "Essay for the Recording of Illustrious Providences" (1684) had been an attempt to collect evidence of God's favors to New England. Cotton inserted a few remarkable cases into his epic history of New England.

Source: Cotton Mather, *Magnalia Christi Americana* (2 vols., London, 1702; reprinted Hartford, 1852), II, 355–356.

The good people of New England may tune their praises to a consort with those of the good Psalmist: "He that is our God, is the God of salvation, and unto God the Lord belong the issues from death." How many extraordinary salvations have been granted unto particular persons among that good people, a small volume could not enumerate.

Remarkable answers of prayer have been received by the most of those who have experimentally known the meaning of wrestlings in prayer among us. How many thousands have upon very notable experiments been able to say, "This poor man cried, and the Lord heard and saved him!" One very surprising instance hath been seen several times in this land, when infinite swarms of caterpillars have devoured our fields, and carried whole fields before them; some very pious and praying husbandmen in the extreme exigency, when the devourers have just been entering on their fields, have poured out their fervent prayers unto the God of Heaven for their deliverance; immediately hereupon flocks of birds have arrived that have devoured the devourers and preserved those particular fields, when others have been horribly wasted. Moreover, when any neighbors have labored under desperate maladies or been tempted, or distracted, or possessed, it hath been a common thing for a knot of godly people to meet and fast and pray, and see the afflicted gloriously delivered. Furthermore, when any droughts or floods have threatened the ruin of our harvests, these and those congregations mostly concerned have prayed with fasting on those occasions, and God hath wondrously delivered them, with a distinction from others that have not so called upon Him. The very Pagans in this wilderness have been sometimes amazed at what they have seen of this nature among us, and cried out that "the Englishman's God was a great and a good God!" It may be added, some of our churches have once in a considerable while kept a day of prayer for the success of the word of Christ upon the souls of their children in rising generations among them; and the success hath been such that all the churches in the land have took notice of it.

Again, remarkable rescues from death have been received by so many thousands among us that there hath been scarce one devout family which hath not been able to bring in something unto the heap of these experiences. Fallen persons that have had carts and ploughs just running over them, the beasts which drew them have suddenly stopped, unto the surprise of the spectators. Persons on the very point of mortal bruising or drowning have been snatched out of the jaws of destruction in ways that are not accountable. Even ejaculatory prayers have had astonishing answers. For instance:

An honest carpenter being at work upon an house, where eight children were sitting in a ring at some childish play on the floor below, he let fall accidentally, from an upper story, a bulky piece of timber just over these little children. The good man, with inexpressible agony, cried out, "O Lord, direct it!" and the Lord did so direct it, that it fell on end in the midst of the little children and then canted along on the floor between two of the children, without ever touching one of them all. But the instances of such things would be numberless. And if I should with a most religious veracity relate what wounds many persons have survived, I should puzzle Philosophy and make her have some recourse unto Divinity.

One Abigail Eliot had an iron struck into her head, which drew out part of her brains with it. A silver plate she afterwards wore on her skull where the orifice remained as big as an half crown. The brains left in the child's head would swell and swag, according to the tides. Her intellectuals were not hurt by this disaster, and she lived to be a mother of several children.

One John Symonds, about the age of ten years, had some affrighted oxen with a plough running over him; the share took hold of his ribs, a little below the left pap, and rent an hole in his breast so large that a man might have put in his four fingers. His very heart became visible; his lungs would fly out sundry inches, as often as the place was dressed. In seven or eight weeks he recovered and became an healthy man. But an history of rare cures in this country would fill more pages than may here be allowed. Yet let me take the leave to enquire, what shall be thought of the case of one Sarah Wilkinson, who died of a dropsie? For a long while before her death she had no evacuation, except only by a frequent and forced vomit of water in huge quantities, with which her dissolved bowels came up in successive portions of them. When she was opened, there were no bowels to be found in her, except her heart, which was exceeding small and as it were parboiled; and her milt or spleen, one end whereof stuck to her back and the other to her ribs; as also a small part of her liver or lungs, corrupted so much that they knew not which of the two it was, and this no bigger than the palm of one's hand. Other bowels, none could be found; yet in this condition she lived a long while and retained her senses to the last.

32. Wonders of the Invisible World

With belief in witchcraft almost universal in Europe and America in the seventeenth century, the New England Puritans had no need to invent a theory of demonology. But as Puritans they applied such notions with a vigor and persistence unrivaled among their fellow colonists. Only in New England did persecution of witches assume epidemic proportions; only there did people die for consorting with Satan. The precise reasons for the outbreaks in Connecticut and Massachusetts remain obscure, but there seems little doubt that a causal connection obtained between the hyper-religiosity of the Puritan mind and the rooting out of the devil's agents from New Zion.

Until late in the seventeenth century, when Increase and Cotton Mather turned their literary energies to the subject, William Perkins's Discourse on the Damned Art of Witchcraft served as the Puritans' basic tract. In many respects, Perkins was more temperate and scrupulous than his followers. For this reason, in 1693 Cotton Mather paraphrased Perkins's rules for discovering witches, for by then it had become clear that the courts of Connecticut and Massachusetts had strayed disastrously far from his guidelines. New England courts now accepted, as Perkins had not, the testimony of persons claiming to be molested by specters of persons accused of witchcraft. Today we would question the sanity of the person who claims to see strange shapes, feel blows and pinches, hear voices. In the seventeenth century, that was presumed normal; guilt fell on the "witch" who "caused" such symptoms—usually an old woman or a somewhat eccentric old man—and a trial soon followed.

A. Trial of a Witch

The first recorded case of witchcraft in New England occurred in 1647 in Connecticut when, according to Governor Winthrop of Massachusetts, "one [blank] of Windsor [was] arraigned and executed at Hartford for a witch." During the next two decades, eight or nine more persons (the records are not clear) were hanged in Connecticut, and several others in Massachusetts. But the early cases pale in comparison to the outburst of 1692 in Salem Village (now Danvers) in the Bay Colony.

There is no simple explanation of why such an unprecedented mania hit that community at that time. Probably the traumatic experiences of the previous two decades—King Philip's War, continuing Indian attacks along the northern frontier, the political uncertainties that accompanied the Dominion of New England and the loss of the old charter, and perhaps the clergy's shrill insistence that New England was fast declining from its earlier virtues—helped to create a fertile soil in which local tensions and individual neuroses could take root. Perhaps too, the situation was exacerbated by Cotton Mather and others who in the late 1680s heightened public awareness of the ways of witches by publishing vivid descriptions of cases they had observed. In any event, in the spring of 1692 scores of New Englanders found themselves before hostile courts and hysterical witnesses. Among the accused was George Jacobs.

Source: William E. Woodward, ed., *Records of Salem Witchcraft* (2 vols., Roxbury, Mass., 1864–1865), I, 254–265.

INDICTMENT V. GEORGE JACOBS, SR.

. . . That George Jacobs, Sr., of Salem in the county of Essex, the 11th day of May in the fourth year of the reign of our Sovereign Lord and Lady William and Mary, by the grace of God of England, Scotland, France, and Ireland King and Queen, Defenders of the Faith, etc., and divers other days and times as well before as after, certain detestable arts called witchcrafts and sorceries wickedly and feloniously hath used, practiced, and exercised at and within the township of Salem in the county of Essex aforesaid, in upon and against one Mercy Lewis of Salem village, single woman, by which said wicked arts the said Mercy Lewis the 11th day of May in the fourth year abovesaid, and divers other days and times as well before as after, was and is tortured, afflicted, pinned, consumed, wasted, and tormented; and also for sundry other acts of witchcraft by said George Jacobs committed and done before and since that time against the peace of our Sovereign Lord and Lady the King and Queen, their crown and dignity, and against the form of the statutes in that case made and provided.

Witnesses: Mercy Lewis   Elizabeth Hubbard
                   Mary Walcott   Sarah Churchill

EXAMINATION OF GEORGE JACOBS, SR.

THE EXAMINATION OF GEORGE JACOBS, SR., 10 MAY 1692

[Judge] Here are them that accuse you of acts of witchcraft.

[Jacobs] Well, let us hear who are they and what are they.

[Judge] Abigail Williams—(Jacobs laughed.)

[Jacobs] Because I am falsely accused. Your worship, all of you, do you think this is true?

[Judge] Nay, what do you think?

[Jacobs] I never did it.

[Judge] Who did it?

[Jacobs] Don't ask me.

[Judge] Why should we not ask you? Sarah Churchill accuseth you; there she is.

[Jacobs] I am as innocent as the child born tonight. I have lived 33 years here in Salem.

[Judge] What then?

[Jacobs] If you can prove I am guilty, I will lie under it.

Sarah Churchill said, "Last night I was afflicted at Deacon Ingersall's," and Mary Walcott said, "It was a man with two staves; it was my master."

[Jacobs] Pray do not accuse me; I am as clear as your worships. You must do right judgments.

[Judge] What book did he bring you, Sarah?

[Sarah] The same that the other woman brought.

[Jacobs] The devil can go in any shape.

[Judge] Did he not . . . appear on the other side of the river and hurt you? Did not you see him?

[Sarah] Yes, he did.

[Judge]   Look there, she accuseth you to your face; she chargeth you that you hurt her twice. Is it not true?

[Jacobs] What would you have me say? I never wronged no man in word nor deed.

[Judge]   Here are three evidences [i.e., Abigail, Sarah, and Mary].

[Jacobs] You tax me for a wizard; you may as well tax me for a buzzard. I have done no harm.

[Judge]   It is no harm to afflict these?

[Jacobs] I never did it.

[Judge]   But how comes it to be in your appearance?

[Jacobs] The devil can take any likeness.

[Judge]   Not without their consent.

[Jacobs] Please your worship, it is untrue; I never showed the book. I am silly about these things as the child born last night.

[Judge]   That is your saying. You argue you have lived so long, but what then Cain might [have] lived long before he killed Abel, and you might live long before the devil had so prevailed on you.

[Jacobs] Christ hath suffered three times for me.

[Judge]   What three times?

[Jacobs] He suffered the Cross and jail—

"You had as good confess," said Sarah Churchill, "if you are guilty."

[Jacobs] Have you heard that I have any witchcraft?

[Sarah]   I know you live a wicked life.

[Jacobs] Let her make it out.

[Judge]   Doth he ever pray in his family?

[Sarah]   Not unless by himself.

[Judge]   Why do you not pray in your family?

[Jacobs] I cannot read.

[Judge]   Well, but you may pray for all that. Can you say the Lord's prayer? Let us hear you.

He might in several parts of it, and could not repeat it right after Mary Mialls.

[Judge]   Sarah Churchill, when you wrote in the book, you was showed your master's name, you said.

[Sarah]   Yes, sir.

[Jacobs] If she say so, if you do not know it, what will you say?

[Judge] But she saw you or your likeness tempt her to write.

[Jacobs] One in my likeness; the devil may present my likeness.

[Judge] Were you not frighted, Sarah Churchill, when the representation of your master came to you?

[Sarah] Yes.

[Jacobs] Well! Burn me or hang me, I will stand in the truth of Christ; I know nothing of it.

[Judge] Do you know nothing of getting your son George and his daughter Margaret to sign?

[Jacobs] No, nothing at all.

THE SECOND EXAMINATION OF SAID GEORGE JACOBS, 11 MAY 1692

The bewitched fell into most grievous fits and screechings when he came in.

[Judge] Is this the man that hurts you?

Abigail Williams cried out, "This is the man," and fell into a violent fit.

Ann Putnam said, "This is the man," and he hurts her and brings the book to her and would have her write in the book, and she should be as well as his granddaughter.

[Judge] Mercy Lewis, is this the man?

[Mercy] This is the man; (after much interruptions by fits) he almost kills me.

Elizabeth Hubbard said the man never hurt her till today he came upon the table.

[Judge] Mary Walcot, is this the man?

After much interruptions by fits she said, "This is the man"; he used to come with two staves and beat her with one of them.

[Judge] What do you say, are you not a witch?

[Jacobs] No, I know it not, if I were to die presently.

Mercy Lewis went to come near him but fell into great fits. Mercy Lewis's testimony read.

[Judge] What do you say to this?

[Jacobs] Why, it is false; I know not of it any more than the child that was born tonight.

Ann Putnam said, "Yes, you told me so, that you had been so this 40 years."

Ann Putnam and Abigail Williams had each of them a pin stuck in their hands and they said it was this old Jacobs. Abigail Williams' testimony read.

[Judge] Are you the man that made disturbance at a lecture in Salem?

[Jacobs] No great disturbance. Do you think I use witchcraft?

[Judge] Yes indeed.

[Jacobs] No, I use none of them. . . .

GEORGE HERRICK V. GEORGE JACOBS, SR.

The testimony of George Herrick, aged thirty-four years or thereabouts, testifieth and saith: some time in May last, by order of their Majesties' justices, I went to the prison in Salem to search George Jacobs, Sr.—and likewise William Dounton, the jail keeper, and Joseph Neal, constable, was in presence and concerned with me in the search—where under the said Jacobs his right shoulder we found a teat about a quarter of an inch long or better, with a sharp point drooping downwards, so that I took a pin from said Dounton and run it through the said teat, but there was neither water, blood, nor corruption, nor any other matter, and so we make return.

William Dounton testifieth the above written; and we farther testify and say that said Jacobs was not in the least sensible in what we had done, for after I had made return to the magistrates and returned, I told the said Jacobs, and he knew nothing before.

Sworn in Court, August 4, 1692.

MARY WARREN V. GEORGE JACOBS, SR.

Mary Warren affirmed before the jury of inquest that George Jacobs, Sr., has afflicted her, said Warren, and beat her with his staff, he or his apparition. Said Warren says she has seen said Jacobs or apparition afflict Mary Walcot and beat her with his staff. She said also that said Jacobs has afflict Ann Putnam. Said Warren verily thinks said George Jacobs is a wizard. August, 1692, upon her oath. *Jurat in curia.*

MERCY LEWIS V. GEORGE JACOBS, SR.

The deposition of Mercy Lewis, who testifieth and saith that on 20th April 1692 at or about midnight there appeared to me the apparition of an old, very gray-headed man and told me that his name was George Jacobs, and that he had had two wives; and he did torture me and beat me with a stick which he had in his hand, and urged me to write in his book, which I refused to do. And so he hath continued ever since by times, coming sometimes with two sticks in his hands to afflict me, still tempting me to write in his book, but most dreadful he fell upon me and did torture me on the 9th of May at evening, after I came home from the examination of his maid, threating to kill me that night if I would not write in his book, because I did witness against his maid and persuaded her to confess. But because I would not yield to his hellish temptations, he did torture me most cruelly by beating me with the two sticks which he had in his hands and almost ready to put all my bones out of joint till my strength and heart was ready to fail. But being upheld by an Almighty hand and encouraged by them that stood by, I endured his tortures that night. The 10th May he again set upon me and afflicted me most grievously a great many times in the day, still urging me to write in his book, but at evening he again tortured me most grievously by pinching me and beating me black and blue and threating to kill me if I would not write in his book. But I told him I would not write in his book though he did kill me and tear me all to pieces. Then he proffered me to give me gold and many fine things if I would write in his book, but I told him I would not write in his book if he would give me all the world. Then again he did torture me most grievously but at last went away from me. Also on the 15th May 1692, being the day of the examination of George Jacobs, then I saw that it was that very man that told me his name was George Jacobs, and he did also most dreadfully torment me, almost ready to kill me, and I verily believe in my heart that George Jacobs is a most dreadful wizard and that he hath very often afflicted and tormented me by his acts of witch-craft. . . .

B. Retraction

The Salem trials ground to a halt in the fall of 1692, but not until nineteen persons, among them George Jacobs, and two dogs had been hanged, and a man pressed to death for refusing to plead. The jails teemed with accused witches; several prominent citizens of the colony now feared prosecution, even Lady Mary Phips, wife of the governor. At this point, several leading clergymen, most notably Increase Mather, convinced Governor Phips that spectral evidence could not be sanctioned. Phips dissolved the special court, issued a proclamation of general pardon, and released the prisoners, including seven who were awaiting execution. Within the next few years, several of the accusers—mostly teen-age girls—admitted that they had fabricated their charges. In 1697, Judge Samuel Sewall, a member of the special court, begged public forgiveness for his part in the affair, while the more cautious Cotton Mather confided to his diary that he feared divine punishment "for my not appearing with Vigor enough to stop the proceedings of the Judges, when the Inextricable Storm from the Invisible World assaulted the Countrey." Finally in 1711 the Massachusetts legislature annulled the convictions.

Source: William E. Woodward, ed., *Records of Salem Witchcraft* (2 vols., Roxbury, Mass., 1864–1865), II, 216–218.

Province of the Massachusetts Bay: *Anno Regni Anna Reginae Decimo.* An Act to reverse the attainders of George Burroughs and others for witchcraft.

Forasmuch as in the year of our Lord, one thousand six hundred ninety-two, two several towns within this province were infested with a horrible witchcraft or possession of devils, and at a special Court of Oyer and Terminer holden at Salem in the County of Essex in the same year, 1692, George Burroughs of Wells; John Proctor, George Jacobs, John Willard, Giles Corey, and Martha his wife, Rebecca Nurse, and Sarah Good, all of Salem aforesaid; Elizabeth How of Ipswich; Mary Eastey, Sarah Wild, and Abigail Hobbs, all of Topsfield; Samuel Wardell, Mary Parker, Martha Carrier, Abigail Falkner, Anne Foster, Rebecca Eames, Mary Post, and Mary Lacey, all of Andover; Mary Bradbury of Salisbury; and Dorcas Hoar of Beverly were severally indicted, convicted, and attainted of witchcraft, and some of them put to death, others lying still under the like sentence of the said court and liable to have the same executed upon them.

The influence and energy of the evil spirits so great at that time, acting in and upon those who were the principal accusers and witnesses, proceeding so far as to cause a prosecution to be had of persons of known and good reputation, which caused a great dissatisfaction and a stop to be put thereunto until their Majesties' pleasure should be known therein; and upon a representation thereof accordingly made her late Majesty Queen Mary the Second, of blessed memory, by her royal letter given at her court at Whitehall the fifteenth of April, 1693, was graciously pleased to approve the care and circumspection therein, and to will and require that in all proceedings against persons accused for witchcraft, or being possessed by the devil, the greatest moderation and all due circumspection be used, so far as the same may be without impediment to the ordinary course of justice.

And some of the principal accusers and witnesses in those dark and severe prosecutions have since discovered themselves to be persons of profligate and vicious conversation.

Upon the humble petition and suit of several of the said persons and of the children of others of them whose parents were executed: Be it declared and enacted by his Excellency the Governor, Council and Representatives in General Court assembled, and by the authority of the same, that the several convictions, judgments, and attainders against the said George Burroughs, [etc.] . . . be and hereby are reversed, made, and declared to be null and void to all intents, constructions, and purposes whatsoever, as if no such convictions, judgments, or attainders had ever been had or given. And that no penalties or forfeitures of goods or chattels be by the said judgments and attainders, or either of them, had or incurred, any law, usage, or custom to the contrary notwithstanding. And that no sheriff, constable, jailer or other officer shall be liable to any prosecution in the law for anything they then legally did in the execution of their respective offices.

Made and passed by the Great and General Court or Assembly of Her Majesty's Province of the Massachusetts Bay in New England, held at Boston the 17th day of October, 1711.

33. Wonders of the Human Body

The scientific side of Puritanism was evident from the earliest days of New England, in part a heritage of emerging English rationalism, in part a reflection of the Puritan emphasis on the obligation of discovering and praising God's works. During the seventeenth century, several

New England Puritans gave much of their time to science; a conspicuous example is the younger John Winthrop—physician, physicist, chemist, and naturalist as well as diplomat and statesman. But most early settlers had little time for systematic experimentation or observation. By the early eighteenth century, the challenge of the wilderness had been met, and several New England Puritans now had the time as well as the inclination to become active in scientific matters, most notably Thomas Brattle, the Mathers, and John Winthrop IV of Harvard, who achieved at least minor renown for their scientific work.

A. In Defense of Inoculation

In the field of medicine, the pre-eminent figure among American Puritans was the versatile and prolific clergyman-author, Cotton Mather. When a controversy over inoculation for smallpox hit New England, Mather took the lead in advocating the use of new medical discoveries. He had first learned of the practice from "my Negro-man Onesimus, who is a pretty Intelligent Fellow," who told Mather of the use of inoculation in Africa. Mather's final victory, however, owes much to the support of his octogenarian father, who made a clear stand in the following publication, subsequently incorporated almost verbatim in Dr. Zabdiel Boylston's more famous tracts.

The inoculation episode proved dramatic for both Boylston and the Mathers. Not long after the epidemic broke out in Boston in the spring of 1721, Cotton Mather urged the city's physicians to use the inoculation technique he had read about in the Royal Society Transactions. Dr. Boylston agreed and injected his own children and servants. That touched off a pamphlet war between Boylston and the Mathers on one side and Dr. William Douglas and his supporters on the other. Not content with verbal attacks, one member of the opposition loaded an iron ball with gunpowder and turpentine and threw it into Cotton Mather's bedchamber. It failed to explode, leaving the intended victim alive to read the attached message: "Cotton Mather, You Dog; Damn you: I'll inoculate you with this, with a Pox to you." Such vehement resistance to the new methods of disease control cooled rapidly when the survival rate of those inoculated proved the efficacy of the technique, and disappeared altogether after Boylston published detailed treatises on the subject.

Source: Increase Mather, *Several Reasons Proving That Inoculating . . . Is a Lawful Practice. . . .* Boston, 1721.

It has been questioned whether inoculating the smallpox be a lawful practice. I incline to the affirmative for these reasons:

I. Because I have read that in Smyrna, Constantinople, and other places, thousands of lives have been saved by inoculation, and not one of thousands has miscarried by it. This is related by wise and learned men who would not have imposed on the world a false narrative. Which also has been published by the Royal Society; therefore a great regard is due to it.

II. We hear that several physicians have recommended the practice hereof to his Majesty as a means to preserve the lives of his subjects, and that his wise and excellent Majesty King George, as also his Royal Highness the Prince, have approved hereof, and that it is now coming into practice in the nation. In one of the public prints are these words, "Inoculating the smallpox is a safe and universally useful experiment." Several worthy persons lately arrived from England inform us that it is a successful practice there. If wise and learned men in England declare their approbation of this practice, for us to declare our disapprobation will not be for our honor.

III. God has graciously owned the practice of inoculation among us in Boston, where some scores, yea above an hundred, have been inoculated and not one miscarried; but they bless God for his discovering this experiment to them. It has been objected that one that was inoculated died, viz. Mrs. D——ll, but she had the smallpox in the common way before, and her friends and nearest relations declare that she received no hurt by inoculation but was by a fright put into fits that caused her death. It is then a wonderful providence of God that all that were inoculated should have their lives preserved, so that the safety and usefulness of this experiment is confirmed to us by ocular demonstration. I confess I am afraid that the discouraging of this practice may cause many a life to be lost, which for my own part I should be loath to have any hand in because of the Sixth Commandment.

IV. It cannot be denied but that some wise and judicious persons among us approve of inoculation, both magistrates and ministers. Among ministers I am one, who have been a poor preacher of the gospel in Boston above threescore years and am the most aged, weak, and unworthy minister now in New England. My sentiments, and my son's also, about this matter are well known. Also we hear that the Reverend and learned Mr. Solomon Stoddard of Northampton concurs with us; so doth the Reverend Mr. Wise of Ipswich, and many other younger divines, not only in Boston but in the country, join with their fathers. Furthermore, I have made some inquiry whether there are many persons of a profane life and conversation that do approve and defend inoculation, and I have been answered that they know but of very few such. This is to me a weighty consideration, but on the other hand, though there are some worthy persons that are not clear about it, nevertheless it cannot be denied but that the known children of the wicked one are generally fierce enemies to inoculation. It is a grave saying of old Seneca, *Pessimi argumentum turba est*. For my part I should be ashamed to join with such persons: O my soul come not thou into their secret, unto their assembly be not thou united. I am far from reflecting upon all that are against inoculation. I know there are very worthy persons (with whom I desire to live and die) that are not clear in their judgments for it, and they are greatly to be commended and honored in that they will not act against a doubting conscience. Yet it may be some of them might change their minds if they would advise with those who are best able to afford them scripture light in this as well as in other cases of conscience.

November 20, 1721.

B. *"The Angel of Bethesda"*

Cotton Mather's reputation as a scientist long rested on his role in the inoculation controversy. Recently an even stronger claim has been put forward: his book on medicine—written in the early 1720s but not printed in his lifetime—reveals an extraordinary grasp of medical problems and fundamentals for a man whose primary concerns lay elsewhere and whose reading and investigations had to take place far from the centers of medical research. The following selection is taken from one of sixty-two chapters in The Angel of Bethesda.

Source: Otho T. Beall, Jr., and Richard H. Shryock, "Cotton Mather: First Significant Figure in American Medicine," American Antiquarian Society, *Proceedings*, LXIII (1954), 189–194.

Faelix qui potuit rerum cognoscere causas! Of a distemper we commonly say, to know the cause is half the cure. But, alas, how little progress is there yet made in that knowledge. Physicians talk about the causes of diseases, but their talk is very conjectural, very uncertain, very ambiguous, and oftentimes a mere jargon, and in it they are full of contradiction to one another. It may be one of the truest maxims ever yet advanced by any of the gentlemen has been that *ventriculus malis affectus est origo omnium morborum*: a distempered stomach is the origin of all diseases. I am sure 'tis as useful a caution as ever they gave, and it is the very sum of all prophylactic physic. But, sirs, whence is it that the stomach is distempered?

Since we are upon conjectures, I pray let us allow some room to those of Dr. Marten and company. Every part of matter is peopled. Every green leaf swarms with inhabitants. The surfaces of animals are covered with other animals. Yea, the most solid bodies, even marble itself, have innumerable cells which are crowded with imperceptible inmates. As there are infinite numbers of these, which the microscopes bring to our view, so there may be inconceivable myriads yet smaller than these, which no glasses have yet reached unto. The animals that are much more than thousands of times less than the finest grain of sand have their motions, and so their muscles, their tendons, their fibers, their blood, and the eggs wherein their propagation is carried on. The eggs of these insects (and why not the living insects too!) may insinuate themselves by the air, and with our ailments, yea, through the pores of our skin, and soon get into the juices of our bodies. They may be conveyed into our fluids with the nourishment which we received even before we were born, and may lie dormant until the vessels are grown more capable of bringing them into their figure and vigor for operations. Thus may diseases be conveyed from the parents unto their children before they are born into the world—as the eggs whereof cheese mites are produced were either in the milk before it came from the cow, or at least the rennet with which the cheese was coagulated. If they meet with a proper nest in any of our numberless vessels, they soon multiply prodigiously and may have a greater share in producing many of our diseases than is commonly imagined. Being brought into life, then either by their spontaneous run or by their disagreeable shape, they may destroy the texture of the blood and other juices, or they may gnaw and wound the tender vessels. It may be so that one species of these animals may offend in one way and another in another, and the various parts may be variously offended, from whence may flow a variety of diseases. And vast numbers of these animals keeping together may at once make such invasions as to render diseases epidemical, which those particularly are that are called pestilential. Epidemical and almost universal coughs may by this theory be also accounted for.

Strange murrains on cattle seem to have been sometimes of this original. Dr. Slate observes, of the famous one that passed from Switzerland through Germany to Poland, that in its progress it spread still two German miles in twenty-four hours, and he says, "It were worth considering whether this infection is not carried on by some volatile insect that is able to make only such short flights as may amount to such computations."

As for the distempers in human bodies, Kircher and Hauptman assert that malignant fevers never proceed from any other cause than little animals. Blancard affirms that the microscope discovers the blood in fevers to be full of animals. Ettmuller says unwanted swarms of insects resorting to a country foretell a plague impending.

And thus we may conceive how diseases are conveyed from distant countries or climates by the *animalcula*, or their eggs, deposited in the bodies or clothes or goods of travelers. 'Tis generally supposed that Europe is indebted unto America for the *lues venerea*. If so, Europe has paid its debt unto America by making unto it a present of the smallpox, in lieu of the great one.

Dr. Lister having observed that the plague is properly a disease of Asia and still comes from thence, he adds that the smallpox is an exotic disease of the Oriental people and was not known to Europe, or even to the lesser Asia or to Africa, till a spice trade was opened by the latter princes of Egypt unto the remoter parts of the East Indies, from whence it originally came, and where at this day it rages more cruelly than with us. Dr. Oliver likewise gives it as his opinion that we received the smallpox and measles from Arabia, and that Europe was wholly unacquainted with them until by frequent incursions of the Arabians into Africa, and afterwards into Spain, the venom came to be spread as now it is.

The essential cause of the itch appears to be a vast number of minute animals that make furrows under the scarfskin and stimulate the nervous fibers, as may be demonstrated by a microscope examining the humor in the little bladders rising between the fingers. The insects contained in a very small part of that humor, fixed upon the skin of a sound person either by shaking hands with the mangy or using a towel or a glove after him, these do soon insinuate into the pores and then quickly multiply enough to occupy almost all the surface of the body. Hence if the cure be not so closely followed, as not only to check but also to kill all the animals, they soon increase and become as troublesome as they were before. In the like manner is a yet more filthy disease communicated. Thus 'tis that God judges you, O you whore-mongers and adulterers! . . .

While I was thus entertaining myself with the speculations of Dr. Marten and his auxiliaries upon this new theory of diseases, I lit upon Mr. Bradley's new *Improvements of Planting and Gardening*, who maintains that the blights upon the vegetable world are owing to insects, whereof he discovered some (a thousand times less than the least grain of sand) which found the cold so agreeable an element unto them that at a yard's distance from a slow fire the heat would burn them to death. But those insects he thought over-grown monsters [compared] to those which have been discovered by M. Leuwenhoek (and other eyewitnesses) whereof above eight million may be found in one drop of water. And Mr. Hook proceeded so far as to demonstrate millions of millions contained in such a mighty ocean. A very gentle air may carry these from one place to another and so our plants become infested with them.

On this occasion I find his friend Mr. Ball modestly but very learnedly offering his apprehensions that our pestilential diseases may be of the like original. In Europe the plagues are brought by long, dry, easterly winds, which Mr. Ball thinks may bring infinite swarms of these destroyers, and that most probably they come from Tartary, for he has never heard of properly pestilential distempers anywhere in the world but where the Tartarian winds have reached them. When the plague raged in London, those places which had scents that probably killed or chased away these animals were kept from the infection. This conjecture about the origin of diseases may be as good as many that have been more confidently obtruded and more generally received.

But what remarks are to be made upon it; what sentiments of piety to be produced? How much does our life lie at the mercy of our God! How much do we walk through unseen armies of num-berless living things ready to seize and prey upon us! A walk, like the running of the deadly garloup which was of old called a passing through the brick kiln! What unknown armies has the Holy One wherewith to chastise and even destroy the rebellious children of men? Millions of billions of trillions of invisible *velites*! Of sinful men they say, "Our Father, shall we smite them?" On His order they do it immediately; they do it effectually. What a poor thing is man that a worm inconceivably less than the light dust of the balance is too hard for him! How much is it our interest and our prudence to keep resolves in the love of God!

But, oh ye sons of erudition and ye wise men of inquiry, let this inquiry come into a due consideration with you: how far a potent worm-killer that may be safely administered would go further than any remedy yet found out for the cure of many diseases! Mercury, we know thee, but we are afraid thou will kill us too if we employ thee to kill them that kill us. And yet, for the cleansing of the small blood vessels and making way for the free circulation of the blood and lymph, and so to serve the greatest purposes of medicine, there is nothing like mercurial deobstruents, of which the cinnabar of antimony, Aethiop's mineral, and the antihectic of Poterium may be reckoned the principal.

But after all, 'tis time to have done with the metaphysical jargon which for a long time has passed for the rationale of medicine. How much would the art of medicine be improved if our physicians more generally had the mathematical skill of a Dr. Mead or a Dr. Morgan, and would go his way to work mathematically and by the laws of matter and motion to find out the cause and cure of diseases. The words of one of them are worth receiving: "Since the animal body is a machine and diseases are nothing else but its particular irregularities, defects, and disorders, a blind man might as well pretend to regulate a piece of clock work, or a deaf man to tune an organ, as a person ignorant of mathematics and mechanism to cure diseases without understanding the natural organization, structure, and operations of the machine which he undertakes to regulate."

34. Wonders of the Celestial World

Natural phenomena held a particular fascination for the Puritan mind for here unquestionably was the might and majesty of the Lord. In the seventeenth-century most interpreters stressed the message God intended by His display; the eighteenth century thought less of the message and more of the manner of the event. The letter below, written by a Harvard tutor, reflects both the trend toward rational explanations of natural phenomena and the lingering fear of appearing irreligious.

Clearly the Puritan tradition was changing under the impact of new ideas. Thomas Robie (1689–1729) had moved a good distance from the seventeenth century notion that comets foretell events, though many people in the eighteenth century still held that belief; in another generation John Winthrop IV, professor of mathematics and natural philosophy at Harvard, could publicly chide Reverend Thomas Prince for clinging to the belief that "Earthquakes [are] the Works of God."

Source: Massachusetts Historical Society, Collections, 1 ser. II (1793), 17–20.

Sir:

I understand by a friend of mine you desire my thoughts of the late appearance in the heavens, which was amazing to the people in many parts of the country. I will therefore endeavor to answer your desire, and that . . . by giving an account of it, according as I observed it, and according to what I can learn from others, and then by telling you what may in all probability be looked upon to be the natural cause thereof. And I hope (though I believe I shall differ from some) I shall say nothing that shall be inconsistent either with divinity or philosophy.

I. For the account of it, etc., take in the following words: December 11, 1719. This evening, about eight o'clock, there arose a bright and red light in the east northeast like the light which arises from an house when on fire (as I am told by several credible persons who saw it when it first arose), which soon spread itself through the heavens from east to west, reaching about forty-three or forty-four degrees in height, and was unequally broad. It streamed with white flashes or streams of light down to the horizon (as most tell me) very bright and strong. When I first saw it, which was when it had extended itself over the horizon from east to west, it was brightest in the middle, which was from me northwest, and I could resemble it to nothing but the light of some fire. I could plainly see streams of light redder than ordinary, and there seemed to me to be an undulating motion of the whole light; so thin was this light as that I could see the stars very plainly through it. Below this stream or glade of light there lay in the horizon some thick clouds (which a few hours after arose and covered the heavens), bright on the tops or edges. It lasted somewhat more than an hour, though the height of its red color continued but a few minutes. About eleven the same night, the same appearance was visible again, but the clouds hindered its being so accurately observed as I could wish for. Its appearance was now somewhat dreadful; sometimes it looked of a flame, sometimes a blood red color; and the whole northeast horizon was very light and looked as though the moon had been near her rising. The dreadfulness as well as strangeness of this appearance made me think of Mr. Watt's description of the Day of Judgment in English sapphic:

> When the fierce north wind with his airy forces
> Rears up the Baltic to a foaming fury,
> And the red lightning with a storm of hail comes
> Rushing amain down.

And of these lines in Flatman:

> When from the dungeon of the grave
> The meagre throng themselves shall heave,
> Shake off their linen chains, and gaze
> With wonder when the world shall blaze.

About an hour or two before break of day the next morning, it was seen again, as I am informed, and those who saw it say it was then the most terrible. I saw it but twice, for the heavens being so overcast discouraged me from sitting up longer than my usual time.

This meteor was seen in many places: to those south from us it appeared lower in the horizon, and therefore to the more southern places must be wholly invisible. Thus I have given you the best account I am able of this meteor, which though very unusual here, yet in northern countries more frequent, and seems to me to be what our modern philosophers call *aurora borealis*.

Now, sir, as for the next thing, which is my thoughts on this meteor, you shall have them in the following words:

II. It is well known to all (though but a little read in philosophy) that there is abundance of nitro-sulphureous particles exhaled or forced out of the earth continually, but most of all in summer days, which is the reason why we have thunder more then than in the winter. Now for two or three days before this appearance, we had hot weather for the time of year, and very hot indeed the day immediately preceding, as hot as we commonly have in September, and the air was so warm as that I can almost call it sultry hot. Now I believe there was a very great quantity of such particles exhaled or forced out of the earth in this hot weather, and this evening were fired, which because fire in such inflammable matter moves very quick, was the cause of the quick motion of this light from the east to the west, though not contrary to the wind, yet across it, for the wind was then north. You will now ask me how it came to pass that there were such exhalations more now than at another time. To which I answer, I believe they were occasioned by some subterraneous heat.[1] That there are subterraneous fires is received by all philosophers and demonstrable from those igneous eruptions that are in many places, which fires are the causes of dreadful earthquakes which have sometimes occasioned the rise of mountains and of land, even out of the water itself.[2] And even in watery countries (now ours is a well watered country) there are pits and wells out of which arise such sulphurous streams as that if you hold a candle over them, they will immediately flame (much of the nature I suppose they are of spirits of wine camphorated), insomuch that whole houses have been consumed hereby. (See the late excellent treatise, called the *Religious Philosopher*, vol. 2.) And possibly there may be such in our country which perhaps may occasion the sudden alteration of weather we are so subject to.

To all this I add that though in the summertime we have more hot weather, and so more vapors are without doubt exhaled, yet whenever the weather is what we call sultry hot, we commonly have much thunder and lightning, or a good deal of rain, and so the matter which occasions such meteors is consumed in thunder and lightning or is mixed with the particles of water and so descends to the earth again. And I am confirmed in this opinion in that, as the chemists say, from rain water may be distilled a burning spirit.

Now if you ask me why this meteor appeared in the northeast and so to the northwest, I answer the exhalations were driven there by the southwest winds the day before, and ascending above, even to the upper regions of the air, were not touched by the northwest winds which blew the day preceding the evening on which this meteor appeared.

There remains a difficulty or two more yet to be solved, viz., how it came to be fired, and why it appeared more than once?

1. Dr. Wallis ascribes the ascent of vapors to subterraneous heats. *Phil. Trans. Abr.*, p. 123.
2. See Dr. Hook's *Discourse of Earthquakes*, and Mr. Ray's *Physico-Theo. Discourses*.

To the first I say it may be fired by what the philosophers of old called the antiperistasis of the air, i.e., this inflammable matter meeting with something of a contrary nature to it was by the contest between them put into a flame, for experience shows that if we take nitre, brimstone, and quicklime, mix them in an eggshell, as soon as they touch the water they will fly out in an actual flame, and such is the nature of an acid and an alkali as that the contest between them will heat the plate or vessel in which you endeavor to satiate them, as I have several times experienced. Now according to philosophy, where there is heat there is fire. Or if it was not thus, as has been already explained, I do not see why some fiery vapor or other might not be driven out of the earth or sea and so in its ascent meet with and give fire to this combustible matter.

As to its appearing more than once, the reason is the same as is given for the repetition of the flashes of lightning.

As for the redness of its color, I take it to be nothing but the more thick or gross particles that might be mixed with this inflammable matter. And as for the white streams of light, they were made by the more fine spirituous particles, and that this is very probable may be argued from the quickness of their motion, as well as their issuing down to the horizon, opposite to the place from whence the meteor first arose (as most tell me they did, and I am apt from the nature of the thing to believe it was so).

And this I shall take to be the true solution of this wonderful appearance till somebody will give me, or I can find, a better.

As to prognostications from it, I utterly abhor and detest them all, and look upon these to be but the effect of ignorance and fancy, for I have not so learned philosophy or divinity as to be dismayed at the signs of heaven. This would be to act the part of an heathen, not of a Christian philosopher. See Jer. 10:2. And here I would entreat you to take me right, for I don't mean that this sight was not surprising to me, for I have said it was before, but I only mean that no man should fright himself by supposing that dreadful things will follow, such as famine, sword, or sickness; nor would I be understood to imagine that there will not be fearful sights in the heavens before the great and terrible day of the Lord.

Thus, good sir, I have, as well as I could, given you an account of that unusual meteor, together with my thoughts upon it. If it is acceptable to you, I shall heartily rejoice and allow you to expose it as you please, only concealing my name, hoping what I have said may serve in some measure to illustrate the works of nature which all they who have pleasure therein will inquire into, that so they may be excited to love, honor, and adore the God thereof, to whom be glory forever. Amen.

I am, sir,

Your very humble servant,

[THOMAS ROBIE]

E musaeo meo, 15 December
Anno 1719

VIII

The Erosion
of Puritan Hegemony

FROM 1630 to about 1660, Puritan control of New England was virtually complete. Church, state, and society at large followed guidelines established by the founding fathers; intruders from outside or heretics within were ousted with impunity. Neither foreign powers nor the English crown had much influence on the small cluster of colonies. They minded their own business and asked only to be left alone to pursue their "errand into the wilderness." Indeed, some observers accused the New England settlements of trying to be independent commonwealths, scarcely tied to the British Empire, and in many respects the charges can be supported. But after the Restoration of the Stuart monarchy in 1660, both New England independence and Puritanism's control over the four United Colonies began to disintegrate.

Not all students of New England Puritanism agree that there was a "declension" after 1660—at least to the extent that declension implies decline. Puritanism, it is argued, remained a vital faith, and it continued to provide the principal impetus to New England society long after the Congregational clergy began to lament in endless "jeremiads" the demise of true faith. In fact, in the last third of the seventeenth century church membership probably increased in proportion to the total population. Decline may have been more imaginary than real, more a reflection on the clergymen than on their contemporaries.

Still, there is little doubt that after about 1660 a gap began to grow between the well-ordered, godly, communitarian Bible commonwealth envisioned by John Winthrop, Richard Mather, and John Cotton and the more materialistic, cosmopolitan, heterodox New England of the post-Restoration. For example, the policy established in 1631 that reserved political privilege on the colony level to visible saints began to erode in 1664 when the crown insisted that an Englishman need not be a Congregationalist in order to qualify as a freeman of Massachusetts. As political control began to slip out of Puritan hands—and it did increasingly after the revocation of the Massachusetts charter in 1684—the means diminished for legislative and judicial curbs on social, economic, and religious deviation. Then after mid-century when new waves of immigration brought settlers who were often less committed to the goals of the founding fathers, survivors of the first generation and their more pious offspring thought they saw materialism joining heterodoxy to undermine the old ways. Too many of the post-1660 immigrants made their livings from commerce; New England was becoming less a religious refuge than an economic opportunity. In 1663, John Higginson, son of Salem's first pastor, felt compelled to remind his listeners "that New-England is originally a plantation of Religion, not a plantation of Trade. Let Merchants and such as are increasing Cent per Cent remember this. Let others that have come over since at several times understand this, that worldly gain was not the end and designe of the people of New-England, but Religion. And if any man amongst us make Religion as twelve, and the world as thirteen, let such an one know he hath neither the spirit of a true New-England man, nor yet of a sincere Christian."

More significant perhaps than the gradual erosion of political monopoly and the growth of materialism was the feeling that after the Restoration New Englanders were less determined than their predecessors to fashion a Zion in the wilderness, to make of their society a vigorous example of piety and right-walking. The loss of a sense of mission and the concomitant secularization of New England society is hard to document, for the shift was more a matter of mood than of action or pronouncement. Still, there is little doubt that the reforming zeal of the first generation had evaporated, leaving the form but not the substance of the Puritan tradition. To their credit, the men and women of the late seventeenth and early eighteenth centuries may have been more tolerant, more practical, more humane (though not at Salem Village) than their predecessors, but with the exception of the Mathers and a few other clergymen they were certainly less militant in their attachment to Puritan principles. The erosion was gradual, almost imperceptible, but few historians doubt that it took place or that it contributed significantly to the transformation of the Puritan into a Yankee.

Reasons for the change are complex, but Perry Miller may not have been far from the mark when he observed that "when the belief and the temper which the first settlers brought to America is examined . . . it seems obvious that the reason later generations ceased marching to the Puritan beat was simply that they could no longer stand the pace." Puritanism asked much of its advocates; it was perhaps inevitable that the enthusiasm of the early seventeenth century be followed by a slump in energy.

Of course what seemed decline to those who followed the goals of the first American Puritans may not be decline in the eyes of others then or now. It can be argued that after 1660 New England ascended, threw off the shackles of a narrow theology and a restrictive society, and became a more open, tolerant community. But any view of the evolution of New England must take into account the Puritans' own view of change—the view that measured the events of post-1660 against the hopes and intentions of the first settlers.

35. The Growth of Factionalism

Although the Puritan tradition was no stranger to vehement differences of opinion, in New England theological debate took place within a rather narrow spectrum. Most of the clergymen and leading laymen among the early settlers had been recruited because they adhered to a Congregational viewpoint, and the Puritan colonies continued to attract evangelical Calvinists steeped in Perkins, Ames, and the other English Puritan interpreters of the Reformed tradition. Abundant room remained for debate over specific practices, especially before the promulgation of the Cambridge Platform in 1648, but throughout the first generation of New England settlement, similarity of opinion overshadowed dispute.

After 1660, the relative homogeneity of New England theology began to disintegrate, partly because Congregational polity allowed almost complete autonomy to each church, partly because the growth of New England's population offered a wider base for disagreement, and primarily, perhaps, because the efforts to settle the controversy over baptism and church membership failed to fully satisfy the several factions that had emerged during the formulation of the Half-Way Covenant. In 1671, John Woodbridge, Jr., (1644–1691) a Connecticut clergyman, described in a letter to the prominent English Puritan Richard Baxter the rapid growth of New England's religious controversy and diversity. Like many other Connecticut ministers, Woodbridge favored a position very close to Presbyterianism.

Source: Raymond P. Stearns, ed., "Correspondence of John Woodbridge, Jr., and Richard Baxter," *New England Quarterly*, X (1937), 572–578.

. . . You asked of me a relation of the mold and manners of our churches in this wilderness, and I wish myself as able as I am willing to serve you, but more wish that the knowledge of our churches would tend to their praise and greater glory. A letter is too narrow a table for an history. I shall endeavor to give you a synoptical narrative of them, which I hope is all that you expect. And that I may be the more perspicuous I shall divide the country (as it is divided itself to my hand) into four quarters, viz.: Rhode Island (if 'tis not too sluttish to be handled), Plymouth Colony, the Massachusetts, and Connecticut.

Rhode Island is a chaos of all religions and like *materia prima* susceptive of all forms. Sir Henry Moodyes' short description of it is merry yet true and apt that at Rhode Island there is enough of two good things: fat mutton and liberty of conscience. It is the asylum for all those that are disturbed for heresy, a hive of hornets, and the sink into which all the rest of the colonies empty their heretics, so that the body of the people are an heterogeneous lump of Familists, Antinomians, Quakers, Seekers, and Antisabbatarians. The best limb in it is a church of Anabaptists led by one Mr. Clarke who they say is an *animal rationale*, of competent abilities and moral principles, but ever *duo gladii*: he is both a magistrate and a teacher. I will not say an elder for they hold no such stated office. As for the rest, or at least the generality of them, they neither own nor attend any sacrament. There is a small town called Providence (if the name be not too sacred for the thing) upon the main, yet under the jurisdiction of the island (the nest of that fallen star, Mr. Williams, whose name I presume is not unknown to you), containing about forty or fifty householders, though so small yet tripartited into three distinct churches and congregations, each differing from [the] others in their principles. And the whole jurisdiction, if they agree in any one position [it] is this, that every man though of any hedge religion ought to profess and practice his own tenets without any molestation or disturbance.

Of Plymouth jurisdiction I shall not say much in particular, because they differ but little from the rigid Independents, whose principles and practices I shall speak of a little lower. I question not but God knows many sincere hearts and faithful subjects among them, yet they seem oversprinkled with Brownism and to be woven with some of the finer and more spiritual threads of Anabaptism. The first members of the church of Plymouth (the head town from whence the whole colony is denominated) were (as 'tis possible you have heard) a swarm of Mr. Robinson's church in Holland, and they have not yet thoroughly grown out the cachexy that hung about them when they first transported themselves into the country. I have not heard of any minister or church amongst them as yet that are awakened to open the church doors a little wider for those to enter who are only unholy and unclean, because the porters are so strict. Though in the other colonies, blessed be God, truth and charity have gotten ground of these errors and pinching practices that we are reproached for by the world, and we daily hear of enlargements of the church, unless among some few that grow more strict by an antiperistasis. Some of those of Plymouth are so liberal that they provide the bread for the sacrament (though the communicants are many) in one loaf, because Paul tells us though we are many yet we are one bread.

In the Massachusetts colony there are three forms of disciplinarians, each one step higher than his fellow: rigid Independents, moderate ones, and those that are Presbyterianly addicted, though their numbers are few and their horns kept short. Of the first sort are the gleanings of the clergy and the body of the laity. . . . The persuasions and practices of these girt Independents, sir, you are not ignorant of, yet because error is multifarious and they differ something from their brethren in England, I shall give you a short account of what they are and do amongst us.

Their grand dogma is that a council has no decisive power unless materially, jejunely to propound what is [named?] truth and error and that every church-species has more formal power than an ecumenical council. Also that no person is in proxima potentia a capable subject of baptism but he who either himself or one or both of his parents are in explicit confederation with a particular society, relating the history of their conversion, the manner and steps thereof. This last-mentioned practice begins to steal away ashamed so that whereas the very women were bound (at least in most places) to deliver their relation before the whole congregation, now in many places the men are admitted if their conversion be first judged of by the elder and an understanding brother or two in private, and then approved by the house of commons in public. Every brother has equal power in judgments with the pastor, though the observation of some is not void of all truth, that the Presbyterians take away the power from the people in word and give it them in practice, the Independents take it from the people in practice though they give it them in word: for in all matters that their zeals move in, they are not content only to hold the bridle but also jostle for all the room in the saddle.

They give the power of ordination in every unorganized church to the laity and think that for the elder of one church to impose hands upon a candidate for office in another is not less than peculiar, an example whereof the last October might have been seen in the next town (though through illness I was not present), viz.: Saybrook, where two of the brethren imposed hands on their officer while four or five elders sat by blowing their fingers—which act (now the times begin to see and men's judgments are nine days old) made one of the inhabitants to say that it was matter of indignation to see a cooper and a blacksmith (as the two imposers were by trade) to ordain an elder.

Again, that baptized children do by eating and drinking and the good influence of the sun grow out the membership, and as they become adult they drop their church-relation and become non-subject to the discipline of the church, which made a prompt young man a while ago tell one of the ministers that they dealt with children here as the people with their young shoats in Virginia, to take them up and mark them and then turn them into the woods.

Many of them hold that the civil magistrate has no power in ecclesiastical matters, neither are churches to give account to courts (much less to councils) for any irregular proceeding, and some of them have said to the excommunicate that have complained of maladministration in the church, that if they are wronged they must tarry to be righted at the Day of Judgment.

Now the more moderate and lax Congregational men give some more honor, but very diminutive, unto councils. They allow of ordination by the eldership, which now is most generally practiced. They baptize the grandchildren of members in full communion (as the phrase is) provided their immediate parents solemnly own the parents' covenant in public, as was agreed on at a synod held at Boston in 1662. They acknowledge that the power of rule belongs to rulers, but the power of liberty to the fraternity. Surely that *potestas libertatis* is but a dry bone if 'tis anything.

As for Connecticut colony, that has waded farthest out of Independency and begins now to shew its shoulders above water. There are in the colony about twenty-two towns in all, and among them all about twelve ministers whose judgments are that churches are not *de jure* Independent but integral parts of the whole, though not all of these [are] ordained officers, it being a fashion peculiar to New England—though of no good either aspect or influence for preachers (both Congregational and Presbyterian)—to preach without being sent and to stand long, five, six, ten, or twelve years, unordained. . . .

In other places divisions are the great remove and all things stand at a stay because part of the people pull one way and part the other. The breath of ordination has turned many a smoking into flaming towns, it being so hard to find a minister such an ambidexter as to be able to please both sides. But I am gone from my purpose. The more rigid and also the more unbent Congregationalists are the same in judgment and practice with those in the other colonies, excepting some few punctilios in which almost every church differs from another. The Presbyterians here are more full in their practice, being not only connived at at large but on some considerations tolerated by the law of the commonwealth. But yet for fear of scattering motes in the eyes of some half-enlightened Christians, they suspend the practice of some things that would be not only convenient but commanded, could they be acted without offense.

There are but two towns in the jurisdiction wherein all the Christian inhabitants are under the care, inspection, and government of the eldership, viz., Wethersfield (to whom God has given Mr. Gershom Bulkeley to be their rector—son to Peter Bulkeley, the author of the treatise of the covenant of grace—a man of good parts and spirit), and my own cure in which when I was ordained I found above sixty unbaptized persons, men, women, and children, though the whole plantation consist not of above thirty householders. And till God stirred up the spirits of some in late years (as Mr. Haynes at Hartford, etc.) to roll off from his people the reproach of uncircumcision, the unbaptized began to be the more numerous and the bigger end of the wallet. . . .

But our great wound and disease is a spirit of separation, which so many are drenched with and so few without some tincture of. We ourselves in this town, through the unsettledness of the times, the infancy of the reformation, and the forementioned conditions of the country, are little more than the embryo of a Presbyterian church in its formalities and maturity. Yet our next neighbors have both refused to join with us at the Lord's table and also to admit our members occasionally into their synaxis; yet professing that 'tis not any personal scandal in any of our members already admitted that frights them, but that were there occasion offered, then they that we use would open the door for the scandalous, which if it could be proved I should begin to think evil of it as well as they. . . .

Those that desire to be admitted communicants first come to me and declare their desires; the next Sabbath I signify their desires to the congregation, to the intent that whosoever know them to lie under scandal and unsuitableness for that ordinance would according to rule seek a reformation of it. If nothing appear against them, I examine them concerning their knowledge and proficiency in the way of life, of the understanding of the nature of the sacrament, and the qualifications of every communicant; in which if I find them not deficient before the sacrament, I declare to the church that there is nothing appearing why they should not partake with us in that holy feast. But the common opinion is so riveted in the hearts of men—viz., that the infected and infectious will steal in at the church doors unless every brother be allowed a feeling of his pulse and smelling of his breath and handling of his neck and hands, least he should prove a smooth supplanter—that 'tis extreme difficult (it being so pleasing to natural pride) to make men vomit it up.

The last year was fatal with us for the dichotomizing three churches—Windsor, Hartford, and Stratford—and making them stand out into six. . . . The church at Hartford had very little reason to divide, because Mr. Whiting, the dissatisfied elder, and his adherents (being the minor part of the church), were invited to continue a part of the church and had liberty to practice his own judgment, when in the other churches the Presbyterians, being the minor part, were staved off from the rest. Mr. Whiting, though he had been ordained to the whole church of which his adherents were members, yet when he withdrew, because *pars ecclesiae non est ecclesia*, was reordained.

Sir, I have in some measure pulled off our rags and showed you the wound. I should be prejudicial to the body of which I am a member if I should not desire you, as you have leisure and opportunity, to propound us a salve that our breaches might be healed and paths restored to dwell in. A standerby may see more of our game than we ourselves. I know you will not be unwilling to impart to me the knowledge of what methods of healing for us are with you, though I confess till men are more humble and self-denying amongst us, the most sanative plaisters will be pulled off. . . .

36. God's Controversy with New England

In 1662, clergyman-poet Michael Wigglesworth, author of the best-selling Day of Doom, brooded over the drought that gripped New England. Out of his ruminations came a new epic poem, God's Controversy with New England; although it did not match the fame of his earlier writing, it struck a chord that would be played over and over again in sermons, pamphlets, and legislative decrees for the next half-century: repent, New England, for you have strayed from God's path and from the high achievements of the founding fathers. God will not long tolerate so profligate a people. Already He wonders:

> What should I do with such a stiff-neckt race?
> How shall I ease me of such Foes as they?
> What shall befall despizers of my Grace?
> I'le surely beare their candlestick away.
> And Lamps put out. Their glorious noon-day light
> I'le quickly turn into a dark Egyptian night.

To most New Englanders, it must have seemed that a dark Egyptian night was indeed on its way. The Puritan Commonwealth of Oliver Cromwell had fallen, thus dooming the cause of international Puritanism. Then came the reinstatement of the Stuart monarchy—no friends of Puritanism—and at the same time a smallpox epidemic in Boston. A drought followed in 1662 which, along with other minor calamities, served as prolegomena to the disastrous Indian uprisings of 1675. With timely aid from Christian Indians, the colonists prevailed, but the price was frightfully high. To Puritan minds, there was no doubt that King Philip of the Wampanoags had been the Lord's rod of chastisement, and the clergy responded as they had since the early 1660s with those peculiar lamentations we now call jeremiads. Their culmination came in 1680 with the report of a "reforming synod" that marked a new high in Puritan self-flagellation. Agreeing with Wigglesworth that "God hath a Controversy with his New-England People," the report attempted to catalogue the causes. Regardless of the validity of the argument, the synod's conclusions reveal the extent to which New England Puritans thought they were in decline.

Source: Williston Walker, Creeds and Platforms of Congregationalism (New York, 1893), 426–432.

Question I

What are the evils that have provoked the Lord to bring His judgments on New England?

Answer. . . .

That God hath a controversy with His New England people is undeniable, the Lord having written His displeasure in dismal characters against us. Though personal afflictions do oftentimes come only or chiefly for probation, yet as to public judgments it is not wont to be so; especially when by a continued series of providence, the Lord doth appear and plead against His people. 2 Sam. 21:1. As with us it hath been from year to year. Would the Lord have whetted His glittering sword, and His hand have taken hold on judgment? Would He have sent such a mortal contagion like a besom of destruction in the midst of us? Would He have said, Sword! go through the land, and cut off man and beast? Or would He have kindled such devouring fires, and made such fearful desolations in the earth, if He had not been angry? It is not for nothing that the merciful God, who doth not willingly afflict nor grieve the children of men, hath done all these things unto us; yea and sometimes with a cloud hath covered Himself, that our prayer should not pass through. And although 'tis possible that the Lord may contend with us partly on account of secret unobserved sins (Josh. 7:11, 12; 2 King. 17:9; Psal. 90:8), in which respect, a deep and most serious inquiry into the causes of His controversy ought to be attended. Nevertheless, it is sadly evident that there are visible, manifest evils, which without doubt the Lord is provoked by. For,

I. There is a great and visible decay of the power of godliness amongst many professors in these churches. It may be feared that there is in too many spiritual and heart apostasy from God, whence communion with Him in the ways of His worship, especially in secret, is much neglected, and whereby men cease to know and fear and love and trust in Him, but take up their contentment and satisfaction in something else. This was the ground and bottom of the Lord's controversy with His people of old. Psal. 78:8, 37, and 81:11; Jer. 2:5, 11, 13. And with His people under the New Testament also. Rev. 2:4, 5.

II. The pride that doth abound in New England testifies against us. Hos. 5:5; Ezek. 7:10. Both spiritual pride, Zeph. 3:11. Whence two great evils and provocations have proceeded and prevailed amongst us.

1. A refusing to be subject to order according to divine appointment, Numb. 16:3; 1 Pet. 5:5.

2. Contention. Prov. 13:10. An evil that is most eminently against the solemn charge of the Lord Jesus, Joh. 13:34, 35. And that for which God hath by severe judgments punished His people, both in former and latter ages. This malady hath been very general in the country; we have therefore cause to fear that the wolves which God in His holy providence hath let loose upon us have been sent to chastise His sheep for their dividings and strayings one from another, and that the wars and fightings which have proceeded from the lust of pride in special, have been punished with the sword, Jam. 4:1; Job. 19:29.

Yea, and pride in respect to apparel hath greatly abounded. Servants and the poorer sort of people are notoriously guilty in the matter, who (too generally) go above their estates and degrees, thereby transgressing the laws both of God and man, Math. 11:8. Yea, it is a sin that even the light of nature, and laws of civil nations have condemned. 1 Cor. 11:14. Also, many, not of the meaner sort, have offended God by strange apparel, not becoming serious Christians, especially in these days of affliction and misery, wherein the Lord calls upon men to put off their ornaments, Exod. 33:5; Jer. 4:30. A sin which brings wrath upon the greatest that shall be found guilty of it, Zeph. 1:8; with Jer. 52:13. Particularly, the Lord hath threatened to visit with sword and sickness and with loathsome diseases for this very sin. Isai. 3:16.

III. Inasmuch as it was in a more peculiar manner with respect to the second Commandment, that our fathers did follow the Lord into this wilderness, whilst it was a land not sown, we may fear that the breaches of that Commandment are some part of the Lord's controversy with New England. Church fellowship and other divine institutions are greatly neglected. Many of the rising generation are not mindful of that which their baptism doth engage them unto, viz. to use utmost endeavors that they may be fit for, and so partake in, all the holy ordinances of the Lord Jesus. Math. 28:20. There are too many that with profane Esau slight spiritual privileges. Nor is there so much of discipline extended towards the children of the covenant, as we are generally agreed ought to be done. On the other hand, humane inventions, and will-worship have been set up even in Jerusalem. Men have set up their thresholds by God's threshold, and their posts by His post. Quakers are false worshipers; and such Anabaptists as have risen up amongst us, in opposition to the churches of the Lord Jesus, receiving into their society those that have been for scandal delivered unto Satan, yea, and improving those as administrators of holy things, who have been (as doth appear) justly under Church censures, do no better than set up an altar against the Lord's altar. Wherefore it must needs be provoking to God, if these things be not duly and fully testified against by everyone in their several capacities respectively. Josh. 22:19; 2 King. 23:13; Ezek. 43:8; Psal. 99:8; Hos. 11:6.

IV. The holy and glorious name of God hath been polluted and profaned amongst us, more especially:

1. By oaths, and imprecations in ordinary discourse; yea, and it is too common a thing for men in a more solemn way to swear unnecessary oaths, whenas it is a breach of the third Commandment so to use the blessed name of God. And many (if not the most) of those that swear consider not the rule of an oath. Jer. 4:2. So that we may justly fear that because of swearing the land mourns, Jer. 23:10.

2. There is great profaneness in respect of irreverent behavior in the solemn worship of God. It is a frequent thing for men (though not necessitated thereunto by any infirmity) to sit in prayer time, and some with their heads almost covered, and to give way to their own sloth and sleepiness, when they should be serving God with attention and intention, under the solemn dispensation of His

ordinances. We read but of one man in the scripture that slept at a sermon, and that sin hath like to have cost him his life, Act. 20:9.

V. There is much sabbath-breaking. Since there are multitudes that do profanely absent themselves or theirs from the public worship of God, on His holy day, especially in the most populous places the land, and many under pretense of differing apprehensions about the beginning of the sabbath do not keep a seventh part of time holy unto the Lord, as the fourth Commandment requireth, walking abroad, and traveling (not merely on the account of worshiping God in the solemn assemblies of His people or to attend works of necessity or mercy), being a common practice on the sabbath day, which is contrary unto that rest enjoined by the Commandment. Yea, some that attend their particular servile callings and employments after the sabbath is begun, or before it is ended. Worldly, unsuitable discourses are very common upon the Lord's day, contrary to the scripture which requireth that men should not on holy times find their own pleasure, nor speak their own words, Isai. 58:13. Many that do not take care so to dispatch their worldly businesses, that they may be free and fit for the duties of the sabbath, and that do (if not wholly neglect) after a careless, heartless manner perform the duties that concern the sanctification of the sabbath. This brings wrath, fires, and other judgments upon a professing people, Neh. 3:17, 18; Jer. 17:27.

VI. As to what concerns families and the government thereof, there is much amiss. There are many families that do not pray to God constantly, morning and evening, and many more wherein the scriptures are not daily read, that so the word of Christ might dwell richly with them. Some (and too many) houses that are full of ignorance and profaneness, and these not duly inspected, for which cause wrath may come upon others round about them, as well as upon themselves. Josh. 22:20; Jer. 5:7, and 10:25. And many householders who profess religion do not cause all that are within their gates to become subject unto good order, as ought to be. Exod. 20:10. Nay, children and servants that are not kept in due subjection, their masters, and parents especially, being sinfully indulgent towards them. This is a sin which brings great judgments, as we see in Eli's and David's family. In this respect, Christians in this land, have become too like unto the Indians, and then we need not wonder if the Lord hath afflicted us by them. Sometimes a sin is discerned by the instrument that providence doth punish with. Most of the evils that abound amongst us proceed from defects as to family government.

VII. Inordinate passions. Sinful heats and hatreds, and that amongst church-members themselves, who abound with evil surmisings, uncharitable and unrighteous censures, backbitings, hearing and telling tales, few that remember and duly observe the rule, with an angry countenance to drive away the talebearer; reproachful and reviling expressions, sometimes to or of one another. Hence lawsuits are frequent, brother going to law with brother, and provoking and abusing one another in public courts of judicature, to the scandal of their holy profession, Isai. 58:4; 1 Cor. 6:6, 7. And in managing the discipline of Christ, some (and too many) are acted by their passions and prejudices more than by a spirit of love and faithfulness towards their brother's soul, which things are as against the law of Christ, so dreadful violations of the church covenant, made in the presence of God.

VIII. There is much intemperance. The heathenish and idolatrous practice of health-drinking is too frequent. That shameful iniquity of sinful drinking is become too general a provocation. Days of training, and other public solemnities have been abused in this respect. And not only English but Indians have been debauched by those that call themselves Christians, who have put their bottles to them, and made them drunk also. This is a crying sin, and the more aggravated in that the first planters of this colony did (as is in the patent expressed) come into this land with a design to convert the heathen unto Christ, but if instead of that, they be taught wickedness, which before they were never guilty of, the Lord may well punish us by them. Moreover, the sword, sickness, poverty, and almost all the judgments which have been upon New England, are mentioned in the scripture as the woeful fruit of that sin. Isai. 5:11, 12, and 28:1, 2, and 56:9, 12; Prov. 23:21, 29, 30, and 21:17; Hos. 7:5, and 2:8, 9. There are more temptations and occasions unto that sin, publicly allowed of, than any necessity doth require; the proper end of taverns, etc., being for the entertainment of strangers, which if they were improved to that end only, a far less number would suffice. But it is a common practice for town-dwellers, yea and church-members, to frequent public houses, and there to misspend precious time, unto the dishonor of the gospel, and the scandalizing of others, who are by such examples induced to sin against God. In which respect, for church-members to be unnecessarily in such houses is sinful, scandalous, and provoking to God. 1 Cor. 8:9, 10; Rom. 14:21; Math. 17:27, and 18:7.

And there are other heinous breaches of the seventh Commandment. Temptations thereunto are become too common, viz., such as immodest apparel, Prov. 7:10, laying out of hair, borders, naked necks and arms, or, which is more abominable, naked breasts, and mixed dancings, light behavior and expressions, sinful company-keeping with light and vain persons, unlawful gaming, an abundance of idleness, which brought ruinating judgment upon Sodom, and much more upon Jerusalem (Ezek. 16:49) and doth sorely threaten New England unless effectual remedies be thoroughly and timeously applied.

IX. There is much want of truth amongst men. Promise-breaking is a common sin, for which New England doth hear ill abroad in the world. And the Lord hath threatened for that transgression to give His people into the hands of their enemies, and that their dead bodies should be for meat unto the fowls of heaven and to the beasts of the earth; which judgments have been verified upon us, Jer. 34:18, 20. And false reports have been too common; yea, walking with slanders and reproaches, and that sometimes against the most faithful and eminent servants of God. The Lord is not wont to suffer such iniquity to pass unpunished. Jer. 9:4, 5; Numb. 16:41.

X. Inordinate affection to the world. Idolatry is a God-provoking, judgment-procuring sin. And covetousness is idolatry. Eph. 5:5. There hath been in many professors an insatiable desire after land and worldly accommodations, yea, so as to forsake churches and ordinances, and to live like heathen, only that so they might have elbow-room enough in the world. Farms and merchandising have been preferred before the things of God. In this respect, the interest of New England seemeth to be changed. We differ from other outgoings of our nation in that it was not any worldly consideration that brought our fathers into this wilderness, but religion, even that so they might build a sanctuary unto the Lord's name; whenas now religion is made subservient unto worldly interests. Such iniquity causeth war to be in the gates, and cities to be burnt up. Judg. 8:5; Math. 22:5, 7. Wherefore, we cannot but solemnly bear witness against that practice of settling plantations without any ministry amongst them, which is to prefer the world before the gospel. When Lot did forsake the Land of Canaan, and the church which was in Abraham's family, that so he might have better worldly accommodations in Sodom, God fired him out of all, and he was constrained to leave his goodly pastures, which his heart (though otherwise a good man) was too much set upon. Moreover, that many are under the prevailing power of the sin of worldliness is evident:

1. From that oppression which the land groaneth under. There are some traders who sell their goods at excessive rates, day-laborers and mechanics are unreasonable in their demands. Yea, there have been those that have dealt deceitfully and oppressively towards the heathen amongst whom we live, whereby they have been scandalized and prejudiced against the name of Christ. The scripture doth frequently threaten judgments for the sin of oppression, and in special the oppressing sword cometh as a just punishment for that evil. Ezek. 7:11, and 22:15; Prov. 28:8; Isai. 5:7.

2. It is also evident that men are under the prevailing power of a worldly spirit, by their strait-handedness as to public concernments. God by a continued series of providence, for many years one after another, hath been blasting the fruits of the earth in a great measure, and this year more abundantly. Now if we search the scriptures, we shall find that when the Lord hath been provoked to destroy the fruits of the earth, either by noxious creatures, or by his own immediate hand in blastings or droughts or excessive rains (all which judgments we have experience of), it hath been mostly for this sin of strait-handedness with reference unto public and pious concerns, Hag. 1:9; Mal. 3:8, 9, 11. As when people's hearts and hands are enlarged upon these accounts, God hath promised (and is wont in his faithful providence to do accordingly) to bless with outward plenty and prosperity, Prov. 3:9, 10; Mal. 3:10; I Cor. 9:6, 8, 10; 2 Chron. 31:10. So on the other hand, when men withhold more than is meet, the Lord sends impoverishing judgments upon them, Prov. 11:24.

XI. There hath been opposition unto the work of reformation. Although the Lord hath been calling upon us, not only by the voice of His servants, but by awful judgments, that we should return unto Him who hath been smiting us, and notwithstanding all the good laws that are established for the suppression of growing evils, yet men will not return every one from his evil way. There hath been great incorrigibleness under lesser judgments. Sin and sinners have many advocates. They that have been zealous in bearing witness against the sins of the times have been reproached, and other ways discouraged, which argueth an heart unwilling to reform. Hence the Lord's controversy is not yet done, but His hand is stretched out still, Lev. 26:23, 24; Isai. 12:13.

XII. A public spirit is greatly wanting in the most of men. Few that are of Nehemiah's spirit, Neh. 5:15. All seek their own, not the things that are Jesus Christ's, serving themselves upon Christ and His holy ordinances. Matters appertaining to the Kingdom of God are either not at all regarded or not in the first place. Hence schools of learning and other public concerns are in a languishing state. Hence also are unreasonable complaints and murmurings because of public charges, which is a great sin, and a private self-seeking spirit is one of those evils that renders the last times perilous, 2 Tim. 3:1.

XIII. There are sins against the gospel, whereby the Lord hath been provoked. Christ is not prized and embraced in all His offices and ordinances as ought to be. Manna hath been loathed, the pleasant land despised, Psal. 106:24. Though the gospel and covenant of grace call upon men to repent, yet there are multitudes that refuse to repent, when the Lord doth vouchsafe them time and means. No sins provoke the Lord more than impenitency and unbelief, Jer. 8:6; Zech. 7:11, 12, 13; Heb. 3:17, 18; Rev. 2:21, 22. There is great unfruitfulness under the means of grace, and that brings the most desolating judgments, Isai. 5:4, 5; Math. 3:10, and 21:43.

Finally, there are several considerations which seem to evidence that the evils mentioned are the matters of the Lord's controversy:

1. In that (though not as to all) as to most of them they are sins which many are guilty of,

2. Sins which have been acknowledged before the Lord on days of humiliation appointed by authority, and yet not reformed.

3. Many of them not punished (and some of them not punishable) by men, therefore the Lord Himself doth punish for them.

37. Encroachments from England

Even if the American Puritans had been left to their own devices, changes would no doubt have come to New England. The shifting character of the population, England's growing taste for toleration, and the differing needs of a society rapidly transforming itself from wilderness outposts to mature and complex communities would have prodded changes in any event. There is also reason to believe, however, that resistance would have been fierce and alteration correspondingly slow. By 1660, the founding fathers had already become the objects of considerable veneration; upsetting their precedents would not come easily. Too, there was the Puritan emphasis on order and stability, hardly conducive to experimentation and adaptation. And finally, the passing of the old guard took place gradually, with vacancies in church and state going to men who had themselves arrived in New England as children or who had been raised under the wings of the founders. For example, when Richard Mather died in 1669, his influence survived to a considerable extent in his son Increase (b. 1639) and grandson Cotton (b. 1663), while many other first-generation clergymen left progeny to fill New England's pulpits and public offices, including Thomas Shepard, John Eliot, and John Cotton. It was to be expected, then, that as Puritanism tended increasingly to slip from a faith into an administration, it would attempt to preserve the Bible commonwealth.

Charles II had other ideas. Salutary neglect of the colonies by his father and grandfather had encouraged New England to grow perverse in her Independency and to become oblivious to imperial regulations. He was further annoyed by reports that two of the men who had voted for the execution of his father received asylum in New England.

A. Report on Massachusetts

As the first step in bringing the Puritan colonies into line, Charles in 1664 sent four royal commissioners to look into the affairs of the New England colonies. They found Rhode Island, Connecticut, and Plymouth reasonably cooperative. Massachusetts seemed obstinate, forever evading questions and showing little inclination to mend her ways. Even after the commissioners recommended cancellation of the Massachusetts charter, the Bay Colony refused to send representatives to England to answer charges. Had the King not been busy with more weighty matters, Massachusetts might have forfeited its cherished independence as early as 1665. Instead, little was done by the crown until 1676, when Edward Randolph (c. 1632–1703), a career bureaucrat with no affection for Puritanism or New England, arrived in Boston as a special commissioner. Meeting with no cooperation from the Massachusetts government—which looked on him as a bearer of unwelcome and illegal *tidings from the King and as an agent of the Mason family that was attempting to reassert title to New Hampshire—Randolph complained to Charles II. In 1678, he was rewarded by an appointment as collector of customs in New England, a job that earned him still further enmity in Boston. By 1680, he was back in London making extensive charges against the Bay Colony, most of which are summed up in the following brief document.*

Source: The Prince Society, *Hutchinson Papers* (2 vols., Albany, N.Y., 1865), II, 264–265.

To the King's most excellent Majesty, the humble representation of Edward Randolph humbly sheweth,

That your Majesty was graciously pleased in March 1675–6 to entrust him with your royal letters to the governor of Boston in New England, and also commanded him upon several queries to inform your Majesty of the present state of that government.

In all humble obedience to your Majesty's royal command, he hath reduced his information to these following heads, viz.:

1. That the Bostoners have no right either to land or government in any part of New England, but are usurpers, the inhabitants yielding obedience unto a supposition only of a royal grant from his late Majesty.

2. They have formed themselves into a commonwealth, denying any appeals to England; contrary to other plantations, [they] do not take the oath of allegiance.

3. They have protected the murtherers of your royal father in contempt of your Majesty's proclamation of the 6th June 1660 and your letter of 28th June 1662.

4. They coin money of their own impress.

5. They put your Majesty's subjects to death for religion.

6. In 1665 they did violently oppose your Majesty's commissioners in the settlement of New Hampshire. In the year 1666, by armed force, turned out your Majesty's justices of peace in the province of Maine in opposition to your Majesty's authority and declaration 10th April 1666.

7. They impose an oath of fidelity upon those that inhabit within their territories to be true and faithful to their government.

8. They violate all the acts of trade and navigation, by which they have engrossed the greatest part of the West India trade,

whereby your Majesty is damnified in the customs £100,000 yearly, and the kingdom much more.

All which he is ready to prove.

B. The Dominion of New England

Randolph's efforts to bring New England into line with imperial policy and to subvert Puritan control of Massachusetts met with mixed success until 1684, when the crown revoked the Massachusetts charter. Two years later, all New England colonies were joined with New York and New Jersey in an experiment in colonial consolidation. The Dominion of New England, ruled by royal governor Sir Edmund Andros, brought the Puritan experiment to a temporary end. Not only did authority now rest in men selected by the crown, but in 1687 South Meetinghouse opened its doors to Anglican services. Samuel Sewall's diary entries tell the story without embellishment: "Wednesday, March 23. The Governour sends Mr. Randolph for the Keys of our Meetinghouse, that may say Prayers there. Mr. Eliot, Frary, Oliver, Savage, Davis and my Self wait on his Excellency, shew that the Land and House is ours, and that we can't consent to part with it to such use. . . . Friday, March 25, 1687. The Governour has service in the South Meetinghouse. . . ."

England's Glorious Revolution of 1688–1689, which saw the overthrow of James II by William of Orange, gave the Puritans a long-awaited chance to oust the Dominion of New England. Soon after news reached Boston of the landing of William in England, a Boston mob incarcerated Randolph, Andros, and several of their followers. Puritan pamphleteers lost no time in justifying the expulsion of what many believed to be a Catholic conspiracy to undermine the liberties of both old and New England.

Source: Peter Force, ed., Tracts and Other Papers Relating Principally to the . . . Colonies in North America (4 vols., Washington, 1836–1847), IV, No. 10.

THE DECLARATION OF THE
GENTLEMEN, MERCHANTS, AND INHABITANTS OF BOSTON,
AND THE COUNTRY ADJACENT. APRIL 18, 1689

I. We have seen more than a decade of years rolled away since the English world had the discovery of an horrid Popish plot, wherein the bloody devotees of Rome had in their design and prospect no less than the extinction of the Protestant religion, which mighty work they called the utter subduing of a pestilent heresy, wherein (they said) there never were such hopes of success since the death of Queen Mary as now in our days. And we were of all men the most insensible if we should apprehend a country so remarkable for the true profession and pure exercise of the Protestant religion as New England is, wholly unconcerned in the infamous plot. To crush and break a country so entirely and signally made up of reformed churches, and at length to involve it in the miseries of an utter extirpation, must needs carry even a supererogation of merit with it among such as were intoxicated with a bigotry inspired into them by the great scarlet whore.

II. To get us within the reach of the desolation desired for us, it was no improper thing that we should first have our charter vacated and the hedge which kept us from the wild beast of the field effectually broken down. The accomplishment of this was hastened by the unwearied solicitations and slanderous accusations of a man for his malice and falsehood well known unto us all. Our charter was with a most injurious pretense (and scarce that) of law condemned before it was possible for us to appear at Westminster in the legal defense of it; and without a fair leave to answer for ourselves concerning the crimes falsely laid to our charge, we were put under a president and council without any liberty for an assembly, which the other American plantations have by a commission from his Majesty.

III. The commission was as illegal for the form of it, as the way of obtaining it was malicious and unreasonable; yet we made no resistance thereunto as we could easily have done, but chose to give all mankind a demonstration of our being a people sufficiently dutiful and loyal to our King. And this with yet more satisfaction, because we took pains to make ourselves believe as much as ever we could of the wheedle then offered unto us, that his Majesty's desire was no other than the happy increase and advance of these provinces by their more immediate dependence on the Crown of England. And we were convinced of it by the courses immediately taken to damp and spoil our trade, whereof decays and complaints presently filled all the country, while in the meantime neither the honor nor the treasure of the King was at all advanced by this new model of our affairs, but a considerable charge added unto the Crown.

IV. In little more than half a year, we saw this commission superseded by another yet more absolute and arbitrary, with which Sir Edmund Andros arrived as our governor, who besides his power—with the advice and consent of his council—to make laws and raise taxes as he pleased had also authority by himself to muster and employ all persons residing in the territory as occasion shall serve, and to transfer such forces to any English plantation in America as occasion shall require. And several companies of soldiers were now brought from Europe to support what was to be imposed upon us, not without repeated menaces that some hundreds more were intended for us.

V. The government was no sooner in these hands but care was taken to load preferments principally upon such men as were strangers to and haters of the people; and everyone's observation hath noted what qualifications recommended a man to public offices and employment, only here and there a good man was used, where others could not easily be had. The governor himself, with assertions now and then falling from him, made us jealous that it would be thought for his Majesty's interest if this people were removed and another succeeded in their room. And his far-fetched instruments that were growing rich among us would gravely inform us that it was not for his Majesty's interest that we should thrive. But of all our oppressors we were chiefly squeezed by a crew of abject persons, fetched from New York to be the tools of the adversary, standing at our right hand. By these were extraordinary and intolerable fees extorted from everyone upon all occasions, without any rules but those of their own insatiable avarice and beggary; and even the probate of a will must now cost as many pounds perhaps as it did shillings heretofore. Nor could a small volume contain the other illegalities done by these horse-leeches in the two or three years that they have been sucking of us; and what laws they made it was as impossible for us to know as dangerous for us to break. But we shall leave the men of Ipswich and of Plymouth (among others) to tell the story of the kindness which has been shown them upon this account. [*Marginal note:* He would neither suffer them to be printed nor fairly published.] Doubtless a land so ruled as once New England was has not without many fears and sighs beheld the wicked walking on every side, and the vilest men exalted.

VI. It was now plainly affirmed, both by some in open council and by the same in private converse, that the people in New England were all slaves, and the only difference between them and slaves is their not being bought and sold. And it was a maxim delivered in open court unto us by one of the council that we must not think the privileges of Englishmen would follow us to the end of the world. Accordingly we have been treated with multiplied contradictions to Magna Charta, the rights of which we laid claim unto. Persons who did but peaceably object against the raising of taxes without an assembly have been for it fined, some twenty, some thirty, and others fifty pounds. Packed and picked juries have been very common things among us, when, under a pretended form of law, the trouble of some honest and worthy men has been aimed at; but when some of this gang have been brought upon the stage for the most detestable enormities that ever the sun beheld, all men have with admiration seen what methods have been taken that they might not be treated according to their crimes. Without a verdict, yea, without a jury sometimes, have people been fined most unrighteously, and some not of the meanest quality have been kept in long and close imprisonment without any the least information appearing against them, or an *habeas corpus* allowed unto them. In short, when our oppressors have been a little out of money, 'twas but pretending some offense to be inquired into and the most innocent of men were continually put into no small expense to answer the demands of the officers, who must have money of them, or a prison for them, though none could accuse them of any misdemeanor.

VII. To plunge the poor people everywhere into deeper incapacities, there was one very comprehensive abuse given to us: multitudes of pious and sober men through the land, scrupled the mode of swearing on the Book, desiring that they might swear with an uplifted hand agreeable to the ancient custom of the colony, and though we think we can prove that the common law amongst us (as well as in some other places under the English Crown) not only indulges but even commands and enjoins the rite of lifting the hand in swearing, yet they that had this doubt were still put by from serving upon any juries, and many of them were most unaccountably fined and imprisoned. Thus one grievance is a Trojan horse in the belly of which it is not easy to recount how many insufferable vexations have been contained.

VIII. Because these things could not make us miserable fast enough, there was a notable discovery made of we know not what flaw in all our titles to our lands. And though besides our purchase of them from the natives, and besides our actual peaceable unquestioned possession of them for near threescore years, and besides the promise of King Charles II in his proclamation sent over to us in the year 1683 that no man here shall receive any prejudice in his freehold or estate, we had the grant of our lands under the seal of the Council of Plymouth, which grant was renewed and confirmed unto us by King Charles I, under the great seal of England. And the General Court, which consisted of the patentees and their associates, had made particular grants hereof to the several towns (though 'twas now denied by the governor that there was any such thing as a town) among us, to all which grants the General Court annexed for the further securing of them a General Act, published under the seal of the colony in the year 1684. Yet we were every day told that no man was owner of a foot of land in all the colony. Accordingly, writs of intrusion began everywhere to be served on people, that after all their sweat and their cost upon their formerly purchased lands thought themselves freeholders of what they had. And the governor caused the lands pertaining to these and those particular men to be measured out for his creatures to take possession of, and the right owners, for pulling up the stakes, have passed through molestations enough to tire all the patience in the world. They are more than a few that were by terrors driven to take patents for their lands at excessive rates, to save them from the next that might petition for them. And we fear that the forcing of the people at the eastward hereunto gave too much rise to the late unhappy invasion made by the Indians on them. Blank patents were got ready for the rest of us, to be sold at a price that all the money and movables in the territory could scarce have paid. And several towns in the country had their commons begged by persons (even by some of the council themselves) who have been privately encouraged thereunto by those that sought for occasions to impoverish a land already peeled, meeted out, and trodden down.

IX. All the council were not engaged in these ill actions, but those of them which were true lovers of their country were seldom admitted to and seldomer consulted at the debates which produced these unrighteous things. Care was taken to keep them under disadvantages, and the governor—with five or six more—did what they would. We bore all these and many more such things without making any attempt for any relief, only Mr. Mather, purely out of respect unto the good of his afflicted country, undertook a voyage into England, which when these men suspected him to be preparing for, they used all manner of craft and rage not only to interrupt his voyage but to ruin his person too. God having through many difficulties given him to arrive at Whitehall, the King more than once or twice promised him a certain Magna Charta for a speedy redress of many things which we were groaning under, and in the meantime said that our governor should be written unto to forbear the measures that he was upon. However, after this we were injured in those very things which were complained of; and besides what wrong hath been done in our civil concerns, we suppose the ministers and the churches everywhere have seen our sacred concerns apace going after them. How they have been discountenanced has had a room in the reflections of every man that is not a stranger in our Israel.

X. And yet that our calamity might not be terminated here, we are again briered in the perplexities of another Indian War; how or why is a mystery too deep for us to unfold. And though 'tis judged that our Indian enemies are not above 100 in number, yet an army of one thousand English hath been raised for the conquering of them, which army of our poor friends and brethren now under Popish commanders (for in the army as well as in the council Pappists are in commission) has been under such a conduct that not one Indian hath been killed, but more English are supposed to have died through sickness and hardship than we have adversaries there alive. And the whole war hath been so managed that we cannot but suspect in it a branch of the plot to bring us low, which we leave to be further inquired into in due time.

XI. We did nothing against these proceedings but only cry to our God; they have caused the cry of the poor to come unto Him and He hears the cry of the afflicted. We have been quiet hitherto, and so still we should have been had not the great God at this time laid us under a double engagement to do something for our security, besides what we have in the strangely unanimous inclination which our countrymen by extremest necessities are driven unto. For first, we are informed that the rest of the English America is alarmed with just and great fears that they may be attacked by the French, who have lately ('tis said) already treated many of the English with worse than Turkish cruelties; and while we are in equal danger of being surprised by them, it is high time we should be better guarded than we are like to be while the government remains in the hands by which it hath been held of late. Moreover, we have understood (though the governor has taken all imaginable care to keep us all ignorant thereof) that the Almighty God hath been pleased to prosper the noble undertaking of the Prince of Orange to preserve the three kingdoms from the horrible brinks of Popery and slavery, and to bring to a condign punishment those worst of men by whom English liberties have been destroyed; in compliance with which glorious action we ought surely to follow the patterns which the nobility, gentry, and commonalty in several parts of those kindgoms have set before us, though they therein chiefly proposed to prevent what we already endure.

XII. We do therefore seize upon the persons of those few ill men which have been (next to our sins) the grand authors of our miseries, resolving to secure them for what justice, orders from his Highness, with the English Parliament, shall direct, lest ere we are aware we find (what we may fear being on all sides in danger) ourselves to be by them given away to a foreign power before such orders can reach unto us—for which orders we now humbly wait. In the meantime firmly believing that we have endeavored nothing but what mere duty to God and our country calls for at our hands, we commit our enterprise unto the blessing of Him who hears the cry of the oppressed, and advise all our neighbors for whom we have thus ventured ourselves to join with us in prayers and all just actions for the defense of the land.

C. A New Constitution

Even before the Glorious Revolution, the New England colonies sought a return of their pre-Dominion rights. Connecticut and Rhode Island succeeded in regaining their old charters from William and Mary, but despite the efforts of Increase Mather, the Bay Colony's agent, the new monarchs refused to reissue the Massachusetts charter of 1629. While William and Mary had little sympathy for the hostile view of Massachusetts epitomized by Edward Randolph, they were not unaware of the need to bring the Bay Colony into closer harmony with the administration of British America. Accordingly, the new charter for Massachusetts struck a compromise between the model followed by the other royal provinces and that long enjoyed by the Massachusetts Puritans. Taking a page from the Dominion of New England, the charter of 1691 incorporated Plymouth and Maine into the colony of Massachusetts; in matters of self-government the charter returned many of the privileges denied under the Dominion and also permitted the combined houses of the legislature to select the upper house, rather than having it selected by the governor and Board of Trade. Still, Puritan control could never function as it once had: gone was the colony's right to select its own governor, to limit the franchise to church members, and to dismiss heretics.

Source: Francis N. Thorpe, ed., *The Federal and State Constitutions, Colonial Charters, and Other Organic Laws* (7 vols., Washington, 1909), III, 1870–1886.

. . . We will and by these presents for us, our heirs, and successors do ordain and grant that there shall and may be convened, held, and kept by the governor, for the time being, upon every last Wednesday in the month of May, every year forever, and at all such other times as the governor of our said province shall think fit and appoint, a great and General Court of Assembly, which said great and General Court of Assembly shall consist of the governor and council or assistants, for the time being, and of such freeholders of our said province or territory as shall be from time to time elected or deputed by the major part of the freeholders and other inhabitants of the respective towns or places who shall be present at such elections, each of the said towns and places being hereby empowered to elect and depute two persons and no more to serve for and represent them respectively in the said great and General Court or Assembly. To which great and General Court or Assembly to be held as aforesaid, we do hereby for us, our heirs, and successors give and grant full power and authority from time to time to direct, appoint, and declare what number each country, town, and place shall elect and depute to serve for and represent them respectively in the said great and General Court or Assembly, provided always that no freeholder or other person shall have a vote in the election of members to serve in any great and General Court or Assembly to be held as aforesaid, what at the time of such election shall not have an estate of freehold in land within our said province or territory to the value of forty shillings per annum, at the least, or other estate to the value of forty pounds sterling. And that every person who shall be so elected shall, before he sit or act in the said great and General Court or Assembly, take the oaths mentioned in an Act of Parliament, made in the first year of our reign. . . .

And our will and pleasure is and we do hereby for us, our heirs, and successors grant, establish, and ordain that yearly, once in every year forever hereafter, the aforesaid number of eight and twenty councilors or assistants shall be by the General Court or Assembly newly chosen, that is to say eighteen at least of the inhabitants of or proprietors of lands within the territory formerly called the Colony of the Massachusetts Bay, and four at the least of the inhabitants of or proprietors of lands within the territory formerly called New Plymouth, and three at the least of the inhabitants of or proprietors of land within the territory formerly called the Province of Maine, and one at the least of the inhabitants of or proprietors of land within the territory lying between the river of Sagadahoc and Nova Scotia. . . .

And further our will and pleasure is, and we do hereby for us, our heirs, and successors grant, establish, and ordain that all and every of the subjects of us, our heirs, and successors which shall go to and inhabit within our said province and territory, and every of their children which shall happen to be born there or on the seas in going thither or returning from thence, shall have and enjoy all liberties and immunities of free and natural subjects within any of the dominions of us, our heirs, and successors, to all intents, constructions, and purposes whatsoever, as if they and every of them were born within this our realm of England. And for the greater ease and encouragement of our loving subjects inhabiting our said province or territory of the Massachusetts Bay, and of such as shall come to inhabit there, we do by these presents for us, our heirs, and successors grant, establish, and ordain that forever hereafter there shall be a liberty of conscience allowed in the worship of God to all Christians (except Papists) inhabiting or which shall inhabit or be resident within our said province or territory. . . .

38. New Directions in Puritanism

As the end of the seventeenth century approached, two areas of controversy within Puritan Congregationalism took on new fervor: the old question of the requirements for admission to communion (should it be limited to those who could demonstrate a conversion experience or open to all "right-walking" Christians?), and the equally ancient question of collective church supervision (how could the churches advise and restrain individual congregations?). The answers that emerged in the late seventeenth century did more than offer new options for Congregationalism; in the eyes of orthodox Puritans the new doctrines threatened the unity and tranquility of church, state, and society. In 1700, Increase Mather, a leader of the conservative clergymen, decried experimentation in the churches and its impact on Harvard, of which he was then president: "Let the Churches Pray for the Colledge particularly, that God may ever Bless that Society with faithful Tutors that will be true to Christs Interest and theirs, and not Hanker after new and loose wayes." Many Puritans, especially those with strong ties to New England's first generation, nodded in agreement. Heedless of such advice, the reformers strode confidently ahead.

A. New Definitions

One of the first clergymen to openly challenge traditional guidelines for admission to communion was Solomon Stoddard (1643-1729), pastor of the church at Northampton, Massachusetts. Stoddard contended that a policy in which none could partake of the Lord's Supper unless he had first experienced conversion and could convince the congregation of it imposed too great a barrier to the most important Christian ceremony. Far better, he believed, to open the gates to all sincere and upright Christians and let the bread and wine help bring true grace to willing souls. As early as the 1670s, Stoddard was preaching and practicing his liberalized standards in the Connecticut Valley, though his first published exposition on the subject did not appear until 1700.

Source: Solomon Stoddard, The Doctrine of Instituted Churches, Explained and Proved from the Word of God (London, 1700), 18-22.

. . . Three things are requisite in order to [gain] admission to the Lord's Supper: first, visible saintship, and that is found in such persons; all professors walking blamelessly are visible saints. The members of the Jewish church are often called saints in the scripture, who did give no further evidence of their saintship. A profession of the faith joined with a good conversation is a sufficient ground for charity; these are marks that we are directed in the scripture to judge of men's saintship by; the Apostle did accept of such persons for visible saints. Men that have these characters are not visibly wicked, therefore they are visible saints. These properties are the proper fruits of saintship and therefore constitute men visible saints: such a profession as being sincere makes a man a real saint; being morally sincere makes a man a visible saint. That whereby godly men do make their saintship visible does make men

visible saints, viz., a profession of the truth and a good conversation.

A second requisite is that they be not scandalous; a man that is
really and visibly godly may fall into a scandal and upon that
account be forbidden to participate at the Lord's table, but when
their conversation is good, they cannot be hindered upon that
account.

A third requisite is that they have knowledge to examine themselves and discern the Lord's body; for the want of this, infants are
denied the Lord's Supper.

Those adult persons that are fit to be admitted into the church
are to be admitted to the Lord's Supper.

All adult persons that are fit to be admitted into the church
ordinarily have all those qualifications requisite to the participation
of the Lord's Supper: they make profession of the true faith and
are of good conversation; they have knowledge of the principles of
religion and so are able to examine themselves, and if any of them
should not understand the nature of that ordinance, they may soon
be sufficiently informed.

Two things are evident in the practice of the Apostles: one is
that they readily admitted such into the church as made a profession of the Christian faith, Act. 2; Act. 6. We never read that ever
they denied admission to any man or woman that made that profession; the other is that all that were thus received by them were
admitted to the Lord's Supper, 1 Cor. 10:17; Act. 2:24. They made
no distinction of the adult members of the church into communicants and non-communicants.

Those that are commanded by God to participate of the Lord's
Supper are to be admitted to the Lord's Supper, but all professors
that have a good conversation and knowledge are commanded by
God to participate in the Lord's Supper. If men have not these
qualifications, they are not obliged immediately to participate in
the Lord's Supper, for it would be a sin if they should. But having
these qualifications they are bound, provided they have opportunity. Christ has laid this law upon professors, 1 Cor. 11:24, 25.
The persons here commanded are not only true believers, then
none can do it with a good conscience but those that know themselves to be true believers; then the church authority can require
none but true believers to come. The persons therefore required to
partake are such professors as carry it inoffensively, and if such are

bound to come, the church is bound to receive them; they may not hinder any man from doing his duty.

There can be no just cause assigned why such men should be debarred from coming to the Lord's Supper; they are not to be debarred for not giving the highest evidence of sincerity. There never was any such law in the church of God that any should be debarred church privileges because they did not give the highest evidence of sincerity, nor for want of the exercise of faith. It is unreasonable to believe men to be visible saints from their infancy till they be forty or fifty years of age and yet not capable of coming to the Lord's Supper for want of the exercise of faith. They are not to be denied because of the weakness of grace; they that have the least grace need to have it nourished and cherished.

Such adult persons as are worthy to be admitted into the church, or being in the church are worthy to be continued without censure, are to be admitted to the Lord's Supper. It is utterly unreasonable to deny the adult members of the church the Lord's Supper and yet not lay them under censure. If they are guilty of any such offense as to be denied the Lord's Supper, why are they not censured? If they are not worthy to be censured, why are they kept from the Lord's Supper?

There are some scriptures that have been thought to hold forth a need of somewhat further, in order to participation in the Lord's Supper, which if they be examined will be found to be strained beyond the import of them. Psal. 66:16, David saith, "I will tell you what the Lord hath done for my soul." Hence it is argued that men should give an account of the manner of their conversion in order to their admission, but if it should be granted that David doth respect the work of regeneration, doth it follow because he was willing to talk of it that they might make a law to bind him to do it in the synagogue, or doth it follow that David offered to do it in order to his joining with the Jewish church, Act. 2:37? They were pricked at the heart before they were admitted into the church, but let it be considered that many others were joined to the Christian church of whom we read no such thing, and here is no living rule that others must declare that they are pricked in the heart before their admission. Yea, it is certain that these did not declare their trouble in order to their admission into the church, but in order to their direction. Yea, it doth not appear that these men were under a work of conversion at this time. They might be godly men before; the thing that stung them was a national sin, which in probability they had no hand in. For the greater part of them were strangers, come up to keep the feast of Pentecost, and were greatly affected with the sin which the nation of the Jews were guilty of in crucifying of Christ, Act. 9:26, 27. The church at Jerusalem refused to admit Paul to their communion till they were informed by Barnabas of his conversion, but it doth not appear that Paul did then desire to participate with them in the Lord's Supper. Possibly it might be only in hearing of the word and prayer, and the reason why they were unwilling to receive him was not any doubt whether his conversion was sincere, but whether he was a Christian. As if in a Popish country, one who had been a violent persecutor should essay to join himself to a Protestant congregation: it would be no wonder if they should be afraid of him until they were informed that he was become a Protestant. This is no foundation to require of all that join to the church an account about the manner of their conversion, 1 Pet. 3:15. Men are required to be ready to give an answer to everyone that asketh them a reason of the hope that is in them, but here by the reason of the hope that is in them we are not to understand their experiences of the grace of God, but the grounds of their faith, the reason why they did believe the Christian doctrine? This is evident because he is speaking of persecution, v. 14, and because he directs them to give their answer with meekness and fear.

Question. Here it may be inquired whether such persons as have a good conversation and a competent knowledge may come to the Lord's Supper with a good conscience, in case they know themselves to be in a natural condition?

Answer. They may and ought to come though they know themselves to be in a natural condition. This ordinance is instituted for all the adult members of the church who are not scandalous, and therefore must be attended by them. As no man may neglect prayer, or hearing the word, because he cannot do it in faith, so he may not neglect the Lord's Supper.

The Lord's Supper is instituted to be a means of regeneration; it is not appointed for the converting of men to the Christian religion, for only such as are converted may partake of it. But it is not only for the strengthening of saints but a means also to work saving regeneration.

There be many, according to the ordinance of Christ, to be admitted to the Lord's Supper who are not regenerate, Matth. 25:1, 2. The kindgom of heaven is like ten virgins, five of them were wise, and five foolish, and it can have no other immediate end respecting these but their conversion. The end of all ordinances is salvation, and therefore to these men it must be regeneration, for without it they cannot be saved.

This ordinance hath a proper tendency to draw sinners to Christ; in this ordinance there is a particular invitation to sinners to come to Christ for pardon. Here is an affecting representation of the virtue of Christ's sufferings; here is a seal whereby the truth of the gospel is confirmed, all which are very proper to draw sinners to Christ. . . .

B. New Congregations

Boston as well as Northampton felt the impact of new theories. While Solomon Stoddard practiced a relatively open communion in the Connecticut Valley, the idea of a church open to all professing Christians gained advocates among some of the Harvard faculty and among residents of the colonial capital. In 1699, a fourth Congregational church in Boston was founded. On matters of faith, the new Brattle Street Church claimed to be in full agreement with its neighbors, but in matters of baptism, the rights of members who had not experienced saving grace, and the use of prayer and Holy Scripture in church services, it departed significantly from traditional Puritan formulas. Many Puritans must have shared the venom Cotton Mather confided to his diary: "I see Satan beginning a terrible Shake unto the Churches of New England; and the Innovators, that have sett up a new Church in Boston, (a new one indeed!) have made a Day of Temptation among us. The Men are ignorant, arrogant, obstinate, and full of Malice and Slander, and they fill the Land with Lyes. . . ."

Source: S. K. Lothrop, *History of the Church in Brattle Street, Boston* (Boston, 1851), 20–26.

A MANIFESTO OR DECLARATION SET FORTH
BY THE UNDERTAKERS OF THE NEW CHURCH
NOW ERECTED IN BOSTON IN NEW ENGLAND,
NOVEMBER 17TH, 1699

Inasmuch as God hath put it into our hearts to undertake the building a new meetinghouse in this town for his public worship, and whereas through the gracious smiles of divine providence on this our undertaking, we now see the same erected and near finished, we think it convenient for preventing all misapprehensions and jealousies to publish our aims and designs herein, together with those principles and rules we intend by God's grace to adhere unto.

We do therefore as in the presence of God our judge, and with all the sincerity and seriousness which the nature of our present engagement commands from us, profess and declare both to one another, and to all the world, as follows:

I.

First of all, we approve and subscribe the Confession of Faith put forth by the assembly of divines at Westminster.

II.

We design only the true and pure worship of God, according to the rules appearing plainly to us in His word, conformably to the known practice of many of the churches of the United Brethren in London, and throughout all England.

We judge it therefore most suitable and convenient that in our public worship some part of the Holy Scripture be read by the minister at his discretion. In all other parts of divine worship as prayer, singing, preaching, blessing the people, and administering the sacraments, we conform to the ordinary practice of the Churches of Christ in this country.

III.

It is our sincere desire and intention to hold communion with the churches here as true churches, and we openly protest against all suspicion and jealousies to the contrary as most injurious to us.

IV.

And although in some circumstances we may vary from many of them, yet we jointly profess to maintain such order and rules of discipline as may preserve, as far as in us lies, evangelical purity and holiness in our communion.

V.

In pursuance whereof we further declare that we allow of baptism to those only who profess their faith in Christ and obedience to Him, and to the children of such, yet we dare not refuse it to any child offered to us by any professed Christian upon his engagement to see it educated, if God give life and ability, in the Christian religion. But this being a ministerial act, we think it the pastor's province to receive such professions and engagements, in whose prudence and conscience we acquiesce.

VI.

As to the sacrament of the Lord's Supper, we believe that as the ordinance is holy, so the partakers in it (that it may not be visibly profaned) must be persons of visible sanctity.

VII.

We judge it therefore fitting and expedient that whoever would be admitted to partake with us in this holy sacrament be accountable to the pastor to whom it belongs to inquire into their knowledge and spiritual state, and to require the renewal of their baptismal covenant.

VIII.

But we assume not to ourselves to impose upon any a public relation of their experiences; however if anyone think himself bound in conscience to make such a relation, let him do it. For we conceive it sufficient if the pastor publicly declare himself satisfied in the person offered to our communion, and seasonably propound him.

IX.

We also think ourselves obliged in faithfulness to God, our own souls, and theirs who seek our communion, to inquire into the life and conversation of those who are so propounded; and if we have just matter of objection to prefer it against them.

X.

But if no objection be made before the time of their standing propounded is expired, it shall be esteemed a sufficient consent and concurrence of the brethren, and the person propounded shall be received to our communion.

XI.

If ever any of our communion should be so unhappy as to fall into any scandalous sin (which God by His grace prevent), we profess all dutiful submission to those censures which the scripture directs and the churches here practice.

XII.

Forasmuch as the same power that admits should also exclude, we judge it reasonable that the pastor in suspending or excommunicating an offender have the consent and concurrence of the brethren.

XIII.

We apprehend that a particular church, as such, is a society of Christians by mutual agreement, usually meeting together for public worship in the same place and under the same ministry, attending on the ordinances of God there.

XIV.

In every such society the law of nature dictates to us that there is implied a mutual promise and engagement of being faithful to the relations they bear to each other, whither as private Christians or as pastor and flock, so long as the providence of God continues them in those relations.

XV.

We moreover declare ourselves for communion of churches, freely allowing our members occasionally to communicate with other Churches of Christ, and receiving theirs occasionally to the table of the Lord with us. And in extraordinary cases, when the providence of God makes it needful, we conceive that any authorized minister of Christ may, upon our request, administer the sacraments unto us.

XVI.

Finally, we cannot confine the right of choosing a minister to the male communicants alone, but we think that every baptized adult person who contributes to the maintenance should have a vote in electing. Yet it seems but just that persons of the greatest piety, gravity, wisdom, authority, or other endowments should be leading and influential to the society in that affair.

These are the principles we profess and the rules we propose through the grace of God to govern ourselves by; and in some of these particulars only, and in no other, do we see cause to depart from what is ordinarily professed and practiced by the Churches of Christ here in New England.

The liberal policy of the Brattle Street Church attracted many adherents, as well as the enmity of the Mathers and other guardians of the old order who thought the ideas of the innovators to "utterly subvert our churches." Yet the Brattle Street Church fell short of being a popular revolt against an aristocratic church: one wit, noting its high proportion of merchants, including wealthy John Mico, and its bewigged clergymen, rhymed:

> Our Merchants cum Mico do stand sacro vico
> Our Churches turn genteel;
> Our Parsons grow trig with Wealth, Wine and Wig,
> And their heads are covered with meal.

In the 1730s, a reaction would set in; Jonathan Edwards and other neo-Calvinist preachers would re-emphasize strict standards of church admission. In the long run, though, the less rigorous policies toward membership and the sacraments put forward by Stoddard and the Brattles carried the day.

C. New Organizations

Although most New England Puritans preferred a Congregational form of church polity, some shared with Presbyterians the belief that totally independent congregations comported neither with scripture nor with the realities of human society. The answer, they argued, lay not in a hierarchy in the Anglican sense, but in a system of representative assemblies with authority to make decisions for the common good. The synods held in New England from time to time were a partial response to such sentiments, though even the synods came under attack from staunch Independents. But as the problems of the Puritan church seemed to multiply toward the end of the seventeenth century, clergymen in both Connecticut and Massachusetts increasingly advocated the creation of permanent ministerial assemblies. In the Bay Colony, this took the form of annual conventions of the ministers and of several district associations that met more often. Both had advisory functions only. An attempt of 1705 to establish a standing council with extensive powers of regulation over the congregations met with a loud rebuff in two pamphlets by John Wise of Ipswich and more silently by the General Court, which declined to endorse the scheme.

In Connecticut, however, a sympathetic governor and legislature gave their blessings to the recommendations of a synod held at Saybrook in September, 1708, at which lay and clerical representatives of the Connecticut churches proposed the creation of county-wide consociations of all congregations, administered by representative councils, and county-wide associations of clergymen. Both organizations were accorded broad *powers over individual congregations and their clergymen. For example, a church failing to abide by decisions of its county consociation was to be "Reputed guilty of Scandalous Contempt" and denied communion with all other congregations.*

Source: Williston Walker, *Creeds and Platforms of Congregationalism* (New York, 1893), 503–506.

. . . For the better regulation of the administration of church discipline in relation to all cases ecclesiastical, both in particular churches and in councils, to the full determining and executing of the rules in all such cases, it is agreed:

First, That the elder or elders of a particular church, with the consent of the brethren of the same, have power and ought to exercise church discipline according to the rule of God's word in relation to all scandals that fall out within the same. And it may be meet in all cases of difficulty for the respective pastors of particular churches to take advice of the elders of the churches in the neighborhood before they proceed to censure in such cases.

2. That the churches which are neighboring each to other shall consociate for the mutual affording to each other such assistance as may be requisite upon all occasions ecclesiastical; and that the particular pastors and churches within the respective counties in this government shall be one consociation (or more if they judge meet) for the end aforesaid.

3. That all cases of scandal that fall out within the circuit of any of the aforesaid consociations shall be brought to a council of the elders and also messengers of the churches within the said circuit, i.e., the churches of one consociation if they see cause to send messengers when there shall be need of a council for the determination of them.

4. That according to the common practice of our churches, nothing shall be deemed an act or judgment of any council which hath not the major part of the elders present concurring and such a number of the messengers present as make the majority of the council, provided that if any church shall not see cause to send any messenger to the council, or the persons chosen by them shall not attend, neither of these shall be any obstruction to the proceedings of the council or invalidate any of their acts.

5. That when any case is orderly brought before any council of

the churches, it shall there be heard and determined which (unless utterly removed from thence) shall be a final issue, and all parties therein concerned shall sit down and be determined thereby. And the council so hearing and giving the result or final issue in the said case as aforesaid shall see their determinations or judgment duly executed and attended in such way or manner as shall in their judgment be most suitable and agreeable to the word of God.

6. That if any pastor and church doth obstinately refuse a due attendance and conformity to the determination of the council that has cognizance of the case and determines it as above, after due patience used they shall be reputed guilty of scandalous contempt and dealt with as the rule of God's word in such case doth provide; and the sentence of non-communion shall be declared against such pastor and church, and the churches are to approve of the said sentence by withdrawing from the communion of the pastor and church which so refuseth to be healed.

7. That in case any difficulties shall arise in any of the churches in this colony which cannot be issued without considerable disquiet, that church in which they arise or that minister or member aggrieved with them shall apply themselves to the council of the consociated churches of the circuit to which the said church belongs, who if they see cause shall thereon convene, hear, and determine such cases of difficulty unless the matter brought before them shall be judged so great in the nature of it, or so doubtful in the issue, or of such general concern that the said council shall judge best that it be referred to a fuller council consisting of the churches of the other consociation within the same county (or of the next adjoining consociation of another county if there be not two consociations in the county where the difficulty ariseth), who together with themselves shall hear, judge, determine, and finally issue such case according to the word of God.

8. That a particular church in which any difficulty doth arise may, if they see cause, call a council of the consociated churches of the circuit to which the said church belongs before they proceed to sentence therein, but there is not the same liberty to an offending brother to call the said council before the church to which he belongs proceed to excommunication in the said case, unless with the consent of the church.

9. That all the churches of the respective consociations shall choose, if they see cause, one or two members of each church to

represent them in the councils of the said churches as occasion may call for them, who shall stand in that capacity till new be chosen for the same service, unless any church shall incline to choose their messengers anew upon the convening of such councils.

10. That the minister or ministers of the county towns, and where there are no ministers in such town the two next ministers to the said town, shall as soon as conveniently may be appoint a time and place for the meeting of the elders and messengers of the churches in the said county in order to their forming themselves into one or more consociations, and notify the said time and place to the elders and churches of that county, who shall attend at the same—the elders in their own persons and the churches by their messengers if they see cause to send them. Which elders and messengers so assembled in councils, as also any other council hereby allowed of, shall have power to adjourn themselves as need shall be for the space of one year after the beginning or first session of the said council and no longer, and that minister who was chosen at the last session of any council to be moderator shall with the advice and consent of two more elders (or in case of the moderator's death, any two elders of the same consociation) call another council within the circuit when they shall judge there is need thereof, and all councils may prescribe rules as occasion may require, and whatsoever they shall judge needful within their circuit, for the well performing and orderly managing the several acts to be attended by them, or matters that come under their cognizance.

11. That if any person or persons orderly complained of to a council, or that are witnesses to such complaints, have regular notification to appear, shall refuse or neglect so to do in the place and at the time specified in the warning given, except they or he give some satisfying reason thereof to the said council, they shall be judged guilty of scandalous contempt.

12. That the teaching elders of each county shall be one association (or more if they see cause), which association or associations shall assemble twice a year at least at such time and place as they shall appoint, to consult the duties of their office and the common interest of the churches, who shall consider and resolve questions and cases of importance which shall be offered by any among themselves or others, who shall have power of examining and recommending the candidates of the ministry to the work thereof.

13. That the said associated elders shall take notice of any

among themselves that may be accused of scandal or heresy unto or cognizable by them, examine the matters, and if they find just occasion, shall direct to the calling of the council where such offenders shall be duly proceeded against.

14. That the associated pastors shall also be consulted by bereaved churches belonging to their association, and recommend to such churches such persons as may be fit to be called and settled in the work of the gospel ministry among them. And if such bereaved churches shall not seasonably call and settle a minister among them, the said associated pastors shall lay the state of such bereaved church before the General Assembly of this colony, that they may take such order concerning them as shall be found necessary for their peace and edification.

15. That it be recommended as expedient that all the associations of this colony do meet in the general association by their respective delegates, one or more out of each association, once a year, the first meeting to be at Hartford at the time of the general election next ensuing the date hereof, and so annually in all the counties successively at such time and place as they, the said delegates, shall in their annual meeting appoint.

In October, 1708, the Connecticut legislature decreed that "all the churches within this government that are or shall be thus united in doctrine, worship, and discipline, be . . . established by law." Not all of the colony's congregations accepted the new system, some deeming it too close to Presbyterianism, others too far from it, but by 1709 the Saybrook Platform had the endorsement of most Connecticut churches. The New England Way no longer meant quite the same thing in Massachusetts Bay and Connecticut, which because of mergers—New Haven into Connecticut in 1664 and Plymouth into Massachusetts in 1691— now encompassed the vast majority of Puritan congregations. The search for consensus, so long a part of Puritan tradition, had failed to solve New England's ecclesiastical differences.

39. Retrospect

The year 1730 marked the centennial of the arrival of John Winthrop and the Massachusetts Bay charter in New England. To celebrate that anniversary, Thomas Prince (1687–1758), prominent clergyman and historian, delivered an election-day sermon, "The People of New England . . .," in which he wove together several major strands of the

Puritan tradition: the parallel between the American Puritans and the ancient Jews, the special signs of God's favor to New England, the inevitable punishment for backsliding, and the necessity to return to the ways and aspirations of the founding fathers.

Prince's words may be read as an obituary as well as a celebration, for the great age of Puritanism was dead. By 1730, New England bore little resemblance to the Bible commonwealth envisioned by Winthrop, Shepard, and Hooker. Even the Great Awakening of the 1730s and 1740s could not revive its spiritual fervor, let alone its social and political institutions. To be sure, New England, even all America, would long bear the impact of the Puritan tradition, but from the perspective of more than two centuries we can see what Thomas Prince could not—that his sermon marks the symbolic end of Puritan hegemony.

Source: Thomas Prince, *The People of New England Put in Mind of the Righteous Acts of the Lord to Them and Their Fathers, and Reasoned with Concerning Them* (Boston, 1730), 21–39.

. . . Here I cannot forbear observing that there never was any people on earth so parallel in their general history to that of the ancient Israelites as this of New England. To no other country of people could there ever be so directly applied a multitude of Scripture passages in the literal sense as to this particular country; that excepting miracles and changing names, one would be ready to think the greater part of the Old Testament were written about us, or that we, though in a lower degree, were the particular antitypes of that primitive people. . . .

And how extremely proper is it upon the close of the first century of our settlement in this chief part of the land, which will now within a few weeks expire, to look back to the beginning of this remarkable transaction, and first commemorate the righteous and signal works of God towards us both in our own days and in the days of our fathers, and then consider the great and special obligations they have laid upon us, with the nature of our carriage towards Him for the time past, and our interest and wisdom for the future. . . .

First let us consider who the fathers of these plantations were and what were their distinguishing characters, that we may give to God the glory of the excellent honor He was pleased to put upon them and see our own obligations to Him for deriving us from such eminent ancestors.

For the generality of them, they were the near descendants of the first reformers in England. They were born of pious parents who brought them up in a course of strict religion and under the ministry of the most awakening preachers of those days. Like so many Timothies, they were from their childhood taught to know the holy Scriptures, to reverence them as the inspirations of God, as the only rule of faith and piety, and to aim at both a pure scriptural way of worship and at the vital power and practice of godliness; and they continued in the things they had learned and had been assured of, as knowing of whom they had learned them. Under such means as these they became inspired with a spirit of piety and with a growing zeal to reform the worship of God to the most beautiful and perfect model of his own institutions.

In points of doctrine they entirely held with the Church of England, their judgment of orthodoxy being the very same; but they apprehended it to be the sole prerogative of God Himself, and a glory that He would not give to another, to appoint the orders of His own house and the acceptable ways of His own worship; that religion is a free obedience to the known laws of God and it is neither in the power of men or angels to make that religion which He has not made so Himself; that His own institutions ought not to be set on a level, mixed or debased with the low devices of men; and that it is a plain, full, and decisive rule of His own injunction—to the law and to the testimony; if they speak not according to this Word, it is because there is no light in them.

This is the pure religion which our fathers admired and aimed at, and at nothing in religion but what was inspired of God. This and nothing else they earnestly breathed and labored after; but for laboring after it, though some of the most pious on earth, they were censured, pursued, seized, imprisoned, fined, and suffered a world of hardship not now to be named. Their native country, which ever since the Glorious Revolution has been an happy land of ease and liberty, was in those former times as the land of Egypt to those pious men; and their lives were made exceeding bitter with religious bondage.

However, through the infinite mercy and wisdom of God, it was well for our fathers, and for us in the end, that they were thus afflicted. For had there been then a succession of such indulgent princes and bishops in England as there have since the Prince of Orange ascended the throne, there never had been such a country as this for religion, good order, liberty, learning, and flourishing towns and churches, which have given us a distinguishing name in the world and have reflected a singular honor to the persons and principles of its original settlers for this hundred years. But having a rougher surface, a barrener soil, a more inclement air than the southern countries, it would in all human prospect have been at this day as the wastes of New Scotland or the wilder deserts between us, but abundantly fuller of barbarous natives; or at most in no better condition than the bordering plantations.

But the omniscient and sovereign God had espied and chosen this land for our fathers, for a refuge and heritage for them and their children, that here they might set up His worship and churches according to the inspired pattern, behold the beauty of the divine appointments in their scriptural purity, and leave these inestimable privileges which they justly preferred above all things else in the world as a blessed inheritance to their posterity, as we see at this day.

And now let us look back and behold in what a remarkable manner the God of our fathers was pleased to bring them out of the land of their sorrows to this far distant and quiet recess of the earth and put it into their hands.

First, He sends a smaller company into a neighboring state,[1] that there they might form themselves into a regular ecclesiastical body till this hidden part of the earth should appear to the light, and yet come under such a discouraging character that none but men inspired with a zeal for religion would go on to settle it. He disappoints the successive endeavors of others who came hither only out of secular views, till the country comes to be given up and abandoned as not worthy the looking after by any trading nation. And then He sends both wasting diseases among the native inhabitants and fierce contentions among the survivors that greatly diminished their numbers and made room for His people.

But O how horrid and dismal do these new-found regions appear! On the shores and rivers nothing but sights of wretched, naked, and barbarous nations, adorers of devils—the earth covered with hideous thickets that require infinite toils to subdue—a rigorous winter for a third part of the year—not a house to live in—not a Christian to see—none but heathen of a strange and hard lan-

1. Viz., into Holland in 1610.

guage to speak with—not a friend within three thousand miles to help in any emergency—and a vast and dangerous ocean to pass over to this!

But the Almighty inspires with a zeal and courage that nothing can daunt, with a faith and patience that nothing can break. He raises up men of superior piety, resolution, and wisdom to lead and animate in the great design.[2] And on they come, all alone, a small and feeble number, through contrary storms and boisterous seas they were never used to, though twice driven back, a terrible winter approaching, their wives and poor piteous children with them, and like Abraham of old they know not whither. But the Lord is their guide; He divides the seas before them; He leads them through in safety; He brings them with joy to the border of His designed sanctuary, to this mountainous country which His right hand had purchased. And having cast out multitudes of heathens before their arrival, He gives them favor in the sight of the rest; He divides His people an inheritance by line and makes them to dwell in peace in the midst of many powerful nations that could have swallowed them up in a moment, for above fifty years together.

But a greater colony is now coming on to strengthen the other and to fill up the land from sea to sea and from the river to the ends of the earth. And here, behold and wonder how this is also accomplished.

Great numbers of eminent persons and others of the same pious and pure dispositions in the main with the former yet continued in the churches of England and in communion with them as long as the higher powers indulged them, with earnest desires, labors, and hopes of a farther reformation of worship. But a spirit of severe imposition is now let loose upon these. The *Book of Sports* on the holy sabbath of God must be read by the ministers in the public assemblies, and their assent to unscriptural ways of worship must be subscribed as a necessry term of their preaching, even though they were solemnly ordained in the church to the office, required by Christ Himself to discharge it, and had a woe laid on them if they desisted to do it. And for preserving their consciences pure, they are driven out of their churches, they are forced from their

2. Such as Mr. Carver, Mr. Bradford, and Mr. Winslow, successive governors of Plymouth Colony, who came together in the first ship which set sail the last time from Plymouth in England on Sept. 6, and arrived in Cape Cod harbor on November 11th, 1620.

flocks that loved them as the light of their eyes, and are more harassed and worried than the vilest of men.

And now at once, to the surprise of the nation, in almost every corner they are moved of God to look to this part of the wilderness He had been preparing for them. Many persons of shining figures are raised up to espouse their cause and venture with them. Their Prince is prevailed on to grant them a charter of distinguishing privileges. They hear, they rise, they flow together; their flocks in great numbers attend and follow them. They all relinquish their delightful seats and their dearest friends, they put off their fair estates, they cast themselves and their children on the tumultuous ocean, and nothing can move them, so they may come into a wilderness rude and hideous to hear the voice of their teachers, become a covenant people of God, observe His laws, set up His tabernacle, behold His glory, and leave these things to their off-spring forever.

And the Lord preserves them; He makes the depths of the sea a way for the ransomed to pass over; He brings them in thousands to these peaceful shores, and here, they that knew not each other before salute and embrace with joy; He unites them in the most lovely agreement to profess and serve Him; they publicly and solemnly enter into covenant with Him, to love and obey Him, to make His doctrines the only rule of faith and His institutions the only rule of worship; and with united joy they sing to the Lord:

> Thou in Thy mercy hast led forth the people which Thou hast redeemed: Thou hast guided them in Thy strength to Thy holy habitation. Thou hast brought them in, and planted them in the mountain of Thine inheritance, in the place, O Lord, which Thou hast made for Thee to dwell in, in the sanctuary which Thy hands have established. And the Lord shall reign for ever and ever.

At first indeed they met with very grievous trials and endured a world of hardship and affliction. . . . But they endure with patience and cry to God and He sends relief. . . .

And now the wilderness and the solitary place is glad for them; the desert rejoices and blossoms as a rose; it blossoms abundantly with peace and righteousness; it rejoices with joy and singing. The glory of Lebanon is given to it, the excellency of Carmel and Sharon; they see the glory of the Lord and the excellency of our God. The waters of the divine influence break out in the wilderness and the streams in the desert; the parched ground becomes a pool and the thirsty land, springs of water; in the habitations of dragons where they lay there grows up the grass, and an highway now is there which is called the way of holiness over which the unclean do not pass and the wayfaring men do not err therein.

And to the great glory of God be it spoken—there never was perhaps before seen such a body of pious people together on the face of the earth. For those who came over at first came hither for the sake of religion and for that pure religion which was entirely hated by the loose and profane of the world. Their civil and ecclesiastical leaders were exemplary patterns of piety; they encouraged only the virtuous to come with and follow them; they were so strict on the vicious both in the church and state that the incorrigible could not endure to live in the country and went back again. Profane swearers and drunkards are not known in the land. And it quickly grew so famous for religion abroad that scarce any other but those who liked it came over for many years after. And indeed such vast numbers were coming that the crown was obliged to stop them, or a great part of the nation had soon emptied itself into these American regions.

And for those who were here, the Spirit from on high is poured upon them and the wilderness becomes a fruitful field; judgment and righteousness continue in it and the effect of righteousness is peace. While a cruel war rages in the kingdom they left, lays it waste, and drowns it in blood, the people here dwell in peaceable habitations, in sure dwellings, in quiet resting places. And the Lord enlarges the bounds of their tents; He stretches forth the curtains of their habitations; He makes them to break forth on the right hand and on the left; He makes their seed to inherit the lands of the Gentiles, the desolate places to be inhabited. And in fifty-four years from the first plantation there appear above fourscore English churches,[3] composed only of known, pious, and faithful professors, dispersed through the wilderness.

But now comes on a cloud which covers our glory! This excellent generation passes away and there arises another which provokes the holy One of Israel to anger.

3. Twelve or 13 in Plymouth Colony, 47 in the Massachusetts, 19 in Connecticut, 3 in Long Island, and 1 at Martha's Vineyard.

The Lord set up our neighboring enemies against us; He united them together who never could unite till now, the western Indians before and the eastern behind; they devoured our Israel with open mouth.

The western nations first came up[4] like the waters of a flood, strong and many; they came up over all our banks, they passed through our country, they overflowed and came over, they reached to the neck and filled the breadth of our land! They lay our country desolate; they burn our towns round about with fire; they devour our land in our presence! They draw near and threaten even the chief and central town itself; and there are those now living who remember that every man therein was ready to shut up his house and go out for the preservation of the remnant of the people! There was the noise of a multitude in the mountains, like as of a great people; a tumultuous noise of the kingdoms and nations gathered together; the Lord of hosts mustered the host of the battle! All hands grew faint and every heart melted; we were afraid; pangs and sorrows took hold of us; we were in pain as a woman that travaileth; we were amazed at one another, for the day of the Lord came, cruel both with wrath and fierce anger, to lay the land desolate!

But when the Lord had brought us to the brink of destruction, then He heard our earnest cries and arose for our rescue. At the lifting up of Himself, the nations were scattered—He rebuked and set them against one another; He made them to flee afar off; He chased them as the chaff of the mountains before the wind and like a rolling thing before the whirlwind. As smoke is driven away, so He drove them away; as wax melteth before the fire, so they perished at the presence of God. . . .

I might go on to mention a great variety of other righteous acts of the Lord our God to this covenant people, both corrective and merciful—as distressing droughts and scarcities; contagious and wasting sicknesses; impoverishing disappointments, fires, and losses of a public nature and influence; vexations from those that have envied and hated us; the cruel taking away of our most dear bought privileges (the most grievous affliction of all others) and their wonderful restoration; the insupportable power of strange oppressors and the surprising appearance of God for our rescue

4. In 1675 and 1676.

when no other arm could save us and our hope was almost perished from before Him—but the time would fail me.

I shall therefore only mention one remarkable work of God which appears to me to be full of wonder and a visible and constant monument of His special favor and appearance for us—and that is this: on the account of our pure religion we have been all along a people misrepresented, envied, and maligned above any other on earth. We have had continually for this hundred years many powerful and active enemies and but few and feeble friends to stand up for us and plead our cause. How comes it then to pass that we have greater civil and religious privileges than almost any others? The most high God has been our mighty Friend. To Him have our dear forefathers and we consigned our greatest interests and He has stood up for us; He has removed kings and set up kings; He has carried the devices of the crafty headlong, that those who mourned might be raised to safety; and when our case has been so helpless that we could only pray, we have then stood still and seen the salvation of God. It is all a continued work of His; it can be ascribed to nothing else; let it be ever marvelous in our eyes; and let Him have all the glory. . . . He formed us of a pious people devoted to Him and He brought them and their offspring into a special, open, express, and solemn covenant with Him. . . .

Now the substance of this covenant is that He will deal with us and we will carry to Him according to His inspired Word. The sacred Scriptures, the promises and threatenings exhibited in them, are the declared rule of His dispensations to us; and the same divine writings, the doctrines and injunctions represented in them, are the professed rule of our carriage to Him. This is the rule and the only rule for the people, churches, and religion of New England. We hold to nothing but what we apprehend to be revealed, taught, and required in them; and we leave everyone to search and judge for themselves.

By our sacred covenant we are therefore under the most solemn obligations to preserve an entire and strict adherence to this divine standard, both in belief and practice, both in life and worship; and woe unto us if we depart therefrom! For if we do, we break our covenant with the holy God and become exposed to all the fearful and signal judgments denounced in Scripture upon the violators of it; and He is a true and jealous God and will signally avenge the quarrel of His broken covenant. But if we faithfully keep to this holy engagement, then we are entitled to all the distinguishing promises which God has made to His covenant people; and He is a gracious and a faithful God and will surely fulfill them for us.

We are also to look on all His past dealings, both afflictive and merciful, both with us and our fathers, as His righteous and faithful acts according to His wise and well-ordered covenant; they are nothing else but His just and faithful performance of it, and by the tenor of this sacred indenture we are to expect His treatment of us for the future. But then, O the extraordinary obligations we are under, both from the covenant of the Lord our God and from all His signal works both of judgment and of favor to us!

Have any of the other plantations suffered so much as we by cruel wars, depredations and bloodshed, impoverishing disappointments, fires and losses, both by sea and land, contagious sicknesses and other evils, which have marked us out for the censure and condemnation of the world?

And yet, what people on earth have had more distinguishing advantages than we? Derived of pious ancestors; possessed of a good and large land with commodious harbors and fruitful seas; living in a clear and healthy air and in the enjoyment of great privileges civil and sacred; having wise and religious laws, pious and learned magistrates and ministers, sober and virtuous educations, grammar schools in every town of an hundred families free for the poorest without expense, well-ordered colleges to perfect the accomplishments of our growing youth for the public service—in fine, free and pure churches,[5] divine institutions, sacred sabbaths for the preservation of religion in its power and practice—and as the effect of this, in general, a sober, civil, charitable, quiet, loyal people; who earnestly wished and prayed for and now greatly rejoice in the happy advancement and succession of the illustrious House of Hanover to the British throne in which, alone under God, we trust

5. Purity in churches is opposed to human mixtures, and the freer they are from these the purer they are; which is the great and professed design of ours who in religious matters make the revelations of God their only rule and admit of nothing but what they apprehend these revelations require, both in discipline and worship as well as doctrine and manners. And freedom in churches is a liberty to judge of the meaning of these revelations, and of professing and acting according to our judgment of the meaning of them; and in particular the free choice of our own pastors and ways of discipline and worship, and our consciences in these things not subjected to any power on earth.

to preserve our constitution, laws, and liberties, and desire nothing but the continuance of all these things—and where can they be found in so great a measure as in this happy land? . . .

But O! Alas! Our great and dangerous declensions! To what an awful measure are they gone already, how transcendently guilty do they make us, how threatening do they grow! What a melancholy prospect would lie before us were we to draw the parallel between the first and present generation! In comparison with this they made a heaven upon earth; but as when their heads were laid in the grave there arose another generation after them which did not so much know the Lord nor the works He had done for Israel, so the following generation has still declined further; and now we are risen up in our fathers' stead, an increase of sinful men, to augment the fierce anger of the Lord against His people.

. . . Though 'tis true we still maintain in general the same religious principles and professions with our pious fathers, yet how greatly is the spirit of piety declined among us, how sadly is religion turning more and more into a mere form of godliness, as the apostle speaks, without the power, and how dreadfully is the love of the world prevailing more and more upon this professing people! And this notwithstanding all the zealous testimonies which have from time to time for above this threescore years been borne against these growing evils.

Like as to Israel of old, so the Lord has sent us from the early days of our apostasy His faithful ministers to testify against it and to warn us of the fatal consequence. With what wonderful life and earnestness have they upon all occasions, and especially on such as these, delivered their anxious souls and mourned over us, as their printed sermons show;[6] and how solemn, plain, and faithful in their public admonitions of our sin and danger! But like that ancient people also, we have not hearkened to the voice of God but hardened our necks against Him and have done worse and worse in every generation. And what will be the consequence of this—unless a reformation save us—but severer chastisements than others suffer, a growing separation between our God and us, the withdrawment of His Holy Spirit from us, the loss of piety, the increase of all corruption both in worship and in manners (as they usually

6. See the excellent election sermons of Mr. Higginson, Mitchel, Stoughton, Danforth, Shepard, Oakes, Torrey, etc., which might be of public service were they reprinted and dispersed.

go together), and a terrible entail of vice and ruin to our dear posterity! . . .

Now then let the affecting view of all these things, both present, past, and future, excite us all in our several places to do our utmost that we may not share in the dreadful guilt of this declension, nor have our part in drawing on the lamentable consequences of it. But let us lay it to heart and mourn before the Lord, first our own apostasies and sins and then the apostasies and sins prevailing among this people. Let us cry earnestly for the spirit of grace to be poured forth on us and them, that the hearts of the children may be returned to the God of their fathers and may continue steadfast in His sacred covenant. And being revived ourselves, let us labor to revive religion in our several families, and then rise up for God in this evil day, bear our open witness also against the public degeneracy, and do what in us lies for the revival of the power of piety among all about us.